MONSTERS WITHIN

THE UNOFFICIAL AND UNAUTHORISED GUIDE TO *DOCTOR WHO* 2008

MONSTERS WITHIN

THE UNOFFICIAL AND UNAUTHORISED GUIDE TO *DOCTOR WHO* 2008

STEPHEN JAMES WALKER

First published in England in 2008 by
Telos Publishing Ltd
139 Whitstable Road, Canterbury, Kent, CT2 8EQ

www.telos.co.uk

This edition 2021

Telos Publishing Ltd values feedback. Please e-mail us with any comments you may have about this book to: feedback@telos.co.uk

ISBN: 978-1-84583-177-6

British Library Cataloguing in Publication Data.
A catalogue record for this book is available from the British Library.

TABLE OF CONTENTS

INTRODUCTION

Welcome to the latest in Telos's series of comprehensive annual guides to *Doctor Who*.

2008 was a year when the world's longest-running science-fiction show attained a previously undreamt-of level of popularity in the UK, and indeed around the world, rising to a peak with the transmission of the final episode of Series Four, the extraordinary 'Journey's End'. But it was also in many ways the end of an era, as showrunner Russell T Davies - the man who had brought *Doctor Who* back to the screen in 2005 after an absence of some 16 years from regular production - announced that he was giving up the job and handing over to one of his most accomplished writing colleagues, Steven Moffat, who would take charge from 2010, after four seasonal specials in 2009.

The first section of this book notes all the main events, news stories, promotional activities and so forth that occurred in the *Doctor Who* world between the end of Series Three and the end of Series Four, pausing along the way to discuss in more detail the main developments, in what is designed to serve as a useful record of this period from the 'outside looking in' perspective of the viewing public. Following this, there are capsule biographies for all the main cast and production team members who worked on Series Four. Then comes the most substantial section of the book, which consists of a detailed guide to and analysis of all 14 episodes, including the Christmas special 'Voyage of the Damned', plus the two mini-episodes 'Time Crash' and 'Music of the Spheres'. Lastly there are five appendices, covering more peripheral matters: Series Four of *Doctor Who Confidential*; the series' ratings and fan rankings; original *Doctor Who* novels published during the timeframe covered by this book; original *Doctor Who* comic strip stories published during the same period; and other officially-sanctioned original fiction based on the new series.

If you are reading this book, the chances are that you are already an avid follower of the good Doctor's adventures, but I hope that in the following pages you will find much to interest, inform and enlighten you, and ultimately to enhance your appreciation and enjoyment of the latest run of episodes in what is undoubtedly my favourite TV series of all time!

Stephen James Walker
24 October 2008

PART ONE
THE YEAR AS IT HAPPENED

CHAPTER ONE
ON COURSE FOR CHRISTMAS

The first week of July 2007 was an exciting time for *Doctor Who* fans as, following the debut transmission of the dramatic Series Three finale on the last day of the previous month, the BBC issued a flurry of press releases concerning major casting developments on the show. These revealed that Freema Agyeman would be returning as Martha Jones after a three episode crossover visit to the adult spin-off *Torchwood;* that - as previously rumoured - Kylie Minogue would be appearing as the major guest star in the forthcoming Christmas special 'Voyage of the Damned'; and that Catherine Tate had agreed to reprise her role as Donna Noble throughout the whole of Series Four.[1] After this, things understandably quietened down a little. The next major public event on the horizon was the transmission of 'Voyage of the Damned', expected to form part of BBC One's prestigious Christmas Night schedule, as had been the case for its two predecessors, 'The Christmas Invasion' and 'The Runaway Bride'. Nevertheless, there was still plenty going on in the *Doctor Who* world in the meantime.

July 2007

On 3 July, the BBC Trust and the BBC Executive published their joint annual report, which cited *Doctor Who* as a major drama success, noted that it had 'exceeded all expectations and [become] a national talking point' and identified it as one of the shows responsible for a 19 percent boost in profits from global TV sales. Less positively, the report said that the 'Tardisode' teasers produced for Series Two for viewing via mobile phones and bbc.co.uk had not been quite the hit that had been hoped for, although they had proved 'popular on broadband'.

While newspapers and websites around the world continued to run stories about Minogue's forthcoming appearance in 'Voyage of the Damned', 5 July saw a number of sources naming American film star Dennis Hopper as another possible addition to the special's cast list. As it turned out, these reports were not without substance, but were somewhat out of date: the idea of Hopper appearing had already fallen through by this point. On 8 July, the *Jewish Telegraph* carried the news that British character actor Clive Swift had been cast in the role for which Hopper had been considered, that of Mr Copper. The following day, the *Sun* named another cast member for the special: veteran actor Geoffrey Palmer, who had appeared twice previously in *Doctor Who*, in 'Doctor Who and the Silurians' (1970) and 'The Mutants' (1972).

Series Three began its debut screening on the Sci-Fi Channel in the USA on the evening of 6 July, opening with a double bill of 'The Runaway Bride' and 'Smith and Jones'. As usual, the episodes were quite heavily edited by the channel to bring them

---

[1] For further details of these press releases, see *Third Dimension: The Unofficial and Unauthorised Guide to Doctor Who 2007* (Telos Publishing 2007).

down to the length required to fit slots that included numerous commercial breaks. ABC in Australia meanwhile continued its own Series Three screenings, which had begun on 30 June with 'Smith and Jones'.

6 July was also the date when *Daily Mail* showbiz correspondent Baz Bamigboye broke the story that David Tennant was in talks with the Royal Shakespeare Company with a view to playing the lead role in a new production of *Hamlet* due to be staged in the summer of the following year. This immediately rang alarm bells for many fans, as it suggested that Tennant might be unavailable to make a new run of *Doctor Who* episodes in 2008, which some took to indicate that he might have decided to give up the role of the Doctor.

Tennant was in the news again on 9 July when the *Guardian* put him in twenty-fourth place in its annual Media 100 list, making him – in their estimation, at least – the most powerful actor in television. Showrunner Russell T Davies took fifteenth place in the list, up from twenty-eighth the previous year.

As production on 'Voyage of the Damned' got under way in Cardiff, the BBC Press Office released the first official publicity photo from the special on 11 July. This showed Tennant and Minogue in costume on one of the *Titanic* interior sets. The official *Doctor Who* website – at bbc.co.uk/doctorwho – announced the Minogue would be playing a waitress called Astrid, confirmed the casting of both Swift and Palmer and revealed the names of a number of other actors taking part in the production: Gray O'Brien, Debbie Chazen, Clive Rowe, Russell Tovey, George Costigan and Jimmy Vee. Several newspapers used the release of the publicity photo as an opportunity to run further stories about Minogue's appearance in the special, some of them also including approving quotes from BBC One Controller Peter Fincham, who happened to appear the same day at a press launch for the channel's autumn season.

A brief unscheduled break in recording of 'Voyage of the Damned' took place toward the end of the month as Tennant returned to his family home in Scotland to attend the funeral of his mother Helen, who had sadly died of cancer on 15 July. Fans of the actor who wished to show their support were encouraged to make donations to the ACCORD hospice in Paisley, where his mother had been treated in the last weeks of her life, and where she had previously worked. Reportedly over £6,000 was eventually raised.

25 July saw the official *Doctor Who* website revealing that Series Four would feature the return of the Ood, the popular monsters introduced in Series Two's 'The Impossible Planet'/'The Satan Pit'. The report noted:

> In 'Planet of the Ood', the Doctor and his new companion Donna will travel to a weird and wonderful alien planet, where she will meet the mysterious race for the first time. The episode will allow viewers to discover the origins of the Ood and why they behave the way they do – but will the Doctor become their friend or foe? 'We're delighted the Ood are making a welcome return to *Doctor Who*,' said lead writer and executive producer Russell T Davies. 'They were last seen falling into a black hole back in Series Two and we think it's only fair for the viewers to find out what the Ood have to say for themselves! Donna is certainly in for a shock.'

CHAPTER ONE: ON COURSE FOR CHRISTMAS

On 31 July, under the heading 'Kylie is Pensioner's Cup of Tea', the BBC News website reported a case of mistaken identity that had apparently occurred during 'Voyage of the Damned' location recording:

> Kylie Minogue was mistaken for a real waitress in her role in *Doctor Who* when a pensioner asked her for a cup of tea. While filming a one-off Christmas special outside a Swansea hotel, an elderly customer apparently thought the singer was a member of staff. The 39-year-old star plays a waitress on the *Titanic* in the BBC Wales show. An eye-witness said: 'It was absolutely comical. Kylie is an international star but obviously this old dear didn't know who she was.' He added: 'She said to Kylie: "Excuse me, love, is it too late for a cup of tea?" Kylie saw the funny side and just laughed. I don't think she knew if the lady was serious or not and just carried on into the film set.' The pensioner then walked into Morgan's hotel in Swansea in time for her tea.

August 2007

2 August saw the *Sun* coming up with some unfounded speculation about the identity of the actor who would play the eleventh Doctor:

> Word has reached TV Biz that the Beeb have found the man to take over as Doctor Who from David Tennant - *Cold Feet* star James Nesbitt. David, 36, is expected to quit at the end of the next series and insiders say Irishman James, 42, is a cert to get the TARDIS key. The *Jekyll* star is pals with *Doctor Who* writer Steven Moffat, tipped to replace show chief Russell T Davies when he also stands down at the end of the next series. Our mole said: 'Moffat has worked with James on *Jekyll* and the talk in BBC Drama is that he's a shoo-in as the next Doctor. First a Scottish Doctor - now we could have a Northern Irish one.'

This moved Moffat himself to post a rebuttal the following day on the forum of the Outpost Gallifrey fan website, noting: 'The James Nesbitt story is a total fabrication. Made up. A fantasy. Just a guy sitting at a desk and just inventing stuff. I wasn't going to say anything, but I'm getting embarrassed for the deeply wonderful Jimmy Nesbitt. So tell everyone please, 'cos it's getting very silly.'

Undeterred, the *Sun* unveiled another supposed casting exclusive on 6 August:

> *Doctor Who* bosses are set to sign up *Gandhi* star Sir Ben Kingsley to play the Daleks' creator Davros. Sir Ben, 63 - who won an Oscar for his movie role as India's peace-loving spiritual leader - is in final negotiations to play one of the most dangerous baddies in the galaxy. A source said: 'Ben's agent has been in talks for a while now and he's very keen to play the part of Davros. A deal will be signed any day now.' Fans will be delighted that insane half-man, half-machine Davros is returning for the

> fourth series of the hit BBC One show, which stars David Tennant as the Time Lord. The alien scientist – who first battled the Doctor in 1975 – is hell-bent on destruction with his army of exterminating Daleks.

This story was subsequently repeated by a number of other news outlets. Although the scoop regarding Davros's return would indeed prove to be correct, no contract for Kingsley would be forthcoming.

More reliable information was made available by the BBC itself on 10 August, when the Press Office put out a release that read in part:

> The start of the new series will see Donna tracking down the Time Lord during an alien emergency in modern-day London.
>
> The couple are destined to experience a series of wonderful adventures throughout the new series including meeting one of *Doctor Who*'s most popular aliens, the Ood, in a brand new episode, 'Planet of the Ood'.
>
> Donna and the Doctor ... will also be travelling through time for an encounter with the legendary murder mystery novelist, Agatha Christie.
>
> Agatha Christie will be played by *Jekyll* star Fenella Woolgar, and *The Good Life* actress Felicity Kendal will star as Lady Clemency Eddison.
>
> *Blackadder* and *Notting Hill* actor Tim McInnerny will also guest star later in the series.
>
> *Doctor Who*'s executive producer and head writer Russell T Davies comments: 'Visiting Agatha Christie has been on my wish-list for ages now and, for the Doctor, it's a real meeting of minds! Viewers can expect many more ambitious storylines and a whole host of guest stars in 2008.'
>
> Mathew Prichard, Agatha Christie's grandson, comments: 'What a brilliant idea that Agatha Christie and Doctor Who should meet! Two characters whose contribution to British entertainment is absolutely unrivalled.
>
> 'As far as I know my grandmother, Agatha Christie, never saw *Doctor Who*, but I am sure she would have been intrigued, excited and above all flattered by all this attention in 2007.'[2]
>
> Catherine Tate said: 'I am delighted to be returning to *Doctor Who*. I had a blast last Christmas and look forward to travelling again through time and space with that nice man from Gallifrey.'

This release formed the basis of many news stories in the British press the following day. In most cases these added no further information of their own. The *Sun*, however, had a separate item reporting on an apparent setback to plans for one Series Four episode:

---

[2] The suggestion that Christie never saw *Doctor Who* is, perhaps, surprising, given that she did not die until 1976, part-way through the fourth Doctor's on-screen era.

> Filming on *Doctor Who* was thrown into chaos after an Italian film set bosses planned to use, was hit by a fire. Crew on the BBC One drama flew out to Rome's Cinecittà studios - where the Beeb filmed their epic *Rome* series - earlier this week. They plan to make an Ancient Rome-themed episode for *Doctor Who*'s fourth series there later this year. But on Thursday night a huge blaze ripped through the studio - destroying masses of expensive BBC equipment. An insider said: 'It was a huge blaze. At one point, it looked like the whole studio was a goner. It threw a real spanner in the works for the *Doctor Who* team. They're planning an episode where the Doctor goes back in time to Ancient Rome and thought it would be perfect to use the set.' *Who* bosses still plan to use the set once fire damage has been cleared up, with insiders suggesting crucial parts were still intact. *Doctor Who* executive producer Julie Gardner said: 'Some of the production team have been looking at locations in Italy for the new series. The Doctor will have a Roman adventure.'

The *Sun*'s report also added weight to earlier indications that David Tennant would be taking the lead role in *Hamlet* for the Royal Shakespeare Company in 2008, but went on to add, less accurately: 'Taking the role is likely to mean David is forced to quit *Doctor Who* before the end of Series Four - as we predicted.'

Not to be outdone by the *Sun*'s fanciful casting claims, the Sunday tabloid *News of the World* got in on the act on 19 August with a bizarre report that actress Joan Collins was to appear in Series Four as Time Lady the Rani, who had been played in classic-era *Doctor Who*[3] by her one-time *Dynasty* co-star Kate O'Mara. An 'insider' was quoted as saying: 'The *Doctor Who* team are delighted they've managed to sign Joan. It's a real coup. [She's] perfect for the role ... like Alexis Colby with a sonic screwdriver.'[4]

Also on the same date, an intriguing snippet of news filtered out from a fan convention, A Day with the Doctor, held in Auckland, New Zealand. Seventh Doctor actor Sylvester McCoy, guesting at the event, told attendees of a conversation he had recently had with film director Peter Jackson, in which Jackson had claimed that fifth Doctor actor Peter Davison was to return to *Doctor Who* for a multi-Doctor story. The same story broke in the UK at the beginning of the following week when an uncharacteristically accurate report appeared in the *Sun*:

> *Doctor Who* legend Peter Davison is to step back into the TARDIS - and come face to face with the current Doctor. Peter,

---

[3] The term 'classic-era *Doctor Who*' is now commonly used to describe the original run of the show, encompassing the 26 seasons transmitted between 1963 and 1989 plus the TV movie of 1996, while 'new-era *Doctor Who*' is commonly used for the revived version that began in 2005 - a convention that will be followed throughout this book.

[4] Alexis Colby was the name of Collins' *Dynasty* character. O'Mara had played her younger sister, Cassandra.

> 56, who played the Time Lord in the 1980s, will pull on his famous trenchcoat once again for a *Children in Need* special. Bosses are tight-lipped about the storyline, written by *Who* scribe Steven Moffat. But an insider revealed: 'The Doctor is forever travelling though time so there's no reason why he couldn't catch up with a former incarnation. Peter was top of the writer's list to make a comeback.' This year's *Children in Need* charity telethon takes place on BBC One on Friday, November 16.

The UKTV Drama cable channel meanwhile announced that in a 'Who is the Greatest Doctor Who?' poll conducted via its website, David Tennant had come out top, with 8,866 votes – over three times as many as the runner-up, Tom Baker.

On 23 August, the BBC released a new Series Four publicity photograph, showing the Doctor and Donna outside the TARDIS with Donna wearing a 1920s 'flapper'-style dress for recording of the Agatha Christie episode.

25 August brought welcome news of another awards success for *Doctor Who*. The BBC News website carried a report that read in part:

> BBC One has scooped two awards at the Edinburgh TV Festival, being named terrestrial channel of the year and taking best programme for *Doctor Who* … BBC One's success was described as 'The best thing that's happened to me all month' by Controller Peter Fincham. He has had to apologise for recent scandals including the misleading editing of a film clip of the Queen. Mr Fincham has also had to face criticism over rigged competitions on shows such as *Blue Peter*, but said he was 'very lucky to be running BBC One' and said it was a job he 'loved'. 'I hope I'll be doing it for a good while yet,' he told delegates at the annual festival, which attracts about 2,000 industry figures … The winner of the best programme prize was chosen from a shortlist by almost 200 young people, who were invited to attend the festival as a way of showcasing the next generation of TV talent. *Doctor Who* producer Phil Collinson paid tribute to those delegates, saying that to receive the award 'from young people coming into this industry is a particular honour'. He also praised the BBC, saying that without it, '*Doctor Who* would never be made, would never be so good and would never be so well supported'.

Fincham would in fact be forced to resign from the BBC on 5 October over the scandals referred to in this report.

The latest in the *Sun*'s succession of misleading Series Four casting claims appeared on 30 August:

> Rock legend David Bowie is set to star in *Doctor Who* – as an evil alien abductor. Producers reckon the Ziggy Stardust singer, now 60, makes a perfect villain because of his 'great other-

> worldly look'. And he will cross swords with the TARDIS's Time Lord when he kidnaps crime author Agatha Christie – who in real life mysteriously vanished for 11 days in 1926. Bowie's willingness to appear in the two-part *Doctor Who* special, to be shown on BBC One next year, will surprise many of his fans.

Graeme Harper, director of the forthcoming Agatha Christie story (which was actually to consist of only one episode), had in fact toyed with the idea of casting Bowie as one of its characters, the Reverend Golightly, but this had come to nothing. Bowie himself was quick to rubbish the *Sun*'s story, his official website quoting him as saying it was 'tish and tosh'; these comments were picked up by the BBC News website, which added that a BBC One spokeswoman had also denied the story.

As the Royal Shakespeare Company issued official confirmation that he would be playing the lead in its 2008 production of *Hamlet*, and also the part of Berowne in *Love's Labour's Lost*, David Tennant visited Blackpool on 31 August to switch on its famous annual illuminations, which – as in a number of previous years – were due to incorporate a *Doctor Who* display. A live report on the event was included in Dale Winton's show on BBC Radio 2.

September 2007

Doctor Who racked up another accolade on 1 September when, at the World Science Fiction Convention in Yokohama, Japan, Steven Moffat's script for 'The Girl in the Fireplace' earned him a prestigious Hugo Award in the Best Dramatic Presentation, Shortform category. This matched his win in the same category the previous year for 'The Empty Child'/'The Doctor Dances'. Moffat was quoted on the official *Doctor Who* website as saying: 'Best thing about winning a (second) Hugo, is that it's for *Doctor Who*. 'Cos years ago, when I was a tiny little *Doctor Who* fan, I bought this American magazine called *Starlog*. It was all about *Star Wars* and *Star Trek* (whatever those are) but the reason I bought it was in a tiny box in the corner it said '*Doctor Who*'! And I was so excited that this big important American magazine had an article about my favourite show! And it broke my heart. Because in the article it said 'In all fairness *Doctor Who* is unlikely ever to win a Hugo ...' Two Hugos, I've got!! Two Hugos for *Doctor Who*!! And I'd say more, but I'm off to the *Starlog* offices to dance around and flick v-signs.'

On 3 September, a big story broke when the BBC Press Office made its first major *Doctor Who* announcement since the beginning of July. This read in part:

> After months of media speculation, BBC One can confirm that the BAFTA-award winning *Doctor Who* will return for a fifth series in spring 2010.
>
> Viewers are in for a treat this Christmas, as a special episode starring David Tennant and Kylie Minogue will be broadcast on BBC One in December 2007.
>
> Series Four, which went into production in July 2007, will hit UK screens in spring 2008 with a special episode for Christmas

> 2008.
>
> In 2009, *Doctor Who* will return with three specials starring David Tennant, with head writer, Russell T Davies.
>
> The full length fifth series will transmit in 2010.
>
> Jane Tranter, Controller, BBC Fiction, says: '*Doctor Who* is one of the BBC's best loved and most successful dramas. Its journey over the past three series has been one of the most ambitious and exciting that we have had, and I'm delighted to be able to confirm not only three exciting specials for 2009, but a fifth series in 2010.'
>
> Menna Richards, Controller, BBC Wales, says: 'The success of *Doctor Who* is a fantastic tribute to the dedication and expertise of the production team at BBC Wales who have worked on the project from the outset. This announcement is marvellous news for all involved and, more importantly, for the programme's amazing fan base and audience. BBC Wales is looking forward to producing the fifth series.'

Not all *Doctor Who* fans regarded this as the 'marvellous news' that Richards had suggested they would; many questioned the need for and wisdom of the 2009 'gap year', as it quickly became known, and were concerned that no indication had been given as to whether or not Tennant would remain as the Doctor for Series Five, or whether or not Davies would continue as showrunner. On the other hand, most were at least pleased that the BBC had made what amounted to an expression of long-term commitment to the show. These were issues that would continue to be hotly debated within fandom for many months to come.

With this controversy still at its height, it was perhaps just as well that the rest of September proved to be relatively quiet on the *Doctor Who* news front, with only two other notable stories breaking. First, on 3 September, the Dorchester Hotel in London was the venue for the annual awards show staged jointly by *TV Quick* and *TV Choice* magazines. As in 2006, *Doctor Who* picked up two of these reader-voted prizes, for Best-Loved Show and Best-Loved Actor. David Tennant was present in person to collect the latter, but refused to be drawn when journalists quizzed him on whether or not he would still be the Doctor in 2010.[5] Secondly, on 25 September, the BBC Press Office put out another *Doctor Who* release, this one giving further details of the Series Four story set in Ancient Rome:

> In one of the most ambitious episodes to date, the Doctor … and Donna … arrive in Pompeii in AD 79, on the eve of the historic eruption of Mount Vesuvius. The Time Lord and his companion are posed with an immediate dilemma - should they warn the residents of Pompeii of the forthcoming catastrophe or leave them to fend for themselves? *The Thick Of It* actor Peter Capaldi guest stars as Caecilius and is joined by *Quadrophenia* and *Rose and Maloney* actor Phil Davis who stars as Lucius. Further guest stars include *Howard's Way* and *Born and Bred* actress Tracey

[5] Spin-off show *Torchwood* took the award for Best New Drama at the same event.

> Childs who plays Metella. The filming[6] of the episode took place at Cinecittà studios in Rome, which the *Doctor Who* team expertly transformed into Pompeii for a week ... in September of this year. *Doctor Who*'s executive producer and head writer Russell T Davies says: 'Arriving in Pompeii marks the start of another exciting adventure for the Doctor and Donna. Donna is stunned to find herself in the midst of history's most famous volcanic eruption.'

This press release was accompanied by a new publicity photograph showing David Tennant and Catherine Tate in costume about to record a scene on the Cinecittà lot.

There was one other major development in the *Doctor Who* universe this month: 24 September saw the start of Series One of *The Sarah Jane Adventures*, the second full spin-off show to be produced, with transmission of both episodes of 'Revenge of the Slitheen' (one on BBC One, the other on CBBC).

October 2007

One of the lesser-sung behind-the-scenes talents of *Doctor Who* gained deserved recognition on 1 October when the BBC News website reported that Foley editor Kelly-Marie Angell had won an award for her work on the show:

> Kelly-Marie Angell uses snapped celery sticks to recreate the sound of broken bones and mashed melon for blood spurts as part of her work as a Foley editor.
>
> She was given the Conch award for most promising newcomer in the UK within the post-production sound industry. The 22-year-old was presented with a trophy at a ceremony in London. 'I'm extremely lucky,' said Miss Angell, who also works on the *Doctor Who* spin-offs *Torchwood* and *The Sarah Jane Adventures* at BBC Wales in Llandaff, Cardiff. 'It's not the usual nine-to-five job and I have to explain [what I do] to most people. They think it's really cool, which it is.' As a Foley editor - a title named after pioneering sound engineer Jack Foley - Miss Angell looks at each scene and then decides which sounds should be used with each character's movement.

Further Series Four news arrived on 2 October courtesy of the official *Doctor Who* website, which reported that an old adversary of the Doctor's was due to make a return:

> Christopher Ryan, best known for playing super-cool Mike in

[6] Although the majority of press reports, and, indeed, comments from the production team and cast, refer to the series as being 'filmed', it is in fact recorded on tape. For ease of reading, references to 'filming' have been left intact in quoted sources.

> the classic comedy series *The Young Ones*, is set for a guest-starring role in an upcoming Series Four adventure. Ryan will play a Sontaran leader in the story, due to begin filming in the next few weeks. 'I'm absolutely delighted to be appearing in this new *Doctor Who*,' Chris revealed. 'The last time I appeared in *Doctor Who* was in 1986, Colin Baker was the Doctor and I was still a Young One.' The story in question was 'The Trial of a Time Lord', where Chris starred as the slug-like Mentor Kiv alongside Trevor Laird, who played Martha's dad in 2007. If you know your *Who* lore, the Sontarans will need no introduction. If you're a newer viewer, however, you may not know that the Sontarans are amongst the greatest villains from the classic series of *Doctor Who*. A military, warlike species, able to clone vast armies of themselves, the Sontarans are locked into an eternal struggle with their enemies the Rutans.

On 3 October, the *MediaGuardian* section of the guardian.co.uk website ran an interview with BBC Head of Fiction Jane Tranter, in which she said that she remained open-minded about the possibility of a feature film version of *Doctor Who* being made. The report continued:

> Ms Tranter also hinted that actor David Tennant, who plays the current Doctor, was likely to return to the role for a fifth series, even though he has agreed to play Hamlet for the Royal Shakespeare Company next year. His decision means that the fifth series will not be shown until 2010, two years after the fourth series airs next year, effectively creating a 'gap year' filled by three *Doctor Who* specials starring Tennant and overseen by head writer and executive producer Russell T Davies. Ms Tranter also refused to be drawn on speculation that Steven Moffat was being lined up as a replacement for Davies – who is believed to be on the verge of leaving the show – or that actor James Nesbitt was being lined up take over from Tennant. 'All we can say is that David is a fantastic Doctor and that he is doing *Hamlet*,' she said.

Further suggestions of a *Doctor Who* movie in the offing came the following day in the form of a report in the *Daily Star*. This stated that the production would see David Tennant as the Doctor reunited with Billie Piper as Rose Tyler and quoted an unnamed 'source' as saying: 'It's all been hushed up ... but yes, it's definitely happening. David and Billie were a superb combination on the small screen, so it seems only right that they appear in the film.'

On 6 October, James Nesbitt took the opportunity of an interview in the *Belfast Telegraph* to deny the rumours circulating since August that he was in the frame to play the eleventh Doctor, or that he was even interested in the role.

The *Daily Star* had another, more accurate *Doctor Who* story to offer on 8 October, when it reported:

> *Doctor Who* bosses are set to call back *four* of the Time Lord's favourite assistants - including Billie Piper - for a sensational showdown. The old cast members will be reunited to help the Doc fight evil Dalek creator Davros in an explosive finale to the next series. Leading the way in the line-up will be Billie as Rose Tyler along with the rest of the Tyler family; they will hook up with the TARDIS traveller's latest assistants Martha Jones and Donna Noble. Also on hand to help out the Doc will be his old companion Sarah Jane Smith as well as Torchwood boss Captain Jack Harkness. Even the Time Lord's dog K-9 will make an appearance. The TV source said: 'This is the daddy of all shows. The writer Russell T Davies really wants to pull out all the stops for the finale next year.'

An additional snippet of Series Four casting news emerged on 10 October in a Press Association report stating that Sarah Lancashire, best known for her long stint as a regular in ITV1's *Coronation Street*, would be appearing in the first episode as a villainous character called Miss Foster, an 'enigmatic and powerful businesswoman'. Lancashire was quoted as saying: 'I'm absolutely thrilled to be in *Doctor Who*. It's a brilliant episode and I'm looking forward to taking the Time Lord on.'

16 October saw the *Sun* present some major 'spoilers' for 'Voyage of the Damned' in a report that read in part:

> Kylie Minogue will plant a tender kiss on Doctor Who in the Time Lord's Christmas special ... The tiny pop poppet has to climb on a box to snog the lofty Doctor, played by David Tennant. But romantics will be disappointed to learn there will be no lasting love between the pair. The seasonal spectacular ends on a sad note when Kylie, playing Doctor Who's temporary sidekick, spins off into space in a strange 'half-form' of herself. Kylie's Christmas smacker is revealed in a plot outline for the show. BBC bosses have been desperate to keep it secret - but the *Sun* has seen a copy. We can reveal the special is set on board the *Titanic*, which has become a spaceship run by arch-baddie Max Capricorn.

Other revelations in the *Sun*'s report included the fact that the special would end 'with a stunning scene in which the *Titanic* falls from the sky and looks like crashing on Buckingham Palace'.

On 19 October, the BBC Press Office finally gave official confirmation that the 2007 *Children in Need* telethon would include a special *Doctor Who* scene; and two days later, the official *Doctor Who* website announced that it would indeed feature the return of Peter Davison as the fifth Doctor:

> David Tennant's tenth Doctor is set to meet Peter Davison's fifth Doctor in a special scene commissioned for BBC One's *Children in Need*. The scene, entitled 'Time Crash', was written

> by award-winning *Doctor Who* writer Steven Moffat, and will transmit as part of the *Children in Need* fundraising evening on Friday 16 November 2007. 'It is an honour for me to be able to make the connection between the fifth Doctor and the tenth Doctor,' noted Peter Davison. 'However, now is not the time for sound-bites. I can feel the hand of history on my shoulder, even if I can't do the buttons up!'

On 22 October, fuel was added to the rumours that Russell T Davies might soon be moving on from *Doctor Who* when *MediaGuardian* reported:

> Russell T Davies, the *Doctor Who* executive producer, is developing a BBC drama series about fortysomething gay men, the Corporation has confirmed. Davies, who is taking a break from his duties on *Doctor Who,* is currently developing script ideas for the new project. The *Queer as Folk* writer will oversee the project when he takes a break from working on *Doctor Who* in 2009. Confirming the development, a BBC spokeswoman said that it was 'too early' to say which channel might show the drama or whether it will be produced in-house or by an independent production company. 'It's going to be about fortysomething gay men and how jealous they are of gay teenagers,' Davies said in an interview with the *Guardian* on Saturday. 'I've been longing to write something for adults.'

Fans were able to get an early aural taster of 'Voyage of the Damned' on 29 October when record company Silva Screen made Murray Gold's 'The Stowaway', a song performed by Yamit Mamo in the special, available to hear its MySpace webpage. This was to promote its forthcoming Series Three soundtrack release, on which the track was to be included.

The month then ended as it had begun, with further awards success for *Doctor Who.* At the prestigious National Television Awards ceremony at the Royal Albert Hall in London, it was announced that the show had won the Best Drama category for the third year in a row, and that David Tennant had been named Best Actor for the second year running. Public voting for these awards had opened back on 10 July, and the shortlist had been announced on 15 October. Although included on the shortlist, Freema Agyeman had unfortunately been beaten in the Best Actress category by *EastEnders'* Lacey Turner. Tennant dedicated his award to his late mother, Helen. The BBC News website reported him as having told the audience, in one of his acceptance speeches: 'Thank you for watching [the show]; thank you for enjoying it. I'm having the time of my life, and I'm so glad you're enjoying it.' In their reports the following day, however, the *Guardian,* the *Sun* and the industry journal *The Stage* all focused more on remarks that the actor had made in support of former BBC One Controller and former Head of Publicity Jane Fletcher, who had both resigned from the Corporation in recent weeks in the wake of the 'Crowngate' controversy over the misleading editing of a trailer for a programme about the Queen. In *The Stage,* Tennant was quoted as having said: 'Peter and Jane were fantastic supporters of our show and brilliant at their jobs. It is a real shame they have gone. They were very much a part of our team. It feels very different without them and I am sad about that.' According to the *Guardian*, Agyeman expressed similar sentiments about Fletcher, saying: 'She always had so many other shows [to work on] but it felt like a personal relationship.'

November 2007

3 November saw the BBC release the first publicity photos of one of Series Four's new-look Sontarans - Commander Skorr, played by Dan Starkey. Some of these photos showed the creature posed with David Tennant, Catherine Tate and Freema Agyeman in character as the Doctor, Donna and Martha. This sparked a number of press stories over next couple of days, which contained little in the way of new information, although the BBC News website's report of 4 November confirmed that the Sontaran story would be the one in which Martha made her return to *Doctor Who* after her crossover stint in *Torchwood*.

Doctor Who made its latest appearance on the front cover of the BBC's listings magazine *Radio Times* on 6 November, when newsagents around the country began stocking the edition covering the following week's programmes. The main cover photo showed the fifth Doctor and the tenth Doctor together on the TARDIS interior set in a publicity pose for the 'Time Crash' *Children in Need* special.

On 9 and 10 November, a number of news sources worldwide, including the *Daily Express* in the UK, carried a press agency story about comments made by Kylie Minogue in an interview, suggesting that her appearance in 'Voyage of the Damned' might not be just a one-off. Minogue was quoted as saying: 'It's not up to me, but I know there has been talk that my character could be reintroduced at a later date. We'll have to wait and see. I've always been a fan of *Doctor Who*, and when you think how long it's been running, it is a series that is a unique piece of television history.'

The much-anticipated 'Time Crash' made its debut on BBC One on the evening of 16 November, introduced by *Children in Need* host Terry Wogan and John Barrowman, who also sang during the telethon, as did Kylie Minogue. Official ratings figures would later show that the *Doctor Who* segment had won around 11 million viewers, making it the most-watched part of this year's *Children in Need*, and indeed the most-watched few minutes of TV of the whole week. A repeat transmission at a quarter to one in the morning drew in almost three million additional viewers. A piece of plastic celery worn by Davison on his lapel for the production was subsequently auctioned on the eBay website to raise more money for *Children in Need* and attracted a winning bid of £5,500 from 21-year-old Australian fan Dimitry Telfer.

During a break in location recording for Series Four, Catherine Tate enlisted the aid of David Tennant to tape two humorous skits, of about two minutes each, to be shown at a Hollywood Ball event organised for this weekend by the Laura Crane Trust children's cancer charity, of which she was patron. These skits had them in costume, but not in character, addressing the audience at the event, which Tate had originally hoped to attend in person. Over £25,000 was raised for the charity.

The official *Doctor Who* website had news of yet more awards success for the show in a 19 November report that read in part:

> *Doctor Who* has scooped a prestigious Writers' Guild of Great Britain Award for the Best TV Series beating *Life on Mars* and *New Tricks*. In the presentation on Sunday 19 November, Series Three of the BBC One Drama was named Best TV Series. Paul Cornell, Gareth Roberts and Steven Moffat were in attendance to collect the award on behalf of the Series Three writing team, which also included Russell T Davies, Chris Chibnall, Helen Raynor and Stephen Greenhorn. 'It's a particular honour to receive an award from our peers in the writing community,' said Gareth Roberts, writer of 'The Shakespeare Code'. 'We're all surprised and delighted, and looking forward to bringing more *Doctor Who* to BBC One in 2008.'

A very sad development for the *Doctor Who* world occurred on 22 November, the day before the show's forty-fourth anniversary, when its original producer, Verity Lambert OBE, died of cancer. Many heartfelt tributes poured in, and numerous obituaries were published over the course of the next few days. Controller of BBC Wales Menna Richards was quoted as saying: 'In *Doctor Who*, Verity Lambert has left a legacy that lives on in the new productions BBC Wales has been making since 2004. We in Wales owe her a debt of gratitude for handing on such a treasure which continues to be enjoyed the world over.'

A major news story broke on 26 November when fans who had gone along to watch some of the location recording for the Series Four episode 'Turn Left' and were amazed to see Billie Piper back playing her iconic role of Rose Tyler. The following morning's *Daily Mirror* was the first newspaper to pick up on the story, reporting:

> Doctor Who will have three glamorous assistants in the next series - after Billie Piper agreed to a surprise comeback. BBC chiefs are delighted that Billie, 25, is to star in at least three episodes to round off the next run, which starts in March. The Time Lord, played by David Tennant, starts with Donna (Catherine Tate) as his helper, is then joined by Martha (Freema Agyeman) and then reunites with Billie's character Rose for the finale. A source said: 'With Donna, Martha and Rose competing to assist him, Doctor Who is going to be spoilt for choice.' Since quitting, Billie has often admitted she misses the show, which turned her into a major TV star. The actress told the *Mirror*: '*Doctor Who* is a big part of my life. I've missed it since I left and I love David Tennant.'

As a number of online news outlets began repeating this story, the official *Doctor Who* website issued a brief confirmation:

> Following a series of unconfirmed reports across the media this morning, we're delighted to officially confirm that Billie Piper will return as Rose Tyler in Series Four of *Doctor Who*. Anything you may read elsewhere about when, how or for how long Rose

returns to *Doctor Who* should be treated as pure speculation at this point.

27 November proved to be a particularly busy news day, as this was also the date when the BBC Press Office issued advance information about all the Corporation's forthcoming Christmas programmes, including 'Voyage of the Damned'. 'At the end of the last series,' the release noted, 'viewers witnessed the *Titanic* crash through the TARDIS walls in spectacular style, and tonight's action continues from that moment. Kylie [Minogue], who plays Astrid, a waitress on the *Titanic*, says: "It is an incredible thrill to be joining David and the entire *Doctor Who* production for this year's Christmas special. *Doctor Who* enjoys a unique history and it is going to be very exciting to be a part of that."'

Also on 27 November, BBC Radio 2 broadcast a programme entitled *X-amining Kylie*, in which Minogue was interviewed by David Tennant about her life and career, including her appearance in 'Voyage of the Damned'. It was promised that a revised version of the programme, containing more extensive discussion of 'Voyage of the Damned', would be put out at a later date, after the special had actually been transmitted.

At a ceremony on 29 November, Tennant was named as winner of the Screen category of the Glenfiddich Spirit of Scotland awards, ahead of a number of other Scottish film and TV actors. His father Sandy accepted the award on his behalf, although Tennant sent a short video message recorded on the TARDIS interior set: 'I'm really gutted that I'm not there with you tonight. I'm down in Cardiff saving the universe; well, someone has to. I think that my dad and my sister are there with you tonight, so please look after them.'

As November came to a close, however, the thoughts of all *Doctor Who* fans started to turn to just one thing: the imminent transmission of the latest Christmas special, 'Voyage of the Damned'.

CHAPTER TWO
SEASONAL SUCCESS

On 1 December 2007, the edition of the BBC's *Radio Times* for the week of 8 to 14 December hit the newsstands, and saw *Doctor Who* again take pride of place on the cover. A photograph of David Tennant as the Doctor and Kylie Minogue as Astrid, posed on a specially-constructed *Titanic* prow set designed to pay homage to the hit movie *Titanic* (1997) starring Leonardo diCaprio and Kate Winslet, was accompanied by the strapline: 'It's nearly Christmas: Kylie joins David Tennant for the trip of a lifetime in our exclusive preview of the *Doctor Who* Christmas special.'

1 December was also the date when the first on-screen trailer for BBC One's special Christmas programming was unveiled, between that evening's editions of *Strictly Come Dancing* and *Robin Hood*. This included over a dozen brief clips from 'Voyage of the Damned' – the first to be made available from the special.

The official *Doctor Who* website had some further information to offer in a news item on 6 December:

> With BBC One's Christmas Day schedule just announced, we can confirm that you need to be in front of your telly and tuned in to BBC One at 6.50 pm if you don't want to miss a second of 'Voyage of the Damned'. And there are quite a few seconds too. This year, the *Doctor Who* Christmas special will run for a whopping 71 minutes instead of the usual 60. If that wasn't enough, there will also be a brand new one hour *Doctor Who Confidential* at 8.30 pm on BBC Three. With a whole host of bonus material launching on the website at around 8.00 pm too, that's quite an evening of *Doctor Who* entertainment.

Additional promotion for 'Voyage of the Damned' came in the form of a 90-second-long trailer shown in many British cinemas around this time; and on 8 December BBC One (except in Scotland) gave the first of many screenings to a ten-second-long teaser for the special.

10 December saw Russell T Davies making a brief appearance on BBC News 24's *Entertainment Today* programme, commenting, 'Kylie Minogue is fantastic in the Christmas *Doctor Who*, and I literally can't wait for people to see it. It's my job to say she's fantastic, but she really is! You will see a truly quality performance, and you will see why she is so iconic and successful. No-one's that successful for that long without talent, and she is perfect. Put her together with David Tennant, who is just sizzling on screen and gives even more than ever in this Christmas episode, and I could not be happier. Seriously, it's fantastic entertainment for Christmas Day!'

Important behind-the-scenes changes for *Doctor Who* were foreshadowed in a news release issued by the BBC Press Office on 11 December. This read in part:

> BBC Wales has announced that Piers Wenger is to take over the reins as executive producer for *Doctor Who*'s fifth series and will become the new Head of Drama, BBC Wales when Julie Gardner leaves that role in January 2009. Piers was the producer of the multi-award winning *Housewife, 49* with Victoria Wood and has just finished work on *Ballet Shoes*, Heidi Thomas's adaptation of Noel Streatfield's classic novel to be shown on Boxing Day on BBC One. He left his role as Head of Development at Granada Drama earlier in the year to help set up independent drama producer Mammoth Screen. 'I'm incredibly excited to be joining BBC Wales,' said Piers. 'The success of the drama team there has been extraordinary and I look forward to taking the team to even greater heights. Working with Julie Gardner on *Doctor Who* over the next year will provide an invaluable insight into the secrets and success of the series. I couldn't have a more inspiring leader.' Julie Gardner will continue as executive producer of the fourth *Doctor Who* series and the *Doctor Who* specials to be broadcast during 2009. She will continue to executive produce *Torchwood* and *The Sarah Jane Adventures* for BBC Wales ... [Controller of Fiction] Jane Tranter comments: 'Julie Gardner is one of the most impressive television executives in the UK. Her success over the past four years in BBC Wales drama has been unparalleled; her work on *Doctor Who* has earned her a place in TV history; and I'm delighted that she is committed to working across such a broad range of drama at the BBC for the next few years. She will provide a guiding light for Piers for the next 12 months and this creative collaboration will be an exciting time for BBC Wales drama.' Julie Gardner comments: 'I know that when I hand over my sonic screwdriver to Piers for Series Five of *Doctor Who*, it'll be to someone who loves and understands the show. *Doctor Who* is the most precious TV drama in the galaxy and I'm leaving it in safe and brilliant hands. I've been on the trip of a lifetime in the last five years with the finest writers, actors and crew, and I've got another 18 months of time travel to enjoy.'

Doctor Who Magazine entered into the Christmas spirit in its Issue 390, which went on sale on 13 December. This featured a specially-shot photo of Kylie Minogue posing with a Dalek on the front cover and an exclusive interview with the actress inside. On the same date, the website of genre magazine *SFX* presented the first part of an interview with producer Phil Collinson, in which he said of the special: 'It's jam-packed with Christmas – it's full of it! So it does feel very much in the spirit of all our other specials. It'd have to be really, on Christmas Day – I think it would be odd if they were basking on the beach somewhere, y'know! I'm a traditionalist, I think you've got [to have] a bit of Christmas about it, a bit of snow somewhere and some tinsel and some angels and a Christmas tree thrown in there and a bit of Santa Claus, and we've got all of that.' Asked if Minogue had been nervous returning to acting after a break of a number years, Collinson commented: 'If she was, she didn't talk to me about it, and she didn't appear to be. She came straight into our read-through, sat down and picked up the script and read it, she sat next to David, and it was a brilliant, brilliant read-through – there was chemistry almost immediately ... Obviously, we would want to cast a person who was right for that part and ... we all felt that it felt right. A brilliant off-shoot from that is that she's one of the most famous women on the planet and wanted to be involved with our project. And that's great for *Doctor Who*.'

14 December saw the cinema trailer for 'Voyage of the Damned' made available to view both on the BBC's YouTube channel and on the official *Doctor Who* website. A shorter version, running to just under 40 seconds, was also placed on the website. The following day, the full 90-second version was given its first TV screening, at 6.00 pm on BBC One after the early evening news bulletin – an event considered so significant that, in what may well have been a first for a trailer, it was even listed as a separate schedule item in *Radio Times*! It was also added to the BBC's 'red button' interactive TV service. The 40-second version of the trailer gained a BBC One airing as well, at 10.10 pm after *The Omid Djalili Show*.

Journalist Caitlin Moran, a long-time supporter of *Doctor Who*, presented a major exclusive in the 15 December edition of *The Times* in the form of a lengthy behind-the-scenes article on the production of 'Voyage of the Damned'. This account began in December 2006 at the launch party for 'The Runaway Bride', when the idea of Kylie Minogue taking a part in the show first arose, and ran right through to 28 November 2007 and the viewing of the (near) final edit by Russell T Davies, Julie Gardner and Phil Collinson. 'Although [these days] no-one can fail to be aware of what a communal effort the making of any TV show or film is,' reflected Moran, 'this final screening of "Voyage of the Damned" brings home how many thousands of small acts of uncommon devotion are put into making the average episode of *Doctor Who*. As the *Titanic* majestically ploughs through space, it's partially down to the life-long fan at special effects company The Mill, who spent three days painting in port hole lights on the upper deck. When Kylie's character has a sudden, scene-stealing moment, it's down to Russell T Davies taking his laptop on his first holiday in a year and rewriting scenes as his partner waited by the pool. Despite being set across all space, and all time, this show is made with as many tiny stitches and as much love as a bride's trousseau. And with the fresh edit, the narrative punches straight through like a fist and leaves you, at the end of its hour, feeling that there are short-cuts to distant suns, and big adventures happening out in the black sky, and bursts of heroic reason and uplift, courtesy of a hot 900-year-old time traveller and his magic phone booth.'

Also on 15 December, *Guardian* columnist Charlie Brooker named the Series Three episode 'Blink' his Populist Drama of the Year, opining that it was 'simultaneously the best piece of sci-fi *and* horror the BBC has produced in a decade'.

The same morning, Catherine Tate guested on Jonathan Ross's BBC Radio 2 programme and created something of a stir by saying that Series Four would be her last as Donna and adding: 'I think it's maybe David's last'. This gave rise to a flurry of reports the following day, including in the *Independent*, the *Sun*, the *Daily Mail* and the *People*.

16 December also saw BBC One's *Breakfast* programme presenting a previously-unseen 20-second clip from 'Voyage of the Damned'. Viewers in the USA, meanwhile, got an early Christmas present when HBO gave a debut screening to the seasonal special of Ricky Gervais's sitcom *Extras*, featuring a 50-second scene in which David Tennant as the Doctor and an unnamed new companion played by Claudia Sermbezis encounter a clichéd man-in-a-rubber-suit slug monster, Shlong, portrayed by a heavily-costumed Gervais.

On 17 December, as press reports continued to appear about Tate's comments two days earlier regarding Tennant's future in the show, Davies gave a brief interview to CBBC's *Newsround* programme, which also presented some publicity stills from 'Voyage of the Damned' on its website. 'It is absolutely one of my favourite pieces of work,' Davies said of the special. 'When we finish it, I get a little DVD and I go home with it. I've watched it on my own since then about four times. That's how much I love it. I think it's brilliant.'

The following morning brought the latest of the *Sun*'s fanciful stories speculating about the identity of Tennant's successor as the Doctor:

> Jennifer Saunders is set to be the first female Time Lord – for just one episode. The comic actress is in talks to become Doctor Who as David Tennant, 36, will leave after filming three specials in 2009. TV bosses are keen to get a woman on board the TARDIS for one of those shows. A source said of Jennifer, 49, best known as Edina in *Absolutely Fabulous*: 'She's in the running and we all think she would be fantastic.'

The gist of this story was subsequently repeated elsewhere, including in the *Daily Mail* and *Now* magazine.

Industry journal *Broadcast* meanwhile announced its Hot 100 of 2007 list, which included several *Doctor Who*-related names, including Davies in top place in the category of Producers and Steven Moffat at number 11 in that of Writers.

Also on 18 December, the official *Doctor Who* website announced that Peter Davison's daughter Georgia Moffett would be taking a guest starring role in an unspecified Series Four episode. It also revealed that the first episode would be 'Partners in Crime' by Russell T Davies and the fourth – the beginning of a two-parter – would be 'The Sontaran Stratagem' by Helen Raynor.

The main focus of attention on 18 December, however, was the Science Museum in London, where the press preview screening of 'Voyage of the Damned' took place that evening, followed by the now-traditional launch party for the throng of invited guests and journalists. Amongst the *Doctor Who* names present were stars David Tennant, John Simm (the Master), Elisabeth Sladen (Sarah Jane Smith), Camille Coduri (Jackie Tyler) and Noel Clarke (Mickey Smith) and 'Voyage of the Damned' guest cast members Geoffrey Palmer, Clive Swift, Clive Rowe, Bernard Cribbins and Russell Tovey. Kylie Minogue was unable to attend; she was reportedly in Japan at the time. The event gave rise to a wealth of publicity over the next few days, with most of the main British newspapers devoting coverage to it and many online news outlets running stories, in some cases including video clips of interviews conducted at the event and brief excerpts from the special itself. Many of these pieces again focused on the issue of how long Tennant was planning to remain as the Doctor. The BBC News website reported:

> *Doctor Who* star David Tennant has laughed off speculation that he is planning to quit the show at the end of the next series in 2008. Comic actress Catherine Tate sparked rumours at the weekend when she said in a radio interview that she thought the next series would be Tennant's last ... Tennant, speaking at the launch of the Christmas episode, said: 'Catherine Tate stitched me up good and proper. I started getting all these phone calls on Saturday lunchtime saying apparently you're leaving *Doctor Who*,' Tennant told the BBC. 'Catherine Tate's just announced it on Radio 2 – thanks Catherine!' He added: 'I said to her on Monday morning, "Did you know you've caused a minor diplomatic incident?" She was completely oblivious that the phone had been ringing off the hook.' Tennant confirmed he was doing four *Doctor Who* specials in 2009, but there was no decision about the next series in 2010. 'I'm doing four more specials and beyond that no-one's asked me to make any decisions and I'm quite happy to be enigmatic for as long as possible,' he said.

Eagle-eye fans immediately spotted the possible implication in this report that the number of specials due to be made in 2009 had increased from the originally-announced three to four. Some suspected that this was simply an error, with the 2008 Christmas special being wrongly included in the total, but in fact it was true, as Davies would later confirm in *Doctor Who Magazine*.

On 19 December, the official *Doctor Who* website presented an end-of-year question and answer session with Davies, Gardner and Collinson, while the website of *SFX* magazine made available the second part of its own interview with Collinson, continued from the week before.

20 December brought the news that Tennant had taken third place in a poll of the 100 Coolest Men in Britain voted for by readers of lads' magazine *Zoo* (the top two places being taken by musician Noel Gallagher and soccer ace Steven Gerrard respectively). The *Sun* meanwhile continued its run of far-fetched *Doctor Who* casting claims with a (possibly tongue-in-cheek) story that pop idol Madonna had turned down an invitation to appear in the show as 'the last Cassandra'.

On 21 December, Adam Sherwin of *The Times* reported a minor controversy over the supposed use of religious iconography in 'Voyage of the Damned' – although quite how this controversy had arisen when the special had yet to be seen by the public was something of a mystery. Stephen Green of the evangelical group Christian Voice had apparently commented, 'The Doctor would have to do a lot more than the usual prancing around to be a messiah. He has to save people from their sins.' On the other hand, Malcolm Brown, director of mission and public affairs for the Church of England, was quoted as saying: 'Science fiction at its best helps to illuminate eternal themes, and that's something the Church can happily work with.'

David Tennant could be heard on 22 December playing a part in BBC Radio Four's Mark Gatiss-adapted Saturday afternoon play *The Wooden Overcoat*, and seen on 23 December as the celebrity guest in the top-rated BBC Two show *Top Gear*'s regular 'Star in a Reasonably-Priced Car' slot, which involved him driving a Chevrolet Lacetti around a race track as quickly as he could.

Also on 22 December, 'Voyage of the Damned' attracted some less positive publicity when a number of news outlets reported that the last survivor of the original *Titanic* disaster was upset about the theme of the special. The Scottish newspaper *Daily Record* noted:

> 95-year-old Millvina Dean, the only living survivor of the 1912 sinking, hit out at the BBC bosses for making entertainment out of tragedy. At her nursing home in Hampshire, Millvina said: 'The *Titanic* was a tragedy which tore so many families apart. I lost my father and he lies on that wreck. I think it is disrespectful to make entertainment of such a tragedy.' But a spokeswoman for the show insisted: 'No offence was intended. "Voyage of the Damned" is set on a spaceship called the *Titanic* and not a boat.'

With transmission only a day away, the 24 December editions of a number of newspapers carried appreciative previews of the special or recommended it as a highlight of the Christmas TV schedule. Caitlin Moran of *The Times* was particularly effusive in her piece, which read in part:

> For those who are into the peripatetic Time Fox and his magic turquoise wardrobe ... there is good news: this year's Christmas special is a doozy. Much better than last year's which, God bless it, peaked with the screaming thrill of the TARDIS bouncing along the A40 flyover ten minutes in ... For 2007 ... everything's gone up a few notches. 'Voyage of the Damned' is a disaster movie. More specifically, it's *The Poseidon Adventure* - a ship is damaged, a motley assortment of survivors battle to survive - but in space. The headline on the show is that there's some rather lovely chemistry between Kylie (sexy alien waitress Astrid Peth) and David Tennant (the Doctor) ... Giving the heavily guarded plot away would be an act of borderline Scroogedom - the *Who* team go to immense lengths to make sure every episode comes as a surprise on Christmas Day - but, suffice to say, you should have been both thrilled and ever so completely emotionally devastated by the end. While Kylie is delightful throughout - 'merry and squeezable' pretty much covers it - the show is, with an almost tedious reliability, David Tennant's ... This is someone who can give 110 percent intergalactic sexbrain, even when hanging upside-down, wearing a space helmet, or standing on the other side of a wall.

Following the Christmas Day transmission of 'Voyage and the Damned' and the accompanying *Doctor Who Confidential* documentary, both were made available to view online via bbc.co.uk's pioneering iPlayer service. In order to promote this, it was announced that big-screen outdoor showings of the special would take place continuously between 10.00 am and 4.00 pm on 27 December in public squares in Bradford, Derby, Hull, Leeds, Liverpool, Manchester and Rotherham.

Also on 27 December, at 9.00 pm, BBC One aired the *Extras* Christmas special first seen 11 days earlier in the USA, including Tennant's brief scene in character as the Doctor.

Post-transmission reviews of 'Voyage of the Damned' had started to appear in the press by this point, and on the whole were rather mixed. The *Mirror*'s resident TV critic Jim Shelley wrote in his paper's 27 December edition:

> *Doctor Who* was … hallucinogenic, with some brilliant psychedelic Pink Floyd-esque imagery such as the *Titanic* floating in space or flying over Buckingham Palace. It also had great baddies (gold angelic Cybermen that were very *New Avengers*) and neat jokes. But poor David Tennant had to work his little Converse plimsolls off to keep the whole thing afloat. The plot was a mess, consisting mostly of one hi-tech chase scene after another, and it descended into noise and bluster. As [when she recently appeared] on *The X Factor*, there was something faintly depressing about Kylie Minogue, who just doesn't look vivacious enough to be worth all the fuss.

Tim Teeman of *The Times* was even more scathing in his 26 December-published piece, which read in part:

> Here's a bit of seasonal sacrilege: *Doctor Who* sucks. The Christmas special amounted to a delirious tribute to *The Poseidon Adventure*. It featured, in no particular order, Kylie Minogue, monsters, explosions, a threat to destroy Earth, references to *Titanic* (both the real-life disaster and the film) and *The Apprentice* and murderous angels. It was boring, despite the endless dashing about and CGI flimflam. *Doctor Who* thinks it can do no wrong. Yesterday evening, it did …
>
> *Doctor Who* is now a national treasure of which no ill must be spoken, but for me the show and character [have] become lazy, predictable and indulgent; as evidenced in that ridiculous 'I'm the Time Lord, I'm 903 years old' rallying speech last night. The imminent arrival of Catherine Tate as the Doctor's new assistant will hopefully undercut the self-love sinking the TARDIS.

Far more impressed, however, was the *Telegraph*'s James Walton, who wrote in his piece of the same date:

> As I've had to confess before, I've never quite understood why so many people think that *Doctor Who* is the best thing to have happened to British telly in the 21st Century … Here, though, I think I could begin to see what all the fuss is about. Certainly I

> can't imagine how this episode could have done its job any better.

By this point, most print and online news outlets were also running stories about the outcome of the hotly-fought Christmas Day ratings war between the BBC and ITV; and it was good news for the former. The *Daily Telegraph*'s 28 December report was fairly typical:

> The BBC trounced ITV in this year's festive television ratings war, screening nine of the ten most popular programmes on Christmas Day. *EastEnders* was the biggest draw with 13.9 million people tuning in for the second half of a double bill, making it the most watched show of the year so far. The programme, which focused on the discovery of Stacey Branning's affair with her father-in-law, attracted 55.3 per cent of the total audience share, according to overnight viewing figures. The *Doctor Who* Christmas special starring Kylie Minogue as a waitress on the *Titanic* came second with 12.2 million viewers compared with 8.7 million last year. Other big ratings winners included Penelope Keith and Peter Bowles's reunion as the aristocratic Audrey fforbes-Hamilton and the dashing businessman Richard DeVere in a special edition of *To the Manor Born*.

When the official ratings figures became available early in January, adjusted to include those who had recorded programmes to watch later, *Doctor Who*'s tally would stand at an even more impressive 13.31 million viewers, astonishingly making it the second most-watched TV programme of the year, beaten only by the edition of *EastEnders* that immediately followed it. Its Appreciation Index figure of 86 was also excellent, indicating that the audience had been not only large but also - unlike some of the press commentators - thoroughly entertained.[7]

29 December brought news that Kylie Minogue had been awarded an OBE in the Queen's annual New Year's Honours list - although presumably not for the part she had played, as Astrid, in helping to prevent the replica *Titanic* crashing into Buckingham Palace on Christmas Day! Going from the sublime to the ridiculous, the same day's edition of the *Sun* carried yet another erroneous news item about a Series Four episode:

> BBC bosses are so confident in *Doctor Who* that they are making an episode without him in it. Instead, the Time Lord's three female assistants - Rose, Martha and Donna - take the starring roles. The shock twist comes after the Doctor, played by David Tennant, gets lost in space. His faithful sidekicks - played by Billie Piper, Freema Agyeman and Catherine Tate - are left to take control of the TARDIS as they battle to save the world from

---

[7] See Appendix B for a detailed discussion of all the Series Four ratings and rankings.

> an alien invasion. An insider on the show's top-secret Cardiff set said: 'The chemistry between the three assistants is electric. It is so strong that we realised the Doctor could be in danger of getting in the way. So it is left to the girls to sort things out, having to save civilisation and the Doctor himself.'

A significant piece of genuine news meanwhile emerged from the bbc.co.uk podcast commentary on 'Voyage of the Damned', which became available to download at the end of the month: participants Russell T Davies, Julie Gardner and Phil Collinson revealed that Collinson would be leaving his post as *Doctor Who*'s producer before work began on the post-Series Four specials.

Rounding off the festive season, David Tennant and John Simm were amongst the studio guests seen enjoying themselves on *Jools's Annual Hootenanny*, a pre-recorded programme with which BBC Two ushered in the New Year on 31 December. Kylie Minogue was amongst the musical guests performing on the programme. Then, on New Year's Day, Freema Agyeman served as one of the presenters on BBC Radio 1's *New for 2008* programme, aired between 7.00 pm and midnight; Agyeman's slot ran for an hour from 10.00 pm.

CHAPTER THREE
TOWARD SERIES FOUR

As the New Year began and excitement over 'Voyage of the Damned' died down, there was still a constant stream of *Doctor Who* news to keep fans interested while they waited with increasing impatience for the start of Series Four.

January 2008

While various news outlets published stories on and photos of Billie Piper's New Year's Eve wedding to fellow actor Laurence Fox, which had been attended by David Tennant amongst others, the *Sun* opened its 2008 *Doctor Who* coverage with a 2 January report about Sarah Lancashire's forthcoming appearance in show, illustrated with images taken from the Series Four trailer shown at the end of 'Voyage of the Damned'. It also mentioned some of the other confirmed guest stars for Series Four and concluded, on a slightly more speculative note:

> Billie Piper and Elisabeth Sladen will recreate their roles as Rose Tyler and Sarah Jane Smith. John Barrowman, who plays Captain Jack Harkness in spin-off series *Torchwood*, will also be back. The series is the last for star David Tennant, 36, but he will play the Doctor in four special episodes in 2009 and in a movie version.

8 January marked the one hundredth anniversary of the birth of first Doctor actor William Hartnell, although sadly this landmark seemed to attract little attention outside of fandom.

Issue 391 of *Doctor Who Magazine*, which went on sale on 10 January, confirmed two more Series Four episode titles, 'The Unicorn and the Wasp' and 'Midnight'; and announced that second Doctor actor Patrick Troughton's son David would be taking a guest role in the series, reported by online sources to be named Professor Hobbs.[8]

11 January brought news of yet more awards success for *Doctor Who*, as it was announced that users of the interactive TV guide DigiGuide had voted it Best Sci-Fi show by a huge margin. The *Sun* meanwhile published a further brief casting story, claiming that David Jason had been offered a *Doctor Who* role but had been unable to accept it because he was under exclusive contract to ITV.

On 15 January, the BBC Press Office announced that the BBC iPlayer website had attracted over one million visitors since its marketing launch on Christmas Day. It went on to say:

---

[8] In the event, the name of Troughton's character in 'Midnight' would be spelt slightly differently as 'Hobbes'.

> The BBC favourites that made up the top five most frequently streamed programmes [up to 7 January] are the *Doctor Who* Christmas special (BBC One), *Extras* Christmas special (BBC Two), *Top Gear* (BBC Two), *The Catherine Tate Christmas Show* (BBC One) and the Christmas Day edition of *EastEnders* (BBC One).

This was a further testament to the huge popularity of 'Voyage of the Damned'; and, as fans quickly noted, even the number two, three and four programmes on the list had a *Doctor Who* connection (through Tennant's appearances in the first two and Tate's in her own show). The news of this successful launch spawned a number of stories in the media over the days that followed, most of which made mention of *Doctor Who*'s status as the service's most-watched programme.

15 January brought a live appearance by showrunner Russell T Davies on DJ Nemone's BBC 6 digital radio show, answering a range of *Doctor Who*-related questions. He could then be both heard and seen the following evening on BBC Four, discussing his life and career in depth in a programme entitled *Mark Lawson Talks to Russell T Davies*.

The 19 January edition of the Canadian newspaper *Toronto Star* carried a Catherine Tate interview that mainly covered her comedy work but also touched on her return to *Doctor Who*:

> '["The Runaway Bride"] was supposed to be a one-off,' Tate confirms. 'We didn't know [Donna would be back] when we did it. It was left open, but that was entirely unintentional – you know, he says, "Come with me," and I say "No". And then I ask, "Am I ever going to see you again?" and he says, "If I'm lucky". It just sort of happened that way ... though it did, you know, make it incredibly easy for me to come back in.' The venerable sci-fi series has proved a refreshing change of pace from what has, up till now, been a one-woman show. 'I don't actually think the process is any different than doing comedy, but the results are different,' she allows. 'What's great about doing *Doctor Who* is that it has a narrative, so it means that I can approach it more as a straight acting role. It's just nicer to have a story arc that lasts longer than, like, four minutes. And it's just the one character, and I don't have to have the pressure of writing it. It's a pressure and a privilege, writing. But mainly a pressure.'

Sir Michael Lyons, Chairman of the BBC Trust, praised both *Doctor Who* and *Torchwood* during a 22 January visit to Cardiff, citing them as shining examples of good-value-for-money programme-making and promising more investment for BBC Wales. On the same date, Australia's *New Idea* magazine reported that Kylie Minogue was on the point of signing a deal to return to *Doctor Who* after her well-received appearance in 'Voyage of the Damned'. The following day then saw the OrganGrinder blog on the guardian.co.uk website announcing that *Doctor Who* had been voted its readers' favourite TV show of 2007 – the third year running it had won the poll.

On 24 January, the BBC Press Office put out a further *Doctor Who* news release, revealing two more Series Four guest cast members:

> Alex Kingston, best known for roles in *ER* and *Moll Flanders*, will appear in a Steven Moffat penned two-parter as River Song – a mysterious character who meets the Doctor on an expedition to uncover the secrets of an abandoned library. She is joined by *James Bond* regular Colin Salmon, who also stars in the two episodes. Alex Kingston comments: 'I used to watch *Doctor Who* through the crack in the door. I was so terrified but I couldn't tear myself away. I loved it so much and I'm so delighted to be a part of the new series.'

The long-standing rumours regarding Sarah Jane Smith's return in the Series Four finale were also confirmed on 25 January, in a preview snippet from a forthcoming Elisabeth Sladen interview placed on the *SFX* magazine website.

As the month drew to a close, the 29 January edition of the *Sun* reported that Series One of *Doctor Who* had been sold by BBC Worldwide to the ProSeiben channel in Germany, and that the dialogue of Christopher Eccleston and Billie Piper would be dubbed into German by vocal artists Frank Roth and Maren Rainer respectively.

February 2008

From 1 February, a new, 90-second-long trailer consisting of a montage of clips from Series Four started screening in 142 Empire, 837 Odeon and 736 Cineworld cinemas around the country as part of a deal between the BBC and Carlton Screen Advertising. BBC Vision's head of marketing, Naomi Gibney, was quoted as saying, 'This is a great opportunity for the BBC to reach new audiences with an exciting preview of the new series of *Doctor Who*'.

1 February was also the date when the BBC Press Office officially confirmed that Phil Collinson would shortly be moving on from the *Doctor Who* producer's job, which he had held since 2004. The press release read in part:

> Peter Salmon, Chief Creative Officer, BBC Vision Productions, today announces that Phil Collinson is joining the BBC to become Head of Drama, Manchester, returning to the city where he started his television career.
>
> Collinson will be charged with developing links with both on- and off-screen talent in the region and contributing shows to the overall slate of BBC Drama production when he begins in the spring.
>
> The appointment of the *Doctor Who* producer reflects the commitment of the BBC to grow the drama slate across the UK. Phil will take up his new role after he completes work on Series Four of *Doctor Who* in a few weeks' time ...

> Russell T Davies, executive producer and writer, *Doctor Who*, says: 'Phil has been the secret hero of *Doctor Who* for the past four years, and we'll miss him more than I can say – but the most exciting thing about this new job is that so many more producers, writers and actors will get to work with him. I envy them!'
>
> Phil Collinson comments: 'The four years I've spent producing *Doctor Who* in Cardiff have been incredibly rewarding and I've long wondered how I was ever going to prise myself away from such a thrilling show and inspirational cast and crew.
>
> 'The chance to return home to Manchester though, and start something completely new, is irresistible. Manchester has always been an amazing centre for excellence in drama production and the chance to establish a formal BBC Drama base there, and build on the massive range of local talent, is incredibly exciting. I'm thrilled and honoured to be charged with this task.'

7 February saw Issue 392 of *Doctor Who Magazine* go on sale. This announced that Series Four's Ancient Rome episode would be second in the running order and entitled 'The Fires of Pompeii'; that the sixth episode would be written by Stephen Greenhorn, who had previously been responsible for Series Three's 'The Lazarus Experiment'; and that 'Midnight' would take the tenth slot. The magazine also revealed that Steve Pemberton, one of *Doctor Who* writer and actor Mark Gatiss's colleagues in the League of Gentlemen comedy team, had won a guest starring role in the story that would comprise the eighth and ninth episodes. This formed the basis of a 12 February news item in the *Sun*, which noted:

> Bosses are keeping tight-lipped about *who* he [Pemberton] will play. But insiders said Steve will play a mysterious character called Lux who meets the Doctor during an expedition to uncover the secrets of an abandoned library ... A source said: 'Steve is an obvious choice for *Doctor Who* bosses because he looks so funny and he's used to playing weird characters from his time in League of Gentlemen.'

The 14 and 15 February editions of BBC One's ever-popular soap opera *EastEnders* included scenes set in and around a (fictional) *Doctor Who* convention-cum-exhibition, dubbed '*Doctor Who* – The Time Lord Revisited', in the unlikely venue of St Paul's Cathedral in London. These scenes, which had been shot on 3 and 4 December 2007, involved amongst other things a group of Cybermen, with costumes resembling those from 'Revenge of the Cybermen' (1975), staging a re-enactment (of sorts) of the famous scene from 'The Invasion' (1968) where the creatures march down a flight of steps within sight of the Cathedral. A TARDIS police box, Daleks and a (fan-made) K-9 were also in evidence.

The 20 February edition of the *Sun* revealed that comedian and chat show host Paul O'Grady was to make a celebrity cameo appearance in the Series Four finale, discussing 'strange goings on' on his show. A BBC source was quoted as saying: 'Paul has been desperate to be on the show for ages and asked if he could be a guest star. Fortunately *Who* creator Russell T Davies is a big fan of his too, and jumped at the chance. We've had to wait until his chat show is filming again so we can shoot him on the set. It will be the usual camp Paul – just maybe a bit more sinister.'

Also on 20 February, the BBC Press Office put out a further news release about the ongoing success of the iPlayer service. This noted:

> Over 17 million programmes have been streamed or downloaded on demand on BBC iPlayer in the first seven weeks since its marketing launch, according to the latest figures from the BBC. Daily volumes have been increasing strongly during January and February and last week the total number of streams and downloads in a single day broke through the half a million barrier. During January, more than 2.2 million people watched a programme on BBC iPlayer, with approximately 11 million TV programmes streamed or downloaded on demand.

As of 12 February, 'Voyage of the Damned' was still the number one programme viewed via the iPlayer.

On 21 February, Catherine Tate could be heard interviewing David Tennant in a new edition of BBC Radio 4's *Chain Reaction*. The 'round-robin' format of this show meant that the following week's edition would see Tennant himself become the interviewer, putting questions to actor Richard Wilson, remembered by *Doctor Who* fans for his role as Dr Constantine in 'The Empty Child'/'The Doctor Dances'.

The *Sun* presented its latest *Doctor Who* story on 29 February, gleefully reporting:

> Here's a real Who-dunnit – two top-secret scripts from the hotly awaited new *Doctor Who* series have been leaked to TV Biz. And our mole didn't even need a sonic screwdriver to get hold of the bundle, which features episodes nine and ten of the hit show. *Doctor Who* bosses take security on the programme very seriously and are paranoid about show secrets getting out. So not surprisingly, top brass hit the roof after hearing about our leak. An insider said: 'Bosses are fuming – this is the last thing they would want to happen.' But they needn't worry – we won't be ruining it for the show's 14million fans by serving up all the twists and turns of the plot.

The story went on to reveal a few details of the plot and dialogue of the Steven Moffat two-parter that would ultimately prove to be accurate, suggesting that the paper had indeed managed to obtain illicit copies of the scripts. Elsewhere in the same edition, the *Sun* printed a photo taken on location of a soaking wet David Tennant, recording one of the final scenes of Series Four.

March 2008

On 6 March, the official *Doctor Who* website was given a makeover, its homepage presenting a new image of the Doctor and Donna on the TARDIS interior set both wearing brown pinstripe suits, captioned 'Partners in Stripes'. The BBC at the same time released a number of similar images for promotional purposes.

6 March was also the date when Issue 393 of *Doctor Who Magazine* went on sale. This confirmed that Series Four would begin transmission in April and revealed the title of the eighth episode to be 'Silence in the Library'.

Also on this date, the *Sun* presented the latest in its succession of largely inaccurate Series Four news stories, this one based on an unsubstantiated rumour circulating within fandom:

> PM Harriet Jones becomes a Dalek in the new series of *Doctor Who*, TV Biz can reveal. Penelope Wilton, 61, returns as the somewhat gormless Harriet two years after we last saw her, being brought down by a fuming Time Lord for being too cocky in 'The Christmas Invasion'. She was later deposed when The Master brainwashed voters into putting him in Downing Street under the alias Harold Saxon. Now Harriet is set to become a real threat to the good Doctor - as the daddy of all Daleks. In a shock moment on the BBC One sci-fi hit the casing of one of the metal monsters opens to reveal the ex-PM has been converted into a tyrannical pepper pot.

Issue 168 of genre magazine *SFX* appeared in newsagents on 12 March and contained a lengthy interview with Russell T Davies. Questioned about the logic behind the 'gap year' in 2009, he responded: '*Doctor Who* is now one of the BBC's biggest flagship shows, and this sort of pattern will guarantee it being on air for 20 years. It's no good looking at that American pattern of making seven years if you're lucky - that's just not going to work. Who wants it to die after seven years? It's much bigger than that. It needs looking after, in the sense that it needs pauses, it needs its legend revamping every so often. If you build these pauses in now and say this will always happen, that's part of the plan now - it's literally a 20 year plan, which can't be guaranteed, because different people will be in charge in years to come - but if you present them with something rock solid, that is working, and has a unique transmission pattern that shouldn't be interfered with, then it will stay.' These comments, which were also reported in that day's edition of the *Sun*, added fuel to the debate still ongoing within fandom about the 'gap year' and the show's long-term future.

20 March brought confirmation from the BBC Press Office of an exact start date for Series Four: 5 April. The following brief plot details were also given: 'Donna Noble is determined to find the Doctor again - even if it means braving the villainous Miss Foster and her hordes of sinister Adipose, as Russell T Davies's BAFTA Award-winning time-travelling drama returns for a fourth series. But when the alien threat escalates out of control, can Donna find her Time Lord before the march of the Adipose begins?' Similar details would be made available for subsequent episodes on a weekly basis as part of the Press Office's routine release

of scheduling information for forthcoming programmes.

Following the pattern established with 'Voyage of the Damned', the 90-second trailer previously seen in cinemas was now shown on BBC One as well, debuting at just after 7.00 pm on 22 March, having again been accorded sufficient significance to merit a *Radio Times* listing. It was also placed on the official *Doctor Who* website and in higher quality on the BBC's YouTube channel. Three specially-shot, bronze-hued ten-second teaser trailers, featuring Sontarans, Ood and a Dalek respectively, also made their BBC One debut on this date, just after the late evening news programme, with a different one being shown in each TV region. These too were made available to view (as usual, in the UK only, due to rights restrictions) on the show's website and the BBC's YouTube channel.

26 March brought what would prove to be a controversial announcement from the BBC, in the form of a confirmed start time for transmission of 'Partners in Crime': 6.20 pm – the earliest slot the show had been given since its return in 2005. *Doctor Who Confidential* would follow at 7.10 pm on BBC Three. Two days later, speaking at a conference organised by *Broadcast* magazine, Russell T Davies told the audience that he was distinctly unhappy with the new slot and felt that the BBC had 'cocked up' the scheduling. The BBC's in-house staff magazine *Ariel* reported:

> Russell T Davies is predicting that *Doctor Who* could lose up to 1.5 million viewers when it returns in a new 6.20 pm slot next month. The writer and executive producer of the series told the Broadcast television drama conference today that the BBC should maintain the later 7.00 pm to 7.15 pm slot and the budget for the sci-fi series but it had mucked it up. The BBC believes the programme would do as well in the new slot, he said. 'Well, we'll see, but I think I'm right.' Not all time travel is welcome. He also said he would resist any move to [record] the series in HD – it would be too expensive and it was 'rubbish' to think no-one would watch unless it was in high definition. He said it had always been the plan to rest *Doctor Who* in 2009. He said he would use the time off to work on new projects, for instance for a 9.00 pm slot with more adult, emotional content, although nothing had been commissioned.

The contention over the show's scheduling was a storm that would rumble on into the following month.

28 March saw Tennant joining hosts Alan Carr and Justin Lee Collins on Channel 4's *The Friday Night Project* and appearing in a number of humorous skits, including one in which he donned a false moustache, glasses and a white coat to play a medical doctor called upon to treat a three-breasted alien woman and a 1980s-style Cyberman that had apparently just given birth to a Cyberbaby.

On 29 March, the *Daily Telegraph* published a profile of Davies under the heading '*Doctor Who*'s Russell T Davies Saves Family TV' and an interview with the man himself, in which he was quoted as saying: 'The day I leave *Doctor Who*, I will just walk away. I would never want to hang on as a ghost of what I was. I would be a nightmare! I'd be that voice at the back of the set going, "Oh, I wouldn't do it that way."'. The same day's edition of the *Independent* meanwhile presented a profile of

Tennant, noting, 'The most powerful actor in television is also, by all accounts, the nicest bloke in showbiz'. Davies was again quoted in this piece, waxing lyrical about his lead actor's talents and adding: 'The show's success is so mad that I don't think any of us will get our heads round it till it's all over and we look back on it in ten years' time and say, "Blimey, that was weird". But I think what the public like about David is his energy. He glitters on screen; there's a vitality to him that is undeniably what has worked with the Doctor. On set we're surrounded by props and monsters and explosions, and things often go wrong. When they do, we say to each other, "Well, at least we've got David." We put the camera on him and it just comes to life.' This *Independent* piece was also noteworthy for stating that Tennant was 'informally committed' to appear in Series Five in 2010. Further press interviews with Davies would appear over the next few days – including one in the *Western Mail* and one in the *Scotsman*, both on 31 March – as the promotional effort for the new series went into overdrive.

29 March also saw a new Series Four trailer unveiled, and once more placed on the show's official website and the BBC's YouTube channel. This specially-shot piece was in the same bronze-hued style as the three ten-second teasers but ran to a full 40 seconds. It featured a series of clips of Sontarans, Ood, Daleks and the Doctor, framed by a sequence of Donna seated by a campfire saying: 'There are things waiting in the darkness. Creatures of metal and fire and blood. But he's out there, burning through time, facing a thousand dangers across the stars, and never giving up. He looks like a man, but he's a legend, and his name is the Doctor. He'll come back to save us, and this time, I'm gonna be ready. Then, just like that, we'll be gone.' The final words, 'we'll be gone', had the Doctor's whispered voice joining Donna's. An edited 20-second version of this 'campfire trailer', as it became known, was also shown, beginning on the evening of 31 March.

On 30 March, the Sunday editions of a number of the national newspapers carried pieces on 'Partners in Crime' as part of their preview of the coming week's TV, an advance press screening of both this episode and 'The Fires of Pompeii' having taken place at the BBC's Television Centre on 25 March. The *Sunday Times*'s critic seemed in two minds about the series-opener's merits:

> Written by Russell T Davies with characteristic ingenuity, 'Partners in Crime' is strikingly unscary: the cute alien babies pose no threat and the villainess's sinister scheme only causes one fatality. Humour is pervasive from the silent sequence when [the Doctor and Donna] first spot each other, to the satirising of slimming gurus and supernannies. The closing scene establishes Donna as the Time Lord's new companion, and it is too early to judge whether this gamble – not unlike making Rose's mum his sidekick – will succeed. Some Whovians (painfully reminded of predecessor Bonnie Langford) find Tate's shouty secretary over the top, and she plainly won't match Rose's and Martha's athleticism. But there are signs of comic rapport with Tennant, and Davies must be counting on the different chemistry derived from pairing characters of roughly the same age.

The *Mail on Sunday*, however, was more fully appreciative, making the episode its 'Pick of the Day' and commenting:

> It's a witty, at times borderline daft, scene-setter, but the laugh count, notably the silent comedy exchange between Tate and David Tennant when their characters meet again, remains consistently high. Factor in Sarah Lancashire's power-dressed villain and the cutest monsters (blubber-baby aliens) the show has ever seen, and it's another winner for Russell T and the gang.

On balance, the positive press coverage far outweighed the negative - the *Observer* even went so far as to describe 'Partners in Crime' as 'the strongest opening episode since the revamped *Doctor Who* was launched back in 2005' - and it seemed that viewers were in for a real treat the following Saturday.

CHAPTER FOUR
SERIES FOUR HITS THE SCREEN

On 1 April, with the start of Series Four only days away and excitement within fandom building to fever pitch, the new edition of the BBC's *Radio Times* went on sale and offered a choice of four collectable *Doctor Who* covers, depicting characters and images from 'Partners in Crime', 'The Fires of Pompeii', 'Planet of the Ood' and 'The Unicorn and the Wasp' respectively. Inside the magazine, an extensive preview feature by Russell T Davies confirmed the titles of all the forthcoming episodes bar the twelfth – which was kept under wraps because it was considered too revealing of the plot – and presented intriguing snippets of advance information about each. At this stage, the ninth episode was called 'River's Run', although that would later change.

Also in this edition of *Radio Times*, coincidentally, was an article about *Doctor Who*'s original producer, the recently-deceased Verity Lambert, who was to be the subject of a tribute evening on BBC Four. Davies was quoted as saying that when he relaunched *Doctor Who*, Lambert's version of the show was one that he had turned to for inspiration: 'It was before the series became bogged down in any continuity. There was just mystery. An open road – that's what she created.'

All the rival TV listings magazines also devoted space to *Doctor Who* this week, *TV & Satellite Week* and *TV Guide* both featuring a main front cover photo of the Doctor and Donna and the *TV Times* running a competition to win a new-era-style Dalek constructed by the This Planet Earth licensees.

1 April was also the date when the major Series Four press launch was held in London, the invitation-only audience being treated to previews of both 'Partners in Crime' and 'The Fires of Pompeii' and a trailer for the rest of the series featuring numerous previously-unseen clips. Ian Wylie of the *Manchester Evening News* was one of the first journalists to file a report, which appeared on the newspaper's website later the same night. It read in part:

> Just back from tonight's launch for Series Four of *Doctor Who*. We saw episodes one and two, followed by a Q&A with David Tennant, Catherine Tate and Russell T Davies. The talk was of Doctor Who's daughter, the Time Lord and Donna Noble just being 'mates' and the return of the Sontarans. Both David and Russell refused to comment about their futures with the show after this 13-part series and four further specials.[9] Catherine also said she couldn't comment when asked if she was in the specials ... Controller of BBC Fiction Jane Tranter introduced the screening at a cinema in London's West End. She pointed

---

[9] Including the 2008 Christmas special, there would in fact be five specials before the 2010 series.

> out that the *Doctor Who* team had been involved over the last four years with 56 episodes, including this year's yet to be filmed Christmas special. 'And soon they'll be limbering up for yet another marathon stint with four huge specials and then a fifth series looming,' added Jane. 'For me, this fourth series of *Doctor Who* is our best yet. It is the series that appears to have everyone and everything in it and be about absolutely everything the universe has got to offer. But believe me, there is much more still to come after this.'

A number of TV news bulletins also covered the event, including on BBC News 24, and the BBC News website presented a detailed report, complete with video interviews with Tennant and Tate and some exclusive preview clips from 'Partners in Crime'. Stories were then run the following day by a number of other websites and newspapers, including the *Daily Mirror*, while appreciative reviews of 'Partners in Crime' appeared in both the *Sun* and the *Daily Telegraph*. The latter's critic Neil Midgley commented:

> Tate is reprising her role as Donna Noble, who joined the Doctor in the TARDIS for his 2006 Christmas special. She makes an unlikely assistant - 14 years older than spunky Billie Piper, and trying to save the planet in a sensible trouser suit. After Christmas's Kylie-on-the-*Titanic*-in-the-sky extravaganza, the call-centre setting of this new episode looks rather drab. It also jars with the infuriating and virtually constant orchestral soundtrack on which the BBC now insists. It makes the more mature *Who* fan hanker for the sparse glory of the BBC Radiophonic Workshop. But *Doctor Who* always provides an engrossing romp, with enough layers and asides to keep parents and kids entertained. In this episode, the show is well and truly stolen by the six-inch Adipose aliens themselves. As cute as the Pillsbury Doughboy and apparently as ticklish, they'll win over the most cynical viewer - a bit like the show itself.

The subject of the show's scheduling continued to trouble Davies, the BBC News website's report of the launch quoting him as having said: 'It's not a time slot I agree with. I'd rather it went out later [at 7.00 pm]. But we've been told that it's a gateway to the whole Saturday night. We'll see on Monday morning what [the initial ratings figures are] like.' However, it seemed that the executive producer might be winning this war of words with BBC bosses as, in its report the following day, *Ariel* stated that the show would be moved to the later slot he favoured by around the fifth or sixth episode of the run.

The official *Doctor Who* website was relaunched with a new design for Series Four on the afternoon of 2 April, although heavy demand from fans eager to see the results caused some technical hitches, including very long page loading times, over the next few days - a situation for which the webmasters subsequently apologised. To coincide with the relaunch, the BBC made available a set of new

Series Four publicity images. These consisted of photographs of Tennant and Tate posing in costume against a background of a location dressed as a warehouse for 'Planet of the Ood', with swirls of digitally-added energy beams radiating from behind them. Similar images featuring other companion characters would be issued in the weeks to come.

Also on 2 April, the media promotion of the new series continued as Davies appeared on BBC One's *Breakfast*, Tennant and Tate could be heard both on BBC Radio 1's Chris Moyles show, with Scott Mills standing in for Moyles, and on BBC Digital Radio 1Xtra's *Breakfast*, and Tennant alone guested for half an hour on Simon Mayo's BBC Radio Five Live afternoon show. Even ITV's GMTV got in on the act, presenting an enthusiastic preview of 'Partners in Crime' with a number of clips.

On 3 April, the *MediaGuardian* section of the guardian.co.uk website offered a 'special effects sneak peak' in the form of an article describing how the CGI effects of the Adipose creatures had been achieved for 'Partners in Crime', illustrated with an exclusive image gallery. The article explained:

> In what is believed to be a first for a TV series, The Mill used a programme called Massive, normally used [for] adverts and feature films. Stephen Regelous, the Academy award-winning creator of the technology, flew to London to supervise the effects. [Regelous said:] 'The Mill was one of our very first customers and we've been very excited to see the wonderful work that's been produced over the years there using Massive. When I first found out that the Mill was working on *Doctor Who*, I was quietly hoping that Massive might be used to create hordes of Daleks or Cybermen, and with Series Four, I jumped at the opportunity to be involved. It's been very fulfilling to be a fan from about three or four years old and finally be able to contribute to the *Doctor Who* universe.' Regelous created Massive at digital effects company Weta in the 1990s and it was used in the battle scenes in *The Lord of the Rings* trilogy, generating crowd effects that allowed animators to populate a scene with individuals that behave in unique ways.

3 April also saw the release of Issue 394 of *Doctor Who Magazine*, in which Davies confirmed one piece of news that some fans had already deduced from perusing the TV schedules: there would sadly be no third series of the CBBC children's magazine show *Totally Doctor Who* this year.

On 4 April, the CBBC *Newsround* website reported that the title of Series Four's ninth episode had now been changed from 'River's Run' to 'Forest of the Dead', as exclusively revealed to them by Davies himself, while the *Daily Telegraph* ran an article about *Doctor Who*'s ability to attract big-name guest stars. Also on this date, Tennant and Tate continued their hectic round of promotional activities, dashing from studio to studio to guest on: the breakfast show on BBC Radio London; Christian O'Connell's Virgin Radio breakfast show; the Capital FM breakfast show, on which they were interviewed by Denise van Outen and stand-in presenter John Barrowman; George Lamb's lunchtime show on BBC Radio 6; and Steve Wright's afternoon show on BBC Radio 2. Then, that evening, the two stars made a joint guest appearance on BBC One's pre-recorded *Friday Night With Jonathan Ross* chat show, in what amounted to the final major piece of advance publicity for the new series. This interview lasted a full quarter of an hour, included clips from the cinema trailer and from 'Partners in Crime' (the scene of Stacey being converted into Adipose) and covered subjects as diverse as Tate's initial misapprehension that the Sontarans were remote-controlled mannequins rather than actors in costumes and the problems she had encountered in finding a suitable pet cat.

5 April was the long-awaited start date for Series Four, and again it generated plenty of press coverage. The *Guardian*'s *Weekend* magazine published a lengthy interview feature on Tate, focusing mainly on her comedy work, while *The Times*'s David Chater had good things to say about that evening's episode:

> *Doctor Who* is back for a new series, as fabulous as ever. The great joy of the Russell T Davies revival is the humour that runs through every episode. This has now quadrupled with the arrival of Catherine Tate as his latest assistant. And success breeds success. The series attracts the cream of British acting talent, and tonight Sarah Lancashire makes a guest appearance as a super-nanny from outer space. She oversees a company that makes a virulent variety of diet pill, fashioning excess human fat into alien creatures. But the good news is that these aliens are enchanting little fellows who smile, wave, hop around and wish no-one any harm. I want one as a pet

BBC One's *Breakfast* programme meanwhile featured an item on the new *Doctor Who* exhibition in London and an in-studio interview with 'Voyage of the Damned' director James Strong and Dalek voice artist Nicholas Briggs.

'Partners in Crime' was finally transmitted at 6.19 pm - a minute earlier than scheduled - on BBC One. Despite the early time slot that had so concerned Davies, the unofficial overnight ratings statistics reported the following day indicated that it had done exceptionally well, attracting an estimated 8.4 million viewers - slightly higher than either of the previous two series-openers. (When the final figure was released ten days later, it would be adjusted to an even better 9.14 million.) A BBC spokesperson was quoted as saying: 'This is a great start for the new series of *Doctor Who*. The show kicked off a fantastic night of family entertainment on BBC One which pulled in big audiences across the evening.' The Appreciation Index figure, which became available on 7 April, was an excellent 88, the highest that any programme had scored that Saturday. In short, the episode had proved to be a smash hit with the viewing public. This in turn generated even more positive media coverage, headlines such as the *Daily Star*'s '8.4 Million Viewers See *Doctor Who* Return' being typical.

The more substantial press pieces kept on coming as well. On 6 April, *The Independent on Sunday* boasted a lengthy interview with Davies, in which amongst other things he revealed that evolutionary biologist Richard Dawkins would be making a cameo appearance later in Series Four - 'He was as mad and as barking as you'd want him to be. "Don't touch me, I've got a cold! Don't shake my hand!" Just brilliant. It's like, "Woah!".' The *Sunday Times* meanwhile ran an insightful interview with Tennant, written by his friend and one-time landlady, actress Arabella Weir, under the no doubt deliberately provacative title 'It's okay to think Doctor Who is gay, says David Tennant' – although, as became apparent on reading the piece, what Tennant actually said was that he didn't mind people speculating about his own sexuality, rather than the character's. Recalling how his childhood love of *Doctor Who* went hand-in-hand with his desire to be an actor, Tennant told Weir: 'I remember, after seeing Jon Pertwee turn into Tom Baker in *Doctor Who,* having a conversation with my parents at a very young age about actors and what they did. I remember getting the distinction between a character and an actor, as they explained it. I understood what fiction was very clearly – and I always feel uneasy when people talk about children not understanding the difference between fantasy and reality. I can only have been three, and was just enthralled by [*Doctor Who*]. But I was quite clear that I didn't want to be a Time Lord – I wanted to be the person who played a Time Lord.' Also on this date, the *Sunday Telegraph*'s arts and media editor Christopher Hastings presented another interview with Davies, in a piece entitled 'Finally, Catherine Tate gives us a companion to tame Doctor Who'. This read in part:

> Russell T Davies, the mastermind behind the latest incarnation of the hit BBC television show, which returned for a fresh series last night, told *The Sunday Telegraph* that Donna Noble would become the first equal partner to the Doctor, played by David Tennant, and would never fall in love with him. He said that Noble … would help to bring the Doctor down to earth. 'It's about time we got someone in the TARDIS who is not so doe-eyed,' he said. 'Donna is much more the Doctor's equal than any of the previous assistants. She is older and she is not in love with him, and that also makes a difference. David's Doctor is now so glittering and stellar that he needs bringing down to earth by someone who can question him. In episode two, Donna changes the future of characters by her strength of will. I don't think any other assistant could have pulled off that scene.' He said that Tate's character had more in common with the audience: 'She experiences real moments of terror. She is flawed. It really is like having me or you on the TARDIS.'

Post-transmission press reviews of 'Partners in Crime' reflected the same predominantly positive reaction as pre-transmission ones, albeit with a few dissenters. By any standards, it was clear that Series Four had got off to a cracking start – and there were still 12 more episodes to go!

CHAPTER FIVE
THE SERIES IN PROGRESS

The new series having been launched, the promotional activity surrounding it naturally dropped to a lower level, but nevertheless continued. *Doctor Who* would grace the front cover of the *Radio Times* on a further three occasions during the course of Series Four, and every single episode would be accorded a feature article within the magazine's pages. The show's official website would be updated on a weekly basis with lots of exclusive content, including behind-the-scenes video clips (although as usual these would generally be viewable only in the UK). Members of the cast and crew would also continue to give occasional interviews and make occasional TV appearances in support of the show. Then, as the series finale approached, the publicity machine would go into overdrive once again.

April 2008

9 April brought the news that *Doctor Who*'s incidental music would form the basis of one of this year's BBC Proms concerts. The BBC News website reported:

> Daleks will roam the Royal Albert Hall at the *Doctor Who* Prom in July, which will celebrate music from the popular BBC show … The event, presented by *Doctor Who* actress Freema Agyeman, will feature the show's iconic theme tune alongside other compositions related to time and space, including Holst's 'The Planets - Jupiter', Wagner's 'Die Walkure - The Ride of the Valkyries'. *Doctor Who* star David Tennant will make an on-screen appearance in a pre-recorded scene written by Russell T Davies.

10 April was the date when members of the public first spotted the *Doctor Who* crew out on location to record scenes for the 2008 Christmas special, which was being made as part of the Series Four production schedule immediately after the closing episode 'Journey's End'. The following day, the *South Wales Argus*'s David Deans reported on the newspaper's website:

> The Cybermen are back - and they've come to a city near you. The classic *Doctor Who* villains took over the St Woolos cemetery, Newport while filming yesterday. The BBC Wales drama team covered the site in fake snow for a winter scene. Residents was left wondering whether the team may have been filming a Christmas special. Janet Hancock, who lives in Canberra Crescent, Glasllwch, said she saw the filming yesterday morning while out walking the dog. 'I was going past the cemetery walls

> and saw lots of white smoke. A security guard said they were filming *Doctor Who* – it was very exciting.' She said she peeked over the cemetery walls to take a look ..., and saw people in long black coats running all over the site. Sadly she didn't see any of the stars of the series.'

On 14 April, David Tennant was the guest on Colin Murray's morning show on BBC Radio 1, discussing both *Doctor Who* and his forthcoming roles for the Royal Shakespeare Company.

17 April saw an announcement by the organisers of *The Times*'s Cheltenham Literature Festival, due to take place in October, that Tennant and Catherine Tate would be star speakers at the event, discussing their work on *Doctor Who* and their careers more generally. (As things transpired, neither Tennant nor Tate would be able to attend: Russell T Davies and John Barrowman would take their places, appearing on 12 October.)

A conference entitled Spirituality and *Doctor Who* was held on 19 April at the Wilson Carlile College of Evangelism in Sheffield, Yorkshire. The organisers said, 'Christian themes and images in *Doctor Who* – both classic and new – will be explored. But there will also be a respectful look at other shades and faiths in *Doctor Who,* including ecological and Buddhist themes in the Jon Pertwee era, mystic parables in the Peter Davison era and the optimistic atheism of current *Doctor Who* creator Russell T Davies.' Former *Doctor Who* producer Barry Letts was one of the advertised speakers. The *Daily Telegraph*'s religious affairs correspondent Jonathan Wynne-Jones reported on the event on 4 May:

> Andrew Wooding, a spokesman for the Church Army, which organised the conference, said that its intention was to give vicars new ideas for conveying their message. 'There are countless examples of Christian symbolism in *Doctor Who,* which we can use to get across ideas that can otherwise be difficult to explain. Clergy shouldn't be afraid to engage with popular culture as for many young people television plays a large role in their thinking.' ... Although an atheist, Russell T Davies, the chief writer of the current series, has previously acknowledged the benefits of religion. 'I think religion is a very primal instinct within humans, a very good one, part of our imagination,' he said. While he has talked about the humanism in his work he has never admitted to putting overtly religious messages in the storylines. However, with sessions including titles such as 'Meaningful Monsters: Daleks through the Decades', the clergy looked at several episodes that could have religious meaning.

The edition of the *Radio Times* that went on sale on 22 April, listing details for the following week's programmes, was the next to feature a *Doctor Who* cover photo: a dramatic image of Christopher Ryan as General Staal, publicising the return of the Sontarans in 'The Sontaran Stratagem'. A CD of the first half of the *Doctor Who* audiobook *The Resurrection Casket* was given away free with each copy of the magazine; the second half would follow with the next week's edition.

22 April also brought more reports of the location recording under way for the 2008 Christmas special. A syndicated Press Association story revealed that David Tennant and his one-time *Blackpool* co-star David Morrissey had been spotted performing scenes in the grounds of Gloucester Cathedral:

> College Green was covered with artificial snow for the scene filmed today, in which mourners in Victorian costume marched in front of a horse-drawn cart carrying a coffin. Tennant was dressed in the Doctor's trademark ankle-length brown coat, while Morrissey was kitted out in full period garb - a tan knee-length jacket and red waistcoat. A security guard sat in front of the TARDIS, which was tucked down a nearby alleyway, covered by a white sheet. Tennant waved to the crowds as the crew prepared the intricate set and covered the surrounding historic buildings with fake snow. Secrecy surrounds the Christmas episode's storyline, but it's believed to feature the Cybermen - the Doctor's deadliest enemies.

Fans who had been present on location also recounted having seen actress Dervla Kirwan involved in the recording.

On 27 April, the BAFTA Cymru Awards ceremony at the Millennium Centre in Cardiff saw *Doctor Who* picking up six awards out of the eight for which had been nominated - more than any other programme. These were: Best Drama Series (Phil Collinson, for 'Voyage of the Damned'), Best Screenwriter (Steven Moffat, for 'Blink'), Best Sound (BBC Wales sound team, for 'Voyage of the Damned'), Best Director, Drama (James Strong, for 'Voyage of the Damned'), Best Director of Photography (Ernie Vincze, for 'Voyage of the Damned') and Best Make-Up (Barbara Southcott and Neill Gorton at Millennium FX, for 'The Shakespeare Code'). The spin-off *Torchwood* was also a winner, in the category of Best Costume (Ray Holman, 'Captain Jack Harkness').

<u>May 2008</u>

On 4 May, the *Sunday Mail* carried an exclusive interview with Douglas Mackinnon, director of 'The Sontaran Stratagem'/'The Poison Sky', who had at one time been a photographer for this Scottish newspaper. Mackinnon recalled an amusing incident during recording: 'I was working on the TARDIS and I managed to break the bit in the middle that goes up and down. I wanted it to go too fast for a dramatic scene and it just stopped working. I couldn't believe I'd broken the TARDIS. Thankfully, we managed to fix it half an hour later, but I had this surreal phone call with my nine-year-old son Thomas, who is a massive *Doctor Who* fan, back home in Fife, and said: "You'll never believe what I did today ..." And he shouted to my wife Mandy: "Mum, Dad's broken the TARDIS!"'

There was news this month of forthcoming ventures for two of the *Doctor Who* companion actresses: on 7 May it was announced that Freema Agyeman would be playing Tattycoram in a major new BBC Drama production of Dickens' *Little Dorrit*, to be broadcast later in 2008, while on 11 May the Duke of York's Theatre in London's West End named Catherine Tate as the star of its forthcoming production of the play

Under the Blue Sky, due to open on 15 July.

11 May was also the date when *Doctor Who*'s latest awards triumph was announced. At the BAFTA Craft Awards ceremony, staged in London's Dorchester Hotel, Steven Moffat was named as winner of the Best Writer gong for his script for 'Blink'.

On 14 May, the BBC News website reported that David Tennant was amongst those supporting a campaign to prevent cutbacks at the Royal Scottish Academy of Music and Drama, where he had once trained. 'Nothing I have managed to achieve in my career would have happened without my training at the RSAMD,' the actor was quoted as saying. 'The drama training I received was world class and the idea that the opportunities I got there might be compromised for future generations is deeply upsetting. I am incredibly proud to be a graduate of RSAMD and Scotland is rightly proud to have such an important arts training-ground at its heart. I have seen how Scotland's actors are valued and admired throughout the world. I would hate to see a lack of both immediate and long-term funding jeopardise the future of that hard-won reputation.'

16 May brought confirmation that, as had happened the previous year, *Doctor Who* would be taking a week's break in transmission to make way for BBC One's live coverage of the *Eurovision Song Contest* final on 24 May. It was subsequently announced on the official *Doctor Who* website that, by way of consolation, a new trailer for the remaining Series Four episodes would be shown at 6.45 pm on that date and then made available to view online.

The big news story for this month, however, came on 20 May, when the BBC Press Office confirmed a forthcoming development that had long been the subject of rumour and speculation:

> BBC Wales and BBC Drama has announced that BAFTA and Hugo Award-winning writer Steven Moffat will succeed Russell T Davies as lead writer and executive producer of the fifth series of *Doctor Who*, which will broadcast on BBC One in 2010.
>
> Moffat has penned some of the series' most unforgettable and acclaimed episodes, including 'Blink', with its terrifying Weeping Angels, for which he was awarded the BAFTA Writer Award 2008 on Sunday 11 May.
>
> ...
>
> Steven's career began with the landmark ITV children's drama *Press Gang* in 1989, for which he won his first BAFTA.
>
> *Coupling*, the hugely popular and award-winning sitcom he created and wrote for BBC Two, began in 2000 and ran for four seasons.
>
> *Jekyll*, his six-part thriller starring James Nesbitt and Michelle Ryan, transmitted on BBC One last year.
>
> Steven will continue as one of the directors on the board of Hartswood Films, which produced *Coupling* and *Jekyll*, where he is also working on his new comedy *Adam & Eve* with wife Sue Vertue.
>
> He has just delivered the screenplay for *Tintin* – the first instalment of the trilogy of films featuring the iconic Belgian

comic-strip hero – to Steven Spielberg, who will direct it for DreamWorks. Thomas Sangster and Andy Serkis will star.

Steven Moffat says: 'My entire career has been a Secret Plan to get this job. I applied before but I got knocked back 'cos the BBC wanted someone else. Also I was seven.

'Anyway, I'm glad the BBC has finally seen the light, and it's a huge honour to be following Russell into the best – and the toughest – job in television. I say toughest 'cos Russell's at my window right now, pointing and laughing.'

Lead writer and executive producer Russell T Davies says: 'It's been a delight and an honour working with Steven, and I can't wait to see where his extraordinary imagination takes the Doctor. Best of all, I get to be a viewer again, watching on a Saturday night!'

Jane Tranter, Controller, BBC Fiction, says: 'Scripts and writers are at the heart of what BBC Drama is all about, and especially at the heart of *Doctor Who*. The past four series have been brilliantly helmed by the spectacularly talented Russell T Davies.

'As lead writer and executive producer, he has overseen the creative direction and detail of the 21st Century relaunch of *Doctor Who* and we are delighted to have his continued presence on the specials over the next 18 months.

'But the challenge and excitement of the fifth series is now being handed to Steven Moffat. The TARDIS couldn't be in safer hands. Steven's talents both on *Doctor Who* and beyond are well known. He is a writer of glittering brilliance, comedy and depth, with an extraordinary imagination and a unique voice.

'Steven has a wonderful mix of being a committed *Doctor Who* fan and a true artist, and his plans for the next series are totally thrilling.'

The announcement follows the news that Piers Wenger will take over the role of executive producer from Julie Gardner on Series Five of *Doctor Who*.

Piers Wenger says: 'The challenge of taking *Doctor Who* to a new future is a huge and thrilling one and BBC Wales is blessed to have someone with Steven's extraordinary talent in charge.

'His imagination and creativity have already given birth to some of the series' most unforgettable monsters though in this instance no-one need fear; time, space and the future of the Doctor are safe with him.'

Wenger and Moffat are already working closely together on the planning of the series.

Menna Richards, Controller, BBC Wales, says: 'BBC Wales is very proud of *Doctor Who*'s phenomenal success. Steven Moffat is an extraordinary talent and we are very much looking forward to him joining the *Doctor Who* team.'

This change of showrunner would be by far the most significant behind-the-scenes development since *Doctor Who* returned to production in 2004, and not surprisingly the BBC's announcement provoked intense discussion and debate within the show's fandom and amongst online commentators more generally. It was also covered in most of Britain's national newspapers and industry journals, and even in the influential US publication *Hollywood Reporter*. Most of these media stories were purely factual, reiterating elements from the BBC's press release, but the *Independent*'s Thomas Sutcliffe took the opportunity to offer an opinion piece, in the process demonstrating that he was clearly no fan of *Doctor Who*:

> This seemed to me to be a good news/bad news deal. On the one hand, one of Britain's most interesting television writers has at last been liberated from the task of thinking up silly nonsense for a teatime audience and could be welcomed back to the real world. On the other hand, this had only been achieved by the cultural equivalent of a hostage swap. There are writers one would be quite happy to see chained below decks in the *Doctor Who* galley, so that their energies are entirely consumed in a broadly harmless manner, but Moffat – who can write for grown-ups – is not one of them. He didn't see it this way himself, of course, announcing that it was the 'best and toughest job in television'. I'd beg to differ ... Because although it is undoubtedly quite tricky to come up with a really memorable bit of Gothic for the *Doctor Who* series (Moffat's episode 'Blink' comes to mind as an example, as it happens), it's also true that most episodes of *Doctor Who* are forgivingly predictable in their plot and psychological dynamics. In the wilder extremes of *Who*mania over the past couple of years, I've occasionally felt like the one person on the planet whose brain isn't wired to respond to an alien hypnosis beam – a lucky break obviously not shared by the editor of the *Radio Times*, BBC commissioning editors and, I might as well confess, my own children. Can't everybody see that it's okay for immature audiences but hardly justifies the black hole gravitational pull it seems to exert over genuinely talented writers?

24 May saw the transmission of the promised trailer for the remainder of Series Four. This was a minute long and was particularly notable for including a shot of Dalek base with its upper half shrouded in shadow, leading to much speculation amongst fans that the long-rumoured return of Davros was indeed in prospect in the series finale.

On 27 May, columnist Rich Johnston of the Comic Book Resources website made the intriguing claim that acclaimed novelist and comics writer Neil Gaiman had already been invited by Moffat to write for Series Five of *Doctor Who*. He also took the opportunity to pay tribute to Davies:

> Not only did Russell bring back one of my fondest childhood memories, but he turned it into the country's prime television

> icon. More people in the UK are exposed to science-fiction through modern *Doctor Who* than everything else put together. It's a social phenomenon in a multi-channel, online splintered world. The online geekish criticism Russell gets for his work seems so minor compared with his huge and continuing achievements with the series. Complaints about *deus ex machinas*, power of love endings, discarded plot points, and out of kilter humour seem like pointing out that Mohammed Ali had a pimple during his big fight. They mean nothing compared with the pure joy, excitement, the spread of genuine subversive ideas under a cosy blanket while simultaneously binding the family unit for a shared experience. And doing it all with bloody *Doctor Who* as well.

29 May saw the latest edition of *Doctor Who Magazine* go on sale. This featured an exclusive interview with Billie Piper, in which she spoke of her return to the show after a two year absence. This prompted a number of media reports, including on the BBC News website:

> 'I wouldn't have missed this for anything,' the 25-year-old told *Doctor Who Magazine*. 'It means so much to me, this show, and so do the people that make it, so I really wanted to be here for these final episodes.' Piper admitted she had to do a little homework before slipping back into the role. 'I had to watch a lot of the old stuff, so I could remember certain things about the character, because I've been playing posh birds since I left *Doctor Who*,' she said. 'Rose is a bit of a chav, bless her. I needed to hear the voice and watch the posture and everything, but then the minute you get on set, and you've got Russell T Davies' scripts, and he remembers how to write so well for Rose, you're back there on day one, really.' But Piper, who recently married actor Laurence Fox, promised a few changes for her character. 'She has changed. She's hardened. She's been through a lot in her parallel world. I think she's been through emotional turmoil. She's quite sad and lonely, but also really bolshy and - that great quality that Rose has - just so headstrong and single-minded.'

In the 29 May edition of the Scottish *Big Issue*, meanwhile, journalist Laura Kelly presented the first full-length interview with Moffat since it was announced that he would be taking over as *Doctor Who*'s showrunner:

> 'You wouldn't immediately say yes to that job. You imagine that you would say yes immediately, but it's a huge job, and you have to think about it,' Moffat explains. 'I was speaking to David [Tennant] a few weeks before I was offered it and I said, "It must've been great when you were offered *Doctor Who*, you must've just jumped at the chance". He said, "You know, when

> it really happens, it's not like that". It's kind of weird, it's almost like it's not supposed to happen. You're not supposed to be a grown up that gets offered his childhood favourite.' Moffat even went so far as to offer to write more episodes per series to try and persuade Davies to stay in place. Though he's been the obvious successor for years, Moffat was uncomfortable about the parallels with another Scot who has recently taken centre stage after years in the wings. 'It was fairly easy for me to be the favourite because I was the only one who'd been around since the beginning and turning up every year,' he demures. 'I was kind of the other contender, which puts me kind of in the position of Gordon Brown. And look how that turned out. The surly Scot comes in and it all goes to f**k.'

31 May brought news of another new challenge for Freema Agyeman: the BBC Press Office announced that she would be one of the stars of the BBC's forthcoming remake of Terry Nation's popular 1970s drama series *Survivors,* due to be transmitted on BBC One in the autumn.

Also on this date, David Tennant made a further radio appearance, on Jonathan Ross's show on BBC Radio 2, discussing amongst other things his forthcoming appearance in *Hamlet,* the tickets for which were reportedly selling very briskly, and the 2008 *Doctor Who* Christmas special.

June 2008

BBC One's *The Andrew Marr Show* had David Tennant as a guest on 8 June. Discussion focused mainly on a new DVD release of *Taking Over the Asylum,* the 1994 BBC Two series that had given the actor his first starring role on TV, and on the challenges of playing Hamlet. Inevitably, though, the subject of *Doctor Who* also arose. Asked if would be remaining in the role of the Doctor for Series Five in 2010, Tennant claimed that he had not yet been asked, but would consider it if he was. The following day, it was announced that *Hamlet* would be transferring from Stratford-upon-Avon to the Novello Theatre in London's West End for a short run from 3 December to 10 January. After that date, Tennant would be returning to work on *Doctor Who* for the first of the 2009 specials.

On 13 June, the BBC Press Office's regular release of forthcoming programme information revealed the previously-withheld title of Series Four's penultimate episode: 'The Stolen Earth'. Also on this date, it was widely reported that Russell T Davies had been awarded an OBE in the Queen's Birthday Honours list. 'I'm delighted to accept,' Davies was quoted as saying, 'and I hope it does the whole industry a bit of good, for the writing of television drama to be recognised.' A BBC spokesperson commented: 'We are delighted for Russell – he is one of this country's greatest writers and it is fantastic that his talent has been recognised in this way.'

'Turn Left' became the third Series Four episode to be accorded a *Radio Times* front cover photograph when the edition covering the week of its transmission went on sale on 17 June. This had the strapline 'She's Back!' and featured Rose in the foreground with Donna, Martha and the Doctor behind her. Inside the magazine, a Russell T Davies-written article discussed the different functions that the three female companions had fulfilled in *Doctor Who*. As for 'Partners in Crime', *TV & Satellite Week* and *TV Guide* followed suit by featuring similar cover photographs on their own editions this week. Davies was quoted in *TV Guide*'s article as saying of Rose: 'She's a huge protagonist in the action and we see her meeting Donna for the first time. It explores how the two of them get on and, of course, they both have different agendas.'

Also on 17 June, the *Sun* ran a story presenting positive proof that Davros would be back in the series finale: a photograph that it had somehow managed to obtain of the Daleks' creator in his redesigned form, along with one of a red Supreme Dalek. A similar piece appeared in the *Daily Telegraph*, although with only a classic-era photograph of Davros in this case, and both newspapers stated that the part would be played by actor Julian Bleach, who had previously appeared as the Ghostmaker in the 'From Out of the Rain' episode of *Torchwood*.

From 22 June, the BBC began airing two new trailers for 'The Stolen Earth' in selected programme breaks. One was a ten-second bronze-hued teaser showing the Supreme Dalek flanked by other Daleks, while the other was a full 30-second clips montage showing all the main returning characters featured in the episode with a voiceover from Davros: 'The children of time are moving against us, but everything is falling into place. Welcome to my new empire, Doctor.' As usual, these trailers were placed online as well.

Also on 22 June, the *Sunday Mirror* erroneously reported that supermodel Agyness Deyn was being lined up for a role in the forthcoming Christmas special, quoting a BBC source as saying: '*Doctor Who* remains the Beeb's jewel in the crown and bosses love pulling out the stops to land a big-name star to add a bit of extra showbiz sparkle to the Christmas special. Agyness is the perfect choice. She's talented and fast becoming a household name.'

Freema Agyeman appeared on CBBC's *Blue Peter* on 24 June as part of the ongoing promotion for the series finale. The programme also featured a behind-the-scenes item on presenter Gethin Jones recording a scene as a stand-in Dalek Operator and an exclusive clip from 'Journey's End'.

Issue 397 of *Doctor Who Magazine* went on sale on 26 June and included an interview with John Barrowman in which he talked about his return as Captain Jack in the series finale and his excitement at working with Elisabeth Sladen as Sarah Jane Smith.

Also on 26 June, Bernard Cribbins appeared on BBC One's early evening magazine programme *The One Show* to talk about his role as Donna's grandfather Wilf, and an exclusive clip from 'The Stolen Earth' was shown.

The following morning, Agyeman and Sladen appeared together on Richard Arnold's entertainment news show on ITV's GMTV. A Dalek was also on hand in the studio. Then, that afternoon, actor Michael Brandon, best known for his starring role in the crime drama series *Dempsey & Makepeace* (ITV, 1985-86), guested on Channel 4's *Richard & Judy* show to discuss his appearance in 'The Stolen Earth' as UNIT's US commander General Sanchez, again backed up by a clip from the episode.

That day's edition of the *Scotsman* meanwhile looked to *Doctor Who*'s future, reporting:

> The BBC is rumoured to be ready to pay David Tennant a massive £1.3 million to carry on as Doctor Who. The Bathgate-born actor is expected to be offered a new deal worth up to £100,000 per episode. And he could also be offered other drama projects in a bid to keep him on board. BBC bosses are desperate to stop the 37-year-old from quitting the show, which attracts up to eight million viewers. One senior BBC source was quoted saying: 'Everyone assumes David is quitting but that's not the case. We're hoping he will be back. The situation as it stands is that no deal has been discussed yet for the next series of *Doctor Who*. That, however, is about to change. David is brilliant in the role and naturally we hope he will continue. We're not considering anyone else at this time.'

Following transmission of 'The Stolen Earth' the previous day, the afternoon of 29 June saw a 30-second trailer for 'Journey's End' appearing on BBC One and being placed online on the official *Doctor Who* website, the BBC's YouTube channel and, unusually, on the BBC's Bebo page, along with a 30-second clip of the cliffhanger to 'The Stolen Earth'. Unlike that on the YouTube channel, the content on the Bebo page was viewable internationally, making this a particularly popular move with fans outside the UK.

Also on 29 June, ABC in Australia began its debut run of Series Four, kicking off with 'Voyage of the Damned', which sparked a wealth of media coverage and attracted a very impressive 1.25 million viewers in the five major capital cities – a record-breaking figure for *Doctor Who* down under. Further episodes would follow on a weekly basis, and would continue to do exceptionally well in the ratings. For the first time, the channel had also bought the rights to screen the *Doctor Who Confidential* mini-documentaries (in their *Cutdown* form of approximately 15 minutes each), and these would be shown immediately after the episodes to which they related.

In the week following transmission of 'The Stolen Earth', it seemed that the whole of Britain was talking about its astonishing climax, which had left the Doctor apparently on the point of regenerating. The national newspapers and online media had a field day, devoting an extraordinary amount of coverage to *Doctor Who*, in the form of reviews, comment pieces, speculative items about the possible identity of the next actor to play the Doctor and reports of the show's outstanding ratings figures, the *Sunday Telegraph* even claiming on 29 June that the BBC expected as many as 10 million viewers to tune in to 'Journey's End'.

It seemed that *Doctor Who* was now generating a degree of public interest and debate the like of which it had never seen before.

July 2008

For the second time in three weeks, *Doctor Who* featured on the front cover of *Radio Times* when the edition covering the week of transmission of 'Journey's End' went on sale on 1 July. This time, perhaps inevitably, the cover image was one of Davros, flanked by two Daleks, with the rather obvious strapline, 'It's Davros!' This edition of the magazine also included a special eight-page extra section on the making of

Doctor Who's monsters.

4 July, the day before transmission of 'Journey's End', saw possibly a record number of *Doctor Who*-related items appearing in the media. Seventh Doctor actor Sylvester McCoy was on the sofa for ITV's GMTV early morning show; producer Phil Collinson was interviewed on Radio 5 Live's *Breakfast* programme; Freema Agyeman guested on BBC One's own *Breakfast*; and Russell T Davies appeared both on ITV1's *This Morning* and in a video interview on the BBC News website, answering a range of questions sent in by members of the public and commenting on the high degree of secrecy being maintained around the final episode. This secrecy also formed the basis of a story by Lizo Mzimba on the BBC's main 6.00 pm news bulletin, and was reported at around the same time on BBC Radio 4's own early evening news programme. Channel 4's *Richard & Judy* show also discussed *Doctor Who* for the second time in just over a week. National and local newspapers meanwhile continued to devote huge amounts of coverage to the show.

The media frenzy continued unabated on 5 July. The Doctor Who Appreciation Society's Karen Davies and *Doctor Who Adventures* editor Moray Laing were guests on BBC One's *Breakfast*, which also showed clips from stories featuring all ten Doctors, while Tim Smith's morning show on BBC Radio 2 invited listeners to e-mail and text in suggestions for actors to play the next Doctor. The BBC News website made the excitement surrounding that evening's episode the top story in its Entertainment section. And once again the press gave over an incredible number of column-inches to all manner of *Doctor Who*-related subjects.

Following transmission of 'Journey's End', press interest remained astonishingly high. Many of the national newspapers and online news outlets published reviews, and most also covered the episode's extraordinary ratings success, unofficial overnight figures having accorded it a huge tally of 9.4 million viewers. (This would ultimately be adjusted upwards to a phenomenal 10.57 million when the final figures became available on 16 July.) Interviews with Russell T Davies appeared on 7 July in both the *Daily Telegraph* and the *Guardian*, in the latter of which Davies mischievously suggested that troubled singer Amy Winehouse might make a good future Doctor, while the *Sun* looked forward to the 2008 Christmas special featuring the Cybermen, as seen in the trailer at the end of 'Journey's End'. Even outside the UK, many news sources reported on the amazing interest the finale had provoked.

The fact that there was to be no new series in 2009 really started to hit home for fans, though, when - in stark contrast to the previous year - the BBC Press Office issued no flurry of announcements about the show's future in the wake of the transmission of 'Journey's End'. It seemed that there would be quite a delay before any more official news was released, with the Christmas special still almost five months away from transmission and the following one not even due to go before the cameras until January 2009.

There was however one final treat for fans following the end of Series Four, when the *Doctor Who* Prom took place at the Royal Albert Hall in London on 27 July. Freema Agyeman was the main presenter for the event but had support from Camille Coduri, Noel Clarke and a previously-unannounced Catherine Tate, while assorted Cybermen, Ood, Judoon, Sontarans and Daleks menaced the delighted audience. Even Davros, played as on TV by Julian Bleach, put in a dramatic appearance on a plinth that rose through the floor of the auditorium. A particular highlight was the presentation on a big screen above the stage of a new seven-minute mini-episode, 'Music of the Spheres', specially written for the occasion by Davies.[10] The superbly-staged concert drew a standing ovation from the audience, and served as a further testament to *Doctor Who*'s unparalleled popularity in the summer of 2008.

[10] See Episode Guide for more details.

PART TWO
BIO-DATA

CHAPTER SIX
MAIN CAST

DAVID TENNANT (THE DOCTOR)

David Tennant was born David John McDonald in Bathgate, West Lothian, on 18 April 1971 and grew up in Ralston, Renfrewshire, where his father was a Church of Scotland minister. His later stage name, adopted in order to avoid confusion with another actor called David McDonald, was taken from that of pop star Neil Tennant of the Pet Shop Boys. He became a fan of *Doctor Who* at a young age and, partly inspired by that, made it his ambition to become an actor. He joined a Saturday youth theatre while still attending Paisley Grammar School and went on to train at the Royal Scottish Academy of Music and Drama, to which the youth theatre was affiliated. In his twenties he joined a radical Scottish theatre company called 7:84, making his professional debut in their production of *The Resistable Rise of Arturo Ui*. He broke into TV with small parts in *Strathblair* (BBC One, 1992) and a 1993 episode of *Rab C Nesbitt* (BBC Two, 1988-1999) and then won his first lead role - as a manic-depressive - in a drama called *Takin' Over The Asylum* (BBC Two, 1994). After moving from Scotland to London, where he rented rooms from actress Arabella Weir of *The Fast Show* (BBC, 1994-2000), he gained more theatre work, including in numerous Royal Shakespeare Company productions. He also made his feature film debut in *Jude* (Universal Pictures/PolyGram Filmed Entertainment, 1996), in which he shared a scene with its star Christopher Eccleston, later to play the ninth Doctor. Further film roles followed, including in Stephen Fry's *Bright Young Things* (Film Four, 2003) and *Harry Potter and the Goblet of Fire* (Warner Brothers, 2005). It was for his TV work that he became best known, however, taking parts of increasing prominence in programmes such as: *The Mrs Bradley Mysteries* (BBC One, 1999), in which he appeared opposite fifth Doctor actor Peter Davison; *Randall and Hopkirk (Deceased)* (BBC One, 2000-2001); a first season episode of *Foyle's War* (ITV, 2002-); and *He Knew He Was Right* (BBC One, 2004). His rise to star status came with major roles in two acclaimed series in quick succession: as DI Carlyle in *Blackpool* (BBC One, 2004) and, even more memorably, as the title character in Russell T Davies's *Casanova* (BBC Three, 2005), which gained him his first front cover picture on *Radio Times*. *Casanova* effectively served as Tennant's 'audition' for the part of the tenth Doctor, for which he was the only actor seriously considered when Eccleston departed. He accepted the role after a brief hesitation, and quickly became a household name following his full debut in 'The Christmas Invasion' on Christmas Day 2005. This was not in fact his first connection with *Doctor Who*: he had previously played voice parts in a number of Big Finish's audio CD dramas - 'Colditz' (2001); 'Sympathy for the Devil' (2003); 'Exile' (2003) (one of the *Doctor Who Unbound* range); the spin-off series *Dalek Empire III* (2004); 'Medicinal Purposes' (2004); and 'The Wasting' (2005), an episode of the *UNIT* spin-off - and also in an episode of the webcast story 'Scream of the Shalka' (2003). His portrayal of the tenth Doctor was, however, the first time he had been associated with the series in the general public's eyes, and it saw him becoming Britain's most popular TV actor, winning numerous awards and other accolades. He has still found time to take on a number of other roles during breaks in production on *Doctor Who*, including in the TV plays *Recovery* (BBC One, 2007) and *Learners* (BBC One, 2007), and has made numerous guest appearances on talk shows and the like. Following completion of work on the 2008 *Doctor Who* Christmas special, he joined the Royal Shakespeare Company to appear in new productions of *Hamlet* – as Hamlet – and *Love's Labour's Lost* – as Berowne.

CATHERINE TATE (DONNA NOBLE)

Catherine Tate was born Catherine Ford on 12 May 1968 in Bloomsbury, London. She was raised by her mother and grandmother, her parents having separated when she was very young, and educated at Catholic faith schools, principally St Joseph's in Holborn and Notre Dame High School in Southwark. Deciding that she wanted to pursue a career in acting, she eventually gained a place at the Central School of Speech and Drama, where she studied for three years up to the age of 26. She started out in TV in the early 1990s with minor roles in shows such as *Surgical Spirit* (ITV1), *The Bill* (ITV1), and *Men Behaving Badly* (BBC One). A stint as a stand-up comic in 1996 then led on to numerous appearances in popular comedies of the time, including *The Harry Hill Show* (Channel 4, 1997-1999), *That Peter Kay Thing* (Channel 4, 2000) and *Big Train* (BBC Two, 2002). From that point on, although she continued to take occasional straight acting roles on TV and particularly in the theatre – including a number with the Royal Shakespeare Company and the National Theatre – she acquired a reputation primarily as a comedienne. In 2004, she was given her own BBC Two sketch show, *The Catherine Tate Show*, which ultimately ran for three series and won numerous awards. For this she devised and portrayed a range of memorable comedy characters, such as schoolgirl Lauren Cooper and old lady Joannie 'Nan' Taylor, most of them with catchphrases that became much quoted by the public and sometimes entered into popular culture more widely – the prime example being Lauren's 'Am I bovvered?'. Having decided in 2006 to rest *The Catherine Tate Show* and its characters, save for special occasions, she made her debut as Donna Noble in the 2006 *Doctor Who* Christmas special 'The Runaway Bride'. The same year, she broke into feature films, taking roles in no fewer than five productions: *Starter for 10*, *Sixty-Six*, *Scenes of a Sexual Nature*, *Love and Other Disasters* and *Mrs Ratcliffe's Revolution*. She was then invited to reprise her *Doctor Who* role for the whole of Series Four, and readily accepted. She has since returned to the stage in a production of *Under the Blue Sky* in London's West End. She lives in Mortlake, Surrey, with her long-term partner Twig Clark and their daughter Erin.

BILLIE PIPER (ROSE TYLER)

Billie Piper was born Lianne Paul Piper on 22 September 1982 in Swindon, Wiltshire. She was educated at Brookfield Primary School in the Shaw area of Swindon and at Bradon Forest Secondary School in nearby Purton. Deciding that she wanted to be an actress, she went on to study at the Sylvia Young Stage School in London. Her debut TV appearance came in the mid-1990s in the Saturday morning children's show *Scratchy and Co* (CITV). However, it was as a pop singer that she first came to public prominence after she was spotted by Virgin Records fronting a TV advert for the magazine *Smash Hits*. She recorded two albums, *Honey to the B* (1998) and *Walk of Life* (2000), and enjoyed great success, becoming the youngest artist ever to debut at number one in the UK singles chart when she put out her first release, 'Because We Want To' (1998). In May 2001, she married DJ and TV presenter Chris Evans in Las Vegas, USA, after a whirlwind romance. Not wanting to continue as a singer, she eventually decided to return to her first love, acting, and won roles in two movies, *The Calcium Kid* (2004) and *Things to Do Before You're 30* (2005). She then successfully auditioned for the role of Rose Tyler in the revived *Doctor Who*, which was to bring her arguably her greatest acclaim to date, along with numerous awards. She has since had further success on TV with starring roles in *Much Ado About Nothing* (BBC One, 2005), *The Ruby in the Smoke* (BBC One, 2006), *The Shadow in the Glass* (BBC One, 2007), *Mansfield Park* (ITV1, 2007) and *Secret Diary of a Call Girl* (ITV2, 2007-). Her autobiography, *Growing Pains*, was published by Hodder and Stoughton in October 2006, and she made her stage debut in 2007 in a touring production of the play *Treats*. Having separated from Evans, she had a romantic relationship with law student Amadu Sowe between 2004 and 2006. While she and Evans remained on good terms, they eventually divorced on 31 May 2007. She then married her *Treats* co-star Laurence Fox on New Year's Eve 2007. They live in Easebourne, West Sussex, and at the time of writing are expecting their first child.

FREEMA AGYEMAN (MARTHA JONES)

Freema Agyeman was born in 1979 to an Iranian mother, Azar, and a Ghanaian father, Osei. She is one of three children, with an older sister, Leila, and a younger brother, Domenic. Her parents divorced when she was young, and she lived with her mother and siblings in a flat on the Woodberry Down housing estate in Finsbury Park, North London. She was educated at Our Lady's Convent in Stamford Hill and the Anna Scher Theatre School in Islington. Although as a child she had had ambitions to be a doctor and a marine biologist and had enjoyed science, she eventually chose English, Fine Art and Theatre Studies as her A Level subjects. She later studied at Middlesex University, graduating in 2000 with a BA (Honours) in Performing Arts and Drama, and also at Radford University in Virginia, USA. She had plans to work with children if her acting career stalled, but in fact she soon won a regular role as Lola Wise in the revived soap opera *Crossroads* (Carlton, 2001-2003), and this led on to further TV work, including in a 2004 episode of *Casualty* (BBC One, 1986-), a 2005 episode of *Mile High* (Sky One, 2003-2005), a 2005 episode of *Silent Witness* (BBC One, 1996-) and three episodes between 2004 and 2006 as a semi-regular in *The Bill* (ITV, 1983-). She also played the femme fatale Nana in the independent film production *Rulers and Dealers* (RDL Productions, 2006). Having auditioned unsuccessfully for the part of Sally in the *Doctor Who* Christmas special 'The Christmas Invasion' (2005), she made her debut in the show as Adeola Oshodi in 'Army of Ghosts' (2006) and immediately impressed the production team with her performance and personality. She was earning a living working shifts at a Blockbuster video rental store when, shortly afterwards, she was invited to audition for what she was initially told was a regular role in *Torchwood*. She eventually learned what part she was really being considered for - that of the companion in *Doctor Who* - when she was called back for a further, top-secret audition opposite David Tennant in producer Phil Collinson's Cardiff flat. She won the role, and went on to appear as medical student Martha Jones in every episode of Series Three. Although Martha then parted company with the Doctor, she was soon to return in three episodes of Series Two of *Torchwood* - allowing Agyeman to contribute to the spin-off after all - and in five episodes of Series Four of *Doctor Who*.

JOHN BARROWMAN (CAPTAIN JACK HARKNESS)

John Barrowman was born on 11 March 1967 in Glasgow, Scotland. He grew up in his native city until, when he was aged eight, his family emigrated to live in the USA, in the town of Aurora, just south of Chicago, Illinois. He had always been keen on performing - both acting and singing - and pursued this interest during his education at Joliet West High School, Illinois, where he appeared in a number of student productions between 1983 and 1985. An early job was as a musical entertainer in a Nashville, Tennessee theme park called Opryland. He returned to the UK in 1989, initially to study Shakespeare at a London university, and his theatrical career really took off when he won a role opposite Elaine Paige in *Anything Goes* in London's West End. He also started gaining TV work during the 1990s, including as a regular presenter on the BBC children's series *Live and Kicking* (1993). Roles in the American series *Central Park West* (1996) and *Titans* (2000) followed, and more theatre work, including in a couple of productions on New York's Broadway. His starring roles in the theatre have come mainly in musicals, such as *Chicago, Sunset Boulevard, Miss Saigon, Evita, Beauty and the Beast* and *Phantom of the Opera,* although he has also had a number of non-singing parts, including in productions of *Rope* (1993) - during the run of which he met his long-time partner, architect Scott Gill - and *A Few Good Men* (2005). On the big screen he has appeared in the low-budget shocker *Shark Attack 3: Megalodon* (2002), in *De-Lovely* (2004), a biography of composer Cole Porter, and in Mel Brooks' *The Producers* (2005). He has sung on a number of original-cast soundtrack recordings of musicals, and has also released four solo CDs: *Aspects of Lloyd Webber* (1998), *Reflections from Broadway* (2000), *John Barrowman Swings Cole Porter* (2004) and *Another Side* (2007). When, in 2004, his agent was approached by casting director Andy Prior about the possibility of him playing Captain Jack in *Doctor Who,* he was eager to take the role, having long been a fan. He was, in fact, the first regular to be cast in the revived show. So popular did he prove as Captain Jack that he was soon offered the opportunity to star in his own spin-off, *Torchwood*.

Since 2005, he has made frequent guest appearances on just about every entertainment show and celebrity quiz programme on British TV, cementing his position as one of the nation's most high-profile and popular stars. He performed in pantomime in *Cinderella* at the New Wimbledon Theatre over the 2005/2006 Christmas holiday season, and early in 2006 could again be seen on TV, in the variety shows *The Magic of Musicals* for the BBC and *Dancing on Ice* for ITV1. He also had a stint as a stand-in presenter on the ITV morning talk show *This Morning*. Later in 2006, he was one of the judges on the BBC One show *How Do You Solve a*

Problem Like Maria?, about the search for a newcomer to star in a West End revival of the musical *The Sound of Music*. He was named Entertainer of the Year for 2006 by Stonewall and placed third in a Hottest Commodity poll in *Broadcast* magazine. On 27 December 2006, he and Gill became civil partners in a ceremony in Cardiff, the guests at which included his *Torchwood* co-stars and showrunner Russell T Davies. Further Christmas-season pantomime stints came in *Jack and the Beanstalk* at Cardiff's New Theatre in 2006/2007 and in *Aladdin* at the Birmigham Hippodrome in 2007/2008. In 2007, he amongst other things served as one of the judges on BBC One's *Any Dream Will Do*, a follow-up to *How Do You Solve a Problem Like Maria?*, this time designed to find a star for a new West End production of *Jason and the Amazing Technicolor Dreamcoat*

January 2008 saw the publication by Michael O'Mara Books of his autobiography *Anything Goes*, co-written with his sister, journalist and English professor Carole E Barrowman, which he promoted with a short signing tour of bookshops. During the on-air run of *Torchwood* Series Two, he again served as a judge on the latest BBC One talent-search show, *I'd Do Anything*, this time seeking newcomers to fill the roles of Nancy and Oliver in a West End revival of *Oliver!*, and continued to make various other TV guest appearances, including in an episode of BBC One's *Hotel Babylon* and on a number of occasions as presenter of the same channel's National Lottery Draw programme. In April 2008, he was seen as presenter of a new BBC One game show called *The Kids are All Right*, having recorded a successful pilot the previous year. He also undertook a short concert tour of UK cities.

ELISABETH SLADEN (SARAH JANE SMITH)

Elisabeth Sladen was born on 1 February 1948 in Liverpool. An early aptitude for dance, which saw her appear as a mouse in a Royal Ballet production as a child, led on to an interest in acting. On leaving grammar school, she attended drama school for two years. He first screen appearance was as an uncredited extra in the film *Ferry 'Cross the Mersey* (1965). She joined the local repertory theatre, the Liverpool Playhouse, and during her first production for them worked with actor Brian Miller; they met again in Manchester three years later, and were married in 1968. She had a number of early television roles in Granada productions, including in 1970 a six episode stint as a barmaid in the long-running *Coronation Street* (ITV). When a play she was in transferred to London, she and Miller relocated to the capital. This led to her winning parts in a number of BBC shows, including a 1971 episode of *Z Cars*, a 1972 episode of *Doomwatch* and a 1973 episode of *Some Mothers Do 'Ave 'Em*. It was in 1973, however, that she was cast in the role for which she will always be best known, that of Sarah Jane Smith in *Doctor Who*. Since her regular run in the show ended in 1976, she has returned for a number of guest appearances, recorded two audio CD drama series and starred in the spin-offs *K-9 and Company* (1981), *Downtime* (Reeltime Pictures, 1995) and the ongoing *The Sarah Jane Adventures* (2007-). Her other TV credits include almost 100 episodes as a presenter on the children's show *Stepping Stones* (ITV 1977-78) and roles in *Send in the Girls* (ITV, 1978), *Take My Wife* (ITV, 1979), *Gulliver in Lilliput* (BBC One, 1982), *Alice in Wonderland* (BBC One, 1985) and *Dempsey & Makepeace* (ITV, 1985). In 1980 she appeared in the film *Silver Dream Racer*. Following the birth of her daughter,

Sadie, in 1985, she spent a number of years concentrating on being a mother and a housewife, but continued to make occasional television appearances, including in a 1989 episode of *The Bill* (ITV) and as a semi-regular in the 1996 series of *Peak Practice* (ITV).

JACQUELINE KING (SYLVIA NOBLE)

Jacqueline King trained at the Bristol Old Vic Theatre School and has since worked mainly in the theatre, both in repertory and on tour. Her roles in the plays *Piaf, Swann's Song* and *How the Other Half Loves* have taken her to Toronto, Nairobi, Sri Lanka and the United Arab Emirates. Having had a few small TV roles in the 1980s and 1990s, she started to work more in that medium in the 2000s. Her credits include two episodes of *Casualty* (BBC One) in 2001, 11 episodes of *55 Degrees North* (BBC One) in 2004 and 2005, two episodes of *The Bill* (ITV1) in 2006 and five episodes of *Doctors* (BBC One) in 2007. Her role as Donna Noble's mother Sylvia, originally intended as a one-off in the 2006 *Doctor Who* Christmas special 'The Runaway Bride', became a recurring one in Series Four. However, her first brush with the *Doctor Who* world actually came in 2003, when she guest-starred in the audio CD drama 'Deadline' in the *Doctor Who Unbound* series.

BERNARD CRIBBINS (WILFRED MOTT)

Bernard Cribbins was born Bernard McDermott on 29 December 1928 in Oldham, Lancashire. He joined the Oldham Repertory Theatre at the age of 14 and served an eight year apprenticeship, with a break for National Service in the Parachute Regiment in his late teens. His early work was in the theatre, and he made his West End debut in 1956 at the Arts Theatre playing the two Dromios in Shakespeare's *A Comedy of Errors*. He went on to co-star in the first West End productions of the farces *Not Now Darling, There Goes the Bride* and *Run For Your Wife*. From the late 1950s he started appearing in TV shows and films, in increasingly prominent roles. He also developed a talent for musical comedy, and in 1962 recorded the two hit novelty records 'Right Said Fred' and 'Hole in the Ground'. Some of his most well-remembered film roles came over the next decade, including in the comedies *Carry On Jack* (1963) and *Carry On Spying* (1964), as hapless policeman Tom Cambell alongside Peter Cushing's Dr Who in *Daleks' Invasion Earth 2150 AD* (1966) and as station porter Perks in *The Railway Children* (1970). By the end of the 1960s, he had become one of Britain's best-loved character actors, specialising in comedy roles, and was even given his own series, *Cribbins* (BBC One, 1969). In the 1970s he remained a familiar face in a wide variety of TV shows. He also narrated the animated children's TV series *The Wombles* (BBC One) and a celebrated BBC radio adaptation of *The Wind in the Willows* and provided voices for the Tufty character in the Green Cross Code road safety films and for Buzby, a talking cartoon bird that served as the mascot for the then GPO, which later became BT. He holds the record as the most prolific contributor to the BBC's children's story reading programme *Jackanory*, with over a hundred appearances stretching from the 1960s to the 1990s. His other notable TV credits include a 1975 episode of *Fawlty Towers* and a 2003 stint as the regular character Wally Bannister in *Coronation Street* (ITV1). His role in the 2007 *Doctor Who* Christmas special 'Voyage of the Damned' was originally intended to be a one-off, with his character named Stan, but at producer Phil Collinson's suggestion he was brought back to play Donna Noble's grandfather, named Wilfred Mott by Russell T Davies, after Howard Attfield, who had been intended to reprise his role as her father Geoff, died shortly after recording began. The closing credits of 'Voyage of the Damned' were amended before transmission to reflect the change of the character's name.

CHAPTER SEVEN
PRINCIPAL CREATIVE TEAM

RUSSELL T DAVIES OBE (SHOWRUNNER, EXECUTIVE PRODUCER, LEAD WRITER)

Russell T Davies was born in Swansea, South Wales, in 1963. (The 'T' does not stand for anything: he was born Stephen Russell Davies, decided to use the name Russell Davies for professional purposes and started using 'T' as an initial in the 1980s in order to distinguish himself from an actor, journalist and broadcaster also called Russell Davies.) He was educated at Olchfa School, a huge comprehensive, and had an early involvement with the West Glamorgan Youth Theatre in Swansea. He then studied English Literature at Worcester College, Oxford University, graduating in 1984. His TV career began with posts as a floor manager and production assistant at the BBC, where in the late 1980s he also trained as a director and gained a presenting credit on *Play School* (1987). He produced the children's series *Why Don't You ...?* for BBC Manchester from 1988 to 1992, during which time he also started to work as a writer, gaining credits on *The Flashing Blade* (1989), *Breakfast Serials* (1990) and *Chucklevision* (1991). His writing career moved up a gear when he was responsible for the acclaimed BBC children's serials *Dark Season* (1991) – which he also novelised for BBC Books – and *Century Falls* (1993). In 1992, he moved from the BBC to Granada, where he produced and wrote for the popular children's drama *Children's Ward* (1992-1996). He also started to gain writing credits for family and adult programmes, including *Cluedo* (1993), *Families* (1993), *The House of Windsor* (1994) and *Revelations* (1994). He worked briefly as a storyliner and writer on the hugely popular *Coronation Street* (1996) and contributed to Channel 4's *Springhill* (1996). It was at this time that he had his first professional association with *Doctor Who* – having been a long-time fan of the series – when he wrote the *New Adventures* novel *Damaged Goods* (1996) for Virgin Publishing. The following year, he was commissioned to contribute to the ITV period drama *The Grand* (1997), and ended up scripting the whole series after a number of other writers dropped out. He subsequently left Granada and joined a company called Red Productions, where he had a major success as creator, writer and producer of *Queer as Folk* (1999-2000), a ground-breaking two-season drama series for Channel 4 about a group of gay men in Manchester, which also spawned a US remake. Since then, his career has gone from strength to strength, with writer and executive producer credits on *Bob and Rose* (2001) and *Mine All Mine* (2004) for ITV and *The Second Coming* (2003), *Casanova* (2005) and of course *Doctor Who* (2005-), *Torchwood* (2006-) and *The Sarah Jane Adventures* (2007-) for the BBC. On 20 May 2008, it was announced that he would be relinquishing his showrunner responsibilities on *Doctor Who* the following year, leaving him free to pursue new projects. He is frequently cited as one of the most influential and powerful people in the British TV industry, and was awarded an OBE for services to drama in the Queen's 2008 birthday honours.

JULIE GARDNER (EXECUTIVE PRODUCER)

Julie Gardner was born in South Wales, near Neath, in 1969. Having gained a degree in English at London University, she began her working life as a teacher of English to secondary school pupils in Wales. In her mid-twenties, however, she decided that this was not the career for her, and she successfully applied for a job at the BBC, as the producer's secretary on the series *Our Friends in the North* (1996). She quickly ascended the ladder of promotion to script reader in the Serial Drama Department, then to script editor and then to producer, working on shows including *Silent Witness* (1996), *Sunburn* (1999) and *The Mrs Bradley Mysteries* (2000). In 2000, she left the BBC and took up a post as development producer at London Weekend Television. There she was responsible for dramas including a controversial modern-day retelling of Shakespeare's *Othello* (2001) and *Me and Mrs Jones* (2002). She was working on further ideas at LWT when, in 2003, she was head-hunted to become Head of Drama at BBC Wales. The new *Doctor Who* series gave her one of her first executive producer credits, and she has since gone on to fulfil a similar role on *Torchwood* and *The Sarah Jane Adventures*. Other projects she has overseen at BBC Wales include *Casanova* (2005), *Girl in the Café* (2005) and *Life on Mars* (2006-2007). On 21 September 2006 it was announced that she had been promoted to the post of the BBC's Head of Drama Commissioning, and would have special responsibility for implementing a cohesive independent drama strategy across the UK. She would however remain as Head of Drama, BBC Wales, for the time being, and would continue as executive producer of *Doctor Who*, *Torchwood* and *The Sarah Jane Adventures*. Her role on those shows is due to end in 2009, when she will hand over responsibility to Piers Wenger.

PHIL COLLINSON (EXECUTIVE PRODUCER, PRODUCER)

Phil Collinson started his career as an actor. The major role of Alexander in *Queer as Folk* (Channel 4, 1999-2000) was originally written specially for him by his long-time friend Russell T Davies, but ultimately went to another actor, Antony Cotton, on the strength of a superb audition. Collinson ultimately decided to concentrate on working behind the scenes in TV, having already had stints as a script editor and a writer on series such as *Springhill* (Sky One, 1996-1997) and *Emmerdale* (ITV, 1972-). He gained his first job as a producer on *Peak Practice* (ITV, 1993-2002), then went on to fulfil the same role on a number of series for the BBC, including *Linda Green* (BBC One, 2001-2002) and the first seasons of *Born and Bred* (BBC One, 2002-2005) and *Sea of Souls* (BBC One, 2004-2007). A long-time *Doctor Who* fan, he jumped at the opportunity to become its producer when work began on the revived series in 2004. He continued in that capacity throughout the first four series - save for occasional breaks when Susie Liggat deputised for him, which saw him being accorded an executive producer credit instead - and also served as series producer on the first series of *The Sarah Jane Adventures*. As announced by the BBC on 1 February 2008, he left BBC Wales on completion of his work on Series Four of *Doctor Who* to take up a new post as Head of Drama at BBC Manchester.

SUSIE LIGGAT (PRODUCER)

Susie Liggat's TV credits have come mainly as a first assistant director, including on series such as *Teachers* (Channel 4, 2001-2004) and *Casanova* (BBC Three, 2005). In 2006 she produced both *The Sarah Jane Adventures*: 'Invasion of the Bane' and, standing in for Phil Collinson, one recording block of Series Three of *Doctor Who*, comprising the episodes 'Human Nature' and 'The Family of Blood'. She has since served as producer on five episodes of Series Four.

LINDSEY ALFORD (SCRIPT EDITOR)

Lindsey Alford studied Psychology and Zoology and joined the BBC's Natural History Unit as a researcher on wildlife programming. She then transferred to BBC One's *Casualty*, progressing from researcher to storyliner to script editor over a period of several years. Moving to BBC Wales in 2006, she gained further script editor credits on *Doctor Who* ('Daleks in Manhattan'/'Evolution of the Daleks' and 'Human Nature'/'The Family of Blood') and the whole of the first series of *The Sarah Jane Adventures* before taking on that responsibility on the *Torchwood* episode 'Adrift'. She then became the principal script editor on Series Four of *Doctor Who*.

HELEN RAYNOR (WRITER, SCRIPT EDITOR)

After graduating from Cambridge University in the mid-1990s, Helen Raynor began her career in the theatre, as an assistant director and director for a number of companies, including the Bush Theatre, the Royal Shakespeare Company and the Royal Opera House. She then joined the BBC, where she became script editor of BBC One's daytime serial *Doctors* (2002-2004). This led on to a post as one of the initial two script editors on the new *Doctor Who* (2005-). She has also gained credits as a writer for the theatre (*Waterloo Exit Two*, Young Vic, 2003), for radio (*Running Away With the Hairdresser*, BBC Radio 4, 2005) and for TV (*Cake*, BBC One, 2006). She has now written four episodes for *Doctor Who*, 'Daleks in Manhattan'/'Evolution of the Daleks' and 'The Sontaran Stratagem'/'The Poison Sky', and two for *Torchwood*, 'Ghost Machine' and 'To the Last Man'. She contributed the *Doctor Who* short story *All of Beyond* to the anthology *Short Trips: Snapshots* (Big Finish, 2007).

BRIAN MINCHIN (SCRIPT EDITOR)

Brian Minchin was born in Aberystwyth, Wales, in 1987. He worked for several Welsh independent production companies and served as assistant producer or producer on a number of low-budget films, mainly for Sgrin Wales and ITV Wales, including *Down* (2003), which he also co-wrote, *Work in Progress* (2004) and *Dead Long Enough* (2005). He was script editor on BBC Wales's *Belonging* in 2005 before moving on to work in the same capacity on *Torchwood*. Series Four saw him gain his first credits on *Doctor Who*.

NIKKI SMITH (SCRIPT EDITOR)

After starting out as an actress, Nikki Smith's first work as a TV script editor came on the first five series of the police procedural drama *Trial and Retribution* (ITV1, 1997-), the latter of which also saw her serving as head of development and taking a small role as a showgirl. Other script editor credits came on Lynda La Plante's *Mind Games* (ITV1, 2001) and *The Bill* (ITV1, 2003). Following her work on the Series Four *Doctor Who* story 'The Sontaran Stratagem'/'The Poison Sky', she took over from Matthew Bouch as producer of *The Sarah Jane Adventures* for its second series.

JAMES MORAN (WRITER)

James Moran was born in York. He got his first break as a writer by winning a Sci-Fi Channel competition with his script for the short film *Cheap Rate Gravity*, produced in 2002. He went on to write the successful movie *Severance* (2005). His *Torchwood* episode 'Sleeper' was his first TV work to be produced; he has since written 'The Fires of Pompeii' for Series Four of *Doctor Who* and scripts for forthcoming episodes of *Primeval* (ITV1), *Spooks: Liberty* (BBC Three) and *Law and Order: London* (ITV1). He has his own blog, at www.jamesmoran.blogspot.com, on which he has written extensively about his experiences working on both *Torchwood* and *Doctor Who*.

KEITH TEMPLE (WRITER)

Newcastle-born Keith Temple gained some of his earliest credits on *Children's Ward*, the Granada series produced by Russell T Davies in the mid-1990s. He then had stints working on a number of other shows, including ITV1's *Emmerdale* and *Heartbeat* and the BBC's *Casualty* and *Byker Grove*. One of his biggest successes to date came with the play *Angel Cake* (BBC One, 2006), about a woman who bakes a cake that bears an image thought to resemble the Virgin Mary. His Series Four episode 'Planet of the Ood' was his first contribution to the *Doctor Who* universe.

STEPHEN GREENHORN (WRITER)

Stephen Greenhorn was born on 5 September 1964 in West Lothian, Scotland. He has written extensively for the stage – including the hit play *Passing Places* (2000) and the musical *Sunshine on Leith* (2007) based on the songs of the Proclaimers – as well as for TV. His earliest TV writing credits came on two episodes of *The Bill* (ITV, 1983-) in 1996 and 1998 respectively, and on two episodes of *Where the Heart Is* (ITV1, 1996-2006) in 1998. He went on to script the series *Glasgow Kiss* (BBC One, 2000) and the docudrama *Derailed* (BBC One, 2005) and to create and write for the Scottish soap opera *River City* (BBC One Scotland, 2002-). More recent credits include an acclaimed adaptation of Jean Rhys's novel *Wide Sargasso Sea* (BBC Four, 2007), which led on to him being commissioned to contribute 'The Lazarus Experiment' to Series Three of *Doctor Who*. 'The Doctor's Daughter' was his second script for the show.

GARETH ROBERTS (WRITER)

Gareth Roberts was born in 1968. He studied drama at college and worked as a clerk at the Court of Appeal while also pursuing an interest in writing. In the 1990s he authored seven acclaimed *Doctor Who* novels, plus novelisations of two episodes of *Cracker* (ITV, 1993-1996), for Virgin Publishing. He also wrote for *Doctor Who Magazine* and for Big Finish's tie-in audio CD drama range before coming to work on the TV series via the digital mini-adventure 'Attack of the Graske' and the 'Tardisode' teasers for Series Two. He has written the new series novels *Only Human* (BBC Books, 2005) and *I Am A Dalek* (BBC Books, 2006) and numerous *Doctor Who* short stories. He has also written several episodes of *The Sarah Jane Adventures*. His other TV credits include: storylines for *Springhill* (Sky One, 1996-1997); episodes of *Emmerdale* (ITV, 1972-) in 1998; episodes of *Brookside* (Channel 4, 1982-2003) over a four year period from 1999; and co-written episodes of *Randall and Hopkirk (Deceased)* (BBC One, 2000-2001) and *Swiss Toni* (BBC Three, 2004-2004).

STEVEN MOFFAT (WRITER)

Steven Moffat was born in 1961 in Paisley, Scotland. He had gained a degree in English and begun working as a teacher when a chance encounter between his father and a TV producer led to him being commissioned to write the children's series *Press Gang* (ITV, 1989-1993), which quickly acquired cult status. He went on to create and write the sitcom *Joking Apart* (BBC Two, 1993-1995), which was inspired by the breakdown of his first marriage and won the Bronze Rose of Montreux award, and the less-well-received *Chalk* (BBC One, 1997). One of his biggest successes to date came with the sitcom *Coupling* (BBC Two/BBC Three, 2000-2004), which was also the subject of a short-lived American remake (NBC, 2003). More recently, he wrote the acclaimed drama *Jekyll* (BBC One, 2007) as a modern take on Robert Louis Stevenson's *Strange Case of Dr Jekyll and Mr Hyde* (Longmans, Green & Co, 1886). He scripted the spoof *Doctor Who* story 'The Curse of Fatal Death' for BBC One's *Comic Relief* telethon in 1999 and has contributed a number of short stories to various *Doctor Who* collections. He has the distinction of being the only writer other than Russell T Davies to have contributed episodes to each of the first four series of the new *Doctor Who*, and these scripts have earned him numerous Hugos, BAFTAs and other awards. As announced on 20 May 2008, he is due to take over from Davies as *Doctor Who* showrunner in 2009. His other recent projects include scripting the first of a trilogy of *The Adventures of Tintin* films for directors Steven Spielberg and Peter Jackson, to be produced by DreamWorks; he was due to write the second as well, but passed up this opportunity in favour of working on *Doctor Who*.

JAMES STRONG (DIRECTOR)

James Strong's first TV credits were as a documentary maker, on *Critical Mass* (Carlton, 1998), *World in Action* (ITV, 1998/99), *My FC* (Channel 5, 2000) and *Crimewatch UK* (BBC1, 2000). He then moved into directing comedy and drama programmes, including *Otis Lee Crenshaw* (Channel 4, 2000), *Jack Dee's Happy Hour* (BBC One, 2001), *Doctors* (BBC1, 2000-2001), *Nothing but the Truth* (ITV1, 2001),

Blood on her Hands (ITV1, 2002), *Mile High* (Sky One, 2002), *Holby City* (BBC One, 2002-2004), *Casualty* (BBC One, 2004), *The Good Citizen* (BBC One, 2004) and *Rocket Man* (BBC One, 2005) He both wrote and directed the comedy short film *Sold* (2002) and the TV dramas *Lady Jane* (ITV1, 2003) and *Billie Jo* (ITV1, 2004). Prior to his work on 'Voyage of the Damned' and 'Partners in Crime' for Series Four, he directed four other *Doctor Who* episodes: 'The Impossible Planet'/'The Satan Pit' (BBC One, 2006) and 'Daleks in Manhattan'/'Evolution of the Daleks' (BBC One, 2007). He also directed 'Cyberwoman' and 'They Keep Killing Suzie' for the first series of *Torchwood* (BBC Three, 2006).

GRAEME HARPER (DIRECTOR)

Graeme Harper was born on 11 March 1945. He started his working life as a child actor, appearing in TV adaptations of *The Pickwick Papers* (Associated Redifussion, 1956) and *The Silver Sword* (BBC, 1957), amongst other productions, before becoming a floor assistant at the BBC in 1965. It was in the latter capacity that he first worked on *Doctor Who*, on stories including 'The Power of the Daleks' (1966). He was promoted to assistant floor manager in 1969, being assigned to *Doctor Who* again on 'Colony in Space' (1971), 'Planet of the Daleks' (1973) and 'Planet of the Spiders' (1974). His next promotion, in 1975, was to production assistant, in which capacity he worked on 'The Seeds of Doom' (1976) and 'Warriors' Gate' (1981). He then successfully completed the BBC's directors' course. The fifth Doctor's swansong 'The Caves of Androzani' (1984) was the first job he got as a freelance director, after handling some of the final episodes of the hospital drama *Angels* (BBC One, 1975-1983) in-house at the BBC. He went on to direct one further classic series story, 'Revelation of the Daleks' (1984), and would also have handled the third story of Season 23 had the series not then been put on temporary hiatus by Michael Grade, Controller of BBC One at that time. He subsequently became one of Britain's most sought-after TV directors, building up an impressive list of credits on shows such as: *The District Nurse* (BBC One, 1984-1987); *Star Cops* (BBC Two, 1987); *Boon* (ITV, 1986-1992); *The House of Elliot* (BBC One, 1991-1994); numerous episodes of *Casualty* (BBC One, 1986-); *The Royal* (ITV, 2003-); some 2003 and 2005 episodes of *Byker Grove* (BBC One, 1989-2006); and three episodes of *Robin Hood* (BBC One, 2006-). He came close to working on *Doctor Who* again both in 1989, when he was approached to direct 'Battlefield' (an assignment he was prevented from taking on as he was already committed to *Boon*), and in 1993, when he was scheduled to helm the planned, but ultimately unmade, thirtieth anniversary story 'The Dark Dimension'. He finally returned to direct the episodes 'Rise of the Cybermen', 'The Age of Steel', 'Army of Ghosts' and 'Doomsday' for Series Two, '42' and 'Utopia' for Series Three and 'Planet of the Ood', 'The Unicorn and the Wasp', 'Turn Left', 'The Stolen Earth' and 'Journey's End' for Series Four. He has also directed a number of episodes of *The Sarah Jane Adventures* (CBBC, 2007-).

COLIN TEAGUE (DIRECTOR)

Colin Teague's directorial credits include the feature films *Northwest One* (1999), *Shooters* (2002), *Spivs* (2004) and *The Last Drop* (2005), all of which apart from *Shooters* he also co-wrote, and episodes of *London's Burning* (ITV1, 2002) and *Holby*

City (BBC One, 2003-2006). In addition to his four episodes of *Torchwood* – 'Ghost Machine' and 'Greeks Bearing Gifts' for Series One and 'Meat' and 'Adam' for Series Two – he has also directed the 'Invasion of the Bane' special for *The Sarah Jane Adventures* and three episodes of *Doctor Who* – 'The Sound of Drums' and 'Last of the Time Lords' for Series Three and 'The Fires of Pompeii' for Series Four – making him one of only two directors to date to have worked on all three series (the other being Alice Troughton).

DOUGLAS MACKINNON (DIRECTOR)

Scotland-born Douglas Mackinnon grew up on the Isle of Skye. After working as a newspaper photographer, he cut his directorial teeth in 1992 on the short film *Sealladh*, which he also wrote. He went on to gain numerous TV credits, including as assistant director on a number of 1994 and 1995 episodes of *The Bill* (ITV1) and some 1996 episodes of *Soldier, Soldier* (ITV1), and as director on *The Grand* (ITV1, 1997), some 1999 episodes of *The Vice* (ITV1), *Nice Guy Eddie* (BBC One, 2002), *Murder in Suburbia* (ITV1, 2004), some 2004 episodes of *Silent Witness* (BBC One) and some 2004 and 2005 episodes of *Bodies*. He made his feature film debut on *The Flying Scotsman* (Verve/MGM 2006). In 2007, he was lead director on Steven Moffat's *Jekyll* (BBC One). 'The Sontaran Stratagem'/'The Poison Sky' was his first contribution to *Doctor Who*.

ALICE TROUGHTON (DIRECTOR)

Alice Troughton has directed numerous episodes of *Doctors* (2003-2004), *Holby City* (2004-2005) and *EastEnders* (2006) for the BBC and *No Angels* (2006) for Channel 4. She also directed her own comedy short screenplay *Doris the Builder* (2004). Prior to her work on Series Four of *Doctor Who*, she directed the episodes 'Small Worlds' and 'Out of Time' for *Torchwood* and 'Revenge of the Slitheen' and 'Eye of the Gorgon' for *The Sarah Jane Adventures*.

EUROS LYN (DIRECTOR)

Welsh-born Euros Lyn was born in 1971 and educated at Ysgol Gyfun Ystalyfera and the University of Manchester. He began his career as a TV director in 1997, and gained some of his earliest credits on several episodes of the BBC Wales drama *Belonging* in 2000. Aside from the numerous episodes he has directed for *Doctor Who*, from 'The End of the World' in 2005 to 'Silence in the Library'/'Forest of the Dead' and the Proms special in 2008, he has also worked on, amongst others, *All About George* (ITV1, 2005), *Jane Hall* (ITV1, 2006) and *George Gently* (BBC One, 2007). He is due to direct all five episodes of Series Three of *Torchwood* (BBC One, 2009).

EDWARD THOMAS (PRODUCTION DESIGNER)

Edward Thomas took a foundation course in art and design after leaving school, and then studied at the Wimbledon School of Art, from which he graduated with a BA (Hons) degree in 3-D Design, specialising in theatre. He began his career as a designer on a wide variety of commercials and a number of theatrical productions, including *Turandot* for the Royal Opera Company at Wembley Arena, *Under Milk Wood* for the Dylan Thomas Theatre Company and Shakespeare's *Twelfth Night* and *Cymbeline* for the Ludlow Festival. This was followed by work on numerous feature films, including over a dozen South African productions in the early 1990s and *The Mystery of Edwin Drood* (1993), *Resurrection Man* (1998), *Darkness Falls* (1999) and *The Meeksville Ghost* (2001). He also gained credits on a wide range of TV shows including, for BBC Wales, *Jones*, *The Coal Project* and, of course, *Doctor Who* (2005-), *Torchwood* (2006-) and *The Sarah Jane Adventures* (2007-). He has sometimes been credited as Edward Alan Thomas or simply as Ed Thomas, and is represented by the Creative Media Management agency.

PART THREE
CREDITS

DOCTOR WHO
TIME CRASH (2007)
VOYAGE OF THE DAMNED (2007)
SERIES FOUR (2008)
MUSIC OF THE SPHERES (2008)

CREDITS[11]

Producer: Phil Collinson (4.00, 4.01, 4.02, 4.06, 4.08, 4.09, 4.10, 4.12, 4.13), Susie Liggat (4.03, 4.04, 4.05, 4.07, 4.11), Catrin Lewis Defis (MoS)

MAIN CAST

David Tennant (The Doctor)
Peter Davison (The Doctor) (TC)
Kylie Minogue (Astrid Peth) (4.00)
Catherine Tate (Donna Noble) (all except TC, MoS)
Freema Agyeman (Martha Jones) (4.04, 4.05, 4.06, 4.12, 4.13)
Billie Piper[12] (Rose Tyler) (4.01, 4.05, 4.10, 4.11, 4.12, 4.13)
John Barrowman (Captain Jack Harkness) (4.12, 4.13)
Elisabeth Sladen (Sarah Jane Smith) (4.12, 4.13)
Bernard Cribbins (Wilfred Mott) (4.00, 4.01, 4.04, 4.05, 4.11, 4.12, 4.13)
Jacqueline King (Sylvia Noble) (4.01, 4.04, 4.05, 4.11, 4.12, 4.13)

PRODUCTION TEAM

1st Assistant Director: Peter Bennett (4.00), James Blackwell (4.01), Dan Mumford (4.02, 4.08, 4.09), Gareth Williams (4.03, 4.06, 4.07, 4.10), Francesco Reidy (4.04, 4.05), Simon Morris (4.11, 4.12, 4.13), Rhidian Evans (MoS)
2nd Assistant Director: Jennie Fava (all except 4.11), Guy de Glanville (4.11)
3rd Assistant Director: Sarah Davies (all except 4.11, MoS), Paul Bennett (4.11)

---

11 There were no production team credits at all on 'Time Crash' – although a credit for producer Phil Collinson was added for the DVD release (as was one for director Graeme Harper). Where an episode number (or more than one) – or 'TC' for 'Time Crash' or 'MoS' for 'Music of the Spheres' – appears in brackets after a person's name in the listing, this means that they were credited only on the episode (or episodes) indicated. Otherwise, the person concerned was credited on all episodes bar 'Time Crash'. Some production roles were credited only on certain episodes.
12 Not credited in *Radio Times* for 4.01 or 4.05, to keep her appearance a secret.

Location Manager: Gareth Skelding (4.00, 4.01, 4.02, 4.06, 4.10, 4.12, 4.13), Jonathon Allott (4.03, 4.04, 4.05, 4.07, 4.08, 4.09), Emma Woodcock (4.11)
Unit Manager: Rhys Griffiths (4.00, 4.01, 4.02, 4.03, 4.04, 4.06, 4.07, 4.10)
Production Co-ordinator: Jess Van Niekerk
Production Secretary: Kevin Myers (4.00, 4.01, 4.02, 4.03, 4.04, 4.05, 4.06, 4.07, 4.08, 4.10)
Production/Script Secretary: Claire Thomas (MoS)
Assistant Production Co-ordinator: Debi Griffiths (all except 4.11, 4.12, MoS)
Assistant Production Accountant: Carole Wakefield (MoS)
Production Runner: Nicola Brown (4.00, 4.01, 4.02, 4.03, 4.05), Sian Warrilow (4.08, 4.09, 4.11)
Floor Manager: Sian Warrilow (MoS)
Floor Runner: Heddi Joy Taylor (4.00, 4.02, 4.04, 4.06), Andy Newbery (4.01, 4.03, 4.05)
Driver: Wayne Humphreys (4.00, 4.06, 4.07), Darren Lean[13] (4.00, 4.07), Kevin Kearns (4.06, MoS)
Contracts Assistant: Beth Britton[14] (4.00, 4.03, 4.07), Kath Blackman (4.01, 4.06, 4.10), Lisa Hayward (4.02, 4.08, 4.09, 4.10, MoS)
Continuity: Sheila Johnston (4.00, 4.01, 4.02, 4.03, 4.07), Non Eleri Hughes (4.04, 4.05, 4.06, 4.08, 4.09, 4.10, 4.12, 4.13), Llinos Wyn Jones (4.11), Susannah Unsworth (MoS)
Auto Cue: Delyth Mair Davies (MoS)
Script Editor: Brian Minchin (4.00, 4.02, 4.11), Lindsey Alford (4.01, 4.03, 4.06, 4.07, 4.12, 4.13), Nikki Smith (4.04, 4.05), Helen Raynor (4.08, 4.09, 4.10), Gary Russell (MoS)
Camera Operator: Julian Barber (4.00, 4.01, 4.02, 4.06, 4.10), Rory Taylor (4.01, 4.02, 4.12, 4.13), Steven Hall (4.03, 4.07), James Moss (4.04, 4.05), Joe Russell (4.06, 4.08, 4.09, 4.10), Roger Pearce (4.11, 4.12, 4.13)
Focus Puller: Steve Rees (all except 4.11, MoS), Duncan Fowlie (4.06, 4.07, 4.10), Jamie Southcott (4.08, 4.09, 4.11), Penny Shipton (4.11)
Camera Assistant: Jon Vidgen (4.02, 4.03, 4.07, MoS), Tom Hartley (4.07, 4.10)
Grip: John Robinson (all except 4.11, MoS), Dave Holliday (4.11), Dai Hopkins (MoS)
Boom Operator: Jeff Welch (all except 4.11, MoS), Bryn Thomas (4.02, 4.03, 4.07), Kevin Staples (4.11), Adam Ridge (MoS)
Gaffer: Mark Hutchings (all except 4.11, MoS), Stephen Slocombe (4.11), Peter Chester (MoS)
Best Boy: Peter Chester (all except 4.11, MoS), Chris Davies (4.11)
Electrician: Steve Slocombe (4.01, 4.09, 4.10), Clive Johnson (4.01, 4.09, 4.10), Ben Griffiths (4.01, 4.09, 4.10)
Stunt Co-ordinator: Tom Lucy (4.00, 4.01, 4.02, 4.04, 4.05, 4.08, 4.09), Abbi Collins (4.03, 4.07, 4.12, 4.13), Crispin Layfield (4.06, 4.10), Bill Davy (4.11)
Stunt Performer: Jason Hunjan (4.00), Stephanie Carey (4.00), Danielle Da Costa (4.00)
Choreographer: Ailsa Berk (4.00, 4.02, 4.04, 4.05, 4.08, 4.09, 4.12, 4.13)

---

[13] Credited as 'Darren Leen' on 4.00.

[14] Credited as 'Bethan Britton' on 4.03.

Chief Supervising Art Director: Stephen Nicholas
Art Department Production Manager: Jonathan Allison[15] (all except MoS)
Supervising Art Director: Arwel Wyn Jones (all except MoS)
Associate Designer: James North (all except MoS)
Art Department Co-ordinator: Anna Coote (4.00, 4.03, 4.07), Amy Pope (4.01, 4.02, 4.04, 4.05, 4.06, 4.08, 4.09, 4.10, 4.11, 4.13)
Set Decorator: Tristan Peatfield (4.00), Malin Lindhom (4.01), Tim Dickel (4.02, 4.06, 4.10), David Morison (4.03, 4.07, 4.08, 4.09), Joelle Rumbelow (4.04, 4.05), Keith Dunne (4.11), Julian Luxton (4.12, 4.13), Ben Morris (MoS)
Props Buyer: Joelle Rumbelow (4.00, 4.08, 4.09), Catherine Samuel (4.01, 4.02, 4.06, 4.10), Christina Tom (4.03, 4.07), Sue Jackson Potter (4.04, 4.05), Ben Morris (4.11), Adrian Anscombe (4.12, 4.13)
Graphic Artist: Christina Tom (4.11, 4.13)
Standby Art Director: Rebecca Hemy (4.00), Ciaran Thompson (4.01, 4.03, 4.06, 4.07, 4.10), Jamie Macwilliam (4.02), Alexandra Merchant (4.04, 4.05), Ellen Woods (4.08, 4.09), Nick Murray (4.11, 4.12, 4.13), Julia Challis (MoS)
Design Assistant: Peter McKinstry (4.00, 4.03, 4.05, 4.07, 4.09, 4.11, 4.12), Al Roberts (4.01, 4.06), Sarah Payne (4.02, 4.08), Al Roberts (4.04, 4.10, 4.13)
Storyboard Artist: Shaun Williams (all except 4.05, 4.11 4.13)
Standby Props: Phill Shellard (all except 4.11, MoS), Patrick Deacy (4.00), Nick Murray (4.01, 4.02, 4.03, 4.04, 4.05, 4.06, 4.07, 4.08, 4.09, 4.10), Matthew North (4.11), Jackson Pope (4.11, 4.13)
Standby Carpenter: Will Pope (all except 4.11, 4.13, MoS), Paul Jones (4.11)
Standby Painter: Ellen Woods (4.00, 4.01, 4.02, 4.03, 4.04, 4.05, 4.07, 4.10), Julia Challis (4.08, 4.09, 4.11, 4.12)
Standby Rigger: Keith Freeman (all except 4.11, 4.12, MoS), John Cooling (4.11)
Property Master: Phil Lyons (4.00, 4.02, 4.06, 4.09, 4.10, 4.13), Paul Aitken (4.01, 4.03, 4.04, 4.05, 4.07, 4.08, 4.12), Adrian Anscombe (4.11)
Forward Dresser: Stuart Mackay (4.11)
Dressing Chargehand: Matthew Wild[16] (4.01, 4.03, 4.06, 4.09, 4.10)
Senior Props Maker: Barry Jones (4.00, 4.01, 4.02, 4.03, 4.04, 4.05, 4.06, 4.07, 4.08, 4.09, 4.10), Penny Howarth (4.11, 4.12)
Props Maker: Penny Howarth (4.00, 4.03, 4.05, 4.09, 4.10), Nick Robatto (4.01, 4.04, 4.06, 4.08, 4.11), Jon Grundon (4.02, 4.07)
Practical Electrician: Albert James (4.02, 4.04, 4.07), Gafin Riley (2.08)
Construction Manager: Matthew Hywel-Davies, John Whalley (4.09)
Workshop Manager: Mark Hill (4.03, 4.08)
Construction Chargehand: Scott Fisher (4.02, 4.07), Allen Jones (4.10)
Scenic Artist: John Whalley (4.00, 4.04), Allen Jones (4.00), John Pinkerton (4.01, 4.06, 4.11)
Graphics: BBC Wales Graphics
Costume Supervisor: Lindsay Bonaccorsi (all except 4.11), Charlotte Mitchell (4.11)
Assistant Costume Designer: Rose Goodhart (all except 4.01, 4.11, MoS)
Costume Assistant: Barbara Harrington (all except 4.11), Louise Martin (all except 4.11, MoS), Bobbie Peach (4.11), Sara Morgan (4.11)

---

[15] Credited as 'Jonathan Marquand Allison' on 4.00.
[16] Credited as 'Matt Wild' on 2.09.

Make-Up Supervisor: Olivia Jones (4.11)
Make-Up Artist: Pam Mullins (all except 4.11, MoS), Morag Smith (4.00, 4.02), John Munro (all except 4.11, MoS), Steve Smith (all except 4.00, 4.11), Su Westwood (4.11)
Casting Associate: Andy Brierley, Amy Rogers (4.01, 4.02, 4.04, 4.05)
VFX Editor: Ceres Doyle (all except MoS)
Assistant Editor: Carmen Roberts (4.00, 4.01, 4.06, 4.07, 4.10, MoS)
Post Production Supervisor: Samantha Hall, Chris Blatchford
Post Production Co-ordinator: Marie Brown
SFX Co-ordinator: Ben Ashmore (all except MoS)
SFX Supervisor: Danny Hargreaves (4.00, 4.01, 4.02, 4.04, 4.05, 4.06, 4.08, 4.09, 4.10, 4.12, 4.13), Paul Kelly (4.03, 4.07, 4.11)
Prosthetics Designer: Neill Gorton (all except 4.07, 4.10, MoS), Rob Mayor (MoS)
Prosthetics Supervisor: Rob Mayor (all except 4.07, 4.10, MoS)
On Set Prosthetics Supervisor: Pete Hawkins (4.03), Martin Rezard (4.04)
Prosthetic Make Up Artist: Sarah Lockwood (4.02, MoS)
Prosthetic Technician: Jon Moore (4.02), Sarah Lockwood (4.03), Justin Pickethly (4.03), Victoria Bancroft (4.03), Jo Glover (4.04), Lotta Hagvist (4.04), Helen Rowe (4.05), Lenny Sant (4.05), Lauren Welman (4.06), Helen Walker (4.06), Fiona Walsh (4.06), Tim Berry (4.06), Charlie Bluett (4.11), Chris Clarke (4.11)
Online Editor: Matthew Clarke (all except 4.06, 4.12, MoS), Mark Bright (4.01, 4.02, 4.04, 4.05, 4.06, 4.07, 4.08, 4.09, 4.10, 4.11, 4.12)
Colourist: Mick Vincent (all except MoS)
3D Artist: Jean Claude Deguara (4.00, 4.02, 4.03, 4.07, 4.10, 4.12, 4.13), Nicholas Hernandez (4.00, 4.03, 4.07, 4.10, 4.12, 4.13), Nick Webber (4.00, 4.02, 4.05, 4.11, 4.12), Neil Roche (4.00, 4.02, 4.07), Andy Guest (4.00, 4.02, 4.05, 4.12), Bruce Magroune (4.00, 4.03, 4.10), Matt McKinney (4.00, 4.01, 4.04, 4.05, 4.09, 4.11, 4.13), Mark Wallman (4.00, 4.06, 4.09, 4.11), Jeff North (4.00, 4.03, 4.04, 4.05, 4.06, 4.13), Stephen Regelous (4.01), Dave Levy (4.01, 4.13), Serena Cacciato (4.01, 4.05, 4.06, 4.12), Adam Burnet (4.02), Ruth Bailey (4.02, 4.06), Sam Lucas (4.03, 4.07), Will Pryor (4.03, 4.13), Chris Tucker (4.03, 4.05, 4.09), David Knight (4.11), Jean-Yves Audouard (4.13)
2D Artist: Sara Bennett (4.00, 4.01, 4.03, 4.04, 4.05, 4.06, 4.07, 4.10, 4.11, 4.12, 4.13), Russell Horth (4.00, 4.02, 4.05, 4.06, 4.07, 4.08, 4.13), Bryan Bartlett (4.00, 4.01, 4.02, 4.06, 4.08, 4.09, 4.10, 4.12), Greg Spencer (4.00, 4.01, 4.08, 4.09, 4.11, 4.12), Arianna Lago (4.00, 4.05, 4.06, 4.07, 4.08, 4.09, 4.11, 4.12), Simon C Holden (4.00, 4.01, 4.03, 4.04, 4.09), Isobel Barber (4.00), Tim Barter (4.01), James Moxon (4.01, 4.07, 4.08, 4.09), Murray Barber (4.01, 4.02, 4.03, 4.05, 4.06, 4.07, 4.08, 4.09, 4.11), Loraine Cooper (4.01, 4.03, 4.06), Adrian Cirulli (4.02, 4.06, 4.08, 4.09, 4.10, 4.13), Julie Nixon (4.04, 4.05, 4.07, 4.08, 4.09, 4.11), Lyndall Spagnoletti (4.08, 4.09, 4.10), James Etherington (4.10)
Matte Painter: Simon Wicker (4.00, 4.02, 4.03, 4.04, 4.05, 4.08, 4.09, 4.12, 4.13), Alex Fort (4.02, 4.03, 4.10), Charlie Bennett (4.02, 4.08, 4.09), David Early (4.11, 4.12, 4.13)
VFX Co-ordinator: Jenna Powell (all except 4.12, MoS), Rebecca Johnson (all except 4.13, MoS)
VFX Production Assistant: Marianne Paton (4.00, 4.01, 4.02, 4.03, 4.04, 4.06, 4.07, 4.08)
On Set VFX Supervisor: Tim Barter (4.00, 4.02, 4.03, 4.04, 4.06, 4.07, 4.10, 4.12, 4.13,

MoS), David Bowman (4.08, 4.09)
VFX Supervisor: Barney Curnow (4.01, 4.03)
Dubbing Mixer: Tim Ricketts
Supervising Sound Editor: Paul McFadden
Sound Editor: Doug Sinclair (4.08, 4.09, 4.10, 4.11, 4.12, 4.13)
Sound FX Editor: Paul Jefferies
Foley Editor: Kelly-Marie Angell (4.00, 4.01, 4.06, 4.07, 4.10, MoS)
Finance Manager: Chris Rogers (4.00, 4.01, 4.02, 4.05, 4.06, 4.07, 4.10)
Line Producer Italy: Guido Cerasuolo (4.02)

With thanks to the BBC National Orchestra of Wales

Closing Music: The BBC Radiophonic Workshop (MoS)
Original Theme Music: Ron Grainer
Casting Director: Andy Pryor CDG
Production Executive: Julie Scott
Production Accountant: Oliver Ager
Sound Recordist: Julian Howarth (4.00, 4.01, 4.02, 4.03, 4.06, 4.07, 4.08, 4.09, 4.10, 4.12, 4.13), Brian Milliken (4.04, 4.05), Ray Parker (4.11), Simon Koelmeyer (MoS)
Costume Designer: Louise Page (all except 4.11), Ray Holman (4.11)
Make-Up Designer: Barbara Southcott (all except 4.11), Emma Bailey (4.11)
Music: Murray Gold
Visual Effects: The Mill
Visual FX Producer: Will Cohen (all except 4.13), Marie Jones (all except 4.12)
Visual FX Supervisor: Dave Houghton
Special Effects: Any Effects
Prosthetics: Millennium FX (all except 4.07, 4.10)
Editor: Mike Jones (4.00, 4.01), Mike Hopkins (4.02, 4.04, 4.05), Will Oswald (4.03, 4.07, 4.11, 4.12, 4.13), Philip Kloss (4.07, 4.10), Crispin Green (4.08, 4.09), Ceres Doyle (MoS)
Production Designer: Edward Thomas
Director of Photography: Ernie Vincze BSC[17] (4.00, 4.01, 4.02, 4.06, 4.10, 4.12, 4.13), Rory Taylor (4.03, 4.04, 4.05, 4.07, 4.08, 4.09, 4.11), Roger Pearce (MoS)
Production Manager: Tracie Simpson (4.00, 4.01, 4.02, 4.11), Debbi Slater (4.03, 4.04, 4.05, 4.07, 4.08, 4.09), Peter Bennett (4.06, 4.10, 4.12, 4.13)

Executive Producer: Russell T Davies, Julie Gardner, Phil Collinson (4.04, 4.05, 4.07, 4.11)

BBC Wales

[17] Surname misspelt 'Vince' on 4.02.

PART FOUR
EPISODE GUIDE

The durations quoted in the episode guide below are for the complete versions of the episodes on the BBC's master tapes. The durations on transmission were generally a few seconds shorter, as each episode tended to be cut into slightly by the preceding and/or following continuity caption and announcement.

Readers who have yet to see the episodes may wish to bear in mind that this guide is a comprehensive one that contains many plot 'spoilers'.

CHILDREN IN NEED SPECIAL 2007
TIME CRASH

Writer: Steven Moffat
Director: Graeme Harper

DEBUT TRANSMISSION DETAILS

BBC One
Date: 16 November 2007. Scheduled time: Between 8.00 pm and 8.30 pm.[18] Actual time: 8.17 pm.

Duration: 8' 01"

ADDITIONAL CREDITED CAST

None.[19]

PLOT

The tenth Doctor's TARDIS becomes merged with the fifth Doctor's when he forgets to reset the shields after taking Martha Jones home, bringing the two incarnations of the Time Lord together. The time crash creates a black hole that threatens to devastate the universe, but the tenth Doctor forestalls this by cancelling out the black hole with a supernova – he knew what to do because he remembered watching himself do it when he was the fifth Doctor. The crisis averted, the fifth Doctor fades away, returning to his proper place in the timeline. The tenth Doctor again forgets to reset the shields, and is astonished when the control room wall is suddenly breached by the prow of the famous ocean liner *Titanic* ...

QUOTE, UNQUOTE

- Fifth Doctor: 'Who are you?
  Tenth Doctor: 'Take a look.'
  Fifth Doctor: 'Oh. Oh no.'
  Tenth Doctor: 'Oh yes.'

---

[18] All scheduled transmission times for *Children in Need* items are approximate, due to the nature of the live telethon.

[19] In addition to David Tennant and Peter Davison, Freema Agyeman appears briefly as Martha Jones in a reprise of the end of 'Last of the Time Lords', but is uncredited.

Fifth Doctor: 'You're … Oh no.'
Tenth Doctor: 'Here it comes. Yeah, yeah, I am.'
Fifth Doctor: 'A *fan*.'

- Tenth Doctor: 'Where are you now? Nyssa and Tegan? Cybermen and Mara, and Time Lords in funny hats, and the Master? Oh, he just showed up again. Same as ever.'
  Fifth Doctor: 'Oh no. Really? Does he still have that rubbish beard?'
  Tenth Doctor: 'No, no beard this time. Well, a wife …'
- Fifth Doctor: 'To days to come.'
  Tenth Doctor: 'All my love to long ago.'

CONTINUITY POINTS

- An alert sound is identified by the fifth Doctor as indicating a 'level five' emergency: 'A temporal collision. It's like two TARDISes have merged.' Later, the cloister bell sounds, portending imminent disaster. The idea that the merging of two TARDISes could cause a universal cataclysm was first aired in the classic series story 'The Time Monster' (1972), where it was described as a 'time ram'. The cloister bell was first heard in 'Logopolis' (1980).
- When the fifth Doctor turns down his offer of the use of the sonic screwdriver, the tenth Doctor recalls: 'Oh, no, of course, you mostly went hands-free, didn't you.' This refers to the fact that after the original sonic screwdriver was destroyed in 'The Visitation' (1982), the fifth Doctor never used one again. (The next Doctor seen to use a sonic screwdriver on screen was the seventh, in the *Doctor Who* TV movie (1996).)
- The fifth Doctor mentions 'That LINDA lot', the group of devotees seen in the Series Two episode 'Love & Monsters'.
- The tenth Doctor says: 'I'm you with a new face. Check out this bone structure, Doctor, because one day you're gonna be shaving it.' This gives the first explicit confirmation that the Doctor needs to shave, something he has never been seen to do on screen – although the fact that the Master originally had a beard clearly implied that Time Lords do grow facial hair.
- TARDIS components referred to by the tenth Doctor include the 'thermobuffer' (first mentioned in 'Castrovalva' (1980)), the 'helmic regulator' ('The Ark in Space' (1975)) and the 'Zeiton crystals' ('Vengeance on Varos' (1985)).
- The tenth Doctor mentions the fifth Doctor's companions Tegan and Nyssa, his adversaries the Cybermen and the Mara, and 'Time Lords in funny hats' and the Master. The 'Time Lords in funny hats' comment may refer to Commander Maxil, played by future sixth Doctor actor Colin Baker, in 'Arc of Infinity' (1983). It is not possible to tell definitely from these references, or from other clues such as the design details of his costume, from which point in his time-stream the fifth Doctor is taken at the start of 'Time Crash', although it is probably somewhere between 'Arc of Infinity' (1983) – the first story in which he makes a return visit to the Time Lord home planet Gallifrey – and 'Terminus' (1983) – the story in which Nyssa leaves him.

PRODUCTION NOTES

- This special was shot in a single day, 7 October 2007, on one set, the TARDIS interior, with a small crew directed by Graeme Harper. Harper had also directed Peter Davison's last regular story as the Doctor, 'The Caves of Androzani' (1984).
- There were no production team credits on the transmitted programme – the single caption at the end read '*Doctor Who* returns at Christmas in "Voyage of the Damned"'. Credits for Graeme Harper as director and Phil Collinson as producer were however added for the DVD release.
- The Director of Photography was Rory Taylor.
- The CGI effect of the *Titanic* breaking into the control room was different from that seen at the end of 'Last of the Time Lords', it having been considerably refined in the interim.
- Parts of Murray Gold's score intentionally emulated the style of electronic music created by composers at the BBC Radiophonic Workshop for the fifth Doctor's episodes.
- The special was introduced by host Terry Wogan and guest John Barrowman live from the *Children in Need* studio. A small caption was displayed in the top left corner of the screen throughout transmission, indicating alternately the phone number and website address for making donations to the charity.
- Eleven million viewers tuned in for 'Time Crash', the highest rating gained by any part of this *Children in Need* telethon, and indeed the highest gained by *any* TV programme during the week of its transmission – a first for *Doctor Who*, albeit in exceptional circumstances.

PRESS REACTION

- 'It's a piece written for the fans as much as the general audience, with [Peter] Davison delivering a computer-age update of Patrick Troughton's scornful comments on the TARDIS's redecoration back in "The Three Doctors", a sly explanation for Davison's ageing, and a superb post-[John] Simm reprise of "The Curse of Fatal Death"'s innuendos about the Master's campness and its implications. There's a serious element, with the tenth Doctor knowing that he can afford to have fun until the moment that the danger arrives, but really the joy of this is the characterisation – both Doctors initially too centred on the console to notice each other – and the fourth-wall-breaking acknowledgement of Davison's impact on the series, and how fans like Tennant saw it.' Anthony Brown, *TV Zone* Issue 223, Christmas 2007.

ANALYSIS

There is quite a long history of *Doctor Who* mini-episodes being produced to raise money for charity, but it's a chequered history at best. On the one hand, the 1993 *Doctor Who-EastEnders* crossover for *Children in Need*, 'Dimensions in Time', was a disaster of train-wreck proportions; and the 1999 Steven Moffat-penned *Comic Relief* entry 'The Curse of Fatal Death', although reckoned by many to be one of the best *Doctor Who* spoofs ever committed to tape, was a spoof nonetheless, and as such was not to everyone's taste – certainly not to this author's – and no substitute for the real deal. On the other hand, since the advent of the new, Russell T Davies-helmed *Doctor Who*, things have taken a definite turn for the better: the untitled, seven-minute-long 2005 *Children in Need* scene, written by Davies, which saw the newly-regenerated tenth Doctor reintroduce himself to Rose Tyler, was a *bona fide* addition to the show's mythology, and a highly effective dramatic vignette in its own right. Thankfully, 'Time Crash', although a multi-Doctor story like 'Dimensions in Time' and having a Steven Moffat script like 'The Curse of Fatal Death', is very much in the vein of that 2005 success, presenting what is, in essence, a 'missing scene' linking the close of the preceding series finale with the start of the following Christmas special; and, what's more, it is arguably the best of the charity specials to date - perhaps not surprisingly, given that since 1999 Moffat has gone on to become arguably the very best of the current contingent of *Doctor Who* writers.

Long-term fans have been clamouring for some time for the new series to present a multi-Doctor adventure along the lines of the classic series stories 'The Three Doctors' (1973), 'The Five Doctors' (1983) and 'The Two Doctors' (1985). It has to be said, though, that those earlier team-ups always looked more exciting on paper than they proved to be in practice, each seeming a little more self-indulgent than the last - a clear case of diminishing returns - so if this particular *Doctor Who* tradition was going to be dusted off for a 21st Century revival, then a short *Children in Need* special was probably a better choice of vehicle for it than *Doctor Who* itself. 'Time Crash' is certainly likely to appeal more to those aforementioned long-term fans than to relative newcomers, being a kind of love letter to the classic series, and in particular to Peter Davison's Doctor. As Moffat has astutely observed in interviews, Davison's came the closest of all the classic series Doctors to providing a precedent for the younger, more energetic archetype adopted for the new series; he was, in that sense, the first of the 'modern Doctors'. The enormous regard that both Moffat and David Tennant clearly have for him positively shines through in this fitting and well-judged tribute, the tenth Doctor's 'You were my Doctor' comment - confirming that he is indeed a 'fan', as the fifth Doctor initially suspected - seeming quite appropriate in the circumstances, despite threatening to break the fourth wall between studio and audience, if not actually doing so. While Moffat maintains the established convention of different Doctors having a slightly antagonistic attitude toward each other when they meet - always popular with fans, as it reflects their own friendly disagreements over who was the 'best' Doctor - thankfully the conflict is never allowed to go beyond a degree of short-lived tetchy verbal sparring. Even the worst aspect of Davison's Doctor, his dreadful costume, is paid affectionate respect, with the tenth Doctor's gleeful reference to 'crickety-cricket stuff' and amusing comment, regarding the stick of celery on the lapel, 'Not a lot of men can carry off a decorative vegetable' - a good example of the kind of warm humour that runs through the script.

Moffat even takes the opportunity to iron out, rather brilliantly, some long-standing continuity niggles that have been generally glossed over in the past. First, he neatly explains the fact that the earlier Doctors in multi-Doctor stories always look older than they did during their own eras - inevitably so, due to the ageing of the cast - with a simple, almost throwaway line from the tenth Doctor: 'The two of us together has shorted out the time differential; it should all snap back into place when we get you home.' Secondly, he attributes the numerous variations in the appearance of the TARDIS interior over the years, previously referred to in terms of 'redecorating', to the Doctor having 'changed the desktop theme' - 'What's this one,

Coral? It's worse than the Leopard-skin!' – a far more satisfactory, and certainly far more contemporary, rationalisation – and one that has the added advantage of disproving the rather naff theory, apparently propounded in the first instance by production designer Edward Thomas in the process of creating the current set, that the TARDIS might actually have been grown out of coral. It is a mark of Moffat's consummate skill as a writer that he is able to wrap up what could be seen as rather nerdy, fan-pleasing material such as this in such a delightful sugar-coating of humour that it is sure to keep the general viewing audience entertained as well. That said, it is a moot point whether the former issue really needed to be addressed at all, as Davison has actually aged remarkably well, and still looks quite similar to how he did in the mid-1980s – something that, with all due respect to the actors concerned, could not have been said had some of the other surviving Doctors turned up unexpectedly in the TARDIS.

In one respect, Moffat does depart slightly from the precedent of past multi-Doctor stories. Whereas they always relied on an implicit assumption that when the earlier Doctors returned to their proper point in time and space they would not retain any memory of what had occurred, in 'Time Crash' the crucial factor in the resolution of the plot is that the tenth Doctor knows what to do precisely because he remembers having witnessed it previously as the fifth Doctor – an incidental benefit of which is that it gives Moffat an excellent excuse to reference the celebrated 'wibbly-wobbly, timey-wimey' line from his earlier episode 'Blink'. Even this, though, seems to have been carefully thought out, in that the memory is implied to be a latent one that is reawakened only when the two Doctors actually come together. Not only does this afford an answer to awkward questions such as why the post-Time War Doctor believed himself to be the last of the Time Lords, given that in 'Time Crash' the tenth Doctor tells the fifth that he has just met the Master again, but it also perhaps goes some way to explaining why, in 'Utopia', the Doctor seems to sense intuitively that the Time Lord whose essence is contained within Professor Yana's fob watch is none other than his old arch-enemy.[20] The only thing that isn't explained is why the fifth Doctor doesn't initially realise that he is meeting his tenth incarnation, as in previous multi-Doctor encounters there has always seemed to be an instant recognition.

Over the years, fans have often had to resort to making light of the shortcomings of 'Dimensions in Time' and its ilk with excuses such as, 'It may have been rubbish, but it was all in a good cause', 'It wasn't really meant to be taken seriously' or – a sure sign of desperation – 'It doesn't count as part of the official canon'. Nowadays, fortunately, no such justifications are required. 'Time Crash' is a superb piece of *Doctor Who* by any standards, and a worthy supplement to – and celebration of – the show's rich legacy.

---

[20] When this issue was raised on the online *Doctor Who* Forum, Moffat commented, slightly tongue in cheek: 'While the ninth Doctor recalls his experience of meeting the tenth Doctor as the fifth Doctor, he has his own internal sense that the Time Lords are all gone versus a brief memory of some jokey remarks made by that skinny fellow. Naturally he favours his faculties, especially as time has been rewritten by the Time War. It's only when the Yana's watch is mentioned, that he realises that Skinny Bloke wasn't joking. That's why he instantly concludes that Yana is the Master, not some other Time Lord. This was all planned in advance by myself and Russell using graphs.'

4.00 – VOYAGE OF THE DAMNED

Writer: Russell T Davies
Director: James Strong

DEBUT TRANSMISSION DETAILS

BBC One
Date: 25 December 2007. Scheduled time: 6.50 pm. Actual time: 6.50 pm.

BBC Three
Date: 1 January 2008. Scheduled time: 7.00 pm. Actual time: n/k.

Duration: 71′ 53″

ADDITIONAL CREDITED CAST

Geoffrey Palmer (Captain Hardaker), Russell Tovey (Midshipman Frame[21]), George Costigan (Max Capricorn), Gray O'Brien (Rickston Slade), Andrew Havill (Chief Steward), Bruce Lawrence (Engineer), Debbie Chazen (Foon Van Hoff), Clive Rowe (Morvin Van Hoff), Clive Swift (Mr Copper[22]), Jimmy Vee (Bannakaffalatta), Nicholas Witchell (Himself), Paul Kasey[23] (The Host), Stefan Davis[24] (Kitchen Hand), Jason Mohammad[25] (Newsreader), Colin McFarlane[26] (Alien Voice), Ewan Bailey[27] (Alien Voice), Jessica Martin[28] (Voice of the Queen)

PLOT

The Doctor arrives on a spaceship replica of the famous ocean liner *Titanic*, which is bringing a party of tourists from the planet Sto on a cruise to visit the Earth at Christmastime. Captain Hardaker, who is terminally ill and has been bribed with the promise of money for his family, lowers the ship's shields and allows it to be hit by a meteoroid shower. Many of the ship's passengers and crew are killed outright. Then, belying their angelic design, the robotic Hosts, used throughout the ship as information points, begin to pick off the survivors. The Doctor and a small group of passengers, including a young waitress named Astrid Peth, make their way

[21] First name given in dialogue as 'Alonzo'.
[22] First name given on the official *Doctor Who* website as 'Bayldon'.
[23] Not credited in *Radio Times*.
[24] Not credited in *Radio Times*.
[25] Not credited in *Radio Times*.
[26] Not credited in *Radio Times*.
[27] Not credited in *Radio Times*.
[28] Not credited in *Radio Times*.

through the damaged infrastructure, crossing a narrow strut spanning a chasm above the engines' nuclear storm drive, to try to reach the bridge and prevent the ship from crashing into the Earth. The Doctor learns that there is a sealed chamber on Deck 31 and goes to confront its occupant - Max Capricorn, owner of the cruise line, who is confined to a life-support machine. Max's business has failed and he has caused this disaster in order to exact revenge on his former partners and secure a fortune for his retirement. Astrid uses a fork-lift truck to push Capricorn's life support machine into the chasm, but the truck's brake line has been broken and she too goes over the edge, falling to her death. The Doctor gets to the bridge and manages to prevent the ship from crashing. He then tries to save Astrid by using a stored memory of her in the ship's teleport system, but is only partly successful: she becomes 'stardust', with just a ghost of consciousness, and is set free to fly through space for eternity.

QUOTE, UNQUOTE

- **Rickston Slade:** 'Hang on a minute. Who put you in charge, and who the hell are you, anyway?'
  Doctor: 'I'm the Doctor. I'm a Time Lord. I'm from the planet Gallifrey in the constellation of Kasterborous. I'm 903 years old, and I'm the man who's going to save your lives, and all six billion people on the planet below. You got a problem with that?'
- **Astrid:** 'You might be a Time King from Gallibee, but you still need to eat.'
  Doctor: 'Yeah, thanks.'
  Astrid: 'Though you look good for 903.'
  Doctor: 'You should see me in the mornings.'
  Astrid: 'Okay.'
- **Mr Copper:** 'She's just atoms, Doctor. An echo, with the ghost of consciousness. She's stardust.'

CONTINUITY POINTS

- Captain Hardaker refers to the Earth as a 'Level 5 civilisation', as previously established in 'City of Death' (1979) and the 'Revenge of the Slitheen' story in *The Sarah Jane Adventures*.
- The microphone of the singer in the *Titanic*'s band has a Magpie Electricals logo on it - a reference to the electrical manufacturing company first mentioned in 'The Idiot's Lantern'. Presumably this is one of the details of the ship copied from the real *Titanic* (in the *Doctor Who* universe, at any rate).
- The TV news reports seen in this episode, explaining that most Londoners are spending the festive season away from the capital in case there is an extraterrestrial incident there for the third year running, suggest that by Christmas 2008 - when this is set - the population of the UK are finally coming to accept that aliens have visited the Earth.
- When the TARDIS is set adrift from the *Titanic* by the meteoroid strike, the Doctor says: 'Once it's set adrift, it's programmed to lock on to the nearest centre of gravity' - which in this instance is the Earth. The TARDIS lands automatically - in Cardiff, judging from the final scene where the Doctor

teleports down with Mr Copper to retrieve it.

- The Doctor refers to his home planet Gallifrey being 'in the constellation of Kasterborous', the first time this has been specified since *Doctor Who* returned in 2005, although it was mentioned numerous times in the classic series. He also says that he is '903 years old', which ties in with earlier suggestions regarding his age in the new series but contradicts many classic series episodes – which also contradicted each other – and can probably be taken with a pinch of salt, particularly given that the length of a 'year' will vary from one planet to another.
- Foon says that she and Morvin worked in the 'milk market' back on Sto, and that it has all robot staff.
- The Doctor correctly guesses that the *Titanic* has a 'nuclear storm drive'. He says: 'If we hit the planet, the nuclear storm explodes and wipes out life on Earth.'
- When Astrid asks, 'This Christmas thing, what's it all about?', the Doctor replies, 'Long story. I should know. I was there. I got the last room.' What exactly he means by this is left to the viewer's imagination; however, Paul Cornell's *Doctor Who* short story *Deep and Dreamless Sleep*, published in *The Sunday Times* on 24 December 2006, indicated that the Doctor was indeed present at the Nativity.
- When Astrid asks the Doctor how he knows the Earth so well, he replies: 'A few years ago I was sort of made, well, sort of homeless, and, erm, there was the Earth.' This is presumably a reference to him having come to Earth after Gallifrey was destroyed in the Time War, although he could possibly be thinking of when he was exiled to Earth by the Time Lords at the beginning of his third incarnation, or even of when he originally went on the run from his own people in his first incarnation. The 1996 *Doctor Who* TV movie indicated that the Doctor's mother was from Earth, which would presumably account for his initial interest in this particular planet.
- Max Capricorn states that he has been running his company for 176 years; he has been kept alive by his life support system.
- The Queen's Christmas greeting to the Doctor suggests that he is no longer out of favour with the Royal Family – unlike at the end of the 19th Century, when Queen Victoria set up the Torchwood Institute specifically in order to counter the threat she believed he posed to her Empire.

PRODUCTION NOTES

- This special had the working title 'Starship Titanic'. This was also the title of a Douglas Adams-written computer game released in the 1990s.
- Kylie Minogue's creative director William Baker, being a big *Doctor Who* fan, liaised with the show's production team in order to facilitate Minogue's appearance in this special. Russell T Davies wrote the part of Astrid Peth specially for her. One of the conditions of Minogue's participation was that her personal photographer would be allowed to take all the publicity shots of the special, rather than the BBC's own photographer as would normally be the case.

- Composer Murray Gold revised his arrangement of the show's theme music for this special; the new version would be retained for the whole of Series Four. The format of the closing credits, and speed at which they roll, was also changed at this point, owing to new BBC rules specifying a maximum 30-second duration for the credits of any given programme.
- The sequences set in the *Titanic* teleport area were recorded on 13, 28 and 30 July 2007 inside the Exchange building in Swansea Marina, while those set in the lounge were shot between 16 and 18 July at The Coal Exchange in Mount Stuart Square, Cardiff, with some 50 extras in period costume. The infrastructure sequences were recorded partly in a factory on Mamhilad Park Industrial Estate, Pontypool, on 19-21 July, 23-27 July and 3 and 6 August. The scene set in a deserted London street was taped in St John Street, Cardiff on 31 July. The street was sealed off for security reasons owing to Kylie Minogue's presence. Sixth Doctor actor Colin Baker visited the location during this evening, as he was in the area to appear in a play. The scene of the Doctor and Mr Copper outside the TARDIS at the end was shot on Cargo Road, Cardiff Docks, on 1 August. City Hall, Cardiff, doubled for the interior of Buckingham Palace, recording taking place there on 21 August. The scene where the Queen waves to the *Titanic* passing overhead was taped on the same date outside the National Museum of Wales.
- The survivors' perilous progress across the metal strut was the first part of the story to go before the cameras. This was taped in the show's Upper Boat studios rather than on location, on 9 July 2007. The full studio recording dates for the episode were 9 to 12 and 31 July, 1, 2, 7, 8 and 21 August and (for a final pick-up shot) 20 October at Upper Boat, and 21 August at BBC Broadcasting House in Cardiff.
- Bannakaffalatta's voice was changed at the final mix stage; it was originally to have been much deeper and more guttural.
- In creating Astrid, Russell T Davies was partly inspired by his love of Alan Moore's comic book character Halo Jones from *2000 AD*, who worked as a stewardess on a space voyage. The character's name was strongly, and erroneously, rumoured to have significance to the story: 'Astrid' being an anagram of TARDIS, and 'Peth' meaning 'part of' in Aborigine. (??CHECK??)
- Russell T Davies decided to have Foon and Morvin wearing Western fancy dress costumes solely because he needed a reason for Foon to have a lasso with her in the scene where she sacrifices herself by pulling one of the Host into the chasm.
- In the first draft of the script, Buckingham Palace was to have been partly destroyed by the passing *Titanic*, and the Queen was to have been seen picking herself up from the rubble and cursing the Doctor. This was changed owing to the fact that the model shot of Buckingham Palace could not be afforded.
- It was script editor Brian Minchin's idea that Astrid might be rescued by way of her teleport bracelet, which she would still be wearing from the earlier scene where she and the Doctor visit Earth with the tourists.
- A subplot involving Rickston's mobile phone being used to send out an SOS message was cut from the episode after recording.
- The ship's band is heard performing 'I Wish it Could be Christmas Every Day',

a perennial Christmas favourite, first released as a single by Wizzard in 1973. The most prominently featured song, however, is 'The Stowaway', a piece specially composed by Murray Gold, who makes a cameo appearance as the band's guitarist. Conductor Ben Foster also makes a brief on-screen appearance. The uncredited singer is Yamit Momo.

- The episode ended with an extended 'Coming Soon ...' trailer for Series Four, consisting of numerous clips from the first seven episodes. This was preceded by a caption reading 'In Memory of Verity Lambert OBE 1935-2007' in honour of *Doctor Who*'s first producer, who died on 22 November 2007.

OOPS!

- When the Doctor returns over the strut *en route* to Level 31 of the *Titanic* to find out who is in the sealed chamber down there, he should have no way of opening the door that he sealed earlier on using the sonic screwdriver, as he has left the latter with Rickston.
- After the Doctor says 'Take me to your leader' to the Host, he adds 'I've always wanted to say that'. However, he did say that in 'Aliens of London' (albeit in his previous incarnation).
- When Astrid and Max Capricorn fall into the nuclear storm drive it appears to be still active, even though Capricorn has supposedly just closed it down.
- In the sequence where the *Titanic* is falling toward Earth, there are a number of shots of Rickston and Mr Copper in which the picture is reversed, as is obvious from the fact that writing visible on screen – including the name of the *Titanic* on a lifebelt seen to roll across the floor at one point – is backwards.
- The Doctor says that a million pounds in British money is equivalent to about 50 million credits in Mr Copper's currency – presumably the currency of the planet Sto. Earlier, however, when Foon admits to Morvin that she has run up a bill of 5,000 credits in the phone competition to win their *Titanic* tickets – which at the same rate of exchange would equate to about £100 – this is implied to be a huge sum of money, Foon saying that she might as well have bought the tickets and Morvin adding that they would have to work 20 years to pay it off. (Maybe different parts of Sto have different types of credits, or that there is a large difference between the earning power of Mr Copper and Morvin and Foon?)

PRESS REACTION

- 'For the most part, "Voyage of the Damned" is absolutely smashing. David Tennant's Doctor is commanding and hardly ever OTT, while the supporting cast are, mostly, dandy. The script nips along nicely, the jeopardy feels real, the CGI is grand and the humour, though in shorter supply than in previous years, glimmers still – and is only occasionally cheesy. After previous years' sinister Santas, the Host, the foot soldiers of the Big Bad, once again hail from near the Uncanny Valley, and though the Big Bad itself doesn't have the malignant majesty of the Empress of Racnoss, such is the investment you've built up in the story by its unveiling, it feels churlish to complain about that. (Those who know the story of [the movie] *Voyage of the Damned* (1976) will know that the ship in it was never meant to dock safely and the passengers were doomed from the outset. This too may or may not be relevant.) In fact, *Voyage of the Damned*'s biggest flaw is its unique selling point - the presence of Kylie Minogue. She's just not that good. Truth be told, she's blank and insipid. There's no chemistry between Astrid and the Doctor, she delivers her lines with a real lack of conviction and thus we never really believe in Astrid as a character.' Gareth McLean, guardian.co.uk website, 20 December 2007.

- 'It's that Christmas schedule stalwart *The Poseidon Adventure* spiced up with a measure of *Doctor Who*'s own "The Robots of Death", with a little sprinkling of the Robert Maxwell scandal to taste ... Of course, it all falls apart as soon as you try to analyse events, with the disaster movie "journey through the wreck" scenario abandoned after a couple of set-pieces as the Doctor realises that this being *Doctor Who*, there must be an evil mastermind behind it and heads off to his base in the bowels of the ship rather than leading the survivors to safety.' Anthony Brown, *TV Zone* Issue 224, January 2008.
- 'Even at 70 minutes long, the programme didn't have a moment to spare. After all, it had to combine a proper adventure story with (among other things) a "homage" to 1970s disaster movies, a tale of doomed love, lots of jokes, a few more reminders of the Doctor's fundamental loneliness and a whole new set of baddies. At first, mind you, life on board seemed fine - but only for as long as it took us to meet the other characters who, in best disaster-movie style, would soon be joining the Doctor and Astrid ... to form a little band of survivors. They were, naturally, a mixed bunch: ranging from an intergalactic yuppie to Bannakaffalatta ..., who was ashamed of being a cyborg, even though cyborgs were now allowed to get married. (Later, as you might expect in a Russell T Davies drama, he came out proudly.) With these people - and cyborg - in place, catastrophe duly struck. A rock storm hit the *Titanic*, leaving it with little time before it would plunge to Earth and wipe out everybody on the planet. Meanwhile, any passengers left alive after the initial impact were being systematically slaughtered by a group of robot angels using their haloes as killer Frisbees ... I've never quite understood why so many people think that *Doctor Who* is the best thing to have happened to British telly in the 21st Century ... Here, though, I think I could begin to see what all the fuss is about. Certainly I can't imagine how this episode could have done its job any better.' James Walton, Telegraph.co.uk, 26 December 2007.
- 'Its place in the schedule, sandwiched between two more slices of carnage from Albert Square, suggested that it would have its work cut out to keep us from slipping down to the local mortuary for some light relief, and the episode's title, "Voyage of the Damned", did little to counteract the sense of impending doom. The presence of Kylie, however, should always tell you that everything will be all right, especially when she is playing a waitress on a spaceship named the *Titanic*, on board which robots meant to look like angels but more closely (and perhaps pointedly) resembling BAFTA statuettes have turned evil, under the aegis of sinister captain Geoffrey Palmer ... Admittedly, the body count in "Voyage of the Damned" was high, but with David Tennant in particularly puckish mood and Kylie displaying the pluck and perkiness that is *de rigueur* when an angel-bot is trying to take one's head off with its detachable halo, *Doctor Who* was an oasis of cheeky nonsense and careless

invention featuring, among other delights, Bernard Cribbins, whom aficionados will of course remember from the second *Doctor Who* film, *Daleks' Invasion Earth 2150 AD*.' Alex Clark, the *Observer*, 30 December 2007.

- '*Doctor Who* quite literally pushed the boat out for its Christmas special "Voyage of the Damned", setting its extra-terrestrial shenanigans on board a spaceship replica of the *Titanic*. Cruising around planet Earth, attended to by robotic golden angels, all seemed reassuringly ship-shape for the exclusive clientele on board, until the Doctor helpfully pointed out the three asteroids heading their way. As if space weren't stellar enough, Kylie guested as waitress Astrid, enchanting Doctor Who so comprehensively that he offered her the vacant job as his "assistant" without even so much as an interview or references. Sadly, Astrid fell to her death down a flaming engine shaft before she could take up the post, a tragedy Doctor Who proved remarkably sanguine about. And he's supposed to have two hearts. "Voyage of the Damned" was well up to *Doctor Who*'s impeccably high standards, neatly combining comedy and thrills to stunning effect.' Harry Venning, the *Stage* website, 28 December 2007.
- '*Doctor Who* can usually do no wrong. The same can be said for Kylie Minogue. But put together, this was far from spectacular. The Christmas special was set on the *Titanic*, a space-travelling version of the fated ship. Kylie played a waitress desperate to see new skies. Step in the Doctor, some monsters and a race to save the world (and a rip-off of *The Poseidon Adventure*). The last series of *Doctor Who* was superb. And hopefully next year's offering with Catherine Tate will live up to the hype. But the festive affair lacked a strong story and relied too much on big bang effects, although the ending was a real weepy. Enjoyable, but not up to the usual standard.' Jon Wise, the *People*, 30 December 2007.

ANALYSIS

Russell T Davies-scripted episodes occasionally have something of the feel of a '*Doctor Who*'s Greatest Hits' compilation about them, and that is certainly the case here. The Heavenly Host, for instance, recall not only the Robot Santas from 'The Christmas Invasion' and 'The Runaway Bride' – in that they are a menacing robotic version of a familiar Christmas icon – but even more so the classic series' Voc Robots from 'The Robots of Death' (1977), to which certain scenes in 'Voyage of the Damned' unmistakably pay homage, and – in terms of their design, at least – the humanoid-form Axons from 'The Claws of Axos' (1971).[29] In fact, when the first publicity photos of the Host were released, some long-time fans mistakenly assumed that the Axons were about to make a return appearance – not an entirely far-fetched idea in light of the Macra's surprising comeback in 'Gridlock', 40 years after they first snapped pincers at the Doctor. The threat of a spaceship crashing into the Earth and causing devastation recalls the climax of 'Earthshock' (1982), which also saw one of the Doctor's companions making a heroic self-sacrifice; the concept of a replica seagoing vessel flying through space is reminiscent of that of

[29] The Host also resemble the Weeping Angels from 'Blink'. However, Davies had already had the idea for the Host before he ever read the script of 'Blink'.

the literal space ships in 'Enlightenment' (1983); and the idea of a party of alien tourists visiting the planet in a spaceship with a vintage disguise evokes the premise of 'Delta and the Bannermen' (1987).

These nods to the past aside, however, 'Voyage of the Damned' (the second Christmas special in a row to share a title with a popular movie) is arguably a completely new type of story for *Doctor Who*, in that it derives its impact mainly from blockbuster-style spectacle – an important aspect of which is its big-name guest-star appearance by the iconic Kylie Minogue as one-off companion Astrid Peth. Actually, not only is this a type of story that *Doctor Who* hasn't done before, it is one that it *couldn't* have done before, as only now does it have the resources to pull off the breathtaking visuals, amazing effects and large-scale set-pieces required, and the high profile and reputation to tempt a star of Minogue's magnitude. While the previous Christmas special, 'The Runaway Bride', showed a degree of blockbuster ambition, particularly in its thrilling action sequence of the TARDIS chasing a taxi along a motorway and its star-name attraction of Catherine Tate, 'Voyage of the Damned' takes this to a whole new level, pulling out all the stops to deliver a dazzling homage to the disaster movie genre, with the science fiction twist that all the action centres on a spaceship replica of the *Titanic* – an idea that, even leaving aside its identical working title, would be an obvious homage to Douglas Adams' *Starship Titanic* concept, as mentioned in *The Hitch-Hikers' Guide to the Galaxy*, realised as a computer game in 1998 and adapted as a Terry Jones-penned novelisation in 1997.[30] Although its production values are still not *quite* up to feature film standards – unsurprisingly, given the relatively modest amounts of time and money available to the *Doctor Who* team – there are many stunning sequences in 'Voyage of the Damned' that will live long in the viewer's memory. Perhaps the best of these are the awe-inspiring shots of the replica *Titanic* being bombarded by meteoroids as it flies through space and the nail-biting scenes of the Doctor, Astrid and the other survivors making their way across a narrow metal strut spanning a gaping chasm above the ship's nuclear storm drive (one of the script's more obvious tips of the hat to *The Poseidon Adventure*); but there are other examples too.

The downside to all this is that two of *Doctor Who*'s traditional strengths – clever plotting and skilful characterisation – are less in evidence on this occasion. Despite the extended running time, the story itself is really quite simple and straightforward, focusing mainly on the archetypal disaster movie motif of the perilous journey by the survivors through the damaged infrastructure of the stricken vessel – all seen, for once, from the Doctor's viewpoint, rather than from that of a companion. This maintains the viewer's interest reasonably well but never achieves quite the level of tension it should, owing in part to some curious lapses in pacing – the most glaring example of which comes when, despite the extreme urgency of their situation, the Doctor, Astrid and the other survivors pause in their hazardous passage through the ship to eat some conveniently-discovered sandwiches and have a quiet chat. The plot does eventually depart from the standard disaster movie template, switching to the more familiar *Doctor Who* mode

---

[30] Russell T Davies has also mentioned in interviews the *Futurama* episode 'A Flight to Remember' (Fox, 1999), whiich likewise features a space-going version of the *Titanic*.

of the Doctor heading into danger to confront the man responsible for the calamity; but unfortunately, although George Costigan gives a decent enough performance in the role, Max Capricorn turns out to be one of the weakest villains yet devised for *Doctor Who* since the show returned in 2005. He is basically just an evil businessman trying to guarantee himself a lucrative 'retirement plan' and in the process take revenge on the partners who have ousted him from his failed company; motives that seem altogether too mundane for one of the Doctor's adversaries – a shortcoming that Davies has tried to disguise, not entirely successfully, by giving him a grotesque appearance and placing him in a mobile life-support machine, making him look a bit like a cross between *Batman*'s Mr Freeze and *Doctor Who*'s own Davros or, more obscurely, Arcturus from 'The Curse of Peladon' (1972). It's also never satisfactorily explained why he actually needs to be on board the ship in order for his plan to succeed. Likewise the control protocol for the Host seems a bit muddled; it seems distinctly odd that they should accept the Doctor as the 'voice of authority' after Capricorn's death.

There's not a great deal of depth to most of the supporting characters, either. Rickston Slade is a stereotypical self-interested, avaricious businessman; Foon and Morvin Van Hoff are a sweet, chubby couple whose main function is to provide some light relief, although Foon gets to sacrifice herself to save the others after Morvin falls to his death; and Bannakaffalatta is a clichéd 'loveable little alien', who turns out to be a cyborg and who also gets to sacrifice himself heroically, although his presence does raise the question why, out of all the guests and crew on board the ship, he seems to be the only non-humanoid (the real reason presumably being that the budget wouldn't stretch to any more). Captain Hardaker and Midshipman Frame have a bit more going for them, although this is due more to the excellent performances by Geoffrey Palmer and Russell Tovey respectively than to any significant characterisation in the script – the viewer never learns anything whatsoever about Frame, bar the fact that this is his first voyage and he is a plucky and resourceful young man – oh, and that his first name is 'Alonzo', at last giving the Doctor an opportunity to say '*Allons-y* Alonzo!'. The best of the bunch is Mr Copper, well portrayed by Clive Swift, whose litany of amusing misconceptions about Earth and its culture, based on a bogus degree in 'Earthonomics' obtained from Mrs Golightly's Happy Travelling University and Dry Cleaners, is a real comic highlight. It's also pleasing that Davies' hasn't taken the clichéd approach of having all the 'nice' characters survive while all the 'nasty' ones perish – the fact that Slade is one of the few left alive at the end is refreshingly unexpected.

Inevitably, though, the spotlight of attention in this special is very much on Minogue's guest-star turn as Astrid. Astrid is a character in the Rose Tyler mould – a young woman, trapped in a dull, uninspiring job, who dreams of a better life and has the attributes of curiosity, courage and compassion that mark her out as a potential companion for the Doctor. But Minogue is not as naturally charismatic an actress as Billie Piper, and it is hard to shake the feeling that she would have been better served had Astrid been rethought as a role more in keeping with her sexy, glamorous public image – perhaps, say, as a slinky torch singer in the ship's band, which would have had the added advantage of giving her an opportunity to show off her famous vocal talents. To have her go through the whole production in a 1950s-look waitress's outfit, albeit a cute one, and with her hair up in a rather unprepossessing style, seems frankly a waste of an opportunity to display her full star quality.

It also seems decidedly odd, given that he has spent the whole of Series Three blanking Martha's advances, and has literally only just said goodbye to her on Earth, that the Doctor now seems tempted to rush into what is to all intents and purposes a romantic relationship with someone he has only just met. Perhaps he only goes for blondes, like Rose, Reinette and Astrid ...?[31] (Certainly Mr Copper gets short shrift at the end, the Doctor telling him, 'I travel alone'.) Where Astrid's story does work particularly well, though, is in its fitting resolution. While it is perhaps rather repetitive scripting to have yet another self-sacrifice after Foon's and Bannakaffalatta's, Astrid's is the best-realised and most dramatic of the lot, her use of a fork-lift truck to push Max Capricorn's life-support machine into the chasm obviously recalling the dramatic scene at the end of the movie *Aliens* (1986) where Sigourney Weaver's character Ripley uses a cargo-loader to tackle the Alien Queen. The icing on the cake comes when - in what was, remarkably, quite a late addition to the script - the Doctor manages, with the aid of the ship's teleporter, to preserve Astrid's essence as 'stardust', so that she gets to travel through space after all: 'You're not falling, Astrid, you're flying,' as he poignantly puts it. Can it really be a coincidence that 'Astrid' is an anagram of 'TARDIS'?

In the end, it is probably futile to try to assess 'Voyage of the Damned' by the criteria one would normally apply to *Doctor Who*. Even more so than 'The Christmas Invasion' and 'The Runaway Bride', it is an episode that really has to be judged in the context in which it was originally transmitted: as a seasonal special designed to serve up some spectacular, action-packed and undemanding family entertainment to an audience who, having consumed their turkey and Christmas pudding and settled into their armchairs for the evening, would not have been prepared to watch anything too heavy or challenging. This is why disaster movies themselves have been such a popular Christmas offering on TV over the years; and 'Voyage of the Damned' cleverly combines the established appeal of that genre with a plethora of other Christmassy elements such as robotic angels, seasonal decorations, a pop star guest appearance, a character with the surname 'Slade' (whose 'Merry Xmas Everybody' was apparently at one point planned to be used on the soundtrack, as for the previous two Christmas specials), a role for national treasure Bernard Cribbins, a snowy landscape and even a thrilling climax in which the Queen, perhaps relaxing after recording her customary Christmas message to her subjects, is buzzed by a *Titanic*-shaped spaceship outside Buckingham Palace. What more could one ask for?

Sometimes this feels so different from anything the show has ever presented before that it scarcely seems like *Doctor Who* at all. Viewed on its own terms, though, it can only be considered a great success - as its excellent ratings attest - and as such it has undoubtedly had the very welcome effect of further cementing *Doctor Who*'s status as a now-traditional part of Britain's Christmas Night viewing.

---

[31] In 'The Idiot's Lantern', the Doctor comments at one point, 'It's never too late, as a wise person once said. Kylie, I think!' As this would suggest that he is a fan of Minogue's, perhaps it is Astrid's uncanny resemblence to the Australian pop singer that attracts him ...?

4.01 - PARTNERS IN CRIME

Writer: Russell T Davies
Director: James Strong

DEBUT TRANSMISSION DETAILS

BBC One
Date: 5 April 2008. Scheduled time: 6.20 pm. Actual time: 6.19 pm.

BBC Three
Date: 6 April 2008. Scheduled time: 8.00 pm. Actual time: 8.01 pm.

Duration: 48' 35"

ADDITIONAL CREDITED CAST

Sarah Lancashire (Miss Foster), Verona Joseph (Penny Carter), Jessica Gunning (Stacey Harris[32]), Martin Ball (Roger Davey), Rachid Sabitri (Craig Staniland), Chandra Ruegg (Clare Pope), Sue Kelvin (Suzette Chambers), Jonathan Stratt (Taxi Driver)

In Memory of Howard Attfield 1947-2007

PLOT

The Doctor is investigating Adipose Industries, a London-based company marketing a new type of diet pill – a pill that actually turns its users' excess fat into alien Adipose babies. Donna Noble is also investigating the company in the hope that this will lead her to the Doctor, as she now regrets turning down his offer to become his companion after the incident with the Racnoss. Miss Foster, the nanny employed by the Adiposian First Family to carry out its illicit operation on Earth, tries to advance the birth plan and cause all one million of the company's customers to be totally converted into Adipose, killing them in the process. The Doctor and Donna, finally reunited, are able to prevent this by sabotaging the inducer machine that runs down the centre of the Adipose Industries building. The Adipose that have already been born are taken up in levitation beams to their nursery spaceship, which then departs, but Miss Foster falls to her death. Donna joins the Doctor in the TARDIS, pausing briefly to speak to a young woman in the street: unknown to her, it is Rose Tyler.

---

[32] Named 'Stacey Campbell' in dialogue.

QUOTE, UNQUOTE

- **Wilf:** 'You seem to be drifting, sweetheart.'
  Donna: 'I'm not drifting, I'm waiting.'
  Wilf: 'What for?'
  Donna: 'The right man.'
  Wilf: 'Ha, ha, ha, ha! Same old story. A man. Ha, ha!'
  Donna: 'No, I don't mean like that. But he's real. I've seen him. I've met him, just once. And then I let him fly away.'
- **Penny:** 'What sort of a country do you think this is?'
  Miss Foster: 'Oh, it's a beautifully fat country; and believe me, I've travelled a long way to find obesity on this scale.'
- **Doctor:** 'I thought you were gonna travel the world?'
  Donna: 'Easier said than done. It's like, I had that one day with you, and I was gonna change. I was gonna do so much. Then I woke up the next morning, same old life. It was like you were never there. And I tried. I did try. I went to Egypt. I was gonna go barefoot and everything. And then it's all bus trips and guide books and "Don't drink the water", and two weeks later you're back at home. It's nothing like being with you. I must have been mad turning down that offer.'
  Doctor: 'What offer?'
  Donna: 'To come with you.'
- **Donna:** 'I'm waving at fat.'

CONTINUITY POINTS

- When Roger Davey tells him 'I'm not a cat person', the Doctor replies, 'No, I've met Cat People. You're nothing like them.' This is a reference to his meetings with the Cat-kind in 'New Earth' and 'Gridlock', and possibly to his encounter with the Cheetah People in the classic series story 'Survival'.
- The Adipose pills are intended to be taken at the rate of one per day for three weeks. Each Adipose Industries customer is given a free gold pendant that biotunes itself to him or her on contact. These pendants trigger the Adipose births at an appointed time, in the middle of the night, when the customers are normally asleep. It is implied that Roger Davey has already given birth to 14 Adipose - one per night, each weighing one kilo exactly - in the first two weeks of the treatment. Similarly, Stacey Campbell says that she has lost 11 pounds - equivalent to five kilos, and thus five Adipose - in five days. By taking a second pendant to Stacey's house, Donna inadvertently triggers a premature birth. Miss Foster then initiates total parthenogenesis, transforming Stacey's entire body into multiple Adipose. It is implied that she intends all the Adipose Industries customers to suffer the same fate eventually but decides to advance the 'birth plan' when the Doctor intervenes.
- It is unclear exactly where the Adipose Industries building is situated, but it is likely to be somewhere in West London. Donna says that her grandfather's allotment is two and a half miles away, and that seems to be within walking distance of her home in Chiswick. However, the allotment is also said - and shown - to be up on a hill, and there are no such hills in or near Chiswick.

- The van driven by the 'collection squad' sent by Miss Foster to bring home the Adipose into which Stacey has prematurely transformed has mauve flashing lights. This ties in with the Doctor's comment in 'The Empty Child' that mauve, rather than red, is the universal colour signifying an emergency.
- The taxi that arrives to collect Stacey from her home has 'Atmos' stickers in the front and back windows, foreshadowing events in 'The Sontaran Stratagem'/'The Poison Sky'. So too does the taxi over which the newly-born Adipose crawl later in the episode. In production terms, these scenes were shot using the same vehicle.
- This episode contains Donna's first mention of the strange phenomenon of 'the bees disappearing', which will prove significant later in the series.
- Miss Foster has a sonic pen, akin to the Doctor's sonic screwdriver, indicating that this kind of technology is not unique to the Time Lords.
- Miss Foster says that her real name is 'Matron Cofelia of the Five-Straighten Classabindi Nursery Fleet: Intergalactic Class'. She adds: 'I've been employed by the Adiposian first family to foster a new generation after their breeding planet was lost' – the first of a number of mentions of lost planets during Series Four, the explanation for which will be provided in 'The Stolen Earth'.
- The Doctor tells Miss Foster, 'Seeding a Level 5 planet is against galactic law.' 'Voyage of the Damned' also referred to Earth as a Level 5 planet, as did a number of classic *Doctor Who* episodes.
- Miss Foster assumes that, as an alien, the Doctor will have alerted the Shadow Proclamation to her activities. The Shadow Proclamation was first mentioned by the Doctor in 'Rose', although the implication there seemed to be that it was a document rather than an organisation.
- The episode contains a number of references to Martha and Rose, leading up to Rose's reappearance a few minutes from the end. When Donna asks the Doctor if he is still travelling alone, he replies, 'Yup. Well, no. I had this friend, Martha, she was called. Martha Jones. She was brilliant. And I destroyed half her life. But she's fine, she's good. She's gone.' This suggests that he holds himself responsible for the traumatic experiences that Martha and her family endured, particularly in 'Last of the Time Lords'. Later, on a lighter note, he brags, 'She fancied me,' prompting Donna to describe her as, 'Mad Martha, that one. Blind Martha. Charity Martha.' He subsequently admits, 'The last time, with Martha, like I said, it ... it got complicated, and that was all my fault.' Of Rose, the Doctor simply says that she is 'still lost'.

PRODUCTION NOTES

- Made as a single-episode Block 3 of production.
- Like 'Rose' and 'Smith and Jones', this episode has no introductory sequence before the opening titles. The opening shot of Donna walking down a crowded street intentionally mirrors that of Martha at the start of 'Smith and Jones'.
- Actor Howard Attfield was to have returned as Donna's father Geoff Noble but died part-way through production. The scenes in which he appeared were all reshot later, with Bernard Cribbins substituted as Donna's grandfather Wilf

Mott. Some behind-the-scenes sequences of Attfield participating in the initial cast read-through for the episode are included in the accompanying *Doctor Who Confidential* documentary.

- The scenes outside Stacey's house kicked off location work for this episode on 4 October 2007 in Stallcourt Avenue, Roath. Some extra pick-up shots were done there on 19 November. The Doctor's conversation with Roger about his burglar alarm was recorded outside a house in Glyn Rhymni, Cardiff, on 5 October. The shot of Donna walking up to the hill to the allotment was taped on 8 October at Grangemoor Park, but the re-done scenes on the allotment itself with Bernard Cribbins as Wilf in place of Howard Attfield as Geoff were recorded on 28 November on Lady Mary Allotments in Roath Park. Miss Foster's presentation to the press was taped in the Odeon Cinema, Cardiff, at 4.00 am on 8 October. The location used for the exteriors of the Adipose Industries building was the British Gas offices in Helmont House, Churchill Way, Cardiff, also featured in a number of earlier episodes, as well as in *Torchwood*. The rooftop scenes were shot over two nights on 9 and 10 October. The sequence where the Doctor and Donna run up the staircase to the roof of the Adipose Industries building, as seen from the perspective of a camera positioned in the street outside, was originally done on 9 October but had to be reshot the following day as the lights in the building were mistakenly left on the first time around. The interiors of Miss Foster's office were taped on the sixth floor of Dominion House, Cardiff, over 11 and 12 October. The call centre interiors were shot at night on 13 October, in a genuine call centre operated by a debt management company called Picture Financial Group, and some of the staff seen on screen were its actual employees. The scenes of the Adipose Industries basement where the Doctor hides and later accesses the inducer machine were shot in the same Millennium Stadium corridor seen in numerous previous episodes, including 'The Runaway Bride'. These were taped on 15 October. The street shots for the scenes where the Adipose appear *en masse* were taped on Charles Street on 16 October and Churchill Way on 18 October. Some more exteriors of the Adipose Industries building were recorded at Landmark Place, Churchill Way, also on 18 October. A house in Nant-Fawr Road, Cyncoed, Cardiff, became the exterior of Donna's family home, where recording took place on 17 October and 20 November. The scenes in the women's toilet at Adipose Industries were taped at the Tiger Tiger bar and club in The Friary, Cardiff, on 23 October. Sylvia's meeting with her friends at De Rossi's wine bar was recorded at the Fat Cat Café in Greyfriars Road, Cardiff, on 23 October. The sequence where Donna enters the TARDIS and she and the Doctor have a misunderstanding about his 'I want a mate' comment was originally recorded in noisy conditions outside the Oceana club in Greyfriars Road, Cardiff, on 17 October. This was deemed unusable, so a reshoot was done on Havelock Street, Cardiff, on 19 and 20 November. Part of the original version of the scene can however be seen in the Series Four trailer at the end of 'Voyage of the Damned'.
- The scene where Donna talks to a young woman in the street was shot once with Billie Piper as Rose and once with a blonde extra as a stand-in. This was done in Franklen Road, Cardiff, on 29 November. The intention was that the version with the stand-in would be included in the master tape of 'Partners in

Crime' initially supplied to the BBC in London and used for press previews etc, in order to keep Rose's appearance a total surprise to everyone outside the production team. In the end, however, the scene was simply omitted altogether at that stage. The correct version, with Rose's appearance included, was substituted only just before transmission.

- All the November location recording for this episode was directed by Graeme Harper, during work on 'Turn Left', rather than by James Strong.
- Studio recording for this episode took place on 16, 19 and 20 October and 18 December 2007 at Upper Boat.
- The Adipose Industries advertising catchphrase 'The fat just walks away' was originally to have been set to music as a jingle, but this idea was dropped during production.
- The sequence with Stacey being transformed into Adipose in her bathroom was directed by producer Phil Collinson, as James Strong was unavailable at the time. It reportedly took about eight hours to complete.
- The action scene in the window-cleaner's cradle was originally planned for inclusion in 'Smith and Jones', to take place on the outside of the Royal Hope Hospital building on the Moon, but had to be shelved at that time for budgetary reasons. Davies was then able to work it into his script for 'Partners in Crime'. For safety reasons, parts of the scene were performed by stunt doubles, Gordon Seed and Jo McLaren, while other parts were achieved as green-screen effects.
- The song heard playing in De Rossi's wine bar where Sylvia meets her friends is 'Could it Be Magic' by Take That, the final single from their 1992 album *Take That and Party*. The one that Wilf is listening to on his headphones when he fails to spot the Adipose nursery spaceship flying across the sky behind him is 'Twenty-Four Hours from Tulsa', a 1964 single by Dusty Springfield.
- Miss Foster's rooftop address to the newly-born Adipose was intentionally delivered in the style of Eva Perón, First Lady of Argentina from 1946 to 1952, as indicated in Davies's script.
- There was originally to have been a scene where, after the death of Miss Foster, the Doctor sends a message to the Shadow Proclamation, asking them to intercept the Adipose ship. This was recorded but later cut, partly for timing reasons and partly to avoid the need for an additional visual effect to be added.

OOPS!

- A number of shots in the episode are obviously reversed; one of Donna seated in the audience at Miss Foster's press briefing is probably the most noticeable, as the sequence also includes a near-identical shot the right way round.
- The number plate on Donna's Peugeot 307 car inexplicably changes from YD56 VHG when it is parked outside her family home to LN54 VKR when it is parked near the TARDIS later in the episode. In reality, two different cars were used for recording these scenes.
- Stacey's surname is given as 'Harris' in the closing credits but as 'Campbell' in dialogue and in an on-screen graphic.

- Most of the picture- and photo-frames in Stacey's house are empty; a fact that is never explained.
- The cable that breaks on the window-cleaner's cradle is on the opposite side to the one that Miss Foster is seen cutting through.

PRESS REACTION

- 'It could have been the worst thing ever, but it's not: it's too well constructed for that, too packed with good lines. It's pure Russell T Davies, an absurd super-spy fantasy built around a real-world issue - in this case, the idea that we're all too fat. Indeed, though it sometimes flirts with being a bit too silly, cute and familiar - here's *another* evil mega-corporation with a ludicrous SF invention acting as a front for devious aliens! - it gets better on repeat viewings. There's some memorable writing on display, and great set pieces. The whole window-cleaner's basket thing, Donna's late night chats with Gramps under the stars, and the mute, manic gesticulating of her first face-to-face with the Doctor through two sheets of glass: all will stick long in the memory.' Matt Bielby, *DeathRay* Issue 13, June 2008.
- 'One of the difficulties about being a critic is that unbridled enthusiasm often feels like a bit of a cop-out, that in order to do your job properly you are duty-bound to latch on to some tiny flaw and point out in a regretful sort of way that it rather lets the whole thing down. I therefore wish that I could tell you that the new *Doctor Who* is a pretty so-so affair, showing worrying signs of losing its charm, its inventiveness and general cosmic oomph. And that Catherine Tate is hopelessly miscast as the Doctor's new assistant, Donna. But I'm afraid I can't do that. I can't do it simply because last night's episode struck me as being as close to 50 minutes of pure pleasure as you're likely to get on television. It's a measure of the show's confidence that this time round there are no big scaly monsters with tentacles where their nostrils should be. Instead there are the Adipose, which look like little blocks of lard on legs. And this, it turns out, is exactly what they are.' John Preston, *Sunday Telegraph*, 6 April 2008.
- 'Fact is, David Tennant's rampant sideburns were far scarier than last night's aliens, the Adipose. Cute little Flumps-like blobs who were surely the brainchild of some BBC Worldwide bean-counter. Because if there was a reason for their introduction other than the sound of Christmas toyshop tills ringing I'd love to hear it. The reason for Catherine Tate's reintroduction is less clear. Not an unattractive woman. But in terms of bringing the dads in she's not exactly a Billie or a Freema. And the really bad news is she's still shouting. Maybe not quite as loudly as she did during her *Doctor Who* debut. But my screechometer's needle was still going mental throughout, even during that scene where she only mouthed her words.' Ian Hyland, *News of the World*, 6 April 2008.
- '[Catherine Tate's] not my favourite sidekick: too hysterical, too comedy, not cool enough. I can't quite forgive her for not being Freema Agyeman or Billie Piper, who'll both be dropping in on the series, apparently. You can see what the thinking was: bring in the biggest star, the one the kids all do in the playground, and broaden the appeal of the show still further. But I think

they've overlooked the fact that she's not right for this role. And isn't the appeal broad enough already? I'm also finding the music a bit oppressive, too. Oh, it doesn't really matter. It's still awfully nice television.' Sam Wollaston, *Guardian*, 7 April 2008.

ANALYSIS

One of the things that Russell T Davies absolutely excels at in his scripts is introducing - or, in this case, reintroducing - a companion. 'Rose' was a near-perfect debut for its title character, and indeed for the new *Doctor Who* more generally, and 'Smith and Jones' was if anything even better, giving Martha an excellent launch while at the same time telling a highly entertaining story featuring an excellent new race of monsters in the Judoon. It was always going to be a tall order for 'Partners in Crime' to match that sensational standard, and in the end it doesn't quite manage it - but it does come close.

It would be fair to say that the decision to bring back Catherine Tate's Donna Noble for a full season as companion was controversial, particularly given that her initial - and at the time apparently one-off - appearance in 'The Runaway Bride' drew a mixed reaction at best. Thankfully, she proves to be far less grating in 'Partners in Crime', for two reasons. First, Davies has basically contrived to ditch her original character altogether and give her a brand new one. So, instead of a woman who is so ignorant that she can't even point to Germany on a map, who thinks that the height of excitement is a new flavour Pringle and whose stock reaction to any new situation is to shout raucously at everyone in sight, we now have one who shows enough initiative to be able to carry out an undercover investigation into Adipose Industries, whose earlier encounter with the Doctor has left her eager to see the wonders of the universe and whose tendency to mouth off has been reined in to such an extent that, symbolically, her first conversation with the Doctor on tracking him down is conducted entirely in mime, from opposite sides of two facing windows - a genuinely hilarious sequence. Secondly, Tate has toned down her performance considerably, to the point where it could almost be said to be understated at times, and it is only really when she is given an overtly humorous line to deliver - such as Donna's 'You're not mating with me, sunshine' response to the Doctor's 'I just want a mate' - that she lapses into a jarring 'comedy character' voice. But are these improvements sufficient to make Donna a suitable companion for the Doctor? That is a another question, and one that it is still too early to answer on the evidence of 'Partners in Crime' alone, although the prospect of the Doctor travelling with someone a little more mature and worldly-wise than usual, who brings both metaphorical and literal baggage with her into the TARDIS, certainly holds potential.

It is by this point an established part of the format of Davies's revamped *Doctor Who* that each new regular companion is accompanied by some new semi-regular family members. In this case, though, like Donna herself, the two characters in question are not altogether new: her mother Sylvia, played by Jacqueline King, was first seen in 'The Runaway Bride', and her maternal grandfather Wilf Mott, played by Bernard Cribbins, made his debut in 'Voyage of the Damned' - although at that stage his relationship to Donna had yet to be revealed. Sylvia is depicted here as an all-too-familiar nagging mother figure, constantly belittling her daughter and berating her over her apparent inability to hold down a job. Wilf, by contrast, comes across as a highly endearing character; a sweet but eccentric old man whose hobby of spending his evenings on a hilltop allotment, gazing up into space through his telescope in the hope of catching a glimpse of alien visitors, makes him a kind of kindred spirit to Donna, albeit that her own search for alien life has taken a more direct route. Cribbins' performance as Wilf is wonderful, and although it seems almost uncharitable to say so - given that it was precipitated by the regrettable death of Howard Attfield, who was to have returned as Donna's father Geoff, and to whom this episode is fittingly dedicated - the decision to give him this recurring role in the show was absolutely inspired. Indeed, it would not be going too far to say that Wilf proves to be one of the most delightful supporting characters ever to have featured in *Doctor Who*.

Season openers tend to be relatively light and humorous affairs, and that is very much the case with 'Partners in Crime'. The farce-like early scenes where the Doctor and Donna continually miss bumping into each other as they both try to find out what is going on at Adipose Industries are very funny, and expertly handled - as is the rest of the episode - by director James Strong, getting his first chance to tackle a contemporary-Earth-set story for *Doctor Who*. The showcase action set-piece in which Miss Foster, a kind of evil intergalactic Mary Poppins-cum-Supernanny, tries to prevent the Doctor and Donna from escaping down the outside of the Adipose Industries building in a window-cleaner's cradle - the latest demonstration of Davies's penchant for sequences in which the action moves in a vertical plane rather than a horizontal one - is a real highlight, and superbly achieved by all concerned. Highly memorable, too, is the scene where Stacey is totally converted into Adipose in what amounts to a twisted version of childbirth, which is both gross and amusing at the same time

The Adipose themselves are brilliantly realised, courtesy of some of the most sophisticated CGI ever seen in a British TV show, although perhaps just a little *too* cutesy to be fully effective as *Doctor Who* aliens. The whole idea of sentient beings consisting of walking lumps of fat is admittedly absurd to start with, and obviously does not call for an ultra-serious presentation, but the Adipose look just a bit too much like loveable little creatures from a kids' cartoon series, an advertising campaign or a pop music video - such as Blur's 'Coffee & TV', with its celebrated ambulatory milk carton - to be in any way believable. Prior to transmission, there was a certain amount of speculation amongst fans that they would actually turn out to have modelled their Earthly appearance on the template of an Adipose Industries marketing character created for use in TV commercials and the like - and given that the Pillsbury Doughboy was apparently one of Davies's inspirations for their design, it would have been easy enough for him to have incorporated just such an explanation in only a couple of lines of dialogue - but sadly no clever twist of this sort is forthcoming. It helps that they are supposed to be babies rather than fully grown Adipose, which might conceivably look much fiercer, but nevertheless it seems that even the show's youngest viewers haven't taken to them in quite the way that might have been hoped for - there is certainly no evidence of an Adipose craze having broken out in the nation's primary school playgrounds - so maybe they too prefer their *Doctor Who* monsters to be a bit more plausible and scary than this.

The basic plot of the episode - in which the Adipose seek to turn the Earth into a breeding ground for a new generation of their kind by selling a harmful diet pill – bears strong similarities to that of the 'Invasion of the Bane' special co-written by Davies and Gareth Roberts for *The Sarah Jane Adventures* – in which the Bane seek to turn the human race into a new generation of their kind by selling a harmful fizzy drink – and the former's Miss Foster so resembles the latter's Mrs Wormwood, in terms both of character and of appearance, that apparently some young viewers mistakenly assumed that they were one and the same person.[33] This would not really matter too much if it were not for the fact that 'Partners in Crime' has a far less dramatic resolution than 'Invasion of the Bane' and rather pales by comparison, certainly in that respect if not more generally. Whereas 'Invasion of the Bane' has Sarah Jane and her young friends gaining access to Mrs Wormwood's factory by crashing a bus through a wall and ultimately destroying it in a huge explosion, 'Partners in Crime' has the Doctor curtailing Miss Foster's activities by – wait for it – fiddling with some controls in a cupboard. It's not even as if the Adipose's scheme is inherently evil – although it is certainly criminal. If only Miss Foster could have been relied upon to manage it in a more restrained and responsible way, relieving the diet pill customers of their excess fat without going so far as to try to kill them by converting their bone, muscle and hair as well, then arguably it would not have even warranted the Doctor's involvement. As he himself comments, 'Actually, as a diet plan, it sort of works.' Certainly not something that could be said for the Bane's promotion of a fat-inducing fizzy drink – which suggests that the two races could actually have mounted quite a successful joint venture!

Thankfully, this less-than-thrilling *denouement* is partly compensated for by some further superb effects work as the Adipose spaceship – its design surely paying homage to that of the one in Steven Spielberg's *E.T. The Extraterrestrial* (1982), as also referenced on the soundtrack – flies in to hover over the Adipose Industries building, and all the little Adipose rise up to it in beams of light, waving happily to the Doctor and Donna, while their accomplice – or should that be partner in crime? – Miss Foster is released from her beam and falls to her death. As Donna herself observes, the fact that the Doctor stands by and watches as the Adipose babies depart in their ship makes for an interesting contrast with his actions at the end of 'The Runaway Bride', when he mercilessly destroyed the children of the Racnoss – albeit that the two situations are not strictly comparable, as the Empress of the Racnoss was intent on wreaking havoc on the Earth.

This excellent sequence leads on to the concluding scenes of the episode where, having established that there is no danger of Donna falling for him romantically in the way that Martha did, the Doctor welcomes her on board the TARDIS – complete with pre-packed suitcases and even a hat-box! – and, at her request, gives her delighted grandfather Wilf, up on his allotment with his telescope, a valedictory fly-past – a very touching and joyful moment, in keeping with the overall tone of the episode.

But just prior to Donna joining the Doctor in the TARDIS, she pauses in the street to talk to a young, blonde-haired woman – who then turns around, revealing

[33] Andy Lane's *Torchwood* novel *Slow Decay* also involves an alien parasite being spread via a new diet pill, although that is really where the parallels end in that instance.

to the viewer that she is none other than Rose Tyler! It is a testament to just how iconic a character Rose has become that this short sequence, in which she simply walks away across the street and fades from view without having said a word, proves to be easily the most sensational aspect of the entire episode. How can Rose possibly have appeared here, in an ordinary London street, just metres away from the TARDIS, when she was supposedly trapped forever in a parallel universe at the end of 'Doomsday'? And just what does this signify in terms of future developments in Series Four?

This wonderfully surprising and intriguing development tops off a strong opening episode and suitably whets the viewer's appetite for the adventures still to come.

4.02 - THE FIRES OF POMPEII

Writer: James Moran
Director: Colin Teague

DEBUT TRANSMISSION DETAILS

BBC One
Date: 12 April 2008. Scheduled time: 6.45 pm. Actual time: 6.46 pm.

BBC Three
Date: 13 April 2008. Scheduled time: 8.00 pm. Actual time: 8.02 pm.

Duration: 48′ 17″

ADDITIONAL CREDITED CAST

Phil Cornwell (Stallholder), Karen Gillan (Soothsayer), Sasha Behar (Spurrina), Lorraine Burroughs (Thalina), Peter Capaldi (Caecilius[34]), Tracey Childs (Metella), Francesca Fowler (Evelina), Francois Pandolfo (Quintus), Victoria Wicks (High Priestess), Gerard Bell (Major Domo[35]), Phil Davis (Lucius[36])

PLOT

The TARDIS brings the Doctor and Donna to Pompeii on 23 August in 79 AD, the day before Mount Vesuvius is due to erupt. There they meet a marble dealer named Caecilius, his wife Metella, their children Quintus and Evelina and the city's chief auger Lucius Petrus Dextrus. Evelina is soon to become a member of the Sibylline Sisterhood of seers, and both she and Lucius astound the two time travellers with their accurate psychic abilities. These abilities have been awakened by the Pyroviles, alien creatures of stone who crashed here thousands of years earlier and are now using human subjects to reconstitute themselves. The Pyroviles aim to channel the energy from Vesuvius into the equipment in a surviving escape pod from their ship, supplemented by a stone energy converter with components commissioned by Lucius from local merchants such as Caecilius, and use this to turn the Earth into a new planet for themselves, taking over all human life in the process. In order to prevent this, the Doctor has to tamper with the equipment and ensure that Vesuvius erupts in keeping with established history, condemning

[34] Full name given in dialogue as 'Lobus Caecilius'.
[35] Name given in dialogue as 'Rhombus'.
[36] Full name given in dialoge as 'Lucius Petrus Dextrus' – the 'Petrus Dextrus' part of which roughly translates as 'Stone Right', appropriately enough for a character with a stone right arm.

20,000 citizens of Pompeii to death in the process. At Donna's urging, the Doctor returns in the TARDIS to save Caecilius and his family, depositing them on a hill overlooking the doomed city.

QUOTE, UNQUOTE

- **Donna:** 'I'm not an expert, but there's seven hills of Rome, aren't there? How come they've only got one ... Wait a minute. One mountain, with smoke, which makes this ...'
  Doctor: 'Pompeii. We're in Pompeii. And it's volcano day!'
- **Donna:** 'Listen, I dunno what sort of kids you've been flying around with in outer space, but you're not telling me to shut up!'
- **Donna:** 'What d'you do in old Pompeii, then, girls your age? You got mates? D'you go hanging about round the shops? T K Maximus?'
- **Donna:** 'But your own planet. It burned.'
  Doctor: 'That's just it. Don't you see, Donna? Can't you understand? If I could go back and save them, then I would, but I can't. I can never go back. I can't. I just can't. I can't.'

CONTINUITY POINTS

- The Sisterhood find a reference to the TARDIS – 'the blue box, a temple made of wood' – in the 'thirteenth book of the Sibylline Oracles'. There are, in reality, 12 surviving books of Sibylline Oracles. These contain a mixture of Greek and Roman pagan mythology ascribed to the Sibyls, prophetesses who uttered divine revelations in a frenzied state. They are believed to have been written between about 200 and 500 AD – some time after 'The Fires of Pompeii' is set – but based on earlier, now-lost texts. The Doctor says at one point: 'I met the Sibyl once. Hell of a woman. Blimey, she could dance the tarantella. Nice teeth. Truth be told, I think she had a bit of a thing for me. I said, "It will never last." She said, "I know." Well, she would.' Whether he is telling the truth here or simply spinning a yarn to distract the Sisterhood from their intended sacrifice of Donna is a moot point; although a later comment he makes to the effect that the Sibyl would be ashamed to see how the religion she founded has been corrupted suggests that there may at least be some foundation to his claims.
- When the Doctor says of Donna, 'You must excuse my friend, she's from Barcelona', he is presumably making an in-joke reference to the BBC comedy series *Fawlty Towers* (1975-1979), but could just possibly be referring to the planet Barcelona, where the dogs have no noses, as mentioned in 'The Parting of the Ways'.
- The Pyroviles crashed in their ship on the site of Vesuvius thousands of years earlier. As creatures of stone, they shattered on impact. An earthquake in 62 AD woke them up, and they are now using human subjects to reconstitute themselves. These human subjects have had their latent psychic abilities activated after breathing in fragments of the Pyroviles' bodies in fumes from Vesuvius, channelled into their homes via specially-built hypocausts. The seers' powers of accurate prophesy, on the other hand, are accounted for by a momentary time rift created by the eruption of Vesuvius, the effects of which

have rippled back in time into the 'Pyrovillian alternative' – an alternative that the Doctor eventually extinguishes by ensuring that the eruption goes ahead in accordance with established history and destroys the creatures.

- When Quintus, having been persuaded by the Doctor to take him to Lucius's house, says 'Don't tell my dad,' the Doctor replies 'Only if you don't tell mine.' This is likely to be simply a joke on the Doctor's part, as his father – mentioned previously in the 1996 *Doctor Who* TV movie, and implied to be Gallifreyan – was presumably killed in the Time War, if he was not already dead by that point in Time Lord history.
- The Doctor cites the Shadow Proclamation for the second episode running – in this instance, when demanding to know the species designation of the creature possessing the Sibylline High Priestess.
- Donna says to the Doctor at one point: 'You saved me. In 2008, you saved us all.' It is unclear what exactly she has in mind here. She could possibly be referring to the events of 'The Runaway Bride' or to those of 'Partners in Crime'. However, there is quite a lot of evidence from various other episodes to suggest that the former is set in December 2007 and the latter in spring or summer 2009. A more likely explanation therefore is that, unseen on screen, the Doctor has at some point discussed with Donna the worldwide crisis depicted in 'The Sound of Drums'/'Last of the Time Lords', which does indeed have a 2008 dating, and it is that to which she is alluding.

PRODUCTION NOTES

- Made as a single-episode Block 2 of production.
- The major location shoot for this story took place over 13 and 14 September 2007 at the Cinecittà Studios in Rome, on outdoor standing sets of Ancient Rome previously used for the HBO/RAI/BBC series *Rome* (2005-2007). A fire at the Studios on 10 August destroyed some parts of the sets that the *Doctor Who* team had originally intended to use, but they were able to work around this by recording on other parts instead. The show's special effects team took various reference plate shots of Mount Vesuvius on 15 September to be used as the basis of the matte paintings and CGI effects of the volcano's eruption. The scenes in the temple of the Sibylline Sisterhood were recorded on 18 and 19 September at the Temple of Peace in Cardiff, previously used as a location for 'The End of the World' and 'Gridlock'. The scenes of Lucius and members of the Cult of Vulcan on the slopes of Vesuvius, and of the Doctor and Donna emerging from the Pyrovile escape pod after it is thrown clear of the volcano, were shot in a quarry at Morlais, Merthyr Tydfil, on 1 October. The scenes inside Vesuvius itself were taped on 28 September in Clearwell Caves, Coleford, Gloucestershire – as previously used for the Sycorax spaceship interiors in 'The Christmas Invasion' – and on 2 October at Taffs Well, Pentyrch, Cardiff.
- Sets were built at the Upper Boat studios for the villa where Caecilius and his family live; a conscious effort was made to have these look as spacious as possible, so that the transitions from the Italian location to the Welsh studio would be as seamless as possible. A redressed version of the same sets was used for the villa in Rome seen in the final scene. Studio recording for the

episode took place on 20 to 22 and 24 to 27 September and 20 October 2007.

- The elements that Russell T Davies briefed writer James Moran to include in this episode were: Pompeii; a big moral dilemma for the Doctor; an ordinary family (to give the story a human dimension); creatures of fire living inside Vesuvius; and the Doctor and his companion in a space pod being flung out of the top of the volcano like a cork out of a champagne bottle. Moran had always been fascinated with the subject of Pompeii and aimed to make the episode fun and action-packed while remaining respectful to the memory of the people who died in the tragedy. In the earliest stages of the writing process, the companion was called Penny, described to Moran and the other guest writers as a character similar to Donna. This was to conceal the fact that Catherine Tate was returning as Donna, which was at that point still being kept secret by the production team.
- Actor Peter Capaldi, cast in this story as Caecilius but best known for his role as Malcolm Tucker in the BBC Four comedy series *The Thick of It* (2005-2007), was a *Doctor Who* Appreciation Society member as a young man. Tracey Childs, playing Metella, is also a long-time fan of the show, having avidly watched Jon Pertwee's Doctor as a child.

OOPS!

- There are numerous minor historical inaccuracies, such as the details of how Vesuvius erupted in 79 AD, the design and colour of the dress that Donna changes into (purple being reserved for high-ranking people in Roman society), the breed of chickens seen in the streets, and aspects of the Caecilius household.

PRESS REACTION

- 'It looks amazing, and the story is a meaty one with an opportunity for Donna to provide the first real, angry challenge the Doctor has had to his authority. [Catherine] Tate is proving that she can be strong as the Doctor's conscience. The running gag about her being heard as Welsh whenever she speaks Latin is played well, and it's cute that the TARDIS is built into the Sibylline prophesies.' Dave Bradley, *SFX*, Issue 170, June 2008.
- 'Francesca Fowler as the young soothsayer Evelina [provided] the link between the domestic situation and the real peril behind this week's episode - the augurs and soothsayers who, remarkably, are proving to be always right, but turning to stone in the process. Her scene with Catherine Tate, as Donna struggled to work out why seers could seemingly see the future, but not realise that the city was doomed, really helped cement Tate's character as a genuinely compassionate woman in ways that her previous episodes have only hinted at. And it's when Donna's story takes off that the story really hits its stride. Her pestering of the Doctor, until he tells her that as an immutable point in time Pompeii and its inhabitants must be allowed to die, [is] a mere prelude to some wonderful performances. As the duo struggle to defeat Phil Davis's Lucius and the alien Pyroviles, Donna begins to realise that the enormity of the moral dilemma the Doctor has to deal with - see the Earth destroyed, or

perform the act that will cause Vesuvius to erupt and kill 20,000 people. As the Doctor and Donna race through the ash-strewn city, Tate perfectly portrayed Donna's anguish as she forlornly appealed for people not to run to the beaches and certain death. For me, that short scene was the emotional highpoint of a series of heart-rending scenes, each with Donna at their heart. Despite the earlier shortcomings of the episode, it ensured that the programme ended on a ... positive note.' Scott Matthewman, *The Stage* website, 13 April 2008.

- 'Because Donna is older than Rose or Martha and not in love with the Doctor, she's able to call him out in ways they never did. She questions everything, from small details like how she can understand Latin (and, in a funny running gag, what would happen if she spoke actual Latin while using the TARDIS translator) to the very large, important question of why the Doctor couldn't help evacuate the city before Vesuvius erupted. I don't know how concrete the franchise has been in the past about the Doctor inserting himself into major historical events ... but David Tennant sold the Doctor's frustration with all of Donna's questions. If you had seen your entire species burn, and if you had no doubt been placed in thousands of situations over the years where you knew the rules of time wouldn't allow you to save lives, would you want to debate the ethics of it with your new semi-wanted passenger? And then came the brilliant, tragic turn in the escape pod – the one where Donna truly understood the Doctor's burden and unequivocally became his partner – when they realised that *they* were the cause of the eruption, and if they didn't play their role, then the rest of the world would be destroyed. The needs of the many outweighing the needs of the few is a sensible idea, but it's hard to be sensible when you have to put your hands on the lever that's going to kill off the few, right? I knew the Doctor was going to push it, but having Donna push it with him was a huge step forward for both that character and this relationship.' Alan Sepinwall, New Jersey *Star-Ledger*, 2 May 2008.

ANALYSIS

'The Fires of Pompeii' wastes no time in showing off its stunning visuals, opening with a sequence of the Doctor and Donna exploring the bustling streets of the titular city, recorded entirely on Cinecittà Studios' incredible standing sets of Ancient Rome during *Doctor Who*'s first major overseas location shoot since its return to TV in 2005. As if this were not remarkable enough, the sequence ends with the two time travellers getting their first sight of the smoking Mount Vesuvius in the distance, courtesy of some excellent image manipulation by the CGI wizards at The Mill. This sets the standard for the remainder of the episode, which will prove to be arguably the most ambitious and impressive production the show has ever mounted.

There are two other points of note about this opening sequence. First, it gives the Doctor a chance to explain to Donna that the TARDIS's translation circuits work not only on speech but also on printed words, finally justifying all the many seemingly-incongruous English-language signs seen in foreign countries and on alien planets over the course of the show's 45-year history (although why some have remained in other languages and not been translated is now a puzzle ...). Secondly, it not only makes explicit mention of the Doctor's last televised visit to

Ancient Rome, in 1965's 'The Romans', but even echoes an exchange of dialogue from the end of that story, where he denied that he had inspired the Emperor Nero to set fire to the city but at the same time appeared to accept, and indeed almost to relish, the possibility that he might have done so. 'Before you ask,' he now tells Donna, 'that fire had nothing to do with me. Well, a little bit.' This again demonstrates just how remarkable a phenomenon *Doctor Who* truly is: can there ever have been any other case in the whole history of human creativity where an ongoing work of fiction has intentionally referenced a humorous idea from an incident it originally recounted some 43 years earlier?[37] Crucially, though, it does so in such a way that, while the joke will especially delight those fans who are familiar with the earlier story, it will also be appreciated by, and in no way alienate, those who are completely unaware of it.

Having said all this, in some respects 'The Fires of Pompeii' actually gets off to a slightly shaky start. The quickly-established running joke of the Doctor and Donna using familiar Latin phrases and the locals hearing them as Welsh seems a bit too much like a knowing wink of acknowledgement to the show's Cardiff production base and becomes rather laboured, as does the script's insistence on drawing parallels between the Ancient Roman way of life and our own, starting with the Doctor's likening of its cosmopolitan nature to that of London's Soho and continuing with the Stallholder's use of 'Cockney wide boy' jargon, Caecilius's assumption that the TARDIS is a piece of 'modern art' - referencing a similar joke in 'City of Death' (1979) - and Quintus's display of typical 'unruly teenager' behaviour. Admittedly 79 AD is by far the furthest back into Earth's history that the new *Doctor Who* has yet ventured, but nevertheless it seems quite patronising on the part of the production team to treat the audience as if they won't be able to engage with the drama unless it is presented in simple 'they're just like us' terms. More subtly humorous is the reuse - at Russell T Davies's request - of the names of Caecilius, his wife Metella and their son Quintus from the Cambridge Latin Course (CLC) books, used in teaching the language to generations of secondary school children in the UK. Also amusing is the homage paid to *Mary Poppins* - the second in the space of two stories - as the family assume standard positions to stop vases, ornaments and so on toppling to the floor each time there is an earth tremor, as on occasions when a cannon is fired in that movie. Even so - and despite the intercutting of some intriguing and atmospheric scenes introducing the Sibylline Sisterhood, a convocation of seers reminiscent of the Sisterhood of Karn from 'The Brain of Morbius' (1976) - by ten minutes into the episode, it is starting to seem that this is going to be a disappointingly lightweight affair, and possibly even something of a misfire; more *Up Pompeii!* than *I, Claudius*.

Thankfully, things turn around completely with the arrival at Caecilius's villa of the city's chief auger Lucius - another name taken from the CLC books. At first it appears that he is going to be depicted as a clichéd 'mad old soothsayer' character, raising the terrible prospect of the story degenerating into *Carry On Cleo*-style pastiche, but in an extraordinary twist, it turns out that he is more gifted than

---

[37] This could almost be considered a running joke now, as in 'Pyramids of Mars' (1975) the fourth Doctor implied that he was blamed for starting the Great Fire of London in 1666, and in 'The Visitation' (1982) it was revealed that the fifth Doctor was indeed present in Pudding Lane when that conflagration began.

anyone could have expected, as he and Caecilius's daughter Evelina, in training to join the Sisterhood, vie with each other to come up with ever more amazing revelations about the two strangers in their midst. This starts in quite a low-key way with Evelina correctly identifying them as 'Doctor' and 'Noble' (and not, as they previously claimed, a brother and sister named Spartacus), builds in intensity with Lucius calling the Doctor 'man from Gallifrey' and Donna 'daughter of London', and reaches a dramatic climax as Lucius tells the Doctor 'She is returning' and warns Donna 'There is something on your back' while Evelina declares that the Doctor's real name 'burns in the stars, in the Cascade of Medusa herself' and that he is a 'Lord of Time'. This incredible scene, which leaves the viewer just as astonished as the Doctor and Donna themselves, kicks the story into a higher gear altogether, and from this point on, the action really hots up - both metaphorically and literally.

Anyone anticipating a TV reworking of the seventh Doctor audio CD drama 'The Fires of Vulcan', also set in Pompeii on 23 and 24 August in 79 AD, is in for a disappointment, as apart from the matching titles and some general thematic similarities relating to the volcanic eruption there is no other connection between the two stories - although neither is there any contradiction, and it is actually quite amusing to imagine the seventh Doctor and his companion Mel being in one part of the city while the tenth Doctor and Donna are in another. Presumably conman-era Captain Jack Harkness is also somewhere in the vicinity, as in 'The Doctor Dances' he heavily implies that he has been in Pompeii on 'volcano day' - the first use of that term in the show. However, the real danger to the time-line in 'The Fires of Pompeii' comes not from the Doctor bumping into one of his earlier incarnations or someone he knows but from Donna's determination to alert the locals to the forthcoming eruption, in defiance of his assertion that this is a 'fixed point in history' and that they cannot intervene. Here again, writer James Moran - making his *Doctor Who* debut with this episode after contributing the excellent 'Sleeper' to Series Two of *Torchwood* - tackles head-on an issue that has troubled fans for many a year and that has been at best glossed over in the past: why is it that in some stories, the most notable previous examples probably being 'The Aztecs' (1964) and 'The Massacre of St Bartholomew's Eve' (1966), the Doctor insists that history cannot be changed and must not be interfered with, while in others, generally those set in the viewer's present or future, although 'The Unquiet Dead' is one historical example, he seems to have no qualms about getting involved and altering the course of events quite radically? This 45-year-old mystery is finally solved here as the Doctor tells Donna: 'Some things are fixed, some things are in flux. Pompeii is fixed.' When Donna asks how he knows the difference, he replies: 'Because that's how I see the universe. Every waking second, I can see what is, what was, what could be, what must not. It's the burden of a Time Lord, Donna. And I'm the only one left.'

This is an outstanding piece of writing that affords a fresh insight into the Doctor's alien perspective on time and genuinely enhances our understanding of his character - an achievement few other stories can boast, particularly after all these years - while remaining perfectly consistent with everything that has gone before, such as the Doctor's comment in 'The Unquiet Dead' about time being 'in flux' in that instance, and at last resolving a long-standing awkwardness in the show's treatment of historical subjects. But it is far more than just a fan-pleasing piece of continuity-building; it is, in a sense, the whole crux of the story, as the Doctor eventually realises that the Pyroviles are not responsible for the destruction of Pompeii, as he initially assumed, but are actually working to prevent the volcano erupting by channelling its energy into the equipment from their crashed ship, enabling them to take over the Earth. So it is no longer sufficient for him simply to stand by and do nothing in order for history to take what he knows to be its proper course; he is now faced with the prospect of having to actively intervene, and in the process condemn 20,000 citizens of Pompeii to certain death. Even so, he knows that he really has no choice at all, because if he were to allow the Pyroviles to proceed with their plan, it would ultimately lead to the wiping out of the entire human race. Donna recognises this too, as she places her hands on top of his to share in the awful responsibility of pushing down the lever on the Pyroviles' control panel that will cause Vesuvius to erupt: another strong scene, marred only slightly by the fact that it makes this the second story running in which the Doctor has defeated the aliens by, essentially, just fiddling with some controls in a cupboard - or in this case, to be more precise, in what turns out to be an escape pod, which unfortunately also happens to be a rare example of a very poor piece of design work by the show's behind-the-scenes team, as it is clearly far too small for any Pyrovile to be able to get inside.

The theme of historical inevitability is extended as the Doctor and Donna, having been thrown clear of the erupting volcano in the aforementioned escape pod, make their way through the now-chaotic, ash-choked streets of Pompeii, and Donna finds that all her efforts to warn people to head for the hills rather than the beach fall on deaf ears. The Doctor meanwhile makes no attempt to save anyone and simply heads for the TARDIS as quickly as he can, running right past the cowering Caecilius and his family and starting up the ship's engines even before Donna has come on board. It is only after Donna has joined him and tearfully pleaded with him to save at least *someone* that he relents, takes the TARDIS back to the villa and holds out a hand of salvation to the family, saying 'Come with me' - an incredibly powerful moment. Later, after they have dropped the family off on a hill overlooking the doomed city - the last of a succession of truly wonderful CGI effects supplied by The Mill - the Doctor admits to Donna, 'You were right. Sometimes I need someone. Welcome aboard.' This effectively cements Donna's status as a companion by way of an allusion to the end of 'The Runaway Bride', when she told the Doctor, after his killing of the children of the Racnoss Empress, 'Sometimes I think you need someone to stop you' - a role she was not ready to take on at that time, but now clearly is.

This reference to 'The Runaway Bride' is appropriate for another, less palatable reason too, as 'The Fires of Pompeii' unfortunately sees Donna to some extent reverting to the far less appealing personality of her Christmas special debut. The issue is not so much that she is placed throughout the story in the position of being a kind of nagging human conscience to the Doctor - almost like a Jiminy Cricket character - but that at various points, including when she is about to be sacrificed by the Sisterhood, she resorts to the sort of raucous shouting that proved so irritating originally, even at one stage resurrecting the dismissive 'Spaceman' nickname she coined for the Doctor on their initial meeting. Compounding this is the problem that first became apparent in 'Partners in Crime': although she is excellent in the more emotionally intense scenes, whenever she is given an overtly humorous line to deliver, Catherine Tate seems unable to resist the temptation to adopt an over-the-top 'comedy character' voice. The most grating example of this here comes with Donna's 'I bloody love you' to the Doctor; a declaration made all the more incongruous by the fact that it has been prompted by the Doctor having just fended off the Sibylline High Priestess with a gun. Well, okay, it is not a real gun, it is a yellow water pistol; but it still inflicts real pain in this context, and although there is obviously a risk of becoming over-sensitive about such things in the current climate of increasing concern over real-life gun crime, there just seems to be something not quite *right* about the Doctor being seen to use a weapon, even if it is only a toy replica of a firearm rather than the genuine article. This is an issue that will arise again later in Series Four.

The story closes with a rather curious coda in which Caecilius, Metella, Quintus and Evelina are seen six months later living in a smart new villa in Rome, having obviously done rather well for themselves since their encounter with the Doctor and Donna, whom they now honour as their household gods. It is unclear what inference the viewer is supposed to draw from this. Is it that the Doctor and Donna are indeed deserving of being accorded god-like status for having saved the family from the fate suffered by their fellow citizens? Or that the family's good prospects demonstrate once again the positive impact that contact with the Doctor can have on ordinary people's lives? Or that the Doctor was wrong to resist saving the family, as – like the eruption itself – this is another example of how things were always meant to be? Or conversely that the Doctor was right, and that the consequences of the family's prolonged existence will ripple out from here and cause huge damage to the time-line? He did, after all, ask them to keep his involvement a secret, yet they seem to have ignored this by producing a carving of him, Donna and the TARDIS and placing it in plain sight on their altar. All things considered, it might have been better had this scene been omitted altogether.

It is certainly not as if the episode needed another element, as it is already jam-packed with memorable incident, spectacular action and deeply affecting drama that, along with the superlative production values, give it something of the feel of an epic cinema film condensed into less than 50 minutes of screen time. There are fine performances from all the guest cast, with Peter Capaldi (Caecilius), Phil Davis (Lucius) and Victoria Wicks (High Priestess) being particularly outstanding; the Pyroviles are a cleverly-conceived and well-realised new race of *Doctor Who* monsters, and their affinity with fire and stone is nicely woven into the rest of the story, such as in the plot strand of Lucius commissioning marble dealer Caecilius to produce a component for a stone printed-circuit, and in the idea of inhaled Pyrovile ash from the centre of Vesuvius causing people to turn gradually into stone themselves; and the uncanny inaccuracy of the local seers' prophesies is ingeniously explained as the result of a momentary time rift created by the volcano's eruption that 'echoed back into the Pyrovillian alternative'.

A few reservations aside, this is a superb episode, and one that shows just how much potential there is in stories set in Earth's past – even when they don't conform to the tried-and-trusted 'celebrity historical' template usually adopted in the new *Doctor Who*.

4.03 - PLANET OF THE OOD

Writer: Keith Temple
Director: Graeme Harper

DEBUT TRANSMISSION DETAILS

BBC One
Date: 19 April 2008. Scheduled time: 6.20 pm. Actual time: 6.19 pm.

BBC Three
Date: 20 April 2008. Scheduled time: 8.00 pm. Actual time: 8.00 pm.

Duration: 43' 38"

ADDITIONAL CREDITED CAST

Tim McInnery (Mr Halpen[38]), Ayesha Dharker (Solano Mercurio), Adrian Rawlins (Dr Ryder), Roger Griffiths (Commander Kess), Paul Clayton (Mr Bartle), Paul Kasey (Ood Sigma), Tariq Jordan (Rep), Silas Carson (Voice of the Ood)

PLOT

The Doctor and Donna arrive on the icy surface of the Ood-Sphere in the year 4126, where they discover that a company called Ood Operations is turning natural-born Ood into compliant servants for the Human Empire by cutting off their hind-brains and replacing them with translator balls. Some of the Ood are developing 'red eye' and others even going 'rabid', attacking and killing their human masters. Mr Halpen, the company owner, arrives to investigate, accompanied by his servant, Ood Sigma. However, scientist Dr Ryder is unable to explain what is going wrong. The Doctor eventually discovers that there is a huge principal Ood brain, discovered by Mr Halpen's family buried in the ice some 200 years earlier, which is now held in the company's Warehouse 15, surrounded by a circle of transmitters sending a signal to block the telepathic field it transmits to unify its race. Dr Ryder, who is actually an undercover agent of Friends of the Ood (FOTO), secretly reduces the signal to a minimal level, allowing the Ood to rebel against the company. Mr Halpen meanwhile is transformed into an Ood himself, having been tricked by Ood Sigma into drinking regular doses of Ood-graft in the mistaken belief that he was taking a hair tonic. The circle around the principal Ood brain is finally broken, allowing the creatures to sing their Song of Freedom.

[38] First name intended to be 'Klineman', as confirmed in *Doctor Who Confidential*, but not given in the episode itself.

QUOTE, UNQUOTE

- **Donna:** 'Is that …?'
  Doctor: 'It's a brain. A hind-brain. The Ood are born with a secondary brain. Like the amigdala in humans, it processes memory and emotions; you get rid of that, you wouldn't be Donna anymore, you'd be like an Ood, a processed Ood.'
  Donna: 'So the company cuts off their brains.'
  Doctor: 'And they stitch on the translator.'
  Donna: 'Like a lobotomy. I spent all that time looking for you, Doctor, because I thought it was so wonderful out here. I wanna go home.'
- **Ood Sigma:** 'Take this song with you.'
  Donna: 'We will.'
  Doctor: 'Always.'
  Ood Sigma: 'And know this, Doctor-Donna. You will never be forgotten. Our children will sing of the Doctor-Donna, and our children's children, and the wind and the ice and the snow will carry your names forever.'

CONTINUITY POINTS

- The Doctor tells Donna that they have arrived on the Ood-Sphere in the year 4126. As the narrative indicates that this is some time after the events of 'The Impossible Planet'/'The Satan Pit', that Series Two story must have been set in an earlier year; on screen, the date was given as '43 K 2.1', but it was unclear what that meant in current terms. Members of the production team have stated in interviews that they intended 'The Impossible Planet'/'The Satan Pit' and '42' (undated on screen) to be set around the same time, in the 42nd Century, although it appears that the original scripts for 'The Impossible Planet'/'The Satan Pit' dated it to the 43rd Century.
- The Doctor states that the year 4126 falls during 'the Second Great and Bountiful Human Empire', which spans three galaxies (presumably including the Milky Way, aka Mutter's Spiral). The timeline of human empires in *Doctor Who* appears to be as follows:

  - c 2500 to c 3000: The first Earth Empire, as seen in TV in stories such as 'Frontier in Space' (1973) (set around 2540, when the Empire is just becoming established after a war with Draconia, a competing power in the same galaxy) and 'The Mutants' (1972) (set during the 30th Century, when the Empire is in decline) and featured in numerous tie-in novels. This is presumably the Empire that later becomes known as the First Great and Bountiful Human Empire.
  - c 3800 to sometime after 4126: The Second Great and Bountiful Human Empire, as seen in 'Planet of the Ood' and earlier TV stories such as 'The Daleks' Master Plan' (1965/66), when Mavic Chen is the Guardian of the Solar System in 4000 and meets representatives of 'the Outer Galaxies', possibly implying that the three galaxies controlled from the Solar System are known as 'the Inner Galaxies'; there is also mention of Chen having concluded a mineral agreement with 'the Fourth Galaxy', possibly the

same one as visited by the Doctor in 'Galaxy 4' (1965).
  - Sometime after 5000 to sometime after 12,000: The Third Great and Bountiful Human Empire, possibly also known as the New Roman Empire, as referred to by the Doctor in 'The End of the World'. In 'The Invisible Enemy' (1977), the Doctor says that the year 5000 is the time of 'the Great Breakout', when the human race leapfrogs across 'the galaxy', presumably meaning Mutter's Spiral. This suggests that prior to 5000 there is a period when the influence of the human race contracts to the Solar System after the collapse of the Second Great and Bountiful Human Empire. (The 51st Century is also the era from which Time Agents, including Captain Jack Harkness, originate.)
  - c 200,000. The Fourth Great and Bountiful Human Empire, visited by the Doctor and Rose in 'The End of the World', when the Earth appears to be destroyed.

It is unclear where the period of Earth's membership of the Galactic Federation, as featured in the stories 'The Curse of Peladon' (1972) and 'The Monster of Peladon' (1974), fits in all this, but it is probably either just before or, most likely, just after the first Earth Empire. There is talk in 'The Monster of Peladon' of a 'Galaxy Five', with which the Federation is in conflict.
- Donna says that she learnt to whistle at 'West Ham every Saturday', indicating that she is a supporter of West Ham United football club. In 'The Fires of Pompeii', she mentioned her father having said '*Vene Vidi Vici*' when he 'came back from football'. Possibly they attended West Ham matches together?
- In the scene where the Doctor and Donna find an Ood lying wounded in the snow shortly after their arrival on the Ood-Sphere, Donna refers to the creature as 'it' and the Doctor corrects her, saying, 'It's a "he", not an "it"'. This gives the first indication that the creatures have different genders. Then, in the final scene of the episode, some members of the circle of Ood gathered near the TARDIS have long tabards rather than the creatures' usual costumes; these are presumably intended to be female Ood, previously unseen on screen.
- Ood Sigma tells the Doctor, 'I think your song must end soon'. When the Doctor asks him what this means, he replies simply, 'Every song must end'.

PRODUCTION NOTES

- Made with 'The Unicorn and the Wasp' as part of Block 1 of production.
- The location scenes of the snowy landscape of the Ood-Sphere where shot in Trefil Quarry on the edge of the Brecon Beacons, north of Merthyr Tydfil, on 23 August 2007. Director Graeme Harper had at one point considered using this for the surface of Malcassairo in 'Utopia' in Series Three, but had eventually used a quarry closer to the Cardiff production base on that occasion. The fake snow, composed principally of paper, was supplied by a company called Snow Business, which specialises in this type of work. The sequences in the warehouse where the containers of Ood are stored ready for transportation were taped at the Ministry of Defence's St Athan base in Barry on 24 and 27 August. The containers - more than 20 in total - were hired in by the production team, and digitally multiplied by The Mill. The industrial

exteriors of the Ood Operations base were recorded at the Lefarge Cement works in Aberthaw, near Cardiff Airport, from 28 to 31 August. More base exteriors were shot outside Next Generation Data, Imperial Park, Newport, on 4 September. The interiors of Warehouse 15, where the huge unifying Ood brain is held, were shot in the same Mamhilad Park Industrial Estate factory used as a location for 'Voyage of the Damned'. This was done over 4 and 5 September. A room in Hensol Castle, Glamorgan, doubled for the Ood Operations executive office, recording taking place there on 7 September.

- Studio recording for this episode took place on 21 and 22 August, 1 and 3 September and 16 November 2007 at Upper Boat.
- The early drafts of Keith Temple's script for the episode were judged to be too dark in tone – placing more emphasis on the battery farming metaphor, for instance – and to be too densely plotted, in the manner of a multi-part classic-era *Doctor Who* story; these issues were both addressed in later drafts. The Ood in the warehouse were originally intended to be in open cages rather than closed containers but this was changed partly because it would have been too difficult to achieve technically.
- The graphics displayed on the large video screen in the Ood Operations marketing suite were not added in as green-screen effects in post-production but played in on set by back projection.

OOPS!

- Solano says that according to Mr Halpen's own rules there is no alcohol allowed on the Ood Operations base. Later, however, the prospective buyers attending the company's PR event are seen taking advantage of a 'free bar'.

PRESS REACTION

- 'Before this fourth series of the relaunched *Doctor Who* was broadcast, [Catherine Tate's] jammy enlodgement as the Doctor's assistant was, for many, a source of great sorrow. She had not, let's face it, proved a particularly winsome turn in "The Runaway Bride" – the poorest of all the Christmas specials. With an acting range that seemed to consist wholly of shouting while facing left, shouting while facing right, and shouting in some snow, her Donna Noble was kind of untaken to everyone's bosoms that festive afternoon … Tate is often compared with Marmite – you either love her, or you hate her! – but she's not like Marmite at all. Marmite is an inconsequential sandwich spread, that you can quite easily take or leave simply by deciding whether to put it on your toast or not. Catherine Tate, on the other hand, *is the new assistant in Doctor Who*! There is no taking or leaving there. I mean, it's not like we're ever going to stop watching it, is it? Tsk. Prft. Tsk. Of course not. But … she's not working out too badly at all, now she's up and running in a whole series. The main beneficiary of her enrolment has been the atmosphere in the TARDIS. It is unexpectedly pleasant to be, once again, in a time-travelling wardrobe free of sexual tension. In the latter half of the last series, particularly, the show was starting to feel like some manner of intergalactic *Alfie* – any sentient being with receptive genitals simpering at the Doctor, while he cranked his eyebrows up and down like a seesaw ... ["Planet of the Ood"] is another really, really good episode - one that will have you staring at your screen and asking, once again, "How can something so good be happening so early on a Saturday night, in my own front room?"' Caitlin Moran, *The Times*, 19 April 2008.

- '[One] of [Russell T] Davies's hobby-horses is his cultural relativism. On a principle similar to "One man's terrorist is another man's freedom fighter", he clearly reckons that there's no such thing as a truly evil alien ... and that if they do behave badly it's probably the fault of their wicked, neocolonial human oppressors. This was the theme of this week's Ood episode (written by Keith Temple) in which, despite having glowing red eyes, murderous tendencies and faces like mouldy, vomited spaghetti, the Ood were a delightful, peaceloving race who communicated through beautiful telepathic keening somewhere between whale music and J S Bach. The reason they'd gone rotten, it turned out, was that a nasty capitalist ... had enslaved them. Doctor Who, as is his tiresome wont these days, expressed his horror at this latest example of humans behaving badly. "Oi, don't blame me, innit," went Donna, or something like it. "It's been years since we had slaves on our planet." Oh really, says the Doctor. And who makes your cheap clothes? ... Doctor Who is a genius, a man of the universe ... Since when did he acquire the blinkered values of a bearded '60s sociology lecturer? Why can his superbrain not grasp the point that what may seem like a slave-wage to a bienpensant TV scriptwriter is yet a king's ransom for a South-East Asian textile worker, who only has his job because of the comparative advantage his nation has in cheap labour? This is A-level economics we're talking here, not TARDIS science. I still think *Doctor Who*'s great, by the way - unmissable and one of the best things on TV. It's witty, pacy, well acted, with gripping storylines and increasingly impressive special effects. But everyone says that. I just don't think it should be allowed to get away with its rubbish bits.' James Delingpole, the *Spectator*, 16 April 2008.
- 'An utterly unashamed morality play that wears its values on its sleeve in a way that's rare even by *Doctor Who* standards - in *Doctor Who*, death is usually random, claiming good and bad alike, but here there's a *Primeval*-esque sense that you have to have done something that marks you out as bad for the monsters to get you, whether that be the sadism of the chief guard, the drunken city-boy antics of the potential client or, most obviously, the amoral choice of the PR girl who turns the Doctor in and gets killed within seconds of ordering the guards to kill the Ood. Keith Temple's script could have come over as being as subtle as a sledgehammer in other hands, but Graeme Harper's at the directorial helm, so sheer suspense and well-paced set-pieces hold the attention and keep the message in place.' Anthony Brown, *TV Zone*, Issue 228, May 2008.
- 'While unexceptional in terms of new *Who*'s highest points - "Blink" and so on - "Planet of the Ood" is a paragon of just how slick and polished the show has become. This episode barrels along and looks splendid, everything from the Ood themselves to their beautiful, snowbound planet, the giant CGI claw and the Thunderbird-3-esque spaceship screaming quality. There's a confidence and slickness here that, frankly, just makes you want to cheer.' Jes Bickham, *DeathRay* Issue 14, July 2008.

ANALYSIS

It was always on the cards that the Ood would make a return appearance. Inserted by Russell T Davies into Matt Jones's Series Two story 'The Impossible Planet'/'The Satan Pit' when he went off the original idea of bringing back the Slitheen, they proved to be a huge hit with viewers, and one of the most memorable alien races created for the new *Doctor Who*. Having at one point been considered for inclusion in Chris Chibnall's '42' in Series Three, until plans for that story moved in a different direction, they finally return to the screen here in writer Keith Temple's debut contribution to the show.

Davies has always been up-front about the fact that he based the Ood in part on the eponymous creatures of Peter R Newman's 1964 story 'The Sensorites'. In this instance, the connection is made almost explicit, as the Doctor comments that the Ood-Sphere is 'close to the planet Sense-Sphere' – Sense-Sphere being the name of the Sensorites' home world. This, remarkably, makes 'Planet of the Ood' the second episode running to contain a subtle but explicit reference to one transmitted over 40 years earlier. In an interesting development, though, the glowing spheres that the Ood hold are now revealed to be not simply communications devices, like the telepathic transmitter pads used by the Sensorites, but substitutes for their external hind-brains, which have been removed by the human profiteers of Ood Operations in the process of enslaving the creatures. This gives greater depth to their characters, adds still further to their extraordinary hideous-yet-strangely-appealing quality – surely one of the reasons they are so beloved of children – and at the same time strengthens the parallels with the innately trusting Sensorites, Donna telling Mr Halpen: 'You idiot! They're born with their brains in their hands. Don't you see, that makes them peaceful. They've got to be, because a creature like that would have to trust anyone it meets.' The idea of Ood Sigma being distinguished for the others by way of a black symbol on his tunic also harks back to 'The Sensorites'.

'Planet of the Ood' recalls the early part of the first Doctor's era in another, more significant way too. Specifically, this is that the Doctor and his companion are essentially just observers here rather than active shapers of events. All the indications are that the revolution that takes place on the Ood-Sphere would have panned out in exactly the same way even if they had not been present at all. The Ood would still have developed 'red eye' and gone rabid, Mr Halpen would still have been transformed into one of them, and Dr Ryder would still have completed his undercover mission for the Friends of the Ood to 'break the circle' and free the principal Ood brain. This makes for an interesting contrast to 'The Fires of Pompeii'. Whereas in the latter episode the Doctor initially believed that he had to avoid interfering in events, but eventually discovered that he had to make an active intervention in order to ensure that history followed its proper course, here he actually does remain passive – save for flicking a switch to disarm the bombs placed by Mr Halpen around the Ood brain, which surely either Dr Ryder or Ood Sigma would have done in any case – and the situation resolves itself satisfactorily without his help. There is nothing wrong with this in principle, although it is virtually unprecedented in post-1960s *Doctor Who*, but the downside is that the Ood's moving tribute to the Doctor and Donna outside the TARDIS in the closing scene seems largely unmotivated – certainly by comparison with the Caecilius family's veneration of them at the end of 'The Fires of Pompeii', to which this is curiously analogous. Yes, the two time travellers have shown sympathy and understanding for the creatures' plight, but they haven't really done anything significant to end it, unlike the Friends of the Ood. Possibly the Ood's tribute to Dr Ryder - a true martyr to their cause - takes place off-screen.

One thing that can be said in the closing scene's favour, though, is that it is both poignant and visually stunning - qualities that characterise the episode as a whole. Keith Temple's script is superb, striking just the right balance between quieter moments of genuine dramatic intensity and full-on action scenes. The theme of the human race having advanced itself through a shameful reliance on slavery is quite a thought-provoking and sophisticated one for an early-Saturday-evening family drama show to raise, particularly when, in what is an admirably bold piece of writing, Temple brings it much closer to home by having the Doctor point out that some of the clothes that Donna is wearing - and thus, by implication, some of the clothes that members of the audience at home are wearing - are doubtless the product of virtual slave labour practices. Previously in *Doctor Who*, the idea of humanity breaking free of the solar system and founding an empire out among the stars has been typically presented in very positive terms, as a wonderful testament to our race's indomitable pioneering spirit, but here the tone is far more ambivalent, with Donna asking, 'Is that good or bad, though; I mean, we're like explorers, or more like a virus?', and the Doctor replying, 'Sometimes I wonder.' While this is not the first time a *Doctor Who* story has taken an implicitly critical slant on imperialism - 'The Mutants' (1972) is one notable example that comes to mind - it certainly gives an ironic twist to the Doctor's description of this time period as 'the Second Great and Bountiful Human Empire'.

Another astute move on Temple's part is his depiction of Ood Operations as a family-run enterprise with preoccupations akin to those of a typical 21st Century business. The numerous references to advertising campaigns, sales figures, PR promotions, distribution centres, warehouses, livestock and the like all help to ensure that, even though the action takes place in the far-distant future on an unfamiliar alien world, the viewer is still able to relate quite easily to the drama unfolding on screen. The same goes for the way the show's designers have kept the sets of the company's visitor areas and offices quite similar in appearance to present-day corporate premises -complete with Andy Warhol-style prints of the Ood on the wall - and the costumes of its staff and clients akin to standard business suits, with just small variations such as more rounded collars on the shirts. While some die-hard science-fiction fans might complain that this fails to reflect the cultural seismic shifts that are bound to occur over a period of thousands of years - a criticism that has also been applied to some other episodes, such as 'The Long Game' - it could equally be argued that fashions in commercial design and clothing have not changed all that radically over time - certainly the basic design of a man's business suit has remained pretty constant for almost 100 years now - and may even prove to be to some extent cyclical; and one need only consider the now-laughable attempts of earlier science-fiction productions to depict 'the future', replete with flying cars, moving pavements and spandex jumpsuits, to see the folly of attempting to predict what is inherently unpredictable. 'Planet of the Ood''s more effective approach of taking contemporary industrial settings and giving them just a slight futuristic twist is actually reminiscent of that adopted in numerous stories of the second and third Doctors' eras, adding further to the pleasingly old-school feel of this episode.

Not only is Temple's script a first rate piece of work, but Graeme Harper's direction is also outstanding, even by his own very high standards. He has often in the past proved himself adept at delivering thrilling action sequences for the show, and this is again the case here, the best example probably coming with the scene where the Doctor desperately attempts to outmanoeuvre the crushing grip of a mechanical claw operated by company security man Commander Kess – the claw itself being another superb piece of CGI effects work by The Mill, who really excel themselves on this episode, including also with their seamless digital augmentation of the location-shot snowy landscape of the Ood-Sphere and their realisation of the wonderfully retro-look space rocket, fittingly similar to the one in 'The Impossible Planet'/'The Satan Pit', that the Doctor and Donna see pass overhead. No less adept, though, is Harper's handling of the more emotionally involving, character based scenes, such as the early one where the Doctor and Donna find an Ood felled by a gunshot wound, and the later one where they discover a cage full of unprocessed Ood, cowering in the dark with their hind-brains cupped in their hands. The only slightly questionable aspect of this latter scene is the use of Murray Gold's music to represent the Ood's telepathic 'Song of Captivity', which the Doctor temporarily enables Donna to hear and she finds heartbreakingly moving: as good as Gold's music is, it cannot really hope to live up to the expectations placed on it here, and it would have been better had this been approached in a different way, perhaps through the use of ethereal sound effects, or even simply left to the viewer's imagination. That said, the 'Song of Freedom' that accompanies the later scene of the Ood finally being released from their slavery is far more effective, probably because it seems more clearly intended as a metaphorical representation of the creatures' telepathic communication rather than a literal one.

Another pleasing aspect of 'Planet of the Ood' is that Donna is on much better form here, after 'The Fires of Pompeii' saw her to some extent slipping back into the more irritating traits of her original 'The Runaway Bride' persona. There is a welcome absence of strident shrieking this time around, and the only jarringly misplaced piece of humour – her 'Do I look single?' retort when an Ood refers to her as 'Miss', which is not only an incredibly crass comment to make in the context of the serious discussion she is having but simply defies logic, since she is indeed single and invariably swift to quash any assumption that she and the Doctor are a married couple – is a rare misjudgement in the scripting rather than any lapse on the part of Catherine Tate, who actually delivers the line as well as could be hoped for. Not only that, but Donna shows her true worth here as an audience identification figure. Her reaction on first encountering an Ood, in the aforementioned scene where she and the Doctor find one lying mortally wounded in the snow, is a spot-on mixture of shock, confusion, trepidation and compassion, and throughout the episode she continues to ask just the sort of pointed and challenging questions that a woman of her down-to-earth nature and innate decency might be expected to ask. This even at one point leads the Doctor to admit that the first time he met the Ood he simply took for granted their unnaturally servile behaviour and was too busy to save them; a case of the programme-makers having recognised a problematic issue in 'The Impossible Planet'/'The Satan Pit' – and one that had troubled many fans as well – and, rather wonderfully, having cared enough about it to return to it and address it in this follow-up story. As the

Doctor himself puts it, 'I reckon I owe them one.'

There are relatively few guest cast members in this episode, but they all give very good performances, the best of the lot probably coming from Tim McInnery as the harassed and amoral Mr Halpen, whose final transformation into an Ood - another triumph of prosthetics work by Millennium FX and CGI wizardry by The Mill - is a memorably gruesome moment; Paul Kasey and his fellow monster actors deserve special plaudits for their highly convincing portrayal of the Ood; and the stark industrial locations used for the Ood Operations premises, suitably adorned with fake snow, convey just the right impression of familiar-yet-otherworldly processes grinding away. In fact, every aspect of the production positively shines and, all in all, this is undoubtedly one of the strongest episodes of Series Four. It does, though, leave a few unanswered questions. 'The message has gone out,' says the Doctor, before he and Donna depart in the TARDIS. 'That song resonated across the galaxies. Everyone heard it. Everyone knows. The rockets are bringing them back. The Ood are coming home.' But surely it can't really be as simple as that, can it? The Second Great and Bountiful Human Empire has relied on the Ood to fetch and carry for it for some 200 years. Is it really going to let them all go now, just like that? Potential for another follow-up story there, perhaps, if new showrunner Steven Moffat feels so inclined ...?

4.04 - THE SONTARAN STRATAGEM

Writer: Helen Raynor
Director: Douglas Mackinnon

DEBUT TRANSMISSION DETAILS

BBC One
Date: 26 April 2008. Scheduled time: 6.20 pm. Actual time: 6.19 pm.

BBC Three
Date: 27 April 2008. Scheduled time: 8.00 pm. Actual time: 8.02 pm.

Duration: 44' 33"

ADDITIONAL CREDITED CAST

Ryan Sampson (Luke Rattigan), Rupert Holliday Evans (Colonel Mace), Christopher Ryan (General Staal), Dan Starkey (Commander Skorr), Eleanor Matsuura (Jo Nakashima), Clive Standen (Private Harris), Wesley Theobald (Private Gray), Christian Cooke (Ross Jenkins), Rad Kaim[39] (Worker), Elizabeth Ryder[40] (Atmos Voice)

Sontarans created by: Robert Holmes

PLOT

Martha Jones, now working for UNIT as a fully-qualified medic, calls the Doctor back to Earth to investigate satellite navigation ATMOS devices that are being installed in all the world's cars as a pollution-reducing measure. In light of a spate of mysterious deaths, UNIT believe that the devices have another, more sinister purpose, possibly of an alien nature. The Doctor visits the Rattigan Academy, an elite school set up by teenage millionaire Luke Rattigan, supposedly the inventor of ATMOS. The Doctor realises that the devices contain technology decades ahead of their time, and his suspicions are confirmed when he encounters General Staal of the Tenth Sontaran Battle Fleet. Meanwhile, while Donna returns home to visit her grandfather and mother, Martha is captured by the Sontarans, who produce a clone of her in the ATMOS factory in order to infiltrate UNIT. Escaping from General Staal, the Doctor meets up with Donna at her family home. However, the Sontarans then activate all the ATMOS devices, which start to spew out a noxious gas.

[39] Not credited in *Radio Times*.
[40] Not credited in *Radio Times*.

QUOTE, UNQUOTE

- **Doctor:** 'Martha, Donna. Donna, Martha. Please don't fight. Can't bear fighting.'
  Donna: 'You wish!' [To Martha] 'I've heard all about you. He talks about you all the time.'
  Martha: 'I dread to think.'
  Donna: 'No, no, no. No, he says nice things. Good things. Nice things, really … good things.'
  Martha: 'Oh my god, he's told you everything.'
  Donna (spotting that Martha is wearing an engagement ring): 'Didn't take long to get over it, though. Who's the lucky man?'
  Doctor: 'What, man? Lucky what?'
  Donna: 'She's engaged, you prawn!'
- **Doctor:** 'People with guns are usually the enemy, in my books. You seem quite at home.'
  Martha: 'If anyone got my used to fighting, it was you.'
  Doctor: 'Oh, right, so it's my fault?'
  Martha: 'Well, you got me the job! Besides, look at me. Am I carrying a gun?
  Doctor: 'I suppose not.'
  Martha: 'It's all right for you. You can just come and go. But some of us have got to stay behind. So I've got to work from the inside. And by staying on the inside, maybe I stand a chance of making them better.'
  Doctor: 'Yeah? That's more like Martha Jones!'
  Martha: 'I learnt from the best.'

CONTINUITY POINTS

- The Sontarans have obviously been able to communicate with Rattigan even before the Doctor arrives on the scene. This indicates that, as first established in 'The Time Warrior' (1973/74), they have alien language translator technology.
- Martha contacts the Doctor using the mobile phone she left with him at the end of 'Last of the Time Lords'.
- The Doctor says that he worked with UNIT 'back in the '70s', but then adds in a mutter, 'or was it the '80s?' This is an in-joke reference to a long-standing controversy within *Doctor Who* fandom over the dating of the UNIT stories of the third and fourth Doctors' eras. The overwhelming weight of evidence from the transmitted episodes suggests that they were set in the 1970s. In 'Mawdryn Undead' (1983), for instance, it is explicitly stated that Brigadier Lethbridge-Stewart retired from UNIT in 1977, meaning that all the earlier UNIT stories in which he featured must have taken place prior to that date. There is further evidence to support this from new-era *Doctor Who* and its spin-offs. Most notably, in *The Sarah Jane Adventures*, it is established that Sarah Jane Smith was born in 1950. Given that she was said in her second *Doctor Who* story, 'Invasion of the Dinosaurs' (1974), to be 24 years old, this confirms that the latter story was set in the year of its broadcast. There are, however, two pieces of evidence, of a more tenuous nature, that some fans take to indicate that the UNIT stories could alternatively have been set in the 1980s. First, in 'The Web of Fear' (1968),

Professor Travers states that over 40 years have passed since the events of 'The Abominable Snowmen' (1967), which it is established occurred in 1935, and in 'The Invasion' (1968), Lethbridge-Stewart states that four years have passed since the events of 'The Web of Fear'. This would seem to indicate that 'The Invasion' is set around 1979, rather than 1968 or 1969. However, Professor Travers is intentionally depicted in 'The Web of Fear' as an absent-minded old man, so it is quite possible that when he says 'over 40 years' he actually means 'over 30 years', which would make the dating of 'The Invasion' consistent with all the other, more persuasive, evidence. Secondly, Sarah Jane says in 'Pyramids of Mars' (1975) that she comes 'from 1980'. However, what exactly she means by this is open to question, bearing in mind that she is speaking from the perspective of a time traveller. If she began her travels with the Doctor in 1974 and had been with him for six years by the time of the events of 'Pyramids of Mars' (which is possible, taking into account unscreened 'missing adventures'), she might well think of herself as 'belonging' to 1980 by that point; she would, after all, have aged six years since meeting the Doctor in 1974. Alternatively, perhaps she has spent a period of time living back on Earth in 1980 just prior to 'Pyramids of Mars', as that story does not continue directly on from the previous one, 'Planet of Evil' (1975). On balance, therefore, it seems almost certain that the UNIT stories were indeed set in the 1970s.

- General Staal says that he is of the Tenth Sontaran Battle Fleet and is known as 'Staal the Undefeated'. Commander Skorr reveals that his equivalent nickname is 'the Bloodbringer'.
- The Sontarans' home planet is named for the first time on screen here as 'Sontar'. The Sontarans' creator, Robert Holmes, originally called their planet 'Sontara', in his opening segment of the novelisation of 'The Time Warrior' (a book subsequently completed by Terrance Dicks). The shorter form 'Sontar' was first used in *Doctor Who Magazine*'s tie-in comic strip, specifically in a story called 'The Betrothal of Sontar', where the planet was said to be named after a famous ruler, General Sontar.
- Although the Sontarans are a clone race, they are obviously not all cloned from the same original Sontarans, as there have been numerous small differences in their appearance in the various *Doctor Who* stories in which they have appeared.
- Luke Rattigan, the inventor of ATMOS, is described as a 'child genius' who 'invented the Fountain 6 search engine when he was 12 years old', making him a millionaire overnight. He is now 18 years old and runs the Rattigan Academy, a private school for handpicked students from all over the world, characterised by the Doctor as a 'hothouse for geniuses'.
- The Doctor says that one of the places he wants to take Donna is the 'fifteenth broken moon of the Medusa Cascade'.
- Martha confirms that she has 'security clearance level one' with UNIT.
- This episode is set just 'a few days' after 'Partners in Crime'.
- The way the Doctor prevents General Staal from shooting him on sight by revealing that he knows the name of his race is identical to how Rose stopped a Dalek from exterminating her in 'Doomsday'.
- General Staal complains that the Sontarans were not 'allowed' to take part in the Time War. He does not say who prevented them from doing so, but presumably

it was either the Time Lords or the Daleks. The Sontarans do have primitive time travel technology, as seen in 'The Time Warrior' and implicitly confirmed in this episode with the Doctor's comment that the ATMOS devices contain a 'temporal pocket', and were even able to invade the Time Lords' home planet Gallifrey in 'The Invasion of Time' (1978).

- Wilf says that when Donna was a young girl the family used to call her 'the little general' due to her bossy nature - an interesting nickname, given that this story features another 'little general', Staal.
- An explanation is provided here for Wilf's absence from Donna's wedding in 'The Runaway Bride': Sylvia says that he was laid up with 'Spanish flu'. This was the nickname given to the 1918-1920 flu pandemic, believed to have killed between 50 and 100 million people. Either this virus has made a return in the *Doctor Who* universe, unlike in ours, or else Sylvia is exaggerating the severity of Wilf's illness or, perhaps more likely, making a sarcastic reference to Wilf having done so himself.

BAD WOLF REFERENCES

- There is a graffiti painting of a red wolf on the corrugated fence against which the TARDIS materialises.

PRODUCTION NOTES

- Made with 'The Poison Sky' as Block 4 of production.
- Freema Agyeman's name is included in the opening titles of this episode.
- Extensive location recording was done for this and the following episode. The Rattigan Academy exteriors were taped between 23 and 26 October 2007 at Margam Country Park, a different part of which had been used for scenes in the *Torchwood* episode 'Something Borrowed'. The action at the ATMOS factory was shot on 27, 29 and 30 October and 6 and 8 November at an old shampoo and conditioner factory on the Usk Valley Business Park. A number of the factory's original vats were still in place and can be seen in the transmitted episodes, although the tank in which the clone of Martha is grown was an adapted set element from 'The Fires of Pompeii', and the frame on which the real Martha is kept restrained was previously used in the *Torchwood* episode 'Cyberwoman'. The house used for the Nobles' home was the same private residence on Nant-Fawr Road, Cyncoed, Cardiff, as used previously, recording taking place there on 31 October and 1 and 2 November. The exterior of Orion Electric Ltd in Margam was used for the taping of some further ATMOS factory scenes, and of the supermarket car park sequence where gas is seen spewing from a number of cars. This was done on 9 and 10 November. The scene of journalist Jo Nakashima's car plunging into a canal was recorded on Compass Road Bridge, Cardiff Docks, on 19 November using a 'car cannon', a long metal tube inserted into the body of the car to propel it forward through a release of pressurised gas. On the same date, Cargo Road, Cardiff Docks was used as the location where jeep carrying the Doctor and Ross is taken over by its ATMOS device.
- Studio dates for this story were 12 to 16 and 20 to 22 November and 2 and 18 December 2007 and 24 January and 29 February 2008, all this recording taking

place at Upper Boat.

- Russell T Davies's key tone word for this story was 'military'. His original idea involved family homes being fitted with pollution-reducing chimneys, but writer Helen Raynor thought it would be more realistic and effective to change this to pollution-reducing devices fitted to cars, along with sat-navs.
- The idea of the Sontarans using a 'Cordolaine signal' to stop guns from firing – the copper casings of the bullets being excited by the signal, causing them to expand and jam in the barrel – was devised by Russell T Davies to prevent UNIT appearing too powerful in the story.
- Russell T Davies decided that the acronym 'UNIT' should no longer be said to mean 'United Nations Intelligence Taskforce' in *Doctor Who* or its spin-offs after the real-life United Nations allegedly complained about a fictional UNIT website set up by bbc.co.uk to promote the show. Although the United Nations cannot prevent its name being used in a fictional context in a TV drama, Davies stated that he did not want to risk young fans getting into trouble with the organisation if, for instance, they set up their own websites referring to UNIT by its full name. After much discussion, the revised name 'UNified Intelligence Taskforce' was coined.

OOPS!

- Colonel Mace is not wearing a uniform cap when he salutes first the Doctor and then, at her prompting, Donna, which is contrary to military etiquette.
- There are numerous shot-continuity errors in the episode. Possibly the most noticeable come in the scene where Donna and Wilf are talking in the kitchen of their family home: Bernard Cribbins' hands change positions significantly between different shots.

PRESS REACTION

- 'The narrative is very well plotted and paced, allowing several strands a good amount of exposure before merging together for the exciting cliffhanger. The reintroductions of UNIT, Martha, Donna's family and the war-loving Sontarans are all seamlessly interwoven into Helen Raynor's script … In particular, the interaction between Donna and Martha is charmingly written, confounding the expectations of those who foresaw a full-on cat fight. In addition, the central plot that binds these disparate elements together – the Sontaran plan to gas the Earth via carbon-free sat-nav – is consistently gripping [and] intriguing and benefits from the momentum generated by the pre-credits sequence. Furthermore, Christopher Ryan is superbly cast as General Staal and uses his trademark "constipated" voice and grumpy eyes to great effect. In contrast, Commander Skorr's voice is distinctly lacklustre. "The Sontaran Stratagem" does have one noticeable flaw in the shape of Douglas Mackinnon's inconsistent direction. The first unveiling of an armour-clad Sontaran in the cloning chamber is depicted via a highly underwhelming long shot. Surely the iconic monsters deserve a more tension-filled unveiling to a new generation? The grand reveal of the Martha clone is similarly botched due to shot selection worse than English batsmen during the last Ashes series.' Ben Rawson-Jones, Digital Spy website, 26 April

2008.

- '"The Sontaran Stratagem" is about as deliciously old-fashioned as new *Who* gets. It makes my fan boy sense tingle and makes me grin like an idiot. The Doctor, working with UNIT again, alongside two great companions, and taking on a faithfully realised monster from the classic series. Hurrah! But, as with much of *Doctor Who* in the here and now, the links to the decades of the original series' continuity are done subtly. I get a kick out of them, but if you're not looking for it, it won't spoil your enjoyment of the episode. And there's a lot to enjoy here. David Tennant in particular shows no signs of fatigue in what must have been an exhausting run on this top-rated show. In fact the presence of old touchstones like UNIT seems to have brought out his mischievous side - there's nothing like the Doctor dealing with military types to bring out that traditional, essential "Doctorness". Tennant trips through this with a glint in his eye and a wicked smile on his face, playing the almost naughty child Doctor that we rarely get to see these days.' Mark Wright, *The Stage* website, 27 April 2008.

ANALYSIS

Not for the first time, it seems here that classic-era *Doctor Who* must have been very much on the production team's minds when they were formulating their plans for Series Four. The roots of 'The Sontaran Stratagem'/'The Poison Sky' can be traced right back to 'The War Machines' (1966), the first story to portray the Doctor working alongside the armed forces to defeat a menace threatening contemporary Earth. That successful formula was repeated in 'The Web of Fear' (1968), which in turn led on to 'The Invasion' (1968), the story that introduced UNIT and served as an intentional 'dry run' for the largely Earth-bound stories of the early 1970s. While UNIT has featured a number of times already in new-era *Doctor Who* - most notably in 'Aliens of London'/'World War Three' and 'The Christmas Invasion' - 'The Sontaran Stratagem'/'The Poison Sky' is the first fully-fledged 'UNIT story' of the kind often seen during that earlier decade. Not only that, but it also features the return of the Sontarans, a popular monster race that made its debut during the same decade, in 'The Time Warrior' (1973/74). As such, it affords some fascinating insights into both the similarities and the differences between classic-era and new-era *Doctor Who*.

One of the most remarkable things about 'The War Machines' is the way that the show's newly-recruited scientific adviser Kit Pedler generated the central premise of the story by extrapolating from then-current technological concerns, positing the establishment of a global network of advanced computers communicating via telephone lines - in other words, astonishingly, predicting the advent of the internet years before it actually happened. This was only the second time such an approach had been taken in a *Doctor Who* story - the first having been in 'Planet of Giants' (1964), with its plot about an unscrupulous scientist's creation of an indiscriminately destructive insecticide, inspired by growing disquiet then over the effects of DDT as highlighted in biologist Rachel Carson's book *Silent Spring* (1962) - but over the course of the following decade or so there were many other instances where the show's writers took anxieties over aspects of contemporary life and gave them a slight science fiction twist to make them the basis of a dangerous situation facing the Doctor. Examples of issues addressed in this way included the proliferation of plastic consumer goods in 'Terror of the Autons' (1971), the UK's acceptance into the

Common Market in 'The Curse of Peladon' (1972), chemical waste pollution in 'The Green Death' (1973), unrest amongst mine workers in 'The Monster of Peladon' (1974) and even punitive taxation in 'The Sun Makers' (1977). This is an approach that has been emulated to great effect in new-era *Doctor Who*, including with satellite news services in 'The Long Game', reality TV shows in 'Bad Wolf', Bluetooth mobile phone headsets in 'Rise of the Cybermen'/'The Age of Steel', communications satellites in 'The Sound of Drums' and diet pills in 'Partners in Crime'. In 'The Sontaran Stratagem', it is the turn of sat-nav systems and car exhaust emissions to be given the *Doctor Who* treatment, and writer Helen Raynor has integrated these familiar contemporary elements very well into her narrative, the only possible criticism being that to have both in the same story is almost a case of one idea too many, as the Sontarans could surely have achieved their objectives perfectly well without having remote-control sat-navs fitted to the world's cars as well as their noxious gas-producing devices.

As for the Sontarans themselves, Raynor has made an excellent job of capturing their established characters, and one imagines that their creator, the late Robert Holmes, would heartily approve. She has obviously done her homework on the earlier Sontaran stories, and all the traditional trappings associated with the creatures are present and correct: their bellicose nature, their code of honour, their short stature (which seemed to get overlooked in their previous outing, 'The Two Doctors' (1985)), their probic vent vulnerability, their teleport capability, their jealousy of the Time Lords, even their disdain for the weakness of the human female thorax – a nice nod to a classic line used in both 'The Time Warrior' and 'The Sontaran Experiment' (1975), although it does admittedly seem a little shoehorned in here. Better still, Raynor has also clearly understood that Holmes intended the Sontarans to serve as a satirical embodiment of the more absurd, jingoistic aspects of the military mindset, and thus to be source of mirth as much as fear. This comes across here in their obvious embodiment of 'small man syndrome', their swaggering pomposity and some amusing lines of dialogue, such as where General Staal bemoans the fact that they were not allowed to take part in the Time War. Their haka-like war chant of 'Sontar-ha!' is also very much in keeping with this, and a brilliant innovation by Raynor.

The on-screen realisation of the Sontarans, on the other hand, leaves a lot to be desired, in two respects. First, while Christopher Ryan gives a superb performance as General Staal, delivering his lines with a menacing rasp very much akin to that adopted by the original Sontaran actor, the late Kevin Lindsay, Dan Starkey as Commander Skorr – the only other Sontaran with dialogue in this episode – bizarrely speaks in a completely ordinary, uninflected voice. This is almost as jarring as if a Dalek suddenly adopted a Cockney accent, and while it would be wrong to blame this on Starkey himself, as he must presumably have been directed to speak in that way, or at least not told otherwise, it is badly misjudged. Secondly, and more regrettably still, while the prosthetic head-masks created for Ryan and Starkey are absolutely superb, and very much in keeping with the original Sontaran look, as are their helmets, the new suits of armour designed for the creatures are, frankly, awful. The idea of a body suit bearing a musculature pattern supposedly reflecting that of the wearer is terribly dated, recalling 1980s creations such as the Bat-costume from the movie version of *Batman* (1989), which looked pretty cheesy even then; and the huge shoulder-pads reinforce that impression. The raised collar section also has the unfortunate effect, particularly in low-angle shots, of making it look as if the unmasked Sontaran is peering over the edge, rather in the manner of the Second World War-era graffiti character Chad (asking 'Wot, no Rutans?' perhaps). The new, blue-toned colour scheme is also far less striking and appropriate than the original silver and black. It seems that this may have been chosen in order to avoid the Sontarans appearing too similar to the Judoon, but that is surely turning the problem on its head: the issue is more that the Judoon were made to look too similar to the Sontarans, as indeed many fans commented when they were first seen in 'Smith and Jones'. What makes this even more frustrating is that Peter McKinstry's initial concept art for the new Sontarans, as published on the official *Doctor Who* website, suggests that the original intention was to remain far more faithful to the iconic costumes designed for 'The Time Warrior' by James Acheson - who went on to become a multiple Oscar winner for his feature film work - in which case, as with the new-era Cybermen, this is another unfortunate example of the ideas presented in the concept art being better than those that ended up on screen.

On the plus side, the CGI-created Sontaran mother-ship, and the individual spherical scout ships that fly away from it, are absolutely fantastic, and a brilliant updating of the original 'golf ball' design.

Also updated for this story is the depiction of UNIT, and very effectively so. The *Torchwood* episode 'Fragments' gave the first real indication that the UNIT of this modern era is quite different from the decidedly cosy outfit seen in the stories of the 1970s, having apparently adopted more ruthlessly efficient, uncompromising methods in response to harsher global circumstances; and 'The Sontaran Stratagem' reinforces that impression. As the Doctor himself reflects, 'It was all a bit more home-spun back then.' On the other hand, it could be argued that this is simply a reversion to the way UNIT was first portrayed in 'The Invasion', as a realistic military organisation rather than, as it essentially became during the following decade, a surrogate family for the Doctor. Certainly new commanding officer Colonel Mace, very well played by Rupert Holliday Evans, is a lot closer to the original, suavely-professional, no-nonsense conception of his predecessor Brigadier Lethbridge-Stewart than to the mellower, arguably less credible character he later became; and the field-base-in-a-lorry setup seen here is very reminiscent of the field-base-in-an-aircraft one featured in 'The Invasion'. It is pleasing to note too that the traditional UNIT radio call-sign format - 'Greyhound 16 to Trap 1' and so on - has been retained; and, although they now wear red berets and black uniforms rather than green combat fatigues, the sight of UNIT troops running into action with their machine guns at the ready, or racing to the scene of an incident in their jeeps (or should that be Land Rovers?), will certainly have a warmly nostalgic feel for anyone who followed the Doctor's adventures during the 1970s.

The only slight disappointment in this regard is the change in what the UNIT acronym actually stands for - from United Nations Intelligence Taskforce to UNified Intelligence Taskforce. Having said that, although Russell T Davies's publicly stated reasons for it don't really hold water, this revision does make a certain amount of sense. Back in 1968, when UNIT was first introduced, the United Nations was regarded by most members of the British public in a generally positive light, as an idealistic organisation acting in the best interests of humanity as a whole, above petty national concerns. Whenever, over the course of the following years, UNIT was depicted as being at odds with the British establishment or regular Army - in stories such as 'Spearhead from Space' (1970) and 'The Claws of Axos' (1971) - it was always

UNIT that was shown to have the moral high ground, while the national authorities were portrayed as courting disaster through the pursuit of parochial interests. Since that time, though, a succession of real-world events have arguably led to the United Nations' reputation becoming distinctly tarnished, so that most members of the British public now hold a decidedly more cynical opinion of it. With that in mind, it is perhaps better for UNIT – still intended to be seen as an essentially heroic force, working to the same ends as the Doctor albeit by different means – to be depicted as an independent body rather than one directly affiliated to the United Nations, although Martha does tell the Doctor at one point, 'We've got massive funding from the United Nations', suggesting that there are still close ties there. (Curiously, she also winks at the Doctor at this point, for no apparent reason …)

Another notable shift since the days of classic-era *Doctor Who* comes in the Doctor's own relationship with UNIT. Whereas in his third incarnation he was willing to serve as their scientific adviser – even, for a while, after his exile to Earth by the Time Lords had been lifted and he was free to resume his travels around the cosmos – now he objects to Colonel Mace saluting him and seems embarrassed when it is revealed that he was once 'on staff'. This is not simply because, even back then, he would have insisted that he was an associate rather than an employee, but because he has since developed an aversion to working alongside people who routinely carry guns. Like his wielding of a water pistol in 'The Fires of Pompeii', this raises the issue of his – seemingly ambivalent – attitude toward weapons. Clearly he is squeamish about the deployment of real guns, even by people he is associating with let alone in his own hands, but he seems to have no such qualms when it comes to taking other, usually-innocuous items, and *using* them as weapons – such as where, in this episode, he picks up a squash racket and skilfully hits a ball so that it bounces off a surface and strikes General Staal on the probic vent, incapacitating him. Of course, unlike a gun, this is not a weapon with a lethal capability, but his reservations about UNIT have certainly not stopped him from getting Martha a job with them, as she herself points out, and as Donna is surprised to see, asking him, 'Was that what you did to her: turned her into a soldier?' Does his newfound distaste for UNIT's guns make him more peaceable, or simply more hypocritical? Further attention will be focused on this issue as the series progresses.

One of the most interesting innovations in 'The Sontaran Stratagem' lies in the way that Martha and Donna are used in the narrative. In classic-era *Doctor Who*, it was very often the case that the Doctor and his companion(s) would get split up as a story unfolded, each then acting as the focus of a separate plot strand. In his revived version of the show, by contrast, Russell T Davies initially eschewed this rather clichéd approach, feeling that the audience ought to see the Doctor and his companion enjoying their adventures together, side by side. Here in Series Four, though, the Doctor is reunited with Martha after a pre-planned separation far more extreme than any ever witnessed in classic-era *Doctor Who*. This has seen her being completely absent from the show for three whole episodes and appearing instead in three episodes of the *Torchwood* spin-off. What's more, mid-way through 'The Sontaran Stratagem', Donna too parts company with the Doctor, not because circumstances have forced them to separate but simply because she has decided to pop back to Chiswick to visit her family. So unexpected is this, and so out of keeping with the way the Doctor-companion pairing has been presented before in new-era *Doctor Who*, that it is hardly surprising that the Doctor at first mistakes her intentions and thinks that she is leaving him for good - a misunderstanding set up mainly for comic effect, although sadly the humour falls rather flat here.

This leads on to a remarkable, and surprisingly moving, sequence in which Donna walks down the road toward her family home and reflects on the incredible contrast between the excitement and danger of the life she leads with the Doctor - as illustrated by a number of flashback clips - and the familiarity and mundanity of the one she left behind. The subsequent scene where she sits in the kitchen quietly telling the delighted Wilf about her travels, without revealing anything to Sylvia, who flits around in the background showing her usual lack of sensitivity toward her daughter, cleverly builds on this, reinforcing the characterisation of all three; and it is already evident that this family grouping is going to work far more effectively in the show than the Joneses did the previous year. Again, classic-era *Doctor Who* never did anything remotely like this, and it serves both as a telling reminder of the importance of the domestic context to the Doctor's adventures post-2005, and as a good indication that, even though the show is now arguably becoming a little formulaic - the routine inclusion of a two-part story featuring a classic-era monster at episodes four and five in each series being just one example of this - Davies and his team are still willing to try inventive new approaches from time to time.

As for Martha, her absence from the TARDIS has given her time to get over her crush on the Doctor, to the extent that she has even got engaged - to Tom Milligan, the paediatrician she first met in very different circumstances in 'Last of the Time Lords', who is now away working in Africa. 'Yes, I know,' she jokes to Donna, 'I've got a doctor who disappears off to distant places. Tell me about it.' She has also completed her training and become a full doctor herself, the qualification having been rushed through by UNIT in light of her experience in the field. The net result is that, as first seen in her three *Torchwood* episodes, she now comes across as a more mature and self-assured character than in Series Three. This means amongst other things that, confounding the Doctor's expectations, she and Donna form an amicable relationship right from the outset - making for a nice contrast to the initial animosity seen between Sarah Jane and Rose in 'School Reunion'. Freema Agyeman as always gives a superb, effortlessly charismatic performance in the part, making the viewer realise just how much her presence has been missed; and she even gets to play a dual role here as, in some memorably creepy sequences, the Sontarans create a clone of Martha to do their bidding; another excellent expansion by Raynor on part of the creatures' established backstory, their status as a clone race having not really been exploited in any of their previous stories.

One final way in which 'The Sontaran Stratagem' recalls classic-era *Doctor Who* is that, being the first half of one those now-expected two-parters, it ends on a cliffhanger - and a superb one at that, as the ATMOS devices start pumping out their noxious fumes from cars all over the world and Wilf is trapped inside his family's own vehicle and seemingly doomed to be suffocated, while far above on board their mother-ship the Sontarans exult in their 'Sontar-ha!' chant. Fantastic stuff!

4.05 - THE POISON SKY

Writer: Helen Raynor
Director: Douglas Mackinnon

DEBUT TRANSMISSION DETAILS

BBC One
Date: 3 May 2008. Scheduled time: 6.20 pm. Actual time: 6.19 pm.

BBC Three
Date: 4 May 2008. Scheduled time: 8.00 pm. Actual time: 8.01 pm.

Duration: 44' 40"

ADDITIONAL CREDITED CAST

Ryan Sampson (Luke Rattigan), Rupert Holliday Evans (Colonel Mace), Christopher Ryan (General Staal), Dan Starkey (Commander Skorr), Clive Standen (Private Harris), Wesley Theobald (Private Gray), Christian Cooke (Ross Jenkins), Meryl Fernandes (Female Student), Leeshon Alexander (Male Student), Bridget Hodgson (Captain Price[41]), Kirsty Wark (Herself), Lachele Carl[42] (US Newsreader)

Sontarans created by: Robert Holmes

PLOT

The Sontarans have persuaded Rattigan to help them with an offer to take him and his students to an alien world where he can found a new Earth. When the students find out about this, however, they refuse to participate, and General Staal tells Rattigan that the offer was a lie in any case. The Doctor revives the real Martha, causing the clone to expire, but not before she has revealed the composition of the Sontarans' gas. The Doctor realises that it is 'clone feed', which the Sontarans intend to use to turn the Earth into a hatchery to create billions more of their kind, in furtherance of their centuries-long war against the Rutans. The Doctor, Donna and Martha then travel via the Sontarans' teleport equipment from the ATMOS factory to the Rattigan Academy. There the Doctor assembles an atmospheric converter device and uses this to ignite the Sontarans' gas, causing it to burn away from the air all around the world. He teleports up to the Sontarans' mother-ship with the atmospheric converter, threatening to use it to destroy them unless they leave the Earth. The Sontarans, who are now intending to ravage the planet, are

[41] First name given in dialogue as 'Marion'.
[42] Not credited in *Radio Times*.

unmoved, being unafraid of death. Rattigan uses the teleport equipment to swap places with the Doctor, then activates the atmospheric converter, blowing up the Sontarans and sacrificing his own life in the process. The Doctor, Donna and Martha return to the TARDIS, which suddenly dematerialises, seemingly of its own accord.

QUOTE, UNQUOTE

- **Doctor:** 'Let me talk to the Sontarans.'
  Colonel Mace: 'You're not authorised to speak on behalf of the Earth.'
  Doctor: 'I've got that authority. I earned that a long time ago.'
- **General Staal:** 'Doctor, you impugn my honour!'
  Doctor: 'Yeah ... I'm really glad you didn't say "belittle", because then I'd have a field day.'
- **General Staal:** 'Hah! The planet it going nuclear. I admire them. The bravery of idiots is bravery nonetheless.'
- **Commander Skorr:** 'This is too easy! They're running like slimebait from a speelfox!'

CONTINUITY POINTS

- Some of the TV news reports featured in the episode feature the same American newscaster as seen in a number of previous episodes, played by Lachele Carl.
- The Sontarans' gas is said to be harmful, but not lethal until it reaches 80% density.
- The Doctor says that nuclear missiles won't even scratch the surface of the Sontaran mother-ship. Captain Mace nevertheless prepares to launch a nuclear strike, co-ordinating a 'worldwide nuclear grid' comprising North America, United Kingdom, France, India, Pakistan, China and North Korea. This indicates a far greater degree of worldwide military co-operation in the *Doctor Who* universe than in ours. The inclusion of 'North America' in the list may also mean that in the *Doctor Who* universe the USA and Canada are a single country, or at least work together in military matters.
- The Doctor contacts the Sontaran mother-ship – or 'command ship', as he terms it – under 'Jurisdiction 2 of the Intergalactic Rules of Engagement'. This is the first time that such rules have ever been mentioned in the show.
- The Doctor refers to the war between the Sontarans and their perennial enemies the Rutans, and says, 'It's been raging far out in the stars for 50,000 years.'
- The new planet that the Sontarans have promised to take Rattigan and his students to is referred to as 'Castor 36 ... a new world, far out beyond Alpha Geminorum', although since General Staal later admits that they have lied to him, it is uncertain whether or not any such planet actually exists.
- In a shot of the New York skyline, seen in a montage of gas-shrouded cityscapes in a News 24 report, the name 'Butler Institute' can be glimpsed on the side of one of the skyscrapers. The Butler Institute was a New York-based

organisation featured in Andrew Cartmel's *Doctor Who* novel *Warhead: Cat's Cradle* (Virgin Publishing, 1992) and depicted on the front cover of that book.

- The Doctor says at one point, 'At times like this, I could do with the Brigadier.' This is a reference to the popular classic-era *Doctor Who* character Brigadier Alistair Lethbridge-Stewart. Colonel Mace notes, 'Sir Alistair is a fine man, if not the best. Unfortunately he's stranded in Peru.' The reference to the character as 'Sir Alistair' indicates that he has been knighted by the Queen since last seen on screen in 'Battlefield' (1989). This was first established in the audio CD spin-off series *UNIT*, released by Big Finish in 2004 and 2005. It is unknown why Lethbridge-Stewart happens to be in Peru at this time.
- The beams fired by the *Valiant* at the ATMOS factory look very similar to those fired by Torchwood One at the Sycorax spaceship in 'The Christmas Invasion', later revealed in 'Army of Ghosts' to have come from a captured weapon from a downed Jathaa Sun Glider. This similarity was specified in the script, and suggests that UNIT may have acquired the weapon from Torchwood One after the latter's destruction in 'Doomsday'.
- The Doctor tells the Sontarans that he has a remote control for the TARDIS, but later admits that this was a lie. The fact that the sixth Doctor did not have a TARDIS remote control, while the second Doctor did, featured as a plot point in the previous Sontaran story, 'The Two Doctors' (1985). In the immediately preceding story, 'The Mark of the Rani' (1985), another Time Lord, the Rani, also had a 'Stattenheim remote control' for her TARDIS, and was similarly envied it by the sixth Doctor.
- Before teleporting up to the Sontaran mother-ship, the Doctor states that he has 'recalibrated [the atmospheric converter] for Sontaran air'. This indicates that the atmosphere on board the ship is different in composition from that on Earth, although it seems that humans have no difficulty breathing the former, and Sontarans have no difficulty breathing the latter.
- Sylvia mentions her friend Suzette, as seen in 'Partners in Crime'.

PRODUCTION NOTES

- Made with 'The Sontaran Stratagem' as part of Block 4 of production.
- Freema Agyeman's name is included in the opening titles of this episode
- Some extra studio recording for this episode took place on 22 November 2007 at BBC Broadcasting House in Cardiff.
- The cartoon clip watched by the Doctor on the screen in the UNIT field base was taken from the environmentally-conscious CBeebies show *Tommy Zoom*.
- As originally scripted, the scene where Donna incapacitates a Sontaran by striking it on the probic vent was to have had her using a shoe rather than a mallet from the TARDIS, but this was changed owing to the fact that by this point in the series Donna is wearing trainers.
- The fleeting clip of Rose Tyler displayed on the TARDIS monitor screen was a late addition to the episode, inserted because her brief appearance in 'Partners in Crime' had proved so popular.

OOPS!

- Approximately 28 minutes into the episode, the camera crew can be clearly seen reflected in the glass window of door behind the Doctor and the clone Martha.
- As in 'The Sontaran Stratagem', there are a number of shot-continuity errors in the episode. By far the most noticeable of these come in the scene where the Doctor is threatening to blow up the Sontaran ship using the atmospheric converter: in some shots the Sontarans are aiming their weapons at the Doctor and preparing to fire, while in others they are chanting 'Sontar-ha!' and pounding their fists into their opposite palms.

PRESS REACTION

- 'This is a far stronger two-parter than last year's Dalek-starring equivalent, even if the Sontarans' plan is absurdly convoluted, involving GPS systems, gas, a boy genius and … well, you get the idea. Indeed, said boy genius is, in the final analysis, only here to function as a handy *deus ex machina* when the Doctor decides to become a suicide bomber. (It is, on the surface, noble of him to at least give the Sontarans a choice - but surely he knew that they'd never give in? We already know that they welcome death.) There are other problems, too, and it's here that *Who* seems to be becoming alarmingly formulaic: we have another alien invasion of Earth using consumer devices (hello earpods and Cybermen, hello mobile phones/Archangel network and the Master), the Doctor jury-rigs some contraption to save the day … On it goes. Nevertheless, the two episodes manage to remain terrifically entertaining.' Jes Bickham, *DeathRay* Issue 14, July 2008.
- '"The Poison Sky" is big on action and wit, and that's all to the good. *Doctor Who* can, throughout the course of a season, be all things to all people. If anything, there's so much going on that every now and then, it threatens to overbalance the entire enterprise. Thankfully, Helen Raynor's script manages to keep everything together, and it's no mean feat to juggle everything the story requires. If anything, the Sontarans don't come off all that well - Christopher Ryan, brilliant as General Staal, is reduced to stomping around the bridge of his spaceship. He's very arch, fantastically so, but he could do with something a bit meatier to get his teeth into. Things improve when he receives visits from *uber*-nerd Rattigan, and the Doctor phones him for a screen-to-screen face off, but I wanted more of Tennant and Ryan going toe to toe in person a bit more. And as for the Sontarans' supposed military might - well, as soon as UNIT get the ability to fire their guns again, the bad guys go down a little too easily. A disappointing fate for an entertaining monster While the script is strong, the most disappointing aspect of the "The Poison Sky" is the direction. Douglas Mackinnon handles interplay between the actors well, bringing out the wit of Raynor's script, but things turn decidedly limp when we get to marching Sontarans and gun battles. The Sontarans are supposed to be a military force to be reckoned with, but they stomp around a bit half-heartedly when the battle for the factory kicks off. One thing that *Doctor Who* has done well is monster choreography, but in these sequences it doesn't come

off as well as in previous episodes. Shame, as they look fantastic, but the camera just can't seem to keep with them.' Mark Wright, *The Stage* website, 6 May 2008.

ANALYSIS

One of the great things about the cliffhanger to 'The Sontaran Stratagem' and its resolution in 'The Poison Sky' is that the former will surely have had many viewers asking 'Why don't they just break the car window to get Wilf out?' and, gratifyingly, the latter shows Sylvia doing just that. The immediate danger is thus averted by way of a plausible practical solution rather than, as is so often the case, by the Doctor using the sonic screwdriver (which was shown in 'Army of Ghosts' to be capable of shattering glass) or pulling some other fantastical rabbit out of the hat. This is an approach followed, to excellent effect, throughout most of the rest of the episode, such as when Colonel Mace has his troops issued with more advanced guns with steel-cased bullets to overcome the Sontarans' jamming signal and when he calls in the UNIT carrier ship *Valiant* to clear the gas from the air around the ATMOS factory with its engines, demonstrating that the forces of Earth are not so easily defeated as the Sontarans - and indeed the Doctor himself - have suggested. When, in the closing stages, writer Helen Raynor reverts to having the Doctor assemble an improbable *deus ex machina* in the form of the atmospheric converter, this is far less satisfactory, and raises lots of awkward questions such as how the fire that consumes the Sontarans' gas can possibly spread around the whole world as quickly as it appears to, why it doesn't consume all the oxygen in the atmosphere in the process, what happens to the gas at ground level, why the ATMOS devices don't continue producing more gas (General Staal having just ordered that they be turned up to maximum) and why there aren't lots of fried birds seen falling from the sky - although it is perhaps just about possible to put all this down to 'mysterious features of alien technology', and it certainly holds together better than the terrible resolution to the same writer's Series Three story 'The Daleks in Manhattan'/'Evolution of the Daleks'.

The 'misguided teenage genius' is something of a stock character in genre TV shows, but one that *Doctor Who* has not really featured before, the closest precedent probably being Adam Mitchell from 'Dalek' and 'The Long Game', who failed to make the grade as one of the Doctor's companions. Luke Rattigan falls squarely into this mould, however, and provides a worthwhile extra dimension to the story, aided by an excellent performance from actor Ryan Sampson. His confrontations with the Doctor and his naïve liaisons with his Sontaran 'allies' aboard their mother-ship are particularly effective, while his scheme to found an 'Earth.2' on a new world with a hand-picked group of elite survivors, who are initially ignorant of his true intentions and rebel when they discover them, adds to the 'old school' feel of the story by strongly recalling a key plot element of the third Doctor adventure 'Invasion of the Dinosaurs' (1974). Rattigan's final self-sacrifice is perhaps a little predictable but nevertheless quite fitting, and serves to extricate the Doctor from a situation where - as in 'Evolution of the Daleks' - he has arguably revealed a surprising suicidal tendency by wilfully placing himself in a position where his enemies seem bound to kill him.

This episode is another good one for Donna. Particularly exciting are the scenes where – having failed to catch a blink-and-you'll-miss-it shot of Rose calling the Doctor's name on the TARDIS monitor screen, further whetting the viewer's appetite for events to come – she finds herself alone on board the Sontaran mother-ship, trying to follow the Doctor's phone-relayed instructions. Her terrified reactions here seem absolutely true to life, and far more convincing than the clichéd 'fearless in the face of danger' behaviour typically demonstrated by most of the Doctor's past companions. This is probably the closest that Donna has yet come to showing the full 'down-to-earth everywoman' potential that Russell T Davies and his team saw in her. On the other hand, however, it seems rather out of character for her to agree to retreat to the TARDIS in the first place, leaving the Doctor to get on with the action, and it could be argued that her entire role in the plot of this episode is really just padding. The clear implication is that the Doctor has deliberately contrived to have her teleported to the Sontaran mother-ship in the TARDIS, and yet once she is there, the only thing he wants her to do is to reactivate the teleport equipment – which General Staal has 'deadlocked' after sending his troops to the ATMOS factory, although how the Doctor could have anticipated that is unclear – so that he can use it to get to the Rattigan Academy, which he reached simply by car in the previous episode.

Martha, meanwhile, spends most of the episode unconscious, although Freema Agyeman still gets plenty to do, playing her Sontaran-created clone. The 'evil double' is another stock sci-fi character, and one that was used several times in classic-era *Doctor Who*, but it always seems to work well, and this is no exception. Kudos to David Tennant, too, for skilfully conveying through his performance that the Doctor realises straight away that the clone is not the real Martha, long before he actually reveals how he spotted this through slight imperfections and – ingeniously, something that the viewer could not have realised – the fact that the clone smells! Another unusual and welcome touch is that Martha actually gets to have a heartfelt conversation with the clone before it expires, evoking a degree of sympathy for it that is quite unexpected.

The depiction of the Sontarans is again only partly successful in this episode. Their plan, once it is revealed, seems quite out of character for them, relying on subterfuge and deception rather than a direct approach like bombarding the planet with missiles containing their 'clone feed'. Raynor sort of makes this work, though, by having the Doctor draw attention to it within the narrative itself, in the course of taunting General Staal. It also serves as another effective homage to 'The Invasion' (1968), in which the Cybermen attempted to take over the Earth by stealth using a hypnotic signal transmitted via hidden circuits in transistor radios and the like – that story's equivalent of the ATMOS devices – and with the aid of a duped human electronics tycoon who ultimately turned on them and destroyed them. Less easy to accept is the incredible ease with which the Sontarans are felled by the UNIT soldiers' bullets once the jamming signal is circumvented. It seems that their new body-armour not only looks really naff but is largely ineffective as well. Isn't their probic vent supposed to be their only weak point? That aside, though, the battle sequences are pretty spectacular, depicting the Sontarans going into action in really large numbers for the first time ever in the show, and it was an excellent idea to involve the *Valiant* here. The destruction of the Sontarans' mother-ship in space – paralleling the destruction of the Cybermen's mother-ship at the end of 'The Invasion' – is also stunningly realised. Christopher Ryan's performance as General

Staal continues to impress, but Dan Starkey's as Commander Skorr is again let down by his incongruously ordinary vocal tones, despite the fact that he is actually given the more deliciously memorable dialogue of the two here. A couple of Sontaran minions also get lines to deliver during the course of the episode, and sadly they too talk more like bank clerks from Basingstoke than alien warriors from the planet Sontar.

Now that UNIT has been firmly re-established as a part of modern-day *Doctor Who*, it seems unlikely that this is the last that will be seen of the organisation. Colonel Mace certainly has the potential to become a popular returning character – a true successor to Brigadier Lethbridge-Stewart, who pleasingly gets a quick mention here – as does Captain Price. Whether or not they will fit in with the plans of new showrunner Steven Moffat, however, remains to be seen. The near-present-day-Earth stories might well benefit from a bit of a shake-up, as it is hard to escape the feeling that certain now-customary elements such as the globe-spanning threats and the ersatz TV news reports delivered in some cases by real-life BBC newscasters making cameo appearances – although Kirsty Wark, who fulfils this role in 'The Poison Sky', isn't really a newscaster at all but a senior presenter – are by this point starting to become a little over-familiar and repetitive.

As in 'The Sontaran Stratagem', one aspect of 'The Poison Sky' that doesn't work too well is its occasional touches of humour. These again tend to fall rather flat – the Doctor's joke about not telling Captain Jack about the clone, for instance, works only if one happens to know that 'clone' is a description sometimes applied to a particular stereotype of gay men – and the incident where the Doctor, having been persuaded to don a gasmask, asks Colonel Mace 'Are you my mummy?', referencing the oft-quoted line repeatedly spoken by the gasmask-wearing child in 'The Empty Child'/'The Doctor Dances', is badly misjudged, being far too much of a knowing wink to the audience.

All in all, though, 'The Sontaran Stratagem'/'The Poison Sky', while by no means the best of the show's two-parters, is an entertaining story with some strong central ideas, good characterisation and impressive action set-pieces, and certainly much better than Raynor's Series Three contribution. It ends on another excellent cliffhanger, too, as the TARDIS dematerialises apparently of its own volition, whisking a protesting Martha away from Earth along with the Doctor and Donna, heading toward an adventure that, judging from the 'Next Time ...' trailer, holds out the fascinating prospect of introducing the Doctor's previously-unseen daughter ...

4.06 - THE DOCTOR'S DAUGHTER

Writer: Stephen Greenhorn
Director: Alice Troughton

DEBUT TRANSMISSION DETAILS

BBC One
Date: 10 May 2008. Scheduled time: 6.45 pm. Actual time: 6.44 pm.

BBC Three
Date: 11 May 2008. Scheduled time: 8.00 pm. Actual time: 8.01 pm.

Duration: 45' 12"

ADDITIONAL CREDITED CAST

Georgia Moffett (Jenny), Nigel Terry (Cobb), Joe Dempsie (Cline), Paul Kasey (Hath Peck), Ruari Mears (Hath Gable), Akin Gazi (Carter), Olalekan Lawal Jn (Soldier)

PLOT

The TARDIS deposits the Doctor, Donna and Martha in a colony on the planet Messaline, where a generations-long war is being waged between human and Hath factions. A skin sample is forcibly taken from the Doctor's hand by the human soldiers and processed in one of the progenation machines that both sides use to keep up their numbers. This produces a young woman who is to all intents and purposes the Doctor's daughter, named by Donna as Jenny. Martha is befriended by the Hath when, having been kidnapped by them, she resets the dislocated shoulder of one of their race. The Doctor, Donna and Jenny are meanwhile consigned to a prison cell by the humans' leader, General Cobb, but manage to escape. The warring sides are both seeking an artefact known as the Source, and the Doctor has inadvertently revealed to them how to reach it. Donna deduces from a series of number-plaques on the colony walls that the whole war has actually lasted only seven days. The true history of the conflict - which arose from a power vacuum after the original leader of the joint mission was killed - has become shrouded in myth because of the way that information has passed from one short-lived generation to the next. All sides converge on the Source, which the Doctor identifies as a terraforming device intended to make the planet habitable for the colony. He smashes its central globe on the ground, releasing the terraforming gas to begin its work. The human and Hath sides both lay down their weapons - apart from Cobb, who apparently kills Jenny when she steps into the path of a bullet aimed at the Doctor. However, after the Doctor, Donna and Martha have left in the TARDIS to take Martha home, Jenny revives and escapes from Messaline in a shuttle craft, heading off for a life of adventure.

QUOTE, UNQUOTE

- **Donna:** 'I thought you wanted to go home?'
  Martha: 'I know, but all the same. It's that feeling you get.'
  Donna: 'Like you've swallowed a hamster.'
- **Jenny:** 'Hello Dad!'
- **Donna:** 'Not what you'd call a natural parent, are you?'
  Doctor: 'They stole a tissue sample at gunpoint and processed it. It's not what I call natural parenting.'
  Donna: 'Rubbish. My friend Nerys fathered twins using a turkey baster. It don't bother her.'
  Doctor: 'You can't extrapolate a relationship from a biological accident.'
  Donna: 'Er, Child Support Agency can.'

CONTINUITY POINTS

- Jenny is not a clone of the Doctor but is created through a process of 'progenation'. The Doctor describes this as follows: 'Reproduction from a single organism. It means one parent is biological mother *and* father. You take a sample of diploid cells, split them into haploids, then recombine them in a different arrangement, and grow. Very quickly, apparently.' The people 'born' through this process emerge from the progenation machines in adult form, but not all at the same apparent age: some of the soldiers look older than others, with General Cobb the oldest of all. The machines were originally intended to produce colonists, but were then reconfigured to turn out soldiers, pre-programmed with all the memories and skills needed for the war. When Cline asks Jenny if she is ready to fight, she says, 'Instant mental download of all strategic and military protocols, sir. Generation 5000 soldier primed and in peak physical health.'
- The Doctor describes his newly-created daughter as a 'generated anomaly', and it is this that leads Donna to suggest that she be named 'Jenny'.
- It is unclear how many generations of human soldiers have lived and died in the seven days since the war began. Although Jenny refers to herself as a 'Generation 5000 soldier', this does not necessarily mean that there have been 5000 generations; it seems more likely to be a reference to the type of soldier she is. In one early scene, a loudspeaker announcement is heard reporting a tally of the deceased from various different generations, which are referred to by number. This appears to suggest that there have been about 680 generations, but different interpretations are possible. Later on, the Doctor comments, 'They could have 20 generations in a day,' but again this is not to say that there have actually been that number.
- Donna is aware that the Doctor has two hearts. She must have learned this in some unscreened adventure, as she has never been told it in any televised episode.
- The date is 24 July 6012 in the New Byzantine Calendar, and the spaceship

carrying the humans and Hath arrived on Messaline around seven days earlier. It is unclear how this relates to our current dating system.

- Donna says that she once spent six months temping in Hounslow Library, during which time she mastered the Dewey Decimal system (a library classification system developed in 1876) in two days flat; she is good with numbers.
- The TARDIS has travelled to Messaline of its own accord because of the presence of the Doctor's daughter there, but has arrived too early, hence creating a temporal paradox, as Jenny would not have been born but for the Doctor's visit to the planet.

PRODUCTION NOTES

- Made with 'Midnight' as part of Block 6 of production.
- Freema Agyeman's name is included in the opening titles of this episode
- The Messaline planet exteriors were shot on 12 December 2007 at Kenfig Hill Opencast Mine in Bridgend. The Marble Room of the City Hall, Cardiff, was transformed into the Hath encampment the following day; four hours' recording time was lost due to a public demonstration taking place about the closure of some local primary schools. Newbridge Memo in Newbridge, Gwent, was the theatre used for the human encampment, where recording took place on 14, 17, 18 and 19 December. The Dupont Building on Mamhilad Park Industrial Estate in Pontypool, a regular venue for *Doctor Who* location work, was where the spaceship corridor sequences were taped, on 19 and 20 December. The Source chamber scenes were shot at night on 21 December at Plantasia Botanic Gardens in Swansea, a location suggested by producer Phil Collinson to afford a contrast to the grim industrial settings usually used for spaceship interiors. Following a Christmas break, the underground tunnel scenes were recorded at Rhondda Heritage Park on 7 January 2008. The crew then returned to Mamhilad Park Industrial Estate on 8 and 9 January to tape the action sequence where Jenny acrobatically negotiates a corridor criss-crossed by laser beams. Barry Shooting Range in Barry Island, a disused railway tunnel previously featured as a location on the *Torchwood* episode 'Ghost Machine', was used for the TARDIS's arrival point, recording taking place there on 10 and 11 January. The scene where the Doctor drops Martha home was shot outside a house in Mark Street, Cardiff, on 18 January. The final location work for the episode consisted of some pick-up shots for the Source chamber scenes, recorded this time in the Conservatory at Roath Park, Cardiff, also on 18 January.
- Studio scenes for the episode were taped at Upper Boat on 24 January 2008.
- The Hath were given dialogue in the script, and this was read out loud while the scenes were being recorded so that Freema Agyeman would know what she was supposed to be reacting to as Martha. However, it was always planned that the only thing the viewer would hear on the soundtrack would be the gurgling bubbles-through-liquid noise of the creatures' alien language; this was an element that Russell T Davies added to the script, partly because he thought it would be fun for children to mimic with drinks cartons. The intended implication was that Martha can guess what was being said from the

context, increasingly aided by the TARDIS's translation circuits. Presumably for the same reason, the Hath seem to have no difficulty understanding Martha.

- Writer Stephen Greenhorn gave the Hath names taken from classic Hollywood film stars: Martha is heard to call one of them 'Peck' (after Gregory Peck) in the scene where it sacrifices itself to save her life after she falls into a pit of quicksand; and both 'Hath Peck' and 'Hath Gable' (after Clark Gable) are named in the closing credits.
- Georgia Moffett, who plays Jenny, is the daughter of fifth Doctor actor Peter Davison and his first wife Sandra Dickinson. She auditioned unsuccessfully for the part of Rose Tyler in 2004 and for that of Robina Redmond in the subsequent Series Four episode 'The Unicorn and the Wasp'; in the latter case, the show's production team felt that she would be much better suited to the more significant role of Jenny and asked her if she could wait until they were ready to cast 'The Doctor's Daughter'. Producer Phil Collinson had also recently been reminded of her potential when he and Freema Agyeman bumped into her and her father at an awards ceremony in Monte Carlo. Moffett had previously appeared, in the different role of Tanya Webster, alongside Davison's Doctor in the audio CD drama 'Red Dawn' (Big Finish, 2000).
- Russell T Davies's 'tone word' for this episode was 'subterranean'. The main elements he gave writer Stephen Greenhorn to incorporate were the Doctor's daughter – always intended to be an artificially-created one rather than a long-lost family member – the subterranean war, Martha and the Hath. After the initial draft script was written, Davies also came up with the idea that the whole war should be revealed to have lasted only seven days.
- It was originally intended that Jenny would die after being shot by Cobb. It was at Steven Moffat's urging that Russell T Davies decided to change this and have her survive.

OOPS!

- At the beginning of the episode, when the Doctor rushes over from the TARDIS console to the door, he is not wearing his coat. In the next shot, however, when he steps outside, it has mysteriously appeared.
- About 11 minutes into the episode, a crate visible behind Jenny has a UNIT logo on it. This was a prop reused from the preceding story, and the logo was left on inadvertently.
- In the scene toward the end of the story where the Doctor sets the TARDIS controls to dematerialise, there is a studio light prominently visible on the left hand side of the picture.

PRESS REACTION

- '[The] title is misleading and manipulative, as however much the script and Donna insist that Jenny's the Doctor's daughter, she isn't in any meaningful sense. The Doctor's family is too important a concept to be tossed around for the sake of some cheap publicity and a good closing line to the teaser scene.'

Anthony Brown, *TV Zone* Issue 229, June 2008.

- '"I never would!" consternates the Doctor. "Make the foundation of this society a man who never would!" Now, it's fair enough that he wouldn't shoot a man in the face, but the Doctor deliberately setting himself up as the model for future society is a rare sight. You imagine it *could* happen, what with all the revolutions he's initiated, but he shouldn't be encouraging canonisation, should he? He's not Lenin.' Thom Hutchinson and Matt Bielby, *DeathRay* Issue 15, September 2008.

ANALYSIS

At one point back in the 1980s, *Doctor Who*'s then producer John Nathan-Turner included the fake title 'The Doctor's Wife' in a schedule of forthcoming stories written on his office whiteboard, in the hope of catching out any visiting fan who might then try to spread some inside information. This led to a false rumour spreading through the show's fandom that such a story was indeed in the offing. No doubt Russell T Davies, as a long time fan himself, would have been aware of that rumour, and it is tempting to think that this is what inspired the title of 'The Doctor's Daughter'.[43] Whatever its derivation, it is safe to say that this is one of the most tantalising titles ever to be attached to a *Doctor Who* episode. It seems to hold out the promise of some amazing disclosures in store about the Doctor's past, and inevitably provokes intense speculation in the viewer's mind as to what these might be. Will the title character be revealed to be his genuine, biological daughter? Or an adopted one perhaps (like Miranda from the BBC's Eighth Doctor Adventures novels)? Or just an impostor? If she is indeed his daughter, will she be the mother of Susan, the Doctor's granddaughter, seen travelling with him when the show first began back in 1963? Will she be a Time Lord? If so, why has the Doctor hitherto believed himself to be the last of his race? And, perhaps most intriguing of all, will the identity of her mother be made known?

As it turns out, most of these questions are answered in the first couple of minutes of the episode, in the opening pre-titles teaser, when it transpires that she is an entirely artificial 'daughter' generated almost instantaneously from a skin sample forcibly taken from the Doctor's hand. This is a terrible anticlimax, and leaves the viewer feeling somewhat cheated. The only real mystery remaining is whether or not Jenny - as Donna names her - is sufficiently similar to the Doctor to be considered a female Time Lord (or should that be Time Lady?). When this point is specifically raised by Donna, the Doctor tells Jenny, 'You're an echo, that's all. A Time Lord is so much more. A sum of knowledge, a code, a shared history, a shared suffering.' This may perhaps indicate that, as has long been theorised by

---

[43] Looking even further back into the show's history, first Doctor actor William Hartnell reputedly made a suggestion around 1965 for a story about the Doctor having a wicked son; a part he envisaged playing himself in a dual role. There is no evidence that the production team took this idea seriously, although it is just possible that it was part of the inspiration for 'The Time Meddler' (1965), a story in which the Doctor for the first time encountered a wicked member of his own race, and/or 'The Massacre of St Bartholomew's Eve' (1966), in which Hartnell played the dual role of the Doctor and the corrupt Abbot of Amboise.

some fans, there is a difference between Time Lords and mere Gallifreyans. That said, however, it certainly does not appear to rule out the possibility that Jenny has exactly the same genetic make-up as a Time Lord – she certainly has two hearts like the Doctor, as Donna has already confirmed using the Doctor's stethoscope.

The question arises again toward the end of the episode, after Jenny has been shot. There is no visible wound on her, and the Doctor initially hopes that she may have inherited the Time Lord ability to regenerate, but Martha points out that there is no sign of this, saying, 'She's like you, but maybe not enough.'[44] Further doubt is cast on the matter though when, after the Doctor, Donna and Martha have left, Jenny unexpectedly revives. Has she regenerated after all, or is there some other explanation for this? The glowing substance that emerges from her mouth certainly looks very similar to that exhaled by the Doctor in 'The Christmas Invasion', shortly after his own regeneration. In that instance, however, it was said to be an after-effect of his having absorbed the energy of the time vortex at the end of 'The Parting of the Ways'. That is something Jenny clearly has not done here. Neither has she undergone a change of physical appearance, as usually happens in regeneration. One possibility is that, because this occurs within a few hours of her 'birth', she still has the same healing capacity that allowed the Doctor to grow a new hand when he lost one in a swordfight toward the end of 'The Christmas Invasion'. On balance, though, it seems more likely that she has actually just breathed in some of the life-promoting terraforming gas that the Doctor released earlier, and it is this that has brought about her revival. After all, if it was that easy to make a new Time Lord, or even a new Gallifreyan, it would surely mean that the Doctor could in theory use his own cells to recreate his entire race – a prospect that will, however, seem rather less improbable by the time Series Four reaches its conclusion, with the explanation of how Davros has created a new race of Daleks in 'Journey's End' ...

Issues relating to reproduction have, perhaps surprisingly, emerged as one of the central themes of Series Four by this point. 'Partners in Crime' is all about Matron Cofelia's plan to use the Earth as a new Adipose breeding planet; the Pyroviles want to transform humans into a new generation of their race in 'The Fires of Pompeii'; 'Planet of the Ood' concerns Ood being bred for a life of slavery; and 'The Sontaran Stratagem'/'The Poison Sky' centres around the Sontarans' scheme to turn the Earth into a clone hatchery for their war effort. 'The Doctor's Daughter' fits in well with this, raising questions such as what it means to be a father and the Doctor's grief over the loss of his original family in the Time War – all of them, including presumably Susan, having perished in the conflict, perhaps even at his own hands when he took the as-yet-undisclosed action that ended it. The Doctor's gradual coming to terms with the fact that he now has a new daughter, albeit an artificially created one, and acceptance of the responsibilities this brings with it, is one of the highlights of the episode. Donna plays an important part in this, too. As on a number of previous occasions, most notably in 'The Fires of Pompeii', she effectively acts as the Doctor's human conscience here, keeping him honest. 'Oh, I know that look,' she tells him. 'See it a lot round our way. Blokes

---

[44] The Doctor replies, 'No, too much, that's the truth of it. She was too much like me.' Here, however, he seems to be referring to her character rather than to any physical capability or its lack.

with pushchairs and frowns. You've got dad-shock ... Sudden, unexpected fatherhood. Take a bit of getting used to.'

Picking up another important running theme of Series Four, 'The Doctor's Daughter' also addresses the issue of the Doctor's attitude toward weapons. Jenny has been pre-programmed to use weapons in the humans' war against the Hath - in fact, she could almost be considered a weapon herself - and, as when faced with the UNIT troops' deployment of guns in 'The Sontaran Stratagem'/'The Poison Sky', the Doctor is quick to express his disapproval. Jenny, however, puts up an even more robust defence of her position than either Martha or Colonel Mace did in that preceding story, pointing out that the Doctor is really just like her, always 'drawing up strategies, like a proper general' and effectively using his sonic screwdriver as a weapon. 'You are such a soldier,' she tells him, and it is hard to fault her logic. As David Tennant puts it in the accompanying *Doctor Who Confidential*, 'The Doctor has his own drawer-full of double standards when it comes to behaving as a soldier, something that he clearly has done, and done on quite an epic scale.'

Then there is the scene at the end of the episode where, after Cobb shoots Jenny, the Doctor actually picks up the man's fallen revolver and, shockingly, aims it at his head. Although he eventually lowers it again and declares that he 'never would', it is obvious that it has taken a considerable effort of will for him to restrain himself from pulling the trigger. And what exactly does he mean when he says that he 'never would'? Presumably it is not that he would never kill - which would be disingenuous at best, as he has been either directly or indirectly responsible for the deaths of many of his adversaries in the past - but simply that he would never kill a defenceless man in an act of vengeance. However, although this may indeed be a good basis on which to found a society, as he suggests, it still seems a little odd to hear him actively holding himself up as a role model in this way. Is there perhaps another running theme starting to emerge here, of the lasting influence the Doctor can have on the places he visits? In 'The Fires of Pompeii', he and Donna become worshiped as household gods by the Caecilius family; in 'Planet of the Ood', the Ood promise to sing about them for generations to come; and now, in 'The Doctor's Daughter', he is effectively putting himself forward as the guiding principle of the new society on Messaline. Whatever the answer to that question, one thing that can be said for sure is that, as is almost taken for granted now, David Tennant gives another outstanding performance.

The basic premise of the episode strongly recalls that of the fourth Doctor story 'Underworld' (1978): a generations-long conflict waged in underground tunnels between two factions of the same spaceship crew; periodic machine-aided rejuvenation; a revered technological device sought at the spaceship's heart, its actual purpose long forgotten; the true history of events now corrupted into myth. These ideas are sound enough, and 'The Doctor's Daughter' is certainly far better-realised than 'Underworld'. Where it rather falls down, though, is in its detailed plotting. Pick at it too much, and it all starts to come apart. The first signs of this are seen early on, when the human soldier Cline says in reference to the progenation equipment, 'Everyone gets processed,' and yet neither Donna nor Martha is subjected to this, only the Doctor. Most damagingly, the big revelation at the end, that the whole war has lasted only seven days (an allusion to the Old Testament idea of the world being created in seven days, perhaps?), doesn't really make sense.

The idea that the progenation equipment has enabled the production of multiple generations of human soldiers within this short space of time is just about plausible, but unless every member of each generation, or virtually every member, has been killed simultaneously – in which case, how could they have formed the basis of the *next* generation? – then surely there would have been sufficient transfer of information between the generations that the current one would still be aware of the true origins of the conflict. It is hard to believe that not even a single member of the original generation has made it through the whole week. Seven days is simply too short a time period to allow for myths to have grown up. And how can the surviving soldiers have failed to spot the corpses of all their recently-deceased predecessors that must presumably be lying around somewhere, unseen on screen? If the specified time period had been seven years or even seven months, this might have been more believable, but seven *days* just doesn't work.

If one can overlook this shortcoming, however, 'The Doctor's Daughter' is actually a hugely entertaining episode. The action is virtually non-stop, the pace thrilling, the design superb and the direction brilliant. There are some nice touches of humour – such as in the scene where the Doctor uses a wind-up toy mouse to distract a guard – and the dialogue is razor-sharp throughout. Nigel Terry gives a strong performance as Cobb, and although Martha is perhaps a little underused here – as, strangely, in two of the three *Torchwood* episodes in which she featured – Freema Agyeman again acquits herself very well in this, her last appearance for the time being. The Hath are a nicely-conceived and well-realised new race of monsters for the show – although, as it turns out, they're actually no more monstrous than the humans themselves – and the planetary landscape of Messaline is convincingly depicted by way of some excellent location work and CGI effects.

And then there's Jenny herself. Once one gets past the initial disappointment that she is not, after all, some long-lost daughter from the Doctor's past but a newly-created one, it quickly becomes apparent that she is an absolutely fantastic character, portrayed with winning verve and incredible perkiness by the superbly-cast Georgia Moffett. The scene where she flip-flops acrobatically through a cat's cradle of deadly laser beams – apparently inspired by a similar sequence in Britney Spears' 'Toxic' video – also has the distinction of providing one of this series' most memorable images. If ever a character seemed ideally suited to being brought back for one or more return appearances, or even given her own spin-off show (*Jenny Who*, maybe?), this one does. Surely her swift departure from Messaline at the end of the episode – emulating her father's original departure from Gallifrey by appropriating a shuttle craft and zooming off into the universe in search of 'planets to save, civilisations to rescue, creatures to defeat ... and an awful lot of running to do' – cannot be the last we will see of Jenny, can it ...?

All told, this is a highly enjoyable episode – just provided one doesn't think about the plot too much.

4.07 - THE UNICORN AND THE WASP

Writer: Gareth Roberts
Director: Graeme Harper

DEBUT TRANSMISSION DETAILS

BBC One
Date: 17 May 2008. Scheduled time: 7.00 pm. Actual time: 6.58 pm.

BBC Three
Date: 18 May 2008. Scheduled time: 8.00 pm. Actual time: 8.02 pm.

Duration: 44' 44"

ADDITIONAL CREDITED CAST

Fenella Woolgar (Agatha Christie), Felicity Kendal (Lady Eddison[45]), Tom Goodman-Hill (Reverend Golightly[46]), Christopher Benjamin (Colonel Hugh[47]), Felicity Jones (Robina Redmond), Adam Rayner (Roger Curbishley), David Quilter (Greeves), Daniel King (Davenport), Ian Barritt (Professor Peach), Leena Dhingra (Miss Chandrakala), Charlotte Eaton (Mrs Hart)

PLOT

The Doctor and Donna arrive in England in 1926, where they join a garden party at the house of Lady Clemency Eddison and her husband Colonel Hugh Curbishley. Also amongst the guests is the famous crime novelist Agatha Christie, of whose work Lady Eddison is a great admirer. A spate of murders breaks out at the house, and the Doctor joins forces with Agatha to try to determine which of those present is responsible. Matters take a surprising turn when Donna is attacked by a giant wasp, which the Doctor identifies as an alien Vespiform; a shape-shifter capable of assuming human appearance. It eventually emerges that, while living in India in 1885, Lady Eddison met and fell in love with a man named Christopher, who was really a Vespiform in human disguise. He was killed in monsoon flooding, but on her return to England, Lady Eddison secretly gave birth to his child, which she then gave up for adoption. That child has now returned home - it is the Reverend Golightly, one of the party guests, whose true Vespiform nature emerged only two

[45] First name given in dialogue as 'Clemency'.
[46] First name given in dialogue as 'Arnold'.
[47] Surname given in dialogue as 'Curbishley'.

days earlier when he was angered by a pair of young thieves breaking into his church. Lady Eddison wears a firestone necklace that is actually a Vespiform telepathic recorder given to her by Christopher, and consequently the creature absorbed all her knowledge of Agatha's novels and began committing murders in the same pattern. Agatha takes the necklace and, with the Doctor and Donna in hot pursuit, drives to a nearby lake, luring the Vespiform away from the house. Donna throws the necklace into the lake, and the Vespiform plunges in after it, drowning. Agatha's mental connection to the creature via the firestone causes her to lose all her memory of these events.

QUOTE, UNQUOTE

- **Doctor:** 'Right then. Solving a murder mystery with Agatha Christie. Brilliant!'
  Agatha: 'How like a man to have fun while there's disaster all around him.'
  Doctor: 'Sorry. Yeah.'
  Agatha: 'I'll work with you, gladly, but for the sake of justice, not for your own amusement.'
- **Donna:** 'It's a giant wasp!'
  Doctor: 'What do you mean, a giant wasp?'
  Donna: 'I mean, a *wasp* that's *giant*!'
- **Doctor:** 'People never stopped reading them. She is the best selling novelist of all time.'
  Donna: 'But she never knew.'
  Doctor: 'Well, no-one knows how they're gonna be remembered. All you can do is hope for the best. Maybe that's what kept her writing. Same thing keeps me travelling.'

CONTINUITY POINTS

- In the audio CD drama 'Neverland' (Big Finish, 2002), the eight Doctor says that he owns signed copies of all of Agatha Christie's books. Later, in 'Terror Firma' (Big Finish, 2005), he claims that Christie travelled with him for a time. As 'The Unicorn and the Wasp' appears to show his first meeting with the author, it seems that he was either making up his earlier acquaintance with her, or had forgotten about it by the time of this episode, having been afflicted more than once by amnesia during the course of his eighth incarnation. Since Christie also loses her memory at the end of 'The Unicorn and the Wasp', she would not recall this encounter with the tenth Doctor if she later met the eighth.
- When Agatha Christie introduces herself, the Doctor notes, 'I was just talking about you the other day. I said, "I bet she's brilliant."' This is probably a reference to the closing scene of 'Last of the Time Lords', in which he suggested to Martha that they pay a visit to Christie, although 'the other day' suggests a more recent conversation.
- After the first murder is committed, the Doctor uses his psychic paper to identify himself as 'Chief Inspector Smith from Scotland Yard', maintaining his long-established use of the 'Smith' alias.
- Donna comments, 'Agatha Christie didn't walk around surrounded by

murders. Not really. I mean, that's like meeting Charles Dickens and he's surrounded by ghosts, at Christmas.' The Doctor responds, 'Well ...', no doubt recalling his spooky Christmastime encounter with Dickens in 'The Unquiet Dead'.

- The Doctor briefly refers to an occasion when he was 'deep in the Ardennes, trying to find Charlemagne, who'd be kidnapped by an insane computer.' Full details of this adventure, involving the 8th Century King of the Franks, are given in a short story entitled *The Lonely Computer* by Rupert Laight, illustrated by Brian Williamson, published on the BBC website in the week following transmission of 'The Unicorn and the Wasp'. This was intended in part to help bridge the gap for fans between this episode and the next, which was postponed by a week owing to the BBC's live coverage of the *Eurovision Song Contest* on the Saturday in between.
- On first hearing the buzzing of the Vespiform, Donna comments, 'In 1926 they've still got bees'. This is an allusion to the mysterious disappearance of bees in her own time, as first mentioned in 'Partners in Crime'.
- Donna tells Christie about her fiancé leaving her for a 'giant spider', and as seen in 'The Runaway Bride'.
- Having presumably made an unseen visit back to the TARDIS to analyse the sting of the alien creature, the Doctor identifies it as a Vespiform and says, 'Vespiforms have got hives in the Silfrax Galaxy'.
- The Doctor first showed a liking for ginger beer - one of the items he uses to cure himself of cyanide poisoning in this episode - in his fourth incarnation, in 'The Android Invasion' (1975).
- In reality, Agatha Christie's abandoned car was found at Newlands Corner near Guildford in Surrey. Silent Pool was close by. This indicates that Lady Eddison's house in 'The Unicorn and the Wasp' must also be somewhere in that vicinity.
- The Doctor pulls out from beneath the floor of the TARDIS control room a wooden chest containing items from his past adventures filed under the letter 'C'. These include a Cyberman chest plate, the Carrionite globe from 'The Shakespeare Code' and a bust of one of the Caesars of Ancient Rome, as well as a facsimile edition of one of Christie's novels, *Death in the Clouds*, from the year five billion, an era visited in 'The End of the World', 'New Earth' and 'Gridlock'.

PRODUCTION NOTES

- Made with 'Planet of the Ood' as part of Block 1 of production.
- The brief flashback shot of the Doctor making his way through some trees with a sword, a bow and a quiver of arrows, searching for Charlemagne, was the very first recording to be done for Series Four. The trees in question were actually near Llansannor Court in Llansannor, Glamorgan, the main location used for 'The Unicorn and the Wasp'. All the house exteriors and most of the house interiors were taped there, on 8 to 10, 16 to 18 and 20 August 2007. Tredegar House was used for the other house interiors, including the kitchen. These scenes were taped from 13 to 15 August. The brief sequence in Reverend

Golightly's church was shot at St Senwyr's Church in Cowbridge, a stone's throw away from Llansannor Court, on 18 August. Penylan Road in Newport was used for the road scene of the chase involving the two vintage cars, while Cefn Llwyd in Caerphilly became Silent Pool lake, recording at both these locations being done on 6 September. Hensol Castle in Pontyclun, Mid Glamorgan was the location chosen for the exterior of the Harrogate Hotel, these scenes being taped on 7 September. A small amount of studio recording was also carried out, at Upper Boat, on 21 August and 16 November.

- It was at the suggestion of producer Phil Collinson that Russell T Davies decided to commission a story featuring Agatha Christie. Gareth Roberts' first draft of the script was set in 1966, with Christie as an elderly woman, but it was then decided that it would be better if the action took place in the 1920s instead. This was partly because it allowed for the incorporation of Christie's famous disappearance in 1926, when she went missing for 11 days after discovering that her husband was having an affair, sparking a huge police search that ended only when she was identified amongst the guests staying at a Harrogate hotel, apparently suffering from amnesia. Framing scenes of the elderly Christie on her death-bed in 1976 were recorded, but cut from the final version, mainly for timing reasons. Scenes edited out at the scripting stage included one of Sir Hugh being impaled on the Vespiform's sting and one of the Reverend Golightly's dead body floating to the surface of the lake after the creature has drowned. The sequence where the Doctor is poisoned but saves himself by concocting an antidote from various unlikely foodstuffs was borrowed by Roberts from a ninth Doctor comic strip story that he himself had written for *Doctor Who Magazine*. The idea of the locked, unused nursery was prompted by a similar one in the US series *Will and Grace* (NBC, 1998-2006). The Reverend Golightly's buzzing speech inflection just prior to his transformation into the Vespiform was inspired by the *Tales of the Unexpected* instalment 'Royal Jelly' (ITV, 1980), in which a man played by Timothy West starts buzzing in a similar manner after years of consuming royal jelly from the bees he keeps. Roberts was also influenced by Evelyn Waugh's *Brideshead Revisited*, basing the young heir Roger Curbishley in part on the novel's Sebastian Flyte and including a teddy bear in the nursery scene in homage to the latter's Aloysius.
- While Series Four was being transmitted, the official *Doctor Who* website presented a weekly challenge to assemble a jigsaw puzzle of an image from the following Saturday's episode, the 'reward' for which was to be presented with a short preview script extract from the episode. In the case of 'The Unicorn and the Wasp', part of the extract consisted of lines that were edited out of the episode prior to transmission:

> **Reverend Golightly:** 'Where do you get your ideas from?'
> **Agatha:** 'Murder is easy, Vicar, when you've killed as many people as I have.'

These lines would have come in the opening garden party scene, immediately after Christie jokes that she created a Belgian detective because 'Belgians make such lovely buns'.

- The record playing on the gramophone in the garden party scene is 'Twentieth Century Blues' performed by Al Bowlly. Later, another Al Bowlly record, 'Love is the Sweetest Thing', is heard on the soundtrack over the flashback scene of Roger and Davenport walking in the fields behind the house. The former recording is actually from 1931 and the latter from 1933, making these anachronistic to the episode's 1926 setting.
- David Tennant's father Sandy McDonald makes a cameo appearance as a footman serving drinks in the garden party scene.
- The copy of the paperback edition of Agatha Christie's *Death in the Clouds* seen in the closing scene, with its cover image depicting what appears to be a giant wasp menacing an aeroplane (although the story does not in fact feature a giant wasp), was bought by script editor Lindsey Alford in an eBay auction in case it was needed for the production. It was Russell T Davies's recollection of having seen this cover as a boy that had prompted him to suggest including a giant wasp in the episode. He considered that this fitted well with the idea of the murders interrupting a summer garden party, wasps being a frequent irritant at such events.
- The casting of Fenella Woolgar as Agatha Christie was suggested by David Tennant, who had worked with her before in a number of other productions.
- Agatha Christie's grandson, Mathew Prichard, was kept informed by the production team of plans for the episode, and was present at the cast read-through of the script.

OOPS!

- In the opening scene, the Doctor claims to be able to tell what year it is simply by sense of smell, and yet later on he fails to detect that his drink has been poisoned with cyanide despite this having a distinctive almond-like odour.
- This episode takes a number of historical liberties. Agatha Christie actually went missing on the evening of 3 December 1926, a time of year when it would have been far too cold for the garden party depicted here. Silent Pool, the lake near which her car was abandoned, was dragged (as it was feared she had committed suicide) without - needless to say! - any giant wasp being discovered. The hotel in Harrogate where she was found ten days later was really called the Swan Hydro Hotel, not the Harrogate Hotel as indicated on the sign board seen on screen. (This latter revision may have been made because the hotel is still in business, its name now changed to the Old Swan Hotel.)

PRESS REACTION

- 'I say, old boy, what frightfully spiffing fun! Style and substance merge wonderfully in "The Unicorn and the Wasp", as Gareth Roberts' deceptively frivolous story manages to successfully juggle many elements including the real life disappearance of Agatha Christie, a giant alien bug and a recreation of the classic "whodunnit" murder mystery plot.' Ben Rawson-Jones, Digital Spy website, 17 May 2008.

- 'There is a mystery to be solved. Who is responsible is not immediately clear, but a crime has been perpetrated, of that there can be no doubt. The felony has been uncovered by a curious gentleman who leaves us in no doubt that he has a surfeit of little grey cells. His name is Gareth Roberts, writer of "The Unicorn and the Wasp", 45 minutes of the finest Agatha Christie style murder mystery. The crime? That ITV manages, in two hours, to brutally murder its recent series of *Marple* mysteries, when he is able to produce such a faithful homage to Mrs Christie's work in less than half the time, even though it includes a giant alien shape-changing insect, something that never troubled Poirot. "The Unicorn and the Wasp" is unlike any *Doctor Who* story in the programme's history. Right now, after my third hungry devouring of its glorious combination of melodrama, comedy and high tension, I'd venture that I've just watched the best edition of the show since its 1963 beginnings.' Scott Matthewman, *The Stage* website, 17 May 2008.

ANALYSIS

'The Unicorn and the Wasp' is in some respects very similar to Gareth Roberts' previous *Doctor Who* contribution, 'The Shakespeare Code'. Both take the form of a period-set encounter with a famous writer whose brilliance the Doctor proclaims long and loud throughout; both offer an explanation for a genuine historical mystery, Agatha Christie's 11 day disappearance in 1926 being this episode's equivalent of the fate of Shakespeare's 'lost' play *Love's Labour's Won* in the earlier one; numerous Christie book titles are cleverly incorporated in the dialogue here just as Shakespeare play titles were before; and, more trivially, the Doctor goes through both episodes without once using his sonic screwdriver!

One major difference between the two scenarios, however, is that while few people would dispute Shakespeare's claim to greatness, there are many who would question Christie's. Granted she is the best selling novelist of all time, as the script is at pains to point out, but high sales figures do not necessarily denote high quality. As commentator Lawrence Miles succinctly put it after the episode's transmission, Ronald McDonald may have sold more meals than anyone else, but no-one would argue that he is the world's greatest chef. Even amongst murder mystery fans, Christie's work is far from universally lauded. Particularly sceptical, as a rule, are those who admire the more hardboiled American style of crime story pioneered by writers such as Dashiell Hammett and Raymond Chandler. In his celebrated 1945 essay *The Simple Art of Murder* (essential reading for anyone with an interest in these things), Chandler himself was derisive of Christie's brand of detective fiction, in which typically the plot takes the form of an elaborate puzzle, the motives for the murder are deeply contrived and the means by which it is committed highly improbable, and the characters are an unlikely group of upper-class stereotypes whose pursuits, manners and modes of speech are far removed from most readers' everyday experience. Comparing Hammett's work favourably with this, he noted:

> Hammett wrote at first (and almost to the end) for people with a sharp, aggressive attitude to life. They were not afraid of the seamy side of things; they lived there. Violence did not dismay

> them; it was right down their street. Hammett gave murder back to the people that commit it for reasons, not just to provide a corpse; and with the means at hand, not hand-wrought duelling pistols, curare and tropical fish. He put these people down on paper as they were, and he made them talk and think in the language they customarily used for these purposes.

None of this would matter too much were it not for the fact that, whereas 'The Shakespeare Code' does not actually take the form of a Shakespearean play, 'The Unicorn and the Wasp' is presented very much in the familiar style of an Agatha Christie murder mystery, or at least an affectionate homage to it, as Donna is quick to point out within the narrative itself. This means that the viewer's enjoyment of the episode is likely to depend, in part at least, on the extent to which he or she appreciates Christie's type of crime fiction. Fans of cosy country house detective stories will doubtless be delighted by it, while those who dislike them, or who share this author's strong preference for the tougher, more realistic crime writing of Hammett, Chandler and their ilk, will probably find it harder to swallow.

The Doctor himself finds several things hard to swallow in the scene where he raids Lady Eddison's kitchen for the items he needs to cure the cyanide poisoning to which he has fallen victim, demanding ginger beer (to the initial alarm of gay footman Davenport, who obviously assumes that it is Cockney rhyming slang and his secret has been uncovered), the protein of walnuts, the saltiness of anchovies and finally a shock - provided in the form of a kiss from Donna. This is an absolutely hilarious scene, brilliantly played by David Tennant, and probably the highlight of the entire episode. Elsewhere, though, the humour is rather hit and miss. The idea of Professor Peach being killed in the library with lead piping - an obvious homage to the classic board game Cluedo (called Clue in the USA) - is very funny, as is the running joke of Donna inadvertently referring to Christie stories that have yet to be written, and then trying to claim them as her copyright. Conversely, the numerous flashback sequences, each heralded by a picture wobble in the time-honoured manner of film and TV versions of this type of crime story, are at first amusing but eventually become rather laboured; and the obligatory scene where all the characters are gathered in the drawing room and one by one have the finger of suspicion pointed at them, until the real culprit is finally revealed, raises more of a yawn than a laugh.

On a more positive note, the explanation as to why the Vespiform kills in the manner of a Christie character - that Lady Eddison is a fan of the author's novels and was reading the latest one, *The Murder of Roger Ackroyd*, when the creature first connected with her mind - is very ingenious, and manages to hold the plot together without seeming overly contrived. The flashback-recounted tale of how Lady Eddison's romance with the original human-disguised Vespiform in Delhi in 1885 ultimately led to her bearing its child - the latest of Series Four's many alien-reproduction-themed elements - is excellent too, the only downside being that it risks seeming more intriguing than the main story actually presented on screen.

Also very much in the episode's favour are its very high production values. The well-chosen locations and excellent set, costume and make-up design work all combine to create a perfect impression of the kind of idealised 1920s England so often featured in Christie's novels; and director Graeme Harper again does an excellent job. Fenella Woolgar gives a fine, sensitive performance as Christie herself, skilfully conveying her repressed sorrow at the failure of her marriage and her self-doubt over the merits of her work; and although the stock nature of the other guest roles means that none of them is particularly demanding – that of Lady Eddison doesn't really require an actress of the standing of Felicity Kendall, and she is arguably a little wasted here – they are all well portrayed by their respective cast members. Robina Redmond's descent into a clichéd cor-blimey Cockney as soon as Christie uncovers her true identity as the jewel thief known as the Unicorn – the derivation of which alias is strangely left unexplained – is completely unbelievable, but this is not something for which actress Felicity Jones can be held at fault; it is, again, exactly the kind of development one might expect to find in a Christie novel. This isn't a particularly good episode for Donna, though, as Catherine Tate seems more than ever inclined to resort to an over-the-top comedic delivery of her lines; something that is effectively encouraged by the unusually humorous content of the script. It is worth noting, though, that 'The Unicorn and the Wasp' was in the first block of episodes to go before the cameras for Series Four, so perhaps she was still finding her feet in the role.

One of the real stars of the episode is not actually any of the human cast members but the wasp-like Vespiform, which is certainly amongst the best CGI-rendered creatures ever to be featured in *Doctor Who*, and a tribute to the exceptional work of The Mill. Although it is essentially just a giant version of an ordinary Earth creepy-crawly – recalling previous examples of this kind such as the giant ants of 'The Web Planet' (1965), the giant maggots of 'The Green Death' (1973) and the giant spiders of 'Planet of the Spiders' (1974) – it is really far scarier than many of the alien monsters created for the show, and looks astonishingly lifelike even though presented mostly in the kind of brightly-lit settings that are usually not at all conducive to the success of this type of effect. Actor Tom Goodman-Hill deserves special praise here, too, for his creepily convincing performance in the scenes where the Vespiform's human *alter ego*, the wonderfully named Reverend Golightly, begins to exhibit insect-like buzzing and twitching prior to his full transformation into the creature.

The episode ends strongly, too, with a well-shot vintage car sequence in which Agatha Christie drives away from the house, closely pursued by the Doctor and Donna, in order to lure the Vespiform to the nearby Silent Pool lake, where it is ultimately drowned after Donna throws its telepathic recorder – Lady Eddison's firestone necklace – into the water and the creature plunges in after it. This leads on to the closing scenes, in which Christie loses her memory and, with her car left abandoned by the lake, is taken by the Doctor and Donna to the Harrogate Hotel, where she will eventually be discovered ten days later – ensuring that history keeps to its proper course.

Still, this remains an episode that will be most fully enjoyed by those who share the high regard in which its writer and production team clearly hold Christie's works, and less so by those who are ambivalent about or distinctly unimpressed by them. For the latter group, this is likely to afford at best a lightweight mid-series interlude before things get properly back on track with the first of a Steven Moffat-scripted two-parter, the 'Next Time …' trailer for which seems to hold out a great deal of promise …

4.08 - SILENCE IN THE LIBRARY

Writer: Steven Moffat
Director: Euros Lyn

DEBUT TRANSMISSION DETAILS

BBC One
Date: 31 May 2008. Scheduled time: 7.00 pm. Actual time: 7.02 pm.

BBC Three
Date: 1 June 2008. Scheduled time: 8.00 pm. Actual time: 8.01 pm.

Duration: 43' 05"

ADDITIONAL CREDITED CAST

Alex Kingston (Professor River Song), Colin Salmon (Dr Moon), Eve Newton (The Girl), Mark Dexter (Dad), Sarah Niles (Node 1), Joshua Dallas (Node 2), Jessika Williams (Anita), Steve Pemberton (Strackman Lux), Talulah Riley (Miss Evengelista), O-T Fagbenle (Other Dave), Harry Peacock (Proper Dave)

PLOT

Responding to a mysterious message received via his psychic paper, the Doctor takes Donna to the Library, a planet-sized repository of every book ever written, in the 51st Century. They find the place deserted, although its central computer indicates that there are over a million million non-humanoid life-forms present, and its information nodes warn them to 'count the shadows'. A party of archaeologists arrives, headed by a Professor River Song, who seems to know the Doctor of old, although he has never met her before. It was she who sent him the message to meet her here. The archaeologists explain that the Library sealed itself off 100 years earlier, when some unknown incident occurred that apparently resulted in the deaths of over 4,000 visitors. The Doctor realises that the planet is infested by Vashta Nerada, microscopic carnivores that hunt in the shadows. Two of the archaeologists, Miss Evangelista and Proper Dave, are killed by the creatures, which then take over and animate Proper Dave's spacesuited skeleton, sending it lurching toward the others. The Doctor attempts to teleport Donna back to the safety of the TARDIS, but she fails to arrive, and her face appears on one of the information nodes, seeming to indicate that she has been killed. Meanwhile, a young girl is receiving psychiatric counselling from a man named Dr Moon at her ordinary 21st Century home, but it appears that she has some strange mental connection to the Library and the events unfolding there ...

QUOTE, UNQUOTE

- **Doctor:** 'Books. People never really stop loving books. 51st Century. By now you've got holo-vids, direct-to-brain downloads, fiction-mist, but you need the smell, the smell of books, Donna.'
- **Doctor:** 'Almost every species in the universe has an irrational fear of the dark. But they're wrong. 'Cause it's not irrational. It's Vashta Nerada.'
- **Donna:** 'If they were on Earth, we'd know.'
  Doctor: 'Nah. Normally they live on road-kill. Sometimes people go missing. Not everyone comes back out of the dark.'
  River Song: 'Every shadow?'
  Doctor: 'No, but any shadow.'
  River Song: 'So what do we do?'
  Doctor: 'Daleks, aim for the eyestalk. Sontarans, back of the neck. Vashta Nerada, run. Just run.'
- **Proper Dave:** 'Hey, who turned out the lights?'

CONTINUITY POINTS

- The Doctor tells Donna that the Library occupies a whole world, the core of which is the index computer, the biggest hard-drive ever. The Library contains specially-printed new editions of every book ever written: 'Whole continents of Jeffrey Archer, Bridget Jones, *Monty Python's Big Red Book*.' It is the biggest library in the universe. (In the *Doctor Who* audio CD drama 'The Genocide Machine' (Big Finish, 2000), an ancient library on the planet Kar-Charrat is said to be the biggest in the universe. However, it is destroyed at the end of that story, which takes place in the year 4256, long before the 51st Century setting of 'Silence in the Library', so it must have been superseded by the Library.)
- The message that the Doctor receives from River Song via the psychic paper is: 'The Library. Come as soon as you can. X.' This is only the second time in the show that someone has communicated with the Doctor by this method: the first was when the Face of Boe called him to the hospital in 'New Earth'.
- The Doctor finds himself unable to open a pair of wooden doors that have jammed shut due to warping, because – as Donna incredulously puts it – the sonic screwdriver 'doesn't do wood'. Donna provides the solution herself by kicking the doors open.
- The Doctor mentions that he 'likes a little shop', as previously established in 'New Earth' and 'Smith and Jones'.
- River Song has a diary bearing a blue cover with a design resembling the police box exterior of the TARDIS. Trying to work out at what point in the Doctor's life this meeting occurs, she says, 'Going by your face, I'd say it's early days for you, yeah? So, crash of the *Byzantium*, have we done that yet? Obviously ringing no bells. Right. Oh, picnic at Azgard. Have we done Azgard yet? Obviously not. Blimey, very early days then. Whew, life with a time traveller. I never knew it could be such hard work. Um … Look at you. You're young! … But you are. Your eyes. You're younger than I've ever seen you.' It is uncertain from this whether or not she has met any other, later incarnations of

the Doctor, but clearly the specific incidents she mentions - the crash of the *Byzantium* and the picnic at Azgard - must have occurred for her at some subsequent point in his current incarnation.

- The programme the young girl is seen watching on her TV is an episode of the CBBC cartoon series *Pedro and Frankensheep.*
- Visible on a shelf in the young girl's house is a small model of Robby the Robot from the movie *Forbidden Planet* (MGM, 1956), which - like 'Silence in the Library' - involves a space expedition arriving on a planet, finding only one man and one woman alive there and falling victim to an invisible creature that attacks in the dark.
- The Doctor says that the Vashta Nerada form man-eating swarms and are the 'piranhas of the air ... literally the shadows that melt the flesh.' Most planets have them - 'Where there's meat, there's Vashta Nerada' - but usually in small clusters; the infestation in the Library is the biggest and most aggressive he has ever seen. They latch onto a food source and keep it fresh, in consequence of which the prospective victim appears to have more than one shadow. Light doesn't stop the creatures, but it slows them down.
- The Doctor attempts to teleport Donna back to the safety of the TARDIS but says that he is unable to do the same for the archaeologists as the 'TARDIS won't recognise them'. This is consistent with indications in earlier stories that the TARDIS is normally invulnerable to infiltration by teleport.
- In common with Captain Jack Harkness in 'The Empty Child'/'The Doctor Dances', River Song has a 'squareness gun', the beam from which cuts square holes in things. This is in keeping with the fact that both characters come from the same time period, the 51st Century.
- Believing that Donna has been safely teleported back to the TARDIS, the Doctor says that if he does not join her there in under five hours, 'Emergency Program 1' will activate - which, as River Song realises, means that it will take Donna home. Emergency Program 1 was first featured in 'The Parting of the Ways', when a hologram of the ninth Doctor delivered a recorded message to Rose Tyler prior the TARDIS taking her back to the Powell Estate. However, the Doctor then realises that Donna never reached the TARDIS; the control console should signal his sonic screwdriver if there is a teleport breach, but no such signal has been received.
- In the Series Two episode 'Love & Monsters', Elton Pope's mother is said to have been killed by a 'living shadow'. Could that have been the work of the Vashta Nerada ...? Possibly not, as in a flashback shot, it is clear that her body has not been reduced to a skeleton, as happens to the creatures' victims here. On the other hand, perhaps they were interrupted by the Doctor before they had a chance to complete their work.

BAD WOLF REFERENCES

- On the wall in the girl's home are a child's painting of a young woman with blonde hair and, below it, one of a wolf.

PRODUCTION NOTES

- Recorded with 'Forest of the Dead' as Block 8 of production.
- The interiors of the young girl's house were recorded on 16 January 2008 at 42 Palace Road, Canton, Cardiff. The same location had been used previously for Toshiko Sato's flat in Series Two of *Torchwood*. Brangwyn Hall in Swansea served as the entrance hall of the Library, where the Doctor and Donna consult the computer and discover that they are the only two humanoids present. Recording took place there on 28 January and 2 and 3 February. The main location used for the Library, though, was Central Library in Swansea, where scenes were taped on 31 January and 1, 2 and 4 to 8 February. As this former public library had recently been closed down and cleared of real books, the *Doctor Who* art department had to provide thousands of fakes to fill the shelves and tables. In most cases, these consisted simply of empty ring binders rather than whole books. The same room was used to represent various different areas of the Library simply by varying the predominant colour of the lighting.
- Studio recording for both episodes of the two-part story was carried out at Upper Boat on 23, 24 and 25 January, 14 February and 19 and 20 March 2008.
- The information nodes were originally intended to have a mahogany wood look, like the spherical security camera, but this was changed to pale stone after prosthetics designer Neill Gorton explained that it would otherwise be virtually impossible to blend in the skin tones of the actors required to play the nodes' faces. Early drafts of the script envisaged the nodes skittering across the floor rather than remaining static, but this was ruled out on grounds of practicability.
- This episode was initially found to be under-running, so Steven Moffat had to write some additional material to bring it up to the required length. This included extending the scene where Miss Evangelista's data-ghost gradually expires.
- The archaeologists' spaceship was to have been called the *Kraken*, but this name was ultimately unused on screen. Their spacesuits were racing-drivers' outfits, and their helmets real crash-helmets adapted to include internal lights and ventilation fans.
- Before Alex Kingston was cast, Kate Winslet was considered for the role of River Song.

OOPS!

- The spherical security camera examined by the Doctor and left lying on the floor has inexplicably vanished when, later in the same scene, the archaeologists arrive.
- It is said that there were 4,022 people in the Library when it was sealed 100 years earlier – but surely that is an extraordinarily small number for a planet-sized facility ...? (Possibly there were others who were actually killed by the creatures, as the warning given by the information node at the start of the episode seems to suggest?)

PRESS REACTION

- 'There's a feast of wonderfully inventive concepts at work throughout the story, particularly the data-ghosts and the nodes. Both are used to pack a powerful dramatic punch, with [Miss] Evangelista's "ghosting" scene a perfect example of emotive writing and effective performances being allowed to breathe and flow by non-intrusive direction from the impressive Euros Lyn.' Ben Rawson-Jones, Digital Spy website, 31 May 2008.
- 'All the Moffat trademarks were there, and firing on all cylinders. Childhood fears made real in [a] grandiose adult setting; teasing glimpses of what's really going on; an even more compelling and personal time-travel mystery than in "Blink" (and, at least on the surface, owing even more to *The Time Traveler's Wife* ...); sparkling dialogue; and added in to the mix - something the writer more often than not has no direct control over - some excellent performances from the ensemble cast, featuring Alex Kingston (*Crocodile Shoes, Moll Flanders, ER* - and so good to see her back on our screens again!) and Steve Pemberton (*Benidorm, Blackpool, The League of Gentlemen*).' John Beresford, TV Scoop website, 1 June 2008.
- 'It's a clever, ambitious story that rewards viewers with surprising plot twists and an escalating sense of horror (helped by a weirder-than-usual score). Moffat also has a real skill in crafting well-rounded supporting characters that lesser *Doctor Who* writers lack, and the frightened little girl (played by Eve Newton) and Alex Kingston's mysterious Professor River Song are especially intriguing figures.' James Skipp, Total Sci-Fi website, 13 August 2008.

ANALYSIS

To say that there were high expectations for 'Silence in the Library'/'Forest of the Dead' would be an understatement. Steven Moffat's previous three *Doctor Who* stories, 'The Empty Child'/'The Doctor Dances', 'The Girl in the Fireplace' and 'Blink', had been multiple award winners, bringing him such great acclaim that by this point it was not only the show's fans who knew to anticipate something special whenever his name appeared on the opening credits of an episode, but many members of the general viewing public as well. Not only that, but at the time of transmission, it had just been officially announced that he would be taking over as showrunner from Russell T Davies - one of the few other TV writers whose name is widely recognised outside of fandom - from the 2010 series onwards. Surely this latest two-parter from Moffat could not possibly live up to all the hype. Or could it ...?

Something that Moffat has made almost a personal speciality is mining potent story ideas from the stuff of children's nightmares. 'The Empty Child'/'The Doctor Dances' plays on the innate childhood fear of getting lost, as encapsulated in that ultimate expression of separation anxiety, 'Are you my mummy?'; in 'The Girl in the Fireplace' it is the universal night-time terror of 'monsters under the bed' that is evoked; and in 'Blink' it is the thrilling risk of being caught in a game of Statues, which is really just an attempt to defuse through play the more primal fear of being crept up on by a 'big bad wolf' (a *very* apt theme for new-era *Doctor Who*). Continuing this successful approach, 'Silence in the Library' takes another perennial children's game, that of avoiding stepping on shadows, which in turn taps into the fundamental human fear of the dark, and gives it a classic *Doctor Who* twist by attributing it to a terrifying alien monster, albeit a microscopic one, in the form of the Vashta Nerada, often mistaken for specks of dust caught in a sunbeam. This is a typically simple-yet-brilliant idea from Moffat, and one that has the added benefit in production terms that it can be realised purely through lighting (in some cases enhanced with CGI), without any need to trouble the show's design team.

But, of course, a *Doctor Who* story generally needs a more tangible threat than this if it is to be fully effective – there are certainly never going to be any Vashta Nerada action figures! – and in 'Silence in the Library' that function is fulfilled by the ghoulish form of Proper Dave after he has succumbed to the flesh-eating parasites. It is here that Moffat arguably falls a little short of the dizzy heights he reached in his earlier episodes. This lurching skeleton-in-a-spacesuit menace isn't in the same league as the Weeping Angels in terms of originality – it recalls a type of creature from Daniel Blythe's *New Adventures* novel *Dimension Riders* (Virgin Publishing, 1993) (which incidentally involved a man called Strakk, possibly referenced in the name of Moffat's character Strackman Lux) and is very similar in appearance to the 'space ghost' in the oft-repeated *Scooby-Do, Where are You!* episode 'Spooky Space Kook' (CBS, 1969), which makes amusement a more likely reaction than fear for anyone who remembers that – and its repeated cry of 'Hey, who turned out the lights?' isn't going to rival 'Are you my mummy?' as a playground slogan. However, given that the Weeping Angels are amongst the scariest monsters ever to have featured in *Doctor Who*, and 'Are you my mummy?' amongst the most memorable catchphrases, this is perhaps an unreasonable standard by which to judge it. It is without doubt the best newly-conceived monster to be presented in Series Four, so on that basis alone, it must be considered a success.

In fact, this is an episode packed with strong and imaginative ideas. The planet-sized Library itself is an excellent setting for a story, and the thought of it being entirely deserted is very eerie. The only slight oddity here is that when the Doctor gets the computer to scan for life and it finds two humanoids – him and Donna – but over a million million other organisms, he apparently fails to consider the obvious possibility that these other organisms are microscopic ones such as bacteria, which one would expect to find in any regularly-inhabited environment. The information nodes with their real faces bequeathed by deceased benefactors are also an ingenious creation, and decidedly creepy. More unsettling still is the concept of the data-ghost, the last vestiges of a dead person's consciousness briefly preserved in electronic form in a computerised communications system – apparently not an uncommon phenomenon in this 51st Century time period, as it comes as no surprise to the Doctor. The scene where the ill-fated Miss Evangelista's data-ghost gradually decays and fades away, her last words being the disturbingly repeated 'ice cream' – possibly a corruption of 'I scream', the last thing she actually did in her real life, or the more literal chilled confection as Evangelista reverts in terror to the child everyone thought she was – is incredibly poignant, and a powerful emotional moment for Donna, who earlier befriended the young woman, no doubt recognising in her something of her own former status as an unappreciated temp. The idea of a group of archaeologists arriving by spaceship to explore an apparently deserted yet actually highly dangerous facility effectively pays homage to the classic second Doctor story 'The Tomb of the Cybermen' (1967) - albeit that in this case it has been only 100 years since the Library sealed itself off, which hardly seems a long enough time period to require the involvement of archaeologists - and Strackman Lux is placed in a similar position to Eric Klieg in that earlier story, in that although he has provided the financial backing for the expedition, it is the senior archaeologist who is actually in charge of the operation. Which brings us to the character of River Song.

A space archaeologist from the future who is a close friend, former travelling companion and possibly even one-time lover of the Doctor's and who records all the details of her exploits in a bulging diary. Presented with that character outline prior to transmission of 'Silence in the Library', no dedicated *Doctor Who* fan could have been in any doubt as to who was being described: Professor Bernice Summerfield, possibly the Doctor's most loyal partner ever, who was introduced in Paul Cornell's *New Adventures* novel *Love and War* (Virgin Publishing, 1992), spent several years travelling in the TARDIS and then went on to star in her own spin-off ranges of books and audio CD dramas, which are still going strong today. Perhaps there are all sorts of complicated rights reasons why Bernice could not be brought into the TV show itself - although, having said that, she was at one point planned for inclusion in the ultimately-abandoned thirtieth anniversary story 'The Dark Dimension' back in 1993 - but it has to be said that Professor River Song is so similar a character that she could easily be some parallel-universe version of her, or even the same person now working under an alias. Ironically, in some of Steven Moffat's *Doctor Who Confidential* interviews, recorded at his home, one of the Bernice Summerfield short story anthologies to which he himself contributed some years earlier can be clearly identified amongst the rows of books on the shelves behind his head, as can a number of the *New Adventures* novels in which she features, and it is impossible to believe that he did not have her prominently in mind as an inspiration when he created River Song.

The way that Moffat builds up an aura of mystery around River Song, and in particular around the precise nature of her relationship with the Doctor, by making this his first encounter with her but by no means her first encounter with him, is another masterstroke. Of all the current contingent of *Doctor Who* writers, Moffat is arguably the best at taking full advantage of the show's time travel element, and that is certainly borne out here, with his decision to depict this as one of a series of out-of-sequence meetings between the two characters - possibly inspired by a similar storyline in Audrey Niffenegger's novel *The Time Traveler's Wife* (MacAdam/Cage Publishing, 2003), in which the wife similarly records her husband's visits in a diary.[48] What makes this even more enjoyable is that the Doctor is patently just as keen as the viewer to find out more about the meetings that lie in his future, and just as frustrated when River Song keeps him in the dark by abiding by his own rule of vetoing 'spoilers' - an apt pop-culture allusion by Moffat, somewhat akin to his referencing of DVD Easter Egg extras in 'Blink', and one that will certainly strike a chord with those *Doctor Who* fans who are always eager to discover more details of forthcoming storylines than the production team are prepared to release. Donna too is clearly disconcerted by River Song; and is she

---

[48] This novel also features a 'predestination paradox' of the kind Moffat used in Sally Sparrow's instructions to the Doctor in 'Blink'.

just being protective, or is there actually a hint of jealousy in her rather cool reaction to this fascinating newcomer, who seems to have such intimate knowledge of the Doctor ...?

Adding still further to the appeal of River Song is the superb performance of Alex Kingston in the role. Best known for her portrayal of Dr Elizabeth Corday in over 150 episodes of the US medical drama *ER* (NBC, 1994-), Kingston is a *bona fide* transatlantic star, and engaging her for this *Doctor Who* part has to be considered a real coup by casting director Andy Pryor and his team. What secrets does River Song's diary hold about the Doctor's future? Why does Donna's name seem so significant to her? And how does she come to have what seems to be a modified version of the Doctor's sonic screwdriver? All tantalising questions that may or may not be answered in the following episode ...

As always in one of Moffat's scripts, the good ideas just seem to keep right on coming. Quite apart from those already mentioned, there is the whole parallel storyline of the young girl, her concerned father and the calmly-spoken Dr Moon apparently engaged in some sort of psychiatric consultation in an ordinary 21st Century family home. It is clear that this relates in some way to the events unfolding in the Library; the question is, how? At first it seems that the Library is just a fantasy world in the young girl's mind; then it appears that there is some sort of link between her and its security cameras; and then it transpires that the Doctor can actually communicate with her via her TV set, albeit briefly, and that she in turn can cause books to fly off the Library's shelves by pressing buttons on her remote control handset - another example of Moffat's wonderful ability to take things that will be familiar to young viewers from their own everyday lives and give them an unexpected fantastical twist, stimulating the imagination in a way that is quintessentially *Doctor Who*. The final startling development in this story strand comes when, having requested a moment alone with the young girl, Dr Moon confounds all expectations by telling her: 'The real world is a lie, and your nightmares are real. The Library is real. There *are* people trapped in there; people who need to be saved. The shadows are moving again. Those people are depending on you. Only you can save them. Only you.'

The action in the Library ultimately builds to a thrilling climax, in which Donna's face suddenly appears on one of the information nodes - seemingly implying that she has been killed in a failed attempt by the Doctor to transmat her back to the safety of the TARDIS, although the node's repeated announcement of 'Donna Noble has left the Library; Donna Noble has been saved' is intriguingly cryptic - and the Doctor, River Song and the other archaeologists are apparently left with nowhere to run as the darkness closes in around them and the ghastly figure of Proper Dave's spacesuited skeleton lurches ever closer, eerily demanding to know who turned out the lights.

Now *that's* a cliffhanger!

4.09 - FOREST OF THE DEAD

Writer: Steven Moffat
Director: Euros Lyn

DEBUT TRANSMISSION DETAILS

BBC One
Date: 7 June 2008. Scheduled time: 7.00 pm. Actual time: 7.00 pm.

BBC Three
Date: 8 June 2008. Scheduled time: 8.00 pm. Actual time: 8.01 pm.

Duration: 45′ 21″

ADDITIONAL CREDITED CAST

Alex Kingston (Professor River Song), Colin Salmon (Dr Moon), Harry Peacock (Proper Dave), Steve Pemberton (Strackman Lux), Jessika Williams (Anita), O-T Fagbenle (Other Dave), Eve Newton (The Girl[49]), Mark Dexter (Dad), Jason Pitt (Lee[50]), Eloise Rakic-Platt (Ella), Alex Midwood (Joshua), Talulah Riley[51] (Miss Evangelista), Jonathan Reuben (Man)

PLOT

The Doctor and the archaeologists reach temporary safety from the approaching Vashta Nerada after River Song uses her 'squareness gun' to create an escape route for them. Donna meanwhile finds herself living a new life, with a husband named Lee and twin children, in what turns out to be a virtual reality world within the Library's computer. She and the Library's original 4,022 visitors have all been saved in teleport-signal form to the computer's hard drive in order to protect them from the Vastha Nerada. The Doctor learns that the Vashta Nerada are present in the Library because their spores were in the wood used to make its books. He and the surviving archaeologists make their way to the planet's core, where the expedition's financier, Strackman Lux, explains that the Library was originally built to hold the mind of his grandfather's youngest daughter, Charlotte Abigail Lux, after her premature death. It is she who controls the computer, but the strain of containing over 4,000 other living minds is beginning to tell, and the system is on the point of collapse. Having convinced the Vashta Nerada to allow him one day to

---

[49] Name given in dialogue as 'Charlotte Abigail Lux'.
[50] Surname given in dialogue as 'McAvoy'.
[51] Not credited in *Radio Times* - an intentional move to keep the character's reappearance a secret.

resolve the problem, the Doctor plans to link his own mind to the computer in order to allow for all the saved people to be returned to the Library and then teleported away to safety. Realising that this will kill him, River knocks him unconscious and takes his place. The plan succeeds, but at the cost of River's life. Suddenly, however, the Doctor realises why his future self gave River his sonic screwdriver; the device has preserved her essence as a data-ghost. He enters this into the computer, and River finds herself in a virtual reality afterlife, along with the data-ghosts of her four archaeologist colleagues who were earlier killed by the Vashta Nerada.

QUOTE, UNQUOTE

- **Donna:** 'The Doctor! I saw the Doctor!'
  Dr Moon: 'Yes, you did, Donna. And then you forgot.'
- **Donna:** 'Hang on. So this isn't the real me; this isn't my real body? But I've been dieting!'
- **Ella:** 'Mummy. Joshua and me, we're not real, are we?'
- **Strackman Lux:** 'CAL: Charlotte Abigail Lux. My grandfather's youngest daughter. She was dying, so he built her a library and put her living mind inside, and a moon to watch over her, and all of human history to pass the time; any era to live in, any book to read. She loved books more than anything, and he gave her them all. He asked only that she be left in peace; a secret, not a freak show … Hers is only half a life, of course, but it's forever.'
- **River Song:** 'When you run with the Doctor, it feels like it will never end. But however hard you try, you can't run forever. Everybody knows that everybody dies, and nobody knows it like the Doctor. But I do think that all the skies of all the worlds might just turn dark if he ever, for one moment, accepts it.'

CONTINUITY POINTS

- Speaking to her colleague Anita, River Song says of the Doctor, 'Listen, all you need to know is this. I trust that man to the end of the universe. And actually, we've been.' This seems to indicate that at some future point in his life, the Doctor will return to the era he first visited in 'Utopia', which was set in the year 100 Trillion, explicitly stated by the Doctor to be 'the end of the universe'.
- It is confirmed here that River Song's sonic screwdriver is actually the Doctor's; he will give it to her at some point in his personal future, having adapted it in the interim to include a 'red setting' and 'dampers', as well as the device that stores her data-ghost prior to him transferring it to the Library's computer.
- The Doctor says that 'practically nothing' is strong enough to interfere with his sonic screwdriver, apart from 'some hairdryers, but I'm working on that'.
- The Doctor says that the Vashta Nerada 'live on all the worlds in this system' – presumably meaning the planetary system in which the Library was artificially constructed – and that they 'hunt in forests'.
- River Song is aware that the Doctor has two hearts, and knows of his ability to

regenerate when his body is damaged.

- Just before her death, River tells the Doctor, 'Funny thing is, this means you've always known how I was going to die. All the time we've been together, you knew I was coming here. The last time I saw you, the real you - the future you, I mean - you turned up on my doorstep, with a new haircut and a suit. You took me to Darillium, to see the singing towers. Oh, what a night that was. The towers sang, and you cried. You wouldn't tell me why, but I suppose you knew it was time, my time, time to come to the Library. You even gave me your screwdriver; that should have been a clue.'

PRODUCTION NOTES

- Made with 'Silence in the Library' as Block 8 of production.
- This episode had the working title 'River's Run'.
- Additional location recording done for the second episode of this two-part story was as follows. Hensol Castle in Glamorgan was used for the interior rooms of the sanatorium where Donna and Lee receive treatment, and also for the exterior shots where Donna walks with Dr Moon beside the river; these scenes were all taped on 15 January 2008. The place where Donna meets the veiled form of Miss Evangelista was a children's play area in Victoria Park, Canton, Cardiff, recording taking place there on 16 and 21 January. Still photographs were taken on 16 January at St Mary of the Angels church for the image of Donna getting married to Lee, and at Crwys Medical Centre, Cardiff, for that of her in the hospital after giving birth to her twins. Further interiors of the young girl's house were taped at 42 Palace Road, Canton on 16 to 19 and 21 January. Another house nearby, at 38 Palace Road, became the home of Donna, Lee and their children, these scenes being recorded from 17 to 19 January. The shots of the veiled form of Miss Evangelista in the street were taped just outside the same house on 17 January. The grand Dyffryn House in Dyffryn Gardens, St Nicholas, Vale of Glamorgan, an estate previously featured in 'Tooth and Claw', 'The Girl in the Fireplace' and the *Torchwood* episode 'Something Borrowed', was used for the exteriors of the sanatorium and for the interiors of the children's bedroom. Brangwyn Hall and Central Library in Swansea were again used for the Library interiors, further recording taking place in the former on 28 January and 13 February and in the latter on 6 to 8 and 11 and 12 February. The Library core scenes, however, were taped at a different venue, the disused Alcoa aluminium smelting plant, on 29 and 30 January.
- CAL was originally intended to be a little boy rather than a little girl. Steven Moffat changed this as he thought that it would be more dramatically effective to have a little girl with her father in the virtual reality world, rather than a little boy with his mother.
- The wedding dress worn by Catherine Tate for the virtual reality scene where Donna has just got married to Lee McAvoy was the same one as used in 'The Runaway Bride'.
- In the first draft of the script, the real-world version of Lee was to have been a woman rather than a man, her stammer being the only thing to indicate that this was the same person as was seen in a different, male form in the virtual

reality world of the Library's computer. This was changed as it was felt to overcomplicate the scene.

- Donna's fictional children were named after Steven Moffat's son, Joshua, and a friend's daughter, Ella.

OOPS!

- It is revealed here that the construction of the Library was prompted by the death of the youngest daughter of Strackman Lux's grandfather, i.e. Strackman Lux's aunt (or his mother, but he would surely have said so if that were the case). Unless Lux is very much older than he appears (which is possible, given that humans may have increased longevity at this far-distant point in the future), this implies that the Library cannot have been constructed much more than 100 years earlier; and as it has been sealed for the past 100 years, it must have been only just opened when the Vashta Nerada attacked – which is consistent with the explanation that they hatched from spores contained in the wood used to make the newly-printed books. Possibly this also accounts for the fact that there were only just over 4,000 visitors present at the time. Presumably the Library will never be reopened, either, owing to the ongoing infestation by the Vashta Nerada at the end of the story. This suggests that the total period of time for which it was fully functional and accessible to the public was probably very short indeed. Given this, why at the beginning of 'Silence in the Library' does the Doctor speak of it as if it is universally famous?

PRESS REACTION

- 'These two episodes, criticisms aside, are splendid. Big family science-fiction with a side order of atavistic fear, a splendid setting (the concept of a library planet is brilliant, and it looked incredible), oodles of mysteries and, in Alex Kingston's River Song, a magnificent companion-to-be. Colin Salmon also impresses as the enigmatic Dr Moon, and Catherine Tate further proves that she's the best thing to happen to the show in ages. There [are] also some fascinating hints as to the Doctor's future – when River Song says the Doctor last visited her with a "haircut and a suit", the inference is that she was previously having adventures with a later [incarnation]. Also, she knows his name. What could it be? (The current office joke is that she whispered "Doctor Who" in his ear ...)' Jes Bickham, *DeathRay* Issue 14, July 2008.
- 'It's almost a remake of "The Tomb of the Cybermen" [1967] (archaeologists opening a deserted building) overlaid with a greatest hits of tropes Moffat's used to good effect in the past – a creepy child, romance for the Doctor, a monster with a mindlessly repeated catchphrase (in fact, two of them at once at the cliff-hanger), sight as a danger, a playing with the fourth wall and – finally – everybody lives! ... Yet it works as brilliantly as all of Steven Mofatt's past work, drawing you into the fiction and keeping your mind off the knowledge that this is something that people made, in exactly the way ["The Unicorn and the Wasp"] didn't.' Anthony Brown, *TV Zone* Issue 230, July 2008.

ANALYSIS

Discussing the opening of this episode in its bbc.co.uk podcast commentary, writer Steven Moffat expresses the view, 'Broadly speaking ... episode two of a two-parter of *Doctor Who* should start somewhere else somehow ... You sort of feel, a week later, even though it's a perfectly legitimate continuation, that they've been mucking about in that room for a while ... So I think somehow episode two of a two-parter should have moved on a bit, so you come in at a fresh angle or something.' This is precisely what Moffat achieves here, and arguably in a more startling and effective way than ever before in *Doctor Who*, as after an initial recap and a brief continuation showing how the Doctor and the surviving archaeologists get out of their cliffhanger predicament, the story takes a completely new and unexpected twist.

In a tightly-edited montage of scenes, we see Donna being brought by ambulance to some kind of sanatorium, being treated there by Dr Moon, meeting a fellow patient named Lee McAvoy, marrying him, having twins, and embarking on a fairly ordinary 21st Century family life, in which the Doctor and the Library seem like nothing more than figments of her imagination ... and yet all the while she feels that there is something not quite right about this scenario. A particularly clever aspect of Moffat's writing here is the way he subverts the established conventions of such montage sequences by having Donna actually sense the cuts in the action from one scene to the next, so that she is subliminally aware that developments are occurring in rapid succession rather than, as Dr Moon asserts, over a period of several years.[52] There is an intriguingly multi-layered aspect to this as well, as the strange young girl from 'Silence in the Library' is seen to be watching the events of Donna's new life playing out in the form of a drama on her TV screen, just as the viewer is at home.

It soon starts to become apparent that Donna and the young girl are in essentially the same situation here, living fictional lives inside a virtual reality overseen by the enigmatic Dr Moon. This is confirmed when Donna finds herself called to a children's play park to rendezvous with the cyberspace shade of Miss Evangelista, who now appears as a wonderfully gothic figure in a black Victorian-era dress, the veil of which conceals a face horribly distorted by data transcription errors - as Donna discovers when she pulls the veil aside, in a fantastic shock moment. The Doctor has meanwhile learned from Strackman Lux that the Library has a literal 'doctor moon' - an artificial satellite designed to support and maintain its central computer. All the pieces of the puzzle now start to fall into place. In fact, by the time the Doctor realises that the various references to people having been 'saved' mean that the computer has preserved them in teleport-signal form on its hard drive, this comes as nothing like as big a surprise as the script seems to be suggesting it should; for once, the viewer is liable to be ahead of the game here,

---

[52] Dr Moon says at the sanitorium that he has been treating Donna there for two years. Later, after she has left, married Lee and had her children, he comments, 'You've done so much in seven years, Donna.' It is unclear, though, whether the second period is supposed to include the first or be consecutive to it. If the former were the case, the total supposed period covered by Donna's virtual life would be around seven years; if the latter were the case, it would be around nine years.

and wondering why it has taken the Time Lord so long to catch up – particularly given that this is quite similar to the way that he himself tried to save Astrid at the end of 'Voyage of the Damned'.[53]

Less expected is the explanation of who the young girl really is: the electronically-preserved consciousness of Lux's aunt, Charlotte Abigail Lux (the mysterious 'CAL' alluded to previously in the story), the prospect of whose premature death was the original spur for Lux's grandfather to create the Library, an environment in which she could continue to exist and indulge her love of books forever, in electronic form. It thus turns out that contrary to earlier indications – which will have chimed with the preconceptions of anyone recalling his mendacious antecedent Klieg from 'The Tomb of the Cybermen' (1967) – Lux is not a villainous character after all, but one simply dedicated to preserving his family's heritage; another adroit piece of writing by Moffat.

Moffat also continues in this episode to tease the viewer with intriguing hints as to the precise nature of the spoiler-charged past/future relationship between River Song and the Doctor; although when Lux chides them for squabbling like 'an old married couple', the intended implication seems fairly clear. River's description of the future Doctor she is familiar with makes it sound even more likely than before that she is referring to some later incarnation of the Time Lord; one who can make 'whole armies turn and run away' and then 'just swagger off back to his TARDIS and open the doors with a snap of his fingers'. Having said that, though, the tenth Doctor shows here that he is already capable of persuading the Vashta Nerada to cease their attack simply by dint of his reputation, and by the end of the episode he is able to open the TARDIS doors with a snap of his fingers, so perhaps it is after all only this incarnation that she has met.

Another tantalising development comes when, in order to persuade the Doctor to trust her – as she says he will do completely in his future – River whispers something in his ear, and that something is later revealed to have been his real name. The mystery surrounding the Doctor's name has long been a source of speculation amongst fans. Some have argued that he really is called 'Doctor Who', as appears to have been implied in a few stories such as 'The War Machines' (1966), 'The Highlanders' (1967) and 'The Underwater Menace' (1967), and indeed by the show's closing credits for its first eighteen classic-era seasons[54], while others have maintained that 'Doctor', 'Doctor Who' and 'Doctor John Smith' are all just aliases concealing his true identity.[55] It was once assumed by many that the reason why he avoids using his real name is simply that it is something unintelligible to human ears. Only relatively recently has the idea emerged that it has some greater signficance than that, or possibly even some kind of totemic power, the earliest indications of this arguably coming in 'Silver Nemesis' (1988) but more explicit

---

[53] The Doctor also states in 'Utopia' that the human race will at some point in its history spend '[a] million years as downloads'.

[54] Series One of the new *Doctor Who* also credited the lead character as 'Doctor Who', but this was changed to 'The Doctor' from 'The Christmas Invasion' onwards at the request of David Tennant.

[55] In 'The Armageddon Factor' (1979), the Doctor is referred to by fellow Time Lord Drax as 'Theta Sigma'; however, it is made fairly clear that this is simply a nickname from his days in the Academy on Gallifrey, not his real name.

confirmation being given in new-era stories such as Moffat's 'The Girl in the Fireplace' ('It's more than just a secret, isn't it?' says Reinette). 'Forest of the Dead', though, takes this to a whole new level. 'There's only one reason I would ever tell anyone my name,' the Doctor asserts. 'There's only one time I could.' What exactly those unique circumstances are, however, is left unspoken, so it seems that there is now even more fuel for speculation than ever before.

The way the closing scenes play out is highly dramatic and incredibly moving, with River's self-sacrifice and the Doctor's sudden realisation that his future self has supplied the means for him to give her an eternal afterlife within the idyllic virtual reality of the Library's computer - a science-fiction equivalent to the religious concept of a heaven, as well as a direct parallel to the idea of the minds of deceased Time Lords being stored within the Matrix on Gallifrey, as established in 'The Deadly Assassin' (1976) (a possible inspiration for the movie *The Matrix* (1999), which relies on a similar notion).[56] Could this possibly be what Ood Sigma meant in 'Planet of the Ood' when he said that the Doctor's 'Song' must end soon ...? One point left unexplained is why the computer could not have saved River's data-ghost even without the Doctor's intervention, as it obviously did those of her four colleagues who were earlier killed by the Vashta Nerada. Another is how the data corruption that originally marred Miss Evangelista's virtual reality features has come to be corrected by the end of the episode, restoring her to her real-world beauty. Perhaps though this can all be attributed to the computer crash that River gave her life to circumvent, and to the Doctor's subsequent fixing of the data core. At any rate, the welcome end result is that, as in every previous Moffat-scripted story, nobody really dies; everyone is 'saved'.[57] Even Donna's fictional children, Joshua and Ella, are seen to have a continued existence in the virtual reality world, with River now acting as mother both to them and to Charlotte. In fact, even the Vashta Nerada survive, as the Doctor allows them to continue to infest the Library, presumably rendering it permanently inaccessible (which may be why he seems content to leave behind River's spoiler-filled diary, surely a powerful weapon against him if it fell into the hands of his enemies), provided that they let all the humans leave first - although whether or not he would actually have been capable of destroying them anyway is uncertain, given that he said in 'Silence in the Library' that the only way to fight them was to run.

One consequence of this poignant resolution to the story is that, throughout all his subsequent meetings with River, the Doctor will have to live with the secret foreknowledge of how she will ultimately sacrifice herself to save him. One could even speculate that he will be prompted to cultivate a relationship with her, and ultimately tell her his real name, by his awareness from 'Forest of the Dead' that this is what is supposed to happen; another example of the kind of 'wibbly-wobbly, timey-wimey' pre-destination paradox featured in 'Blink' and 'Time Crash', making it something of a Moffat trademark. This also recalls a key element of the *Doctor Who* audio CD drama 'The Game' (Big Finish, 2005), in which the out-of-sequence friendship between the fifth Doctor and elderly peace negotiator Lord

---

[56] Presumably the Matrix was destroyed in the last great Time War, along with the rest of Gallifrey, although this has not been explicitly confirmed.

[57] 'Blink' does feature one death, that of Billy Shipton, but it is due to old age rather than to any unnatural cause.

Carlisle (William Russell) is closely analogous in form to the one seen here – although that similarity is most likely due to the two stories sharing a common source of inspiration in Audrey Niffenegger's *The Time-Traveler's Wife*.[58]

Like Jenny from 'The Doctor's Daughter', River is clearly a character crying out to be brought back in future stories, perhaps even as a regular companion to the Doctor, although in this particular respect Alex Kingston's casting may prove to have been a mixed blessing, as her star status is likely to limit quite severely her availability to reprise the role, if not rule it out altogether.

Kingston's is not the only notable performance in this story. Also outstanding is Eve Newton's as Charlotte. The inclusion of such a young character – something that Moffat seems particularly inclined to do in his episodes, as further illustrated here by his giving Donna imaginary twins – poses a considerable risk, as high calibre child actors are notoriously hard to find, but that certainly doesn't show in this instance. River's archaeologist colleagues are also a well-cast group, the standout amongst them being Steve Pemberton – best known for his work, alongside sometime *Doctor Who* writer and actor Mark Gatiss, as one of the League of Gentlemen comedy team – in the role of Lux. Kudos too to Colin Salmon for his fine, understated portrayal of Dr Moon.

As for the regulars, David Tennant makes yet another superb contribution as the Doctor. A particular highlight in this regard – as again observed by Moffat in the bbc.co.uk podcast – is the aforementioned scene where River whispers the Doctor's real name in his ear; Tennant's performance here brilliantly conveys just how great an impact this has on the Time Lord, and the conscious effort it then takes for him to compose himself again and reassume his usual confident persona – revealing in the process just how much of a façade that actually is. This also proves to be a particularly strong story for Catherine Tate as Donna. In fact, the scenes of Donna's life with her ersatz family in the virtual reality world arguably represent her very best work on the show. She succeeds here in portraying the character with an unaffected conviction and a degree of touching vulnerability that haven't really been seen before, and it is tempting to think that she is more assured acting in a down-to-earth domestic setting such as this, albeit one with a distinct science-fiction twist, than in the more fantastical situations usually presented by *Doctor Who*. Donna's obvious happiness in the virtual reality world makes it all the more heartrending when she starts to realise that her children are only illusions – as in the distressing scene where they suddenly disappear from their beds before her eyes – and when she is ultimately separated from her new family on being restored to the Library, narrowly missing out on meeting up with the real-world version of Lee as his stammer prevents him from attracting her attention before he is teleported away.

Great credit for the success of this story must also go to director Euros Lyn, not only for bringing the best out of his excellent cast but for his overall handling of the

---

[58] It is tempting to suggest that another source of inspiration for 'Silence in the Library'/'Forest of the Dead' was Michael Jackson's 'Thriller' – the lyrics of which can be heard as 'It's close to "Midnight", and something evil's lurking in the dark; under the Moon light, you see a sight that almost stops your heart' ... 'Night creatures call and the dead start to walk in their masquerade' etc – but this seems highly improbable!

production, which is well-paced, atmospheric and emotionally involving, and looks and sounds superb throughout. The Mill again excel themselves with some truly beautiful CGI shots of the Library; and Murray Gold deserves particular mention, too, as this story boasts one of the most distinctive and effective incidental music scores he has ever provided for *Doctor Who*.

In the final analysis, though, it is more than anything else the exceptional quality of the scripts that makes 'Silence in the Library'/'Forest of the Dead' so special. Everything set up in the first episode is paid off satisfyingly in the second, and the level of invention and skill of execution are just incredible. In short, Steven Moffat has delivered the goods once again, boding very well indeed for his forthcoming tenure as showrunner.

4.10 - MIDNIGHT

Writer: Russell T Davies
Director: Alice Troughton

DEBUT TRANSMISSION DETAILS

BBC One
Date: 14 June 2008. Scheduled time: 7.10 pm. Actual time: 7.10 pm.

BBC Three
Date: 15 June 2008. Scheduled time: 8.30 pm. Actual time: n/k.

Duration: 43' 53"

ADDITIONAL CREDITED CAST

Lesley Sharp (Sky Silvestry), Rakie Ayola (Hostess), David Troughton (Professor Hobbes[59]), Ayesha Antoine (Dee Dee Blasco), Lindsey Coulson (Val Cane), Daniel Ryan (Biff Cane), Colin Morgan (Jethro Cane), Tony Bluto (Driver Joe), Duane Henry (Mechanic Claude)

PLOT

On the diamond planet Midnight, the Doctor leaves Donna to sunbathe in the Leisure Palace – under a thick glass dome, as direct exposure to the X-tonic sunlight here is lethal – while he joins a small party of tourists on a trip aboard the *Crusader 50* space truck to see a spectacular sapphire waterfall that lies four hours' journey away. Taking a detour from its usual route, the vehicle suddenly stops dead, and the passengers and crew hear an inexplicable knocking on the outside of the hull. There is a violent disturbance, and the hostess discovers that the driver's compartment has been completely ripped away. One of the passengers, a woman named Sky Silvestry, seems to have come under the influence of an unseen alien entity. To the alarm of the others, she starts slavishly repeating everything they say, the delay getting progressively shorter until she is actually speaking simultaneously with them. She then focuses this behaviour specifically on the Doctor. Eventually she overtakes him and starts to speak first, compelling him to repeat her words instead. Most of the other passengers are convinced that the entity has now passed from Sky into the Doctor, and they determine to throw him out of the vehicle to his death. However, one of their number, a young girl named Dee Dee Blasco, argues that the entity is actually still within Sky and has just 'stolen' the Doctor's voice. On hearing Sky say '*Molto bene*' and '*Allons-y*' –

[59] First name given in dialogue as 'Winfold'.

distinctive phrases that the Doctor himself used earlier – the hostess realises that this is correct. She opens the cabin door and throws Sky out, sacrificing herself in the process. The entity now gone, silence returns to the cabin as the Doctor and the remaining passengers await the arrival of a rescue ship.

QUOTE, UNQUOTE

- **The Doctor:** 'Taking a big space truck with a bunch of strangers across a diamond planet called Midnight? What could possibly go wrong.'
- **The Doctor:** 'Now listen, all of you. For all we know, that's a brand new life-form over there, and if it's come inside to discover us, then what's it found? This little bunch of humans. What do you amount to? Murder? 'Cause this is where you decide. You decide who you are. Could you actually murder her? Any of you? Really? Or are you better than that?'
  Hostess: 'I'd do it.'
  Biff: 'So would I.'
  Val: 'And me.'
  Dee Dee: 'I think we should.'

CONTINUITY POINTS

- Dee Dee mentions having written a student academic paper on 'the Lost Moon of Poosh'. This ties in with the Series Four theme of missing planets.
- The Doctor tells Sky, 'I had a friend who went to a different universe' – a reference to Rose Tyler.
- Professor Hobbes asserts that there is no life anywhere in the system where Midnight is situated; until the Leisure Palace company moved in, it had never even been visited.
- In testing the extent to which Sky is able to simultaneously mimic his words, the Doctor mentions (amongst other things) the Medusa Cascade, his companions Rose Tyler, Martha Jones and Donna Noble and the TARDIS. In each case, Sky is able to anticipate what he is going to say and utter the same words at the same time.

PRODUCTION NOTES

- Made with 'The Doctor's Daughter' as part of Block 6 of production.
- This episode was a late replacement for one by Tom McRae that fell through at an advanced stage of development. It was written by Russell T Davies over just a couple of days.
- A single day's location recording was done on 11 December 2007 at the Forum Spa, Celtic Manor, Coldra Woods, The Usk Valley, Newport for the Leisure Palace scenes. Studio recording at Upper Boat was done on 27 to 30 November and 3 to 7 and 10 December.
- The pop video seen playing briefly on the truck's entertainment system is the 1978 single 'Do It, Do It Again' by Rafaella Carrà. The black and white cartoon is *Betty Boop and Grampy* (Paramount, 1935).

- David Troughton was a late replacement for Sam Kelly in the role of Professor Hobbes; Kelly broke his leg shortly before he was due to begin work on the episode.
- This is the first story since 'Genesis of the Daleks' (1975) not to feature the TARDIS at all.
- This was originally intended to be the eighth episode of Series Four, which would have made it the fiftieth new-era *Doctor Who* episode to be transmitted (in honour of which, the Crusader Tours truck was named the *Crusader 50*), but was ultimately switched with 'Silence of the Library'/'Forest of the Dead' in the running order.
- The poem from which Dee Dee quotes at one point, her words being simultaneously mimiced by the possessed Sky, is 'Goblin Market' (1862) by Christina Rossetti. The quoted lines are:

  We must not look at goblin men,
  We must not buy their fruits:
  Who knows upon what soil they fed
  Their hungry thirsty roots?

- Billie Piper specially recorded a shot of Rose calling the Doctor's name, to be flashed up on the screen of the *Crusader 50*'s entertainment system, prefiguring her return in the following three episodes.
- Production of this episode placed particularly heavy demands on the *Doctor Who* sound team, as discussed in detail in its accompanying bbc.co.uk podcast and *Doctor Who Confidential* documentary.

OOPS!

- A visual effects green-screen can be clearly seen in shot to the right of the Doctor at the end of his initial phone call to Donna before the opening title sequence.

PRESS REACTION

- 'Movie references were ... to the fore in *Doctor Who*, [and] it was 1970s disaster movies and psychological thrillers getting the nod from writer Russell T Davies. In a creepy tale that relied on acting skills and unseen dangers rather than special effects to crank up the tension, Lesley Sharp stole the show as a woman possessed by a mysterious spirit that allowed her to steal voices. Although the entire episode scarcely strayed outside the cabin of a space shuttle taking tourists around a desolate planet, the pace never flagged, the dynamics of the group panic and the pack mentality turning the cornered tourists into rabid dogs. These mind games were scarier than a million squashed-face monsters.' Keith Watson, *Metro*, 16 June 2008.
- '*Doctor Who*'s retiring big chief, Russell T Davies, decided to show us what he could do without special effects or chases but with sheet upon sheet of dialogue. It was a story of possession and featured something inside Lesley

Sharp (one of his favourite actors) repeating what everyone else said. The episode was largely confined to the four walls of a planetary sight-seeing tour. Think *Stagecoach* and *Huis Clos*. Humanity did not come out of it very well, although personally I could not blame his fellow passengers for turning on David Tennant's increasingly irritating ('I'm clever, I am!') Doctor. 'Midnight' felt too much of a writing exercise to be really scary, but once again it showed that even if it fails as often as it succeeds, this series is not afraid of variety. Like the passengers aboard the charabanc, *Doctor Who* is dead scared of repetition.' Andrew Billen, *The Times*, 16 June 2008.

- 'This episode of *Doctor Who*, written by Russell T Davies, does for space travel what the start of *Lost* did for flying. I'm ripping up my Virgin Galactic ticket right now, even though it cost me $200,000. A nutter on a plane in a far-away galaxy is even more frightening than one at 35,000 feet above the Atlantic. Maybe nutter is not an accurate way of describing Sky, the passenger on a tourist flight the Doctor finds himself on. This is no Naomi Campbell hissy fit. When the aircraft breaks down, a scary thing from outside starts banging on the door, and then somehow enters Sky's mind, taking control of her. She, in turn, takes control of the Doctor. Don't you hate it when that happens? Only a selfless act by the space hostess saves the day. All the action happens inside the plane – this is psychological drama rather than full-blown horror; creepy-unknown scary, not special-effect-monster scary. It's more about the reaction of the passengers inside than what the thing outside (which we never actually see) might be. And it's great. Because what we can't see is much more alarming than what we can. It's tense and claustrophobic, and it gnaws away at you.' Sam Wollaston, *Guardian*, 16 June 2008.

ANALYSIS

Russell T Davies faced quite a challenge in writing 'Midnight'. Not only was he unable to use Donna for more than a couple of brief scenes, because Catherine Tate would be otherwise engaged working on 'Turn Left', but he also had to contend with having a much smaller budget than usual, this episode having been earmarked as a money-saving entry in the schedule. No-one need have had any concerns, though, that he would fail to rise to this challenge, as what he has come up with here is a quite superlative piece of drama that is in some ways archetypal *Doctor Who* and yet in others quite unlike anything ever seen before in the show.

It has often been said that *Doctor Who* does not require spectacular special effects, large-scale action set-pieces or stunning location work in order to succeed, because its greatest strengths lie rather in its brilliant characters, its imaginative concepts and its skilful scripting. This, indeed, was an argument that the show's fans often advanced in the 1990s, when the BBC persisted in keeping it off the air in part because, they maintained, it could not affordably compete with lavishly-produced American science fiction fare such as *Star Trek: The Next Generation* – thus completely missing the point that it did not *need* to compete in that arena, because it was in essence a very different type of show. Never has this been more conclusively demonstrated than in 'Midnight', most of the action of which takes places within the confines of a single, relatively small set of the kind that *Doctor Who* could have comfortably afforded at any point in its long history. In fact,

Davies's script is arguably one that could have been just as readily produced in the 1960s as in the 2000s, notwithstanding all the technical and other limitations of that earlier decade. And yet the end result is superb, and far better than some other episodes on which a great deal more money has been spent.

It could perhaps be argued that this episode represents Davies's attempt to 'do a Steven Moffat' by taking some familiar childhood experience and giving it a sinister twist to make it the basis of a threat faced by the Doctor. This analogy does not quite hold good, however, as while the experiences that Moffat evokes in this way tend to be scary or thrilling ones, such as believing that there are monsters under the bed ('The Girl in the Fireplace') or risking being 'got' in a game of Statues ('Blink'), the one that Davies uses in 'Midnight'– mindlessly repeating everything that someone else says – is something that children do themselves to irritate others, and particularly adults. This literally childish behaviour is transformed here into a truly terrifying phenomenon, as the alien consciousness that gets inside Sky Silvestry's mind not only repeats but ultimately 'steals' the Doctor's words altogether, rendering him immobile and unable to resist as he is then forced to echo what *she* says. The harrowing impact this has on the Time Lord is quite evident – not least from the conversation he has with Donna at the end of the episode where she inadvertently unnerves him by unthinkingly repeating a phrase he has just used ('*Molto bene!*'). This is consistent with indications given in '42' and even as far back as in 'Planet of the Spiders' (1974) that the one thing that scares him more than anything else is the prospect of being possessed – of having his own identity supplanted by that of another, malevolent entity. David Tennant deserves huge praise for the absolute, gut-wrenching conviction with which he conveys these emotions on screen. Every time it seems that his portrayal of the Doctor cannot possibly get any better, he manages to surpass himself again, and that is just what he has done here. Particularly in light of the incredible demands this script places on him – the amount of screen time he has, the technical exigencies of the word-repeating scenes and the sheer quantity of dialogue he is required to cope with – this must surely rank as the most impressive of all his great Series Four performances.

While she doesn't *quite* match this, Lesley Sharp is also absolutely fantastic in the pivotal role of Sky, as she really needed to be if the threat of the alien entity was to be fully effective. She too has some exceptional demands to cope with here – in fact, she has even more repeating to do than Tennant – and she manages this with great distinction, portraying Sky's possession in a chillingly convincing way. In fact, all of the small ensemble cast playing the Crusader Tours passengers and crew are well chosen for their roles and acquit themselves admirably. It is particularly good to see David Troughton, son of second Doctor actor Patrick Troughton, making a further *Doctor Who* appearance, as the pedantic Professor Hobbes, some 36 years after his last part in the TV show, as King Peladon in 'The Curse of Peladon' (1972).[60] Another, unrelated Troughton, director Alice, must also take enormous credit for drawing such great performances out of the cast and maintaining the compelling tension of the drama throughout. Although this is a very different type of episode from her earlier Series Four contribution, 'The

---

[60] In addition to his parts in the TV show, David Troughton has also featured in some of the *Doctor Who* audio plays produced by Big Finish.

Doctor's Daughter', her handling of both is equally adept, marking her out as one of the best of Upper Boat's current stable of directors.

But as much as this story plays to traditional *Doctor Who* strengths - fine scripting, splendid performances, great direction - in other respects it breaks new ground, not just because of its constricted setting, its invisible monster and its psychological horror overtones but also because, uniquely, it sees the Doctor having to deal with a threat without the aid of a companion and amongst a group of complete strangers.[61] While at first he manages to strike up a good rapport with everyone - surreptitiously disabling the vehicle's cacophonous entertainment system with his sonic screwdriver and then, as the journey progresses, chatting cordially with each of them in turn - as soon as danger strikes, things start to turn ugly. It is as much a shock to the viewer as to the Doctor himself when his fellow passengers prove unwilling simply to accept his assertion that he is 'clever', and that they need his help if they are going to survive the situation, but instead challenge his presumption of authority and make him the focus of their suspicion. With no companion to vouch for him on the basis of personal experience, he is unable to convince the passengers to trust him; his self-assured claims appear to them to be simply arrogant, and ultimately they turn on him completely, threatening to throw him out of the truck to his certain death.

One point left intriguingly unanswered by the script is whether this descent into murderous paranoia is due to any extent to the influence of the alien entity, or whether it is attributable entirely to the darker aspects of human nature. Speaking through Sky, the entity at one point says, 'That's how he does it. He makes you fight. Creeps into your head, and whispers.' The truthfulness of this, however, is open to question. The most disturbing aspect of the whole story is the possibility it raises that this perfectly ordinary group of people is quite capable of succumbing to mob mentality and deciding to throw the Doctor out of the ship without the need for any unnatural influence. In the end, the only dissenters amongst the group are Professor Hobbes's put-upon assistant Dee Dee, who shows herself to be far more perceptive than her boss, and the unnamed Crusader Tours hostess, who ultimately sees the truth and - demonstrating, by contrast, the nobler side of human nature - sacrifices her own life to save her passengers.

In many ways, 'Midnight' strongly recalls some of the great entries in Rod Serling's classic US anthology series *The Twilight Zone* (CBS, 1959-1964). That was likewise a show that derived its impact mainly from the inventiveness of its ideas and the superlative quality of its scripts rather than from any reliance on lavish visuals or breathtaking spectacle; and a number of its stories also took as their central premise the capacity of ordinary people to turn on each other with pack-animal ferocity when placed in apparently life-threatening situations. Particularly good examples of this are the Serling-scripted tales 'The Monsters are Due on Maple Street' (1960) and 'The Shelter' (1961). In the former, the residents of Maple Street succumb to paranoia and panic after a strange shadow passes overhead with a loud roar and a young boy mentions a comic-book story about aliens invading by taking on human form. As a number of unsettling incidents occur - lights go on

---

[61] The Doctor was also companionless in one other story, 'The Deadly Assassin' (1976), but that was set on his home planet Gallifrey and featured a number of Time Lord characters who knew him of old.

and off of their own accord, car engines stop and then start up again – a witch-hunt ensues, the finger of suspicion targeting a number of different individuals in turn until one man actually shoots another and a riot breaks out. It transpires that this is indeed the work of aliens, who have realised that all they need to do is to plant the seeds of distrust and the people of Earth will destroy themselves, one street at a time. In the latter episode, also set in a typical suburban community, a man named Dr Stockton who has built a fallout shelter for himself and his family in the basement of his home is turned on by his friends and neighbours after they hear a radio announcement warning that a nuclear attack is imminent. Desperate to survive at any cost, the neighbours end up breaking down the door of the shelter with an improvised battering ram. It is then revealed that the announcement was just a false alarm, but while his neighbours try to apologise for their behaviour and offer to pay him damages, Dr Stockton is left to ponder: 'Damages? I wonder if any of us has any idea what those "damages" really are. Maybe one of them was finding out what we're really like when we're "normal". The kind of people we are, just underneath the skin – and I mean all of us – a lot of naked, wild animals who put such a price on staying alive that they'll claw their own neighbours to death just for the privilege! We were spared a bomb tonight, but I wonder ... if we weren't destroyed even without it.'

In both these episodes, and a number of others, Serling's aim was to highlight the dangers of prejudice and hysteria, and the need for people to remain civilised if civilisation is to survive; and it is easy to see the parallels to this in Davies's 'Midnight'. In Serling's case, these concerns were prompted primarily by the then ongoing Cold War between America and Russia, and it is tempting to wonder if Davies similarly intended the situation in his script to serve as a metaphor for some of the most pernicious manifestations of prejudice in contemporary society. The strongest direct hint of this comes in the scene where the Doctor says, 'I'm just travelling; I'm a traveller, that's all', and the character Val – who arguably drives the hysteria more than anyone else – sneeringly replies, 'Like an immigrant?'; but the overall theme of 'the enemy within', coupled with the setting of the action on a public transport vehicle, inevitably brings to mind the xenophobia whipped up by certain sections of the media over the threat of Muslim extremists carrying out terrorist attacks on aircraft, buses and the like.

Other episodes of *The Twilight Zone* recalled by aspects of 'Midnight' include 'Will the Real Martian Please Stand Up?' (1961) (a party of bus passengers is infiltrated by an alien disguised as one of their number) and 'Nightmare at 20,000 Feet' (1963) (a creature knocks on the outside of an aircraft hull in flight). The idea of a small group of people turning on each other while confined in a cut-off environment meanwhile recalls similar scenarios such as that presented in the Alfred Hitchcock movie *Lifeboat* (1944); the 'witch-hunt' element has numerous precedents, perhaps most notably in Arthur Miller's play *The Crucible*, inspired by the real-life Salem witch trials of 1692; the episode also bears a resemblance to the third ever *Doctor Who* story, 'Inside the Spaceship' (1964), in which the Doctor and his companions are trapped inside the TARDIS and start to succumb to the type of paranoia depicted here, even coming to believe that one of them may have been possessed by an alien entity; and the Leisure Palace recalls the setting of 'The Leisure Hive' (1980), another domed facility on a planet with a lethal environment. Davies has also stated that he wrote 'Midnight' in part as a counterpoint to 'Voyage of the Damned', which features another group of people trapped within a stricken ship, but working together cooperatively and selflessly rather than at each other's throats.

No-one would argue that *Doctor Who* would still be the huge success it is today if every episode was like 'Midnight'; but the fact that it can encompass such a low-budget and closely-constrained one as this, and do it so brilliantly, is testament to the show's ability to tell gripping, inventive and thought-provoking stories even when subject to the tightest of budgetary and other restrictions – provided that there are sufficiently talented people involved, as is most certainly the case here.

4.11 - TURN LEFT

Writer: Russell T Davies
Director: Graeme Harper

DEBUT TRANSMISSION DETAILS

BBC One
Date: 21 June 2008. Scheduled time: 6.40 pm. Actual time: 6.38 pm.

BBC Three
Date: 22 June 2008. Scheduled time: 8.00 pm. Actual time: 8.02 pm.

Duration: 49' 26"

ADDITIONAL CREDITED CAST

Joseph Long (Rocco Colasanto), Noma Dumezweni (Capt Magambo[62]), Chipo Chung[63] (Fortune Teller), Marcia Lecky (Mooky Kahari), Suzann McLean (Veena Brady), Natalie Walter (Alice Coltrane), Neil Clench[64] (Man in Pub), Clive Standen[65] (UNIT Soldier[66]), Bhasker Patel (Jival Chowdry), Catherine York[67] (Female Reporter), Ben Righton (Morgenstern[68]), Loraine Velez (Spanish Maid), Jason Mohammad[69] (Studio News Reader), Sanchia McCormack[70] (Housing Officer), Lawrence Stevenson[71] (Soldier #1), Terri-Ann Brumby[72] (Woman in Doorway), Lachele Carl (Trinity Wells), Paul Richard Biggin[73] (Soldier #2)

PLOT

In an oriental market on the planet Shan Shen, Donna is lured into the booth of a

---

[62] First name given in dialogue as 'Arisa'.
[63] Not credited in *Radio Times*.
[64] Not credited in *Radio Times*.
[65] Not credited in *Radio Times*.
[66] Name established in 'The Sontraran Stratagem'/'The Poison Sky' as 'Private Harris'.
[67] Not credited in *Radio Times*.
[68] First name previously established in 'Smith and Jones' and given in dialogue as 'Oliver'.
[69] Not credited in *Radio Times*.
[70] Not credited in *Radio Times*.
[71] Not credited in *Radio Times*.
[72] Not credited in *Radio Times*.
[73] Not credited in *Radio Times*.

Fortune Teller, who asks her to cast her mind back to the action that ultimately led to her first meeting with the Doctor – a simple decision to turn left in her car rather than right. As a giant beetle crawls onto her back, Donna is persuaded her to make that choice again, and turn right instead. Consequently, a parallel universe forms around her – one in which the Doctor is killed in defeating the Racnoss Empress, the whole of southern England is devastated when Max Capricorn's replica *Titanic* crashes on Buckingham Palace and the Nobles are forced to relocate to Leeds as social order breaks down. Rose Tyler periodically appears in a flash of light to talk to Donna, and eventually explains that she has been able to cross over from her own parallel universe due to an impending 'darkness' that threatens *all* universes. Donna is finally convinced to accompany Rose to a UNIT base where the semi-dormant TARDIS is linked up to a circle of mirrors to form a makeshift time machine. Donna agrees to travel back in time to the day she made her fateful decision. On arriving back in Chiswick, she sacrifices her life by throwing herself in front of a lorry and thus creating a traffic jam that prompts her younger self to turn left instead of right, restoring time to its proper course. The parallel world around Donna vanishes, but not before Rose has whispered two words to her as a message to the Doctor: 'Bad Wolf'. Back on Shan Shen, while the Fortune Teller flees, the time-beetle falls from Donna's back and dies. The Doctor identifies it as one of the Trickster's brigade. When Donna conveys Rose's message, the Doctor races out of the booth to find that all the market signs have changed to read 'Bad Wolf', as have those on the police box exterior of the TARDIS. He grimly explains that this portends the end of the universe.

QUOTE, UNQUOTE

- **Fortune Teller:** 'Make the choice again, Donna Noble, and change your mind. Turn right ... Turn right and never meet that man. Turn right and change the world!'
- **Alice:** 'There's something on your back!'
- **Rose:** 'Something's coming, Donna. Something worse.'
  Donna: 'The whole world is stinking! How could anything be worse than this?'
  Rose: 'Trust me, we need the Doctor more than ever. I've ... I've been pulled across from a different universe, 'cause every single universe is in danger. It's coming, Donna. It's coming from across the stars, and nothing can stop it.
  Donna: 'What is?'
  Rose: 'The darkness.'
- **Fortune Teller:** 'You were so strong! What are you? What will you become?'

CONTINUITY POINTS

- This episode presents alternative versions of numerous events related in *Doctor Who,* and in the spin-off shows *Torchwood* and *The Sarah Jane Adventures*, since the 2006 Christmas special 'The Runaway Bride'. In the alternative universe created by Donna turning right rather than left in her car, she never works for H C Clements and so never becomes a pawn in the plans of the Racnoss Empress. This means that the Doctor must get drawn into thwarting those plans in some other way, as he can no longer have the spur of Donna appearing in the TARDIS in her wedding dress to cause him to investigate. Given that some other hapless victim must be used in place of Donna as a host for the huon particles that the Empress requires, perhaps that person is transported to the TARDIS instead. The presence of Sarah Jane Smith and her young friends at the Royal Hope Hospital when it is attacked by the Judoon, as revealed in a TV news report featuring Oliver Morgenstern, a character seen previously in 'Smith and Jones', is presumably accounted for by her having stepped up her investigatory activities in the wake of the Doctor's death, which she must surely have heard about from her contacts at UNIT. In this timeline, Captain Jack Harkness will never have had the satisfaction of being reunited with the Doctor or indeed the pleasure of meeting Martha Jones, meaning that many of the events of Series Two of *Torchwood* must have played out differently - although apparently not so differently as to have prevented Owen Harper or Toshiko Sato from being killed, as seen in 'Exit Wounds'.

- The idea of the time-beetle clinging to Donna's back recalls, and was partly inspired by, the giant spiders of Metebelis Three clinging to their human hosts' backs in 'Planet of the Spiders' (1974).
- UNIT's Private Harris reports via radio to his commanding officer that the Doctor has been killed having defeated 'some sort of red spider' beneath the Thames Barrier - a reference to the Racnoss Empress, as seen in 'The Runaway Bride', although by the conclusion of these events she would presumably have been in the web-star destroyed while hovering over London rather than in the base beneath the Barrier - and that it 'must have happened too fast for him to regenerate'. This is consistent with other indications, particularly in classic-era *Doctor Who*, that the ability to regenerate allows a Time Lord's body to be restored when it incurs serious damage but does not prevent death in cases where the damage has gone beyond a point of no return.
- A comment made by Donna's boss Jival Chowdry indicates that at least a 'few months' have passed between the Christmas attack on London by the Racnoss Empress and the temporary disappearance of the Royal Hope Hospital. This is consistent with indications from other episodes that the events of 'Smith and Jones' take place around early September 2008, about eight months after those of 'The Runaway Bride'. Donna subsequently tells Rose that Christmas is 'ages away', so it is unlikely to be any later in the year than this. Apparently the Thames has still not been fully reopened at this point, having been drained by the Doctor in defeating the Racnoss Empress, although it is seen in a TV news report that water has now returned to the river.
- The TV news report prior to the crash of the replica *Titanic* refers to the ship's progress being tracked by the 'Guinevere range of satellites'. In 'The Christmas Invasion', Project Guinevere was the name of the mission to send an unmanned probe to Mars.
- It is established here that Donna's father Geoff has died at some point during 2008, probably prior to September. (This was written in due to the death of actor Howard Attfield, who had played Geoff in 'The Runaway Bride'.)
- The American TV news reporter played by Lachele Carl makes a further appearance here, and on this occasion is given a name in the closing credits: Trinity Wells. Previously an item on one of the bbc.co.uk tie-in websites for

Doctor Who suggested that she was called 'Mal Loup' – a rough French translation of 'Bad Wolf'. Presumably however this was simply another sign of super-Rose from 'The Parting of the Ways' having spread those two words throughout history.

- Donna's mother Sylvia says, 'Even the bees are disappearing; you don't see bumble bees anymore' – just the latest of a number of references to this phenomenon in Series Four.
- The linking up of mirrors to the semi-dormant TARDIS to create a time machine recalls the Daleks' use of mirrors to travel through time in 'The Evil of the Daleks' (1967). The way the circle of mirrors is used to show the otherwise invisible time-beetle on Donna's back is also similar to the way the snake-like Mara is revealed in 'Snakedance' (1983).
- The two songs heard being sung by the refugees to keep their spirits up are 'The Wild Rover', a traditional British folk song, and 'Bohemian Rhapsody', written by Freddie Mercury and recorded by Queen for their 1975 album *A Night at the Opera*.
- Donna says to Rose, in reference to the Doctor, 'Were you and him …?', but Rose does not reply.
- Rose says that Donna made her crucial choice between turning left and turning right on 'Monday 21st, at one minute past ten in the morning'. No month is specified, but this is likely to have been sometime in the summer or autumn of 2007, a sufficient period of time before Christmas to allow for her to have begun a relationship and got engaged to Lance Bennett, and in the process become unwittingly infused with huon particles, in the original universe as seen in 'The Runaway Bride'.
- Rose says of the time-beetle: 'It feeds off time, by changing time, by making someone's life take a different turn; like meetings never made, children never born, a life never loved'. The Doctor later describes it as 'one of the Trickster's brigade'. The Trickster was established in 'The Lost Boy', a story in Series One of *The Sarah Jane Adventures,* to be a malevolent creature who feeds on chaos, creating this by altering an individual's timeline and thereby disrupting the course of history. It can do this only with the individual's consent – which must be why, in 'Turn Left', the Fortune Teller has to get Donna to agree to change her original decision to take a job at H C Clements. In 'The Lost Boy', the Trickster contemplated a plan to remove the Doctor from history; foreshadowing the events seen here.
- The Doctor remarks on the fact that in Donna's case, exceptionally, a 'great big parallel world' was created around her as a result of the time-beetle's influence. When Donna queries this, he adds, 'Funny thing is, it seems to be happening a lot, to you … Well, the Library, and then this … Sometimes I think there's way too much coincidence around you, Donna. I met you once, I met your grandfather, then I met you again. In the whole wide universe, I met you for a second time. It's like something's binding us together.' This anticipates events in 'The Stolen Earth'/'Journey's End'.
- At the end of the episode, the Cloister Bell is heard sounding in the TARDIS; a warning of impending disaster, as first established in 'Logopolis' (1980/81).

PRODUCTION NOTES

- Made as a single episode Block 7 of production.
- Billie Piper's name is included in the opening titles of this episode.
- Cardiff location recording for this episode got under way on 26 November 2007 in Bute Street, for the scenes in Chowdry's office, and Hunter Street, for the sequence of the Doctor's dead body being loaded into an ambulance. The following day, Clearwater Way was the venue for Donna's return to 2007 following her trip through time, and a house in Nant-Fawr Road again stood in for the Nobles' residence in the shots of Donna's initial departure in the car with Sylvia. On 28 November, a junction in Court Road was the scene of Donna's dilemma about whether to turn left or right, while Heol Gabriel was the road on which the traffic jam builds up after her older self is run over by a lorry. As Catherine Tate is unable to drive, she was doubled by a stand-in for shots where the Nobles' car was required to be seen in motion. Later the same night, Lady Mary Allotments was used for the sequence where Donna and Wilf see the stars start to go out – although on this occasion it was representing a setting in Leeds, rather than one in Chiswick as in 'Partners in Crime'. On 29 November, recording was carried out in St Isan Road for the scene of Donna's fatal encounter with the lorry, and in Franklen Road for the one where Donna meets Rose by an alleyway. David Tennant joined the unit for a single day on 1 December in the Maltings, which had been extensively dressed by the art department to represent the Shan Shen Market. Recording on this date was hampered by heavy rain, although actress Catherine York, playing a BBC News 24 reporter, was able to shelter beneath an umbrella for the scenes outside the Cardiff Royal Infirmary on Newport Road, doubling for the Royal Hope Hospital. Porthkerry in the Vale of Glamorgan was the next stop for director Graeme Harper and his team. Taping took place there on 3 December on Blackton Road, for the brief scene of the Nobles being relocated to Leeds by bus, at Egerton Grey Country House Hotel for the earlier sequence of them checking into the fictional Firbourne House Hotel for their Christmas break, and on a vantage point overlooking the Porthkerry Viaduct for the effects shot of the mushroom cloud rising in the distance. Egerton Grey Country House Hotel had previously been the location for the Lavender Lawns rest home in the 'Eye of the Gorgon' story in Series One of *The Sarah Jane Adventures*. Machen Street in Penarth doubled for the Nobles' new home in Leeds, recording taking place there on 4 and 5 December. The nearby Rudry Street was the venue for Donna's latest encounter with Rose, also taped on 5 December. The Conway pub in Pontcanna was the setting of the Christmas party attended by Donna, just prior to the arrival of the Racnoss's web-star; these scenes were shot on 6 December. The same date saw recording taking place in Mortimer Road for the sequence of the partygoers looking up at the web-star in the sky above, and in Sophia Gardens – often used as a base by the *Doctor Who* and *Torchwood* location units – for the sequence of Donna and Rose talking on a park bench. Some pick-up shots were also recorded on this Sophia Gardens location for the Shan Shen market scene where the words 'Bad Wolf' appear on the police box signs of the TARDIS. AvestaPolarit steelworks in Panteg, Newport, was the final location to be used for the episode, recording being done there on 7 and 8 December for the UNIT

warehouse scenes. A pick-up shot was taped here too, of the sonic screwdriver falling to the ground after slipping from the Doctor's dead hand.

- Studio recording took place on 22 November 2007 and 31 January 2008 in C2 News Studio of Broadcasting House, Cardiff, for the newscaster scenes. As usual, however, the main studio work was done at Upper Boat. This was on 30 November and 1 December 2007 and 24 January and 20 March 2008. The fortune-teller's booth was a redressed version of the Hub vault set from *Torchwood*.
- Slade's 1973 single 'Merry Xmas Everybody' is heard twice in this episode, having been featured before in both 'The Christmas Invasion' and 'The Runaway Bride'.
- Several clips from 'The Runaway Bride' are seen during the course of the episode, along with reused effects shots from 'Voyage of the Damned', 'Partners in Crime' and 'The Poison Sky'.
- This episode's unusually long running time meant that it was given a 50-minute transmission slot.

OOPS!

- The house from which Donna and Sylvia are seen departing in their car prior to Donna starting her new job is not the one they lived in at the time of 'The Runaway Bride' but the one they had only recently moved into in 'Partners in Crime'.
- When Wilf sees through his telescope that the stars are starting to go out, he apparently fails to consider the point - as any amateur astronomer surely would - that this must have happened many years earlier, due to the time taken for the light to reach the Earth. (Possibly these stars are being removed from time and space altogether, so that they have *never* been there?)

PRESS REACTION

- 'It's great to have [Billie Piper] back. Not least because all we've had in her place is Catherine Tate, a nagging, whining human torture-device of an assistant who always seems to be on the verge of slipping into her "outraged grandmother" character and telling the Daleks, "Well, I never!" … With Steven Moffat … taking over the reins next year, this is clearly a Russell T Davies valedictory tour. Much of this is set-up - the real sparks will fly the week after. But it shows what a punch-the-air (if cheesy), complex (if watered-down) and gripping (if formulaic) show Davies has created, making what TV types long thought was dead: the TV show for all the family.' Stuart McGurk, thelondonpaper, 20 June 2008.
- '*Doctor Who* offered an interesting perspective on the obesity epidemic, cutting to a news report that offered the sound-bite: "America is in crisis. Sixty million people have dissolved into fat - and the fat is walking!" It was as if writer Russell T Davies was e-mailing in from Texas. But the fat jokes were just a side order in a daring *Doctor Who* that cut the Doctor pretty much out of the action. It was Donna who took centre state in a *Sliding Doors*-style scenario ruminating how a life can turn out very differently on the basis of one spur-of-the moment decision … It's taken a while to warm to Catherine Tate as a *Who* sidekick but

her line in moody bafflement was perfectly suited to a complex story that tackled the notion of parallel lives and reversible history while making a stylistic nod to anime along the way ... The fact is, *Doctor Who* could get away with being a lot less clever. But they actually care about what they do.' Keith Watson, *Metro*, 23 June 2008.

ANALYSIS

The obvious reference point for any 'what if?' story such as this is the classic Frank Capra movie *It's a Wonderful Life* (1946), in which a man contemplating suicide is shown by his guardian angel the terrible consequences that would have befallen his local community, and the people he knows and loves, if he had never been born. In 'Turn Left', it is Donna who gets to see what would have happened if she had never met the Doctor, and if he in consequence had been killed in defeating the Racnoss Empress; and the creature that reveals this to her is by no means a guardian angel but 'one of the Trickster's brigade' – an unexpected but welcome cross-franchise reference to the malevolent time-meddling entity introduced in the 'Whatever Happened to Sarah Jane?' story of Series One of *The Sarah Jane Adventures*. The idea of Donna drastically changing her life through the simple action of turning right in her car rather than left also strongly recalls the premise of the movie *Sliding Doors* (1998), in which the whole course of the principal character's future is seen to depend on whether or not she catches a particular tube train.

Given that on *Doctor Who*'s current schedule there has to be a 'Doctor-lite' episode each series, in order to accommodate production of the preceding Christmas special, the idea of having a story centred around the companion instead, with a 'companion-lite' episode elsewhere to compensate for this, seems an ideal compromise, and it is actually rather surprising that this has not been tried before, both 'Love & Monsters' and 'Blink' having taken the alternative approach of featuring neither the Doctor *nor* the companion in the main action. Placed centre-stage for once, Catherine Tate has a real opportunity to shine here, and takes full advantage of it. Although effectively obliged to revert to portraying the original, unenlightened version of Donna as seen in 'The Runaway Bride', she thankfully makes a much better job of it this time around. Even when the script requires her to shout, she manages to avoid unleashing the kind of headache-inducing shriek that grated so badly in her debut. Consequently this Donna seems far removed from the totally unappealing character she was to start with, notwithstanding some excruciating moments such as when she directs the borderline-racist barb 'Now listen, Mussolini!' at the cheery Italian refugee Rocco Colasanto – a brave piece of writing by Russell T Davies, who must also take considerable credit for what is in effect a re-imagining of the original Donna, his script depicting her this time as a believable three-dimensional character rather than a one-dimensional caricature.

But of course Donna is not the only companion of the Doctor's to feature in 'Turn Left': after three brief teaser appearances earlier in Series Four, Rose Tyler is finally back for a full episode. So keenly-anticipated was Billie Piper's return to the show that there was obviously a risk that it could completely overshadow Catherine Tate's contribution. In the event, though, that doesn't really happen, and not only because Piper is on screen for much less of the episode's running time. As phenomenally popular as Rose is, not even her biggest fans would claim that this is her finest hour.

For one thing, the script requires Piper to play a far more serious, subdued version of the character, with none of the zest for life that typified her younger self. But more than that, Piper herself seems distinctly below par here. She looks very underweight, with a gauntness to her features that makes it hard to believe that it is a mere two years since her last appearance in the show, and her speech has a curiously stilted, lisping quality to it that is very distracting. She has since suggested in interviews that this may have been due either to the cold weather on location or to a technical quirk of the final sound mix. Whether that is so, or whether she was actually affected by recent dental work or cosmetic treatment as some have speculated, there is no disputing that she is far from being at her best. To make matters even worse, she has been given a decidedly unattractive new hairstyle. The net result of all these problems is that, while Rose remains arguably the best companion character that *Doctor Who* has ever had, this episode sadly tends to detract from her reputation rather than enhance it.

On the plus side, Rose's glumness does serve to show just how badly she has been affected by her enforced separation from the Doctor since 'Doomsday', and just how serious the situation is that has enabled her to cross between the parallel universes to search for him. The rewriting of history around Donna is an added complication, and although the Doctor himself is largely absent from the episode, in many ways he remains its central character, as it graphically demonstrates the extent to which the Earth and its people rely on him to keep them safe. One of the cleverest aspects of Davies's script is the way it works through all the events of the near-present-day Earth stories since 'The Runaway Bride' and shows how they would have unfolded differently without the Doctor's involvement. In this version of history, as TV news reports reveal, it is Sarah Jane Smith, her adopted son Luke and their young friends Maria Jackson and Clyde Langer who take the Doctor's place when the Royal Hope Hospital gets transported to the Moon by the Judoon - at the cost of all their lives, plus that of Martha Jones. 'Smith and Jones' thus becomes, in effect, the final story of *The Sarah Jane Adventures*, the 'Smith' in this case referring to Sarah Jane rather than the Doctor. Although not alluded to on screen, the events of 'The Lazarus Experiment', 'The Sound of Drums' and 'Last of the Time Lords' must be completely negated, as now the Doctor never travels to Utopia, Professor Yana never becomes the Master and Professor Lazarus never receives Harold Saxon's funding for his experiments. The replica *Titanic* of 'Voyage of the Damned' is no longer prevented from crashing into Buckingham Palace, however, and the whole of southern England is 'flooded with radiation' by the resulting nuclear explosion (although thankfully the Doctor's prediction in the Christmas special that everyone on Earth would be killed if this were to happen proves to have been overly pessimistic). Presumably the explosion wipes out the Slitheen group seen plotting to destroy the Earth in *The Sarah Jane Adventures'* Series One finale 'The Lost Boy'.[74] Certainly it causes Adipose Industries to establish itself in the USA rather than in London, leading to 60 million Americans being transformed into walking lumps of fat (which seems to confirm that Matron Cofelia would indeed have run amuck with

---

[74] The events of 'The Lost Boy' probably occur around January 2009, while those of 'Smith and Jones' probably occur around September 2008 - at which point Sarah Jane, Maria and Luke would have just met Clyde at the beginning of the new school year, as seen in 'Revenge of the Slitheen'.

her scheme even without the Doctor's intervention in 'Partners in Crime'). And when the Sontarans start to choke the world with their ATMOS devices (implying that Luke Rattigan, if not his Academy, must have survived the devastation of southern England), it is this time the Torchwood Three team who step in to save the day, as Rose recounts to Donna, with Gwen Cooper and Ianto Jones losing their lives in the process and Captain Jack Harkness being taken off to the Sontaran home world.

There are a few questions left unanswered here. In particular, it is unclear why, without the Doctor's involvement, the Earth does not fall victim to the Carrionites ('The Shakespeare Code'), the Daleks ('Daleks in Manhattan'/'Evolution of the Daleks') or the Pyroviles ('The Fires of Pompeii') – although in the latter case one might perhaps speculate that the human race again has Captain Jack to thank, a heavy hint having been given in 'The Doctor Dances' that he visited Pompeii on 'volcano day' at some point prior to meeting the Doctor.[75] But Davies was probably wise to draw the line where he did; to have included any more explanations would have risked both devaluing the Doctor's role in averting these historical calamities and also simply overloading 'Turn Left' with continuity references. Even as it stands, this relies to a far greater extent than any previous new-era episode on the viewer having a pre-existing knowledge of many of the Doctor's past exploits. Anyone for whom this was their first experience of watching *Doctor Who* would no doubt be left completely mystified, and at times one is uncomfortably reminded of how the show became over-reliant on allusions to its own mythology back in the mid-1980s. The difference is that *Doctor Who* is a far bigger mainstream success now than it was back then, and can thus be more justifiably confident that such allusions will be understood. There can surely have been very few people in the debut transmission audience for 'Turn Left' who would have had no prior awareness of, for instance, the idea of the Doctor having been on board a replica *Titanic* flying over Buckingham Palace at Christmastime; even those who had not been amongst the phenomenal 13.31 million who tuned in to 'Voyage of the Damned' on Christmas Day 2007 would have had plenty of opportunities to catch up with it on the BBC iPlayer, on repeat screenings or on the DVD releases, or to have heard about it from friends, relatives or work colleagues, or at the very least to have seen mention of it in their newspapers, their TV listings magazines or their children's *Doctor Who Adventures* comics. *Doctor Who* was by this point, after all, the most popular drama programme on British TV – an idea that back in the 1980s would have seemed absolutely absurd.

For a family drama, 'Turn Left' is actually quite adult in tone, venturing into some unexpectedly dark territory at times. The fact that the whole of London has been destroyed is not as immediately shocking as it could have been, the explosion being seen only from a safe distance and consequently being hard to take in, both for the Nobles and for the viewer.[76] What really brings home the magnitude of the disaster is

---

[75] Another possibility is that in this version of history, in which 'The Runaway Bride' never happens, the Doctor defeats the Carrionites, the Daleks and the Pyroviles *before* he encounters the Racnoss Empress in London.

[76] It was also established in 'Voyage of the Damned' that much of the population of London itself goes elsewhere for Christmas 2008, for fear that some disaster might occur; a fact recalled when Wilf mentions that he would have been selling papers in the capital – as seen in the Christmas special – had it not been for Donna winning the raffle that enabled the Nobles to take their holiday.

the stark depiction of its appalling aftermath. As in 'Midnight', Davies highlights the contrasting aspects of human nature here. The positive side is represented by Rocco and the other refugees, including Wilf, who determine to make the best of things in their new billet in Leeds, dividing up the rooms between the different families, remaining resolutely good-humoured and having morale-boosting sing-songs - a clear evocation of the celebrated 'Blitz spirit' of the Second World War. The negative side is seen in the neighbour's resentment of the newcomers' presence, by Sylvia's descent into despair and, most shockingly of all, by the revelation that the 'emergency Government' has set up 'labour camps' for the internment of foreigners - again an obvious Second World War allusion, this time to the horror of the Nazi concentration camps, Wilf grimly noting 'It's happening again' as Rocco and the other non-British refugees are driven off in an army truck.

This of course casts Donna's earlier 'Mussolini' jibe in an even worse light. It seems that, in the wake of the disaster, the UK's own Government has 'turned right' and become a fascist dictatorship; and this time not because it has fallen under some fantastical alien influence - as when infiltrated by the Slitheen in 'Aliens of London'/'World War Three' or taken over by the Master through hypnotism in 'The Sound of Drums'/'Last of the Time Lords' - but simply because ordinary human beings have chosen to take this course themselves. With the entire surviving population of the *Daily Mail*-reading home counties forced to experience living as refugees and asylum-seekers, and troops patrolling the streets pointing guns at unarmed civilians in scenes akin to news reports from Iraq and Afghanistan, it is hard to believe that Davies is not trying to make a veiled political point here - and not all that heavily veiled, either. This is *Doctor Who* at the most subversive it has ever been.

The new version of Donna's life is skilfully related throughout the episode, from her seemingly trivial decision to turn right rather than left *en route* to a new job, to the ups and downs of her time with Jival Chowdry's photocopying business, to her family's enforced relocation to Leeds, to her eventual acceptance of her destiny as revealed to her by Rose - who periodically appears from nowhere in a flash of light to advise her, keep her safe and make the odd portentous remark. This culminates in the fantastic sequence where, positioned within a circle of mirrors linked to the semi-dormant TARDIS, Donna finally gets to see the giant time-beetle on her back - the only downside to this being that the model supplied by Millennium FX to represent the creature is disappointingly artificial-looking - and then travels back in time and sacrifices her life, as Rose has foretold[77], to prevent her younger self from making that fateful decision to turn right. In many ways, the alternative Donna's personal journey here mirrors the original Donna's with the Doctor; she starts out as a blinkered, self-doubting loudmouth, who is too busy complaining about her dismissal by Jival Chowdry to be bothered about the fate of the hundreds of people killed when the Royal Hope Hospital is wrenched to the Moon and back, and gradually has her eyes opened to what is going on in the world around her, and to her true potential in life.

---

[77] This is assuming that Rose was not in fact referring to Donna's later 'death' at the end of 'Journey's End', which is an another possible interpretation, and arguably one that makes more logical sense - although the fact that Donna remembers Rose saying 'You're gonna die' just before she throws herself in front of the lorry indicates that she at least believes that this imminent death is what was meant.

Again, this is brilliant writing by Davies.

Rose's story, on the other hand, is far less well worked out. On her first appearance, she is obviously shocked to learn that the Doctor has been killed, and is not even aware of who Donna is, whereas on subsequent ones she knows all about Donna and her family, has been able to lay plans to ensure that they are away from London when the Christmas Day disaster occurs, has found out all about the changed course of history and the creature on Donna's back, has hooked up with UNIT and made elaborate preparations for Donna to travel back in time, and has even discovered that the Doctor thinks Donna is 'brilliant' and that she will have to die in order to set things to rights – although, paradoxically, she says that she and UNIT (or does she mean the parallel world Torchwood?) aren't sure if their plan will work and are just 'guessing'. How has she managed to acquire all this knowledge and achieve all these things? She refers to having 'readings' indicating that Donna is special and that only the Doctor and Donna together can avert 'the darkness', but she doesn't say where these have come from. Could they have been obtained using the advanced control console that she is seen adjusting in the UNIT warehouse? Quite possibly, but this isn't spelt out. It isn't even made entirely clear whether, when she makes her appearances, she is jumping between parallel universes or travelling via the makeshift time machine that UNIT have rigged up using the abandoned TARDIS – although ultimately the fact that the time machine more or less self-destructs in achieving just a single trip through time for Donna strongly suggests the former, despite the fact that Rose is never actually seen to use one of the yellow-button transporter devices created for this purpose by the parallel world version of Torchwood, as established in 'Doomsday'. It seems that Davies and his team may have been so *au fait* with what they intended here that they simply failed to realise that they had put in insufficient exposition for the viewer.

Rose is wearing the same clothes each time she appears, as Donna herself observes at one point, but it is never explained why. Is it because all this is happening in quick succession from her point of view although over a period of several months from Donna's (in which case, again, how has she managed to achieve so much in between?), or because her jacket has been rigged up to protect her from temporal feedback, like the coat that Donna is given, or even because she is becoming 'Doctor-like' (recalling Donna's comment in 'Partners in Crime' about the Doctor seeming never to change his clothes)? And if she can go back in time and talk to Donna at the point when she dies after being hit by the lorry (an echo of the history-righting resolution to 'Father's Day', where Rose's father Pete similarly commits suicide by throwing himself in front of a car), why couldn't she just have appeared half a mile further down the road and persuaded the younger Donna to turn left rather than right in the first place?[78]

This is all very puzzling and unsatisfactory. It seems strange, too, that UNIT would entrust the execution of such a vitally important mission to a relatively lowly Captain, rather than bring in someone like Colonel Mace to handle it. Is the intended implication here that most of UNIT's top brass in the UK were killed when the replica

---

[78] Also unaddressed here is the question of how Rose came to appear outside the Adipose Industries building at the end of 'Partners in Crime', given that the events of that story occur not in the alternative universe but in the original one where Donna did turn left.

Titanic fell on London? Or even, perhaps, that UNIT don't really believe what Rose has told them, and aren't according it a high priority? Again, this is a point left to the viewer's imagination.

Another mystery is why Rose refuses to tell anyone her name, her only comment on this being, 'Cross too many different realities ... Trust me, the wrong word in the wrong place can change an entire causal nexus.' This appears to allude to the 'power of names' idea previously featured in stories such as 'The Shakespeare Code', 'Last of the Time Lords' and 'Silence in the Library'/'Forest of the Dead', but why Rose should have come to believe that her own name holds such significance is unclear. In dramatic terms, on the other hand, Davies's reason for having Rose conceal her identity is quite apparent: he wanted to set up the ending where she whispers two words to the alternative Donna just before her version of reality blinks out of existence, and those two words are then revealed by the original Donna to have been 'Bad Wolf'. This leads on to the amazing sequence where the Doctor rushes out of the fortune-teller's booth to see the phrase 'Bad Wolf' substituted for all of the words on the Shan Shen market banners and even on the police box signs of the TARDIS itself. Again, though, one has to question whether or not this actually makes sense. The original 'Bad Wolf' idea, as explained in 'The Parting of the Ways', was that Rose, having absorbed the essence of the time vortex, took this phrase from a sign on the wall of Satellite Five in the year 200,100 and spread it back through history as a message to her earlier self to prompt her to take the TARDIS to Satellite Five in the first place. Now, though, it seems to have been accorded a more general association with Rose, making it almost her equivalent of Batman's bat-signal, as David Tennant observes in the accompanying instalment of *Doctor Who Confidential*. One can only assume that the god-like Rose of 'The Parting of the Ways' foresaw these future events even at that time and contrived to have the multiple 'Bad Wolf' images appear to the Doctor as a warning.

That said, these framing scenes in the Shan Shen market top and tail the episode very nicely indeed, featuring some superb CGI effects and excellent design work and affording a deserved second *Doctor Who* role for Chipo Chung as the fortune-teller, her previous appearance having come under heavy prosthetics as Chantho in 'Utopia'.

This episode could scarcely be more different in tone from Graeme Harper's last directorial assignment, 'The Unicorn and the Wasp', and yet he handles it with equal assurance, again demonstrating his incredible versatility. And, in the final analysis, any reservations one might have about the coherence of Rose's involvement in the plot are completely overshadowed by feelings of admiration for the inventiveness, intelligence and sheer boldness of Davies's script. In short, this is not only one of the best stories of Series Four, but also one of the most extraordinary in *Doctor Who*'s long history.

4.12 - THE STOLEN EARTH

Writer: Russell T Davies
Director: Graeme Harper

DEBUT TRANSMISSION DETAILS

BBC One
Date: 28 June 2008. Scheduled time: 7.10 pm. Actual time: 7.11 pm.

BBC Three
Date: 29 June 2008. Scheduled time: 8.00 pm. Actual time: 8.02 pm.

Duration: 45' 41"

ADDITIONAL CREDITED CAST

Penelope Wilton[79] (Harriet Jones), Gareth David-Lloyd (Ianto Jones), Eve Myles (Gwen Cooper), Thomas Knight (Luke Smith), Adjoa Andoh (Francine Jones), Julian Bleach (Davros), Michael Brandon (General Sanchez), Andrea Harris (Suzanne), Lachele Carl (Trinity Wells), Richard Dawkins (Himself), Paul O'Grady (Himself), Marcus Cunningham (Drunk Man), Jason Mohammad (Newsreader), Paul Kasey (Judoon), Kelly Hunter (Shadow Architect), Amy Beth Hayes (Albino Servant), Gary Milner[80] (Scared Man), Barney Edwards[81] (Dalek Operator), Nick Pegg[82] (Dalek Operator), David Hankinson[83] (Dalek Operator), Anthony Spargo[84] (Dalek Operator), Nicholas Briggs[85] (Dalek Voice), Alexander Armstrong[86] (Voice of Mr Smith)

Daleks created by: Terry Nation

---

[79] Not credited in *Radio Times*.
[80] Not credited in *Radio Times*.
[81] Not credited in *Radio Times*. Although credited on previous episodes, and elsewhere, as 'Barnaby Edwards', this regular Dalek Operator is listed with his first name abbreviated to 'Barney' on the closing titles of both 'The Stolen Earth' and 'Journey's End'.
[82] Not credited in *Radio Times*.
[83] Not credited in *Radio Times*.
[84] Not credited in *Radio Times*.
[85] Not credited in *Radio Times*. Briggs also supplied the Judoon voices, for which he was not credited either in *Radio Times* or on screen.
[86] Not credited in *Radio Times*.

4.12 - THE STOLEN EARTH

PLOT

The Earth is removed from its usual place in space and time by the Daleks and taken to the Medusa Cascade along with 26 other planets. As the Daleks start to round up human test subjects, former Prime Minister Harriet Jones uses a piece of sentient software known as the Subwave Network to track down and communicate with the Doctor's former companions Captain Jack Harkness, Sarah Jane Smith and Martha Jones. Rose Tyler has arrived on Earth and made her way to the Nobles' home, hoping to find Donna, but is unable to join in the Subwave Network conference as their laptop does not have a webcam. The Doctor meanwhile takes Donna to the Shadow Proclamation for assistance. He then tracks the stolen Earth to the Medusa Cascade, but is initially unable to find it or the other missing planets. The Doctor's companions are likewise unable to contact him at first, but manage to do so eventually by using Sarah Jane's alien computer Mr Smith to cause every phone on Earth simultaneously to dial the number of Martha's mobile aboard the TARDIS and then boosting the signal via the rift manipulator in the Torchwood Hub. The Doctor now realises that the entire Medusa Cascade has been moved one second out of synch with the rest of the universe. He is able to overcome this barrier and materialise the TARDIS on Earth - but not before receiving a shock when he learns that the Daleks' creator Davros has been rescued from the Time War by Dalek Caan, who has been driven insane in the process, and is now on board the Dalek Crucible at the heart of the system of stolen planets. Rose and Captain Jack converge on the TARDIS's arrival point, but not in time to save the Doctor from being shot by a Dalek. They and Donna help to get him back inside the ship, where he starts to regenerate.

QUOTE, UNQUOTE

- **Albino Servant:** 'I am so sorry for your loss.'
  Donna: 'Yeah. My whole planet's gone.'
  Albino Servant: 'I mean the loss that is yet to come. God save you.'
- **Dalek Caan:** 'He is coming. The threefold man. He dances in the lonely places. O creator of us all, the Doctor is coming.'
- **Davros:** 'Welcome to my new empire, Doctor. It is only fitting that you should bear witness to the resurrection and the triumph of Davros, lord and creator of the Dalek race.'
- **Dalek Caan:** 'I flew into the wild and fire. I danced and died a thousand times.'

CONTINUITY POINTS

- The action of the episode begins at around 8.00 am on a Saturday morning. It is probably the summer of 2009; these events seem to occur not long after the deaths of Owen Harper and Toshiko Sato in *Torchwood*'s Series Two finale 'Exit Wounds', which can be dated to around April 2009, and Maria Jackson and her father Alan from *The Sarah Jane Adventures* are said to be away in Cornwall, presumably on a summer holiday.[87]

- Gwen Cooper phones her husband Rhys and asks him in turn to phone and reassure her mother. However, she makes no mention of her father: is it possible that he has died since being seen in the *Torchwood* episode 'Something Borrowed' …?
- Captain Jack notes that something has established an artificial atmospheric shell around the Earth, keeping in the air and holding in the heat – evidence that the Daleks want to keep the human race alive. Since the Earth's own atmosphere and gravity would normally achieve both these things, this is presumably indicative of the exceptional forces holding the 27 stolen planets in balance.
- Martha Jones has been promoted by UNIT to Medical Director on Project Indigo – an experimental teleport system using technology salvaged from the Sontarans, presumably following their recent attempt to turn Earth into a clone planet for their species, as seen in 'The Sontaran Stratagem'/'The Poison Sky'.
- Gwen Cooper does not know of the Daleks – she asks Jack 'Who are they?' on hearing their war chant of 'Exterminate!' – but Ianto Jones must do, as it has been previously established in *Torchwood* that he worked at Torchwood One at the time of the Battle of Canary Wharf, as seen in 'Doomsday'. He is certainly aware that machine-guns do not work against the Daleks.
- In a shot of the Daleks *en masse* inside their Crucible space station, one of their number can be seen to be riding on a hovering disc resembling the 'hoverbouts' depicted in many Dalek comic strips and illustrations of the 1960s but not previously seen in the TV show itself. Next to it is another piece of hovering equipment of an unfamiliar shape, possibly indicating that it is involved in maintenance or construction work.
- The Doctor describes the Shadow Proclamation as: 'A posh name for police … Outer space police.' Their headquarters stands on a space platform that appears to have been constructed from three artificially-linked asteroids.
- The Doctor initially addresses the Judoon in their native language. This may perhaps suggest that the TARDIS's translation circuits are ineffective in this instance. Although the Judoon are later heard to be speaking in English, they could be using their own translation devices, as established in 'Smith and Jones', possibly for Donna's benefit.
- The Shadow Architect states that 24 planets have been stolen, all at the exact same time. Reading from a monitor screen, the Doctor sees that these include Callufax Minor (possibly a planet from the same system as Calufrax, as seen in 'The Pirate Planet' (1978), despite the slight difference in spelling), Jahoo, Shallacatop, Woman Wept (previously mentioned by Rose in 'Boom Town' as a place that she and the Doctor have visited) and Clom (home of the Abzorbaloff and twin planet to the Slitheen world Raxacoricofallapatorius, as noted in 'Love & Monsters'). With Donna's help, the Doctor deduces that three other planets – Pyrovillia (as mentioned in 'The Fires of Pompeii'), Adipose Three ('Partners in Crime') and the Lost Moon of Poosh ('Midnight') – have also been taken, but

[87] See *Something in the Darkness: The Unofficial and Unauthorised Guide to Torchwood Series Two* (Telos Publishing, 2008), for a timeline of events in the new-era *Doctor Who* universe.

from other points in time, making 27 in total.

- The Daleks destroy the UNIT carrier ship *Valiant*.
- The Doctor states that bees (or a proportion of them, at least) come from the planet Melissa Majoria. These migrant bees have left Earth and travelled home via the Tandocca Scale, a series of wavelengths that they use as carrier signals, described by the Doctor as 'infinitely small'.
- 'Dalek Attack Formation Seven' appears to consist of three Daleks standing side by side in a row.
- The Doctor states that he first came to the Medusa Cascade when he was 'just a kid … 90 years old'. He describes it as 'the centre of a rift in time and space'.
- Harriet Jones describes the Subwave Network as 'a sentient piece of software programmed to seek out anyone and everyone who can help to contact the Doctor'. She says that she 'developed' this 'undetectable' form of communication, but that it was 'created by the Mr Copper Foundation' - a reference to the character Mr Copper from 'Voyage of the Damned', who was left on Earth by the Doctor as a millionaire and promised to put the money to good use.
- The Cardiff time rift remains in place even though the Earth has been transported through space and time to the Medusa Cascade. This confirms that the rift is permanently linked to that point on the Earth's surface (as implied previously by the fact that it is unaffected by other celestial motion, such as the Earth's rotation around the Sun).
- The number of Martha's mobile phone aboard the TARDIS is given on screen as 0770 900461. (This is an unassigned number in reality.)
- The Doctor explains that he was initially unable to detect the stolen planets because 'the entire Medusa Cascade has been put a second out of synch with the rest of the universe - perfect hiding place, a tiny little pocket of time'.
- The Doctor says to Davros: 'But you were destroyed. In the very first year of the Time War, at the Gates of Elysium. I saw your command ship fly into the jaws of the Nightmare Child. I tried to save you.' Davros reveals that he was rescued by Dalek Caan, who used an emergency temporal shift to go back into the Time War itself. The Doctor is astounded by this, responding, 'But that's impossible; the entire War is time-locked'. Davros implies that 'emperors and Time Lords' had previously tried to return to the Time War without success, the reference to 'emperors' possibly alluding to the Dalek Emperor as seen in 'The Parting of the Ways'.

PRODUCTION NOTES

- Made with 'Journey's End' as part of Block 9 of production.
- Credited over the opening titles for this episode are David Tennant, Catherine Tate, Freema Agyeman, John Barrowman, Elisabeth Sladen and Billie Piper. Then, for the first time in the show, additional actor credits are superimposed after the opening titles: these are for Penelope Wilton, Adjoa Andoh, Eve Myles and Gareth David-Lloyd.
- The earliest location recording done for this episode was on 27 and 28 February 2008 for the scenes with Rose inside the Nobles' home, for which the usual house

in Nant-Fawr Road was used. A foyer in the Optometry and Visual Sciences building of Cardiff University became the headquarters of the Shadow Proclamation on 8 March. Ffordd Gerdinan in Tonteg, Mid Glamorgan, was the setting for the TARDIS's initial arrival on Earth on a street where a milkman is making his deliveries; recording took place here on 11 March. The following day, Bernard Cribbins and Jacqueline King taped the scene where Wilf and Slyvia look up into the sky and see that the Earth has moved; this was done outside 18 Hawthorn Road in Pontypridd. Also on the same date, Market Street in Pontypridd represented Camden in London for the sequence of Rose chasing looters away from the Megabyte City computer store and later watching as the Dalek saucers begin their onslaught. On 13 March, taping took place in Penarth for the dramatic sequence where the Doctor and Rose run toward each other, only for the Doctor to be shot by a Dalek, which is then destroyed by Jack. The TARDIS's arrival point was in the High Street; Rose's materialisation was in Queen's Road; the Dalek appeared in Paget Road; and Jack fired his gun from Arcot Street. The next day, recording continued in Cardiff; Brook Street was used for the scene where the Daleks round up human prisoners, while Plantagenet Street saw Wilf and Sylvia confront one of the invaders, which Rose then blows up. South Wales Traffic Management Centre in Coryton was transformed into UNIT's New York base on 16 March. The scenes in Harriet Jones's house were shot in Lower House, Michaelston-le-Pit, on 18 March. On the same date, the Wales Museum Collections Centre in Barry Island was used for the scene where the Project Indigo teleport device is retrieved from storage and Martha is ordered to take the Osterhagen Key. A house in Cwrt-y-Vil Road was used for the interiors of Francine's home, taped over 25 and 26 March. Also on 25 March, the scenes were taped of Sarah Jane leaving her home in Bannerman Road, for which the usual house at 21 Clinton Road, Penarth, was used, and screeching to a halt in her car as she sees two Daleks ahead, for which the nearby Robinswood Crescent was the location.

- The newscast scenes were recorded on 31 January at the usual venue of News Studio C2, Broadcasting House, Llandaff. The main studio recording was then carried out at Upper Boat on 18 to 22 February and 3, 20, 21, 24 and 27 to 29 March, with some extra pick-up shots done on 1 May.
- This episode continues the tradition of celebrity cameo appearances in *Doctor Who*'s series finales. The celebrities on this occasion are biologist and science writer Professor Richard Dawkins, being interviewed on a (fictional) programme called *Universally Speaking*, and popular entertainer Paul O'Grady, appearing on his own chat show (although in our universe this is not transmitted on a Saturday morning). Dawkins is married to actress Lalla Ward, who played the second incarnation of the Doctor's companion Romana in 1979 and 1980, while O'Grady is reported to be a big fan of *Doctor Who*.
- Russell T Davies's original intention was that there should be various other familiar monsters present as well as the Judoon in the Shadow Proclamation scenes. This was to have included the Slitheen. Actress Annette Badland – who had previously played one of the creatures in 'Aliens of London'/'World War Three' and 'Boom Town' – had already recorded some Slitheen dialogue for these scenes before the idea was abandoned, mainly on cost grounds.
- This episode is the first since *Doctor Who* returned in 2005 to involve Daleks

being recorded on location as opposed to only appearing in the studio.

- In place of a 'Next Time ...' trailer, the closing titles of this episode begin with the three words 'TO', 'BE' and 'CONTINUED' superimposed in succession, to the accompaniment of a percussive beat on the soundtrack.

OOPS!

- When the Supreme Dalek arrives on the bridge of the Crucible, it is seen to be positioned beneath a bulkhead door, but in the reverse shot showing the whole chamber full of Daleks, the bulkhead has completely disappeared.
- Even given the gravity of the situation, it seems strange that Captain Jack shows no reaction at all to seeing Rose again, when he must have believed her still to be trapped in a parallel universe.

PRESS REACTION

- 'This episode links together several themes that have been developing throughout the series. From other disappearing planets to the vanishing bees. But the best part of it is seeing so many friends from the Doctor's past linking up for the first time and working together to fight the deadliest threat they've faced yet. Just like last week's episode, people who've followed all the goings on in the *Who*-niverse over the last four years will love the way that so many different themes and characters combine to create one of the best episodes of the series. Because it's the first part of a two-part story, a fair amount of time is spent setting things up which will, no doubt, pay off in the final episode of the series. But even so, it's a cracking adventure that will delight most *Who* fans, while still leaving them desperate to know how it's all going to end in the hour-long finale a week later.' Lizo Mzimba, CBBC Newsround website, undated.
- 'Did you feel the Earth move? Was it a unified, seismic fangasm or seven million viewers falling off the edge of their seats? Probably both. After two episodes proving that he can write taut, edgy, ideas-lead sci fi with the best of 'em, RTD returns to his patented crowd-pleasing, script pyrotechnics in an episode packed with moments that make you go, "Oooooooohhhh!". The returning guest stars all get some meaty moments in the spotlight; Davros is back and creepier than ever (with a fine, restrained performance from Julian Bleach); some of the FX are just outstanding; the pace is breathless; and the dialogue explodes with punchy one liners and audacious continuity references (who'd've thought Mr Copper would get a mention?). Packing all this in does leave the episode feeling occasionally more like an extended movie trailer as Russell resorts to some incredibly broad strokes to kick the plot along; the "call the Doctor" solution borders on cheese while the trail of bees is handier than a sentient Black and Decker workmate. Some character moments don't quite convince, being dropped into the action like little "emotion bombs" with little time to develop amongst the avalanche of revelations. And the Shadow Proclamation - a couple of women in an office block foyer who seriously need to lay off the peroxide - is a severe disappointment after all the foreshadowing. Good to see the Judoon again, though.' Dave Golder, *SFX* website, 28 June 2008.
- 'Starting with a jolt, and ending with what is likely to be the biggest piece of

misdirection in *Doctor Who*'s history, "The Stolen Earth" is everything that new *Who* represents: hope in the face of disaster, gigantic stakes to play for, the return of icons from the classic show suitably redesigned for the new era, and a romantic underpinning. You almost don't notice that the Doctor isn't on screen anywhere near as much as usual, given the wide scope of the episode.' Patrick Holm, Total Sci-Fi website, 30 June 2008.

ANALYSIS

With 'Bad Wolf'/'The Parting of the Ways', Russell T Davies established a precedent that the two-part finale to each series of *Doctor Who* would be the most exciting, dramatic and spectacular story ever. In doing so, however, he arguably made a rod for his own back, as he was then under huge pressure to ensure that each year's run of episodes ended in an even more epic fashion than the last. This was a challenge he successfully met with 'Army of Ghosts'/'Doomsday' in 2006 and 'The Sound of Drums'/'Last of the Time Lords' in 2007, although in the latter case there were some fans who felt that he was in danger of going rather overboard. This raised an interesting question: how could he possibly manage to outdo that in Series Four without going completely over the top? On the basis of 'The Stolen Earth', it seems the answer was that he couldn't.

This is unquestionably the most epic episode that *Doctor Who* has presented to date, but also the most excessive. It appears that Davies has thrown in everything bar the proverbial kitchen sink: the Doctor and Donna; Rose; Martha and UNIT; Captain Jack and his team from *Torchwood*; Sarah Jane and her adopted son Luke from *The Sarah Jane Adventures*; Davros, the Supreme Dalek, the deranged Dalek Caan and a whole army of ordinary Daleks; Wilf and Sylvia; Francine; Harriet Jones; the Shadow Proclamation; the Judoon; Project Indigo; the Osterhagen Key; the Subwave Network; 27 stolen planets; the Medusa Cascade; and, last but by no means least, an apparent regeneration at the cliffhanger. It is undeniably awe-inspiring to see all these fantastic characters and thrilling elements brought together into what amounts to a valedictory celebration by Davies of the show's greatest hits – a kind of new-era equivalent of the classic-era story 'The Five Doctors' (1983) – but the downside is that they are all sold rather short.

With so many different ingredients to incorporate, much of the narrative of 'The Stolen Earth' is given over simply to introducing each of them in turn and then manoeuvring them into the respective positions they need to occupy in order to propel the story forward to its conclusion in 'Journey's End'. The net result is that surprisingly little actually happens in this episode. The Doctor does not even arrive on the main scene of the action until a couple of minutes before the end, having in the meantime hung about in the TARDIS for a while and taken a largely unnecessary detour to visit the Shadow Proclamation – which, after all the intriguing references to it in previous episodes, turns out to be nothing more remarkable than a kind of space police force headed by a strange albino lady known as the Shadow Architect, served by the Judoon and based in a headquarters that, on the inside at least, has the distinctly unimpressive appearance of a starkly-appointed 21st Century office foyer; a classic demonstration of the principle that some things are better left to the viewer's imagination.

As if to compensate for the rather static nature of much of the action being presented, Davies tries to liven things up by incorporating numerous sequences involving impressive displays of pyrotechnics - including in the UNIT base, in the Torchwood Hub, in Sarah Jane's attic, in Harriet Jones's house and in the TARDIS control room. The viewer could be forgiven for becoming a little blasé about this, though, as effects of this kind have been seen so often in *Doctor Who* now - including in the last episode, 'Turn Left', when Rose's makeshift time machine exploded with a profusion of bangs and flashes when activated. Less effective still is Davies's attempt to emphasise the enormity of the threat posed by the Daleks by having Captain Jack and, in particular, Sarah Jane succumb to despair on hearing their familiar war chant of 'Exterminate!' being broadcast by their approaching space fleet. Admittedly the Daleks' grating electronic tones are as chilling as ever - thanks once again to the splendid vocal contributions of Nicholas Briggs - but Captain Jack's fatalistic 'I'm sorry, we're dead!' to his Torchwood colleagues Gwen and Ianto seems overly melodramatic, and obviously ignores the fact that he himself cannot be killed, while Sarah Jane's tearful reaction, although typically very well acted by Elisabeth Sladen, belies the fact that she has come through two previous encounters with the Daleks, and many other perilous exploits besides, without ever going to pieces in this way. Her bravery in the face of danger has always been one of Sarah Jane's defining characteristics, and although it is quite common for people to become more prone to nerves as they get older, she has certainly shown no signs of that in *The Sarah Jane Adventures*, despite now having a son to care for, so this sudden descent into abject terror seems completely incongruous. In fact, it would not be going too far to say that the scene toward the end where she cowers fearfully in her car as the Daleks threaten to exterminate her is almost a betrayal of the character.

The sequence where the Doctor's friends contact him by causing every phone on Earth to dial his number simultaneously also fails to inspire, partly because it is too similar to the one in 'Last of the Time Lords' where the Doctor is restored to full strength by all the survivors of Earth chanting his name simultaneously - which was hardly one of that episode's most appealing aspects in the first place. The idea of the Subwave Network - described by Donna as 'an outer-space Facebook' - is similarly a fairly obvious contrivance to allow for the Doctor's companions to video-conference with each other from their various separate locations; and although it is good to see Penelope Wilton back for a further appearance as Harriet Jones, it is rather a pity that Davies chose to kill off this endearing character in an episode where there are so many different elements vying for attention that she is inevitably given relatively little to do. (Then again, her death is not actually shown on screen, leaving open a slim possibility that she could have escaped somehow ...) The running joke of her unnecessarily identifying herself to everyone she addresses - 'Harriet Jones, former Prime Minster', 'Yes, I know who you are' - is also overused to such an extent that its final pay-off, when it turns out that even the Daleks know who she is, is not quite as amusing as it might have been.

Having said all this, 'The Stolen Earth' is certainly not without its more positive points. It is great to see characters and settings created for the two spin-offs, *Torchwood* and *The Sarah Jane Adventures*, given debut appearances in the parent show, helping to bring a pleasing sense of unity to the whole *Doctor Who* universe. A particularly memorable moment comes just before the cliffhanger, when Gwen and Ianto unleash a volley of machine-gun fire at a Dalek invading the Hub, Gwen roaring in gutsy defiance as they face seemingly certain extermination. This does raise the question why Jack did not take them with him when he teleported away from the Hub (having fixed his vortex manipulator with surprising ease by simply feeding in two digits given to him by Martha from the read-out of her Project Indigo equipment, which doesn't really make any sense at all!), but they had deliberated kept from him the news that a Dalek saucer was approaching, so presumably he thought that they would be safer there than where he was going. There are some fantastic scenes for Wilf and Sylvia, too, such as the one where Wilf uses a paint-gun to try to blind a Dalek, only for the paint to be dispersed by its force-field, leading the Dalek to grate 'My vision is *not* impaired' – a wonderfully humorous inversion of a celebrated phrase from classic-era Dalek stories, as well as a welcome continuation of the process begun back in 'Dalek' of negating previously-perceived weaknesses in the creatures' design (other examples being their assumed inability to climb stairs and the apparent innocuousness of their sucker-cup arm attachments). Further *Doctor Who* appearances by the always-excellent John Barrowman as Captain Jack and Freema Agyeman as Martha – now promoted and working in a UNIT base in New York, the first non-UK branch of the organisation ever to be featured in the show – are also very acceptable.

More pleasing still, Billie Piper is back on much better form as Rose here. Some three months having elapsed since the recording of 'Turn Left', it seems that whatever problems were affecting her speech in that preceding episode have been largely resolved by this point in the production process; and furthermore she has thankfully reverted to the far more attractive hairstyle she wore in Series Two. Unlike in 'Turn Left', it is also made clear now that Rose's sudden jumps through space and time are being effected by someone with whom she is in contact in her parallel universe version of Torchwood, thus remedying a troubling point of confusion. The scenes where she bemoans being excluded from the Subwave Network conversations between the Doctor and his other companions are amusing and poignant at the same time, and also serve to delay her meeting with the Doctor until the last possible moment, when she materialises just a few blocks away from him on a debris-strewn street and they race toward each other to embrace – like Cathy and Heathcliff running across the moors in some clichéd *Wuthering Heights* dramatisation – only for a Dalek to intervene. Davies has by this point abandoned any attempt to disguise the fact that he is writing their relationship as an out-and-out love story – and justifiably so, as the conception that some fans cling to of the Doctor as an entirely asexual hero whose friendships with his companions never go beyond the strictly platonic is at best outdated and at worst completely misconceived, with much evidence to the contrary discernible even in the classic-era stories. The bond between the Doctor and Rose is undeniably an extra-special one, and one of the great things about the dramatic cliffhanger to 'The Stolen Earth' is that it leaves the viewer on tenterhooks to see how their reunion will play out in 'Journey's End'.

In an episode full of talking points, though, one of the biggest is undoubtedly the return of Davros. After the Autons and the Daleks in Series One, the Cybermen in Series Two, the Macra and the Master in Series Three and the Sontarans earlier in Series Four, it was a fairly safe bet that Davros would be the next classic-era adversary to be resurrected, he being one of the few truly iconic characters of that kind remaining to be used. (In fact, it is arguably only the Ice Warriors that are left now, and one has to wonder just how long it will be before they too make a return appearance in the show.) There is no doubt that Davros brings an extra dimension to

Dalek stories, not least because he is able to engage in sustained dialogue and reasoned debate in a way that his creations aren't so well equipped to manage (although this limitation is often exaggerated); and the benefits of this quickly start to become apparent in 'The Stolen Earth', despite the fact that he spends much of his time lurking in the shadows, until the moment of his big reveal. As things stood at the end of 'Evolution of the Daleks' in Series Three, one had to question how Davies and his team could possibly continue their annual run of Dalek stories, Dalek Caan having apparently been left as the only member of the race still in existence. That conundrum is very cleverly resolved here as Davros shockingly reveals that he has created a whole new Dalek army using cells taken from his own body – the latest contribution to the ongoing Series Four theme of unnatural forms of reproduction – Dalek Caan having performed an emergency temporal shift back into the Time War itself in order to rescue him, at the cost of its own sanity.

Not only is Davros extremely well characterised in Davies's script, he is also superbly realised on screen. Neill Gorton and his Millennium FX team have absolutely excelled themselves in crafting his prosthetic head mask. Quite possibly the finest piece of work they have ever done for *Doctor Who*, this essentially harks back to the look of the original 1970s version as first worn by Michael Wisher in 'Genesis of the Daleks' (1975) but also retains some of the modifications seen in the 1980s version as worn by Terry Molloy, making it a perfect synthesis of the best features of both. At the same time, it goes one better than either by giving the character a greater freedom of facial movement and expression than ever before. The new chair created for Davros is also a well-conceived cross between the original design and that of a new-era Dalek base, the only regrettable aspect being the addition of a superfluous rectangular metal piece a bit like a headrest at the back, which detracts from rather than enhances the overall appearance. And giving Davros a mechanical hand was an inspired notion, maintaining continuity with his fingers having been shot off in 'Revelation of the Daleks' (1985). As for Julian Bleach's performance in the role, it would be hard to overstate how impressive this is. Again Michael Wisher's original interpretation is the obvious reference point here, but it is far more than just an expert piece of mimicry; Bleach succeeds in bringing his own extra dimension of villainy to the part, investing the character with a degree of deranged malevolence unmatched by any of his predecessors.

The wrecked form of Dalek Caan is also very well depicted, and Nicholas Briggs again deserves huge credit for his brilliant vocalisation of the character, complete with creepy demented giggle and chilling prediction of 'everlasting death' for the Doctor's 'most faithful companion'. Rather less appealing, sadly, is the design of the new Supreme Dalek. The red colour scheme is suitably bold and distinctive for a Dalek commander – particularly given that Dalek Sec has previously laid claim to the black livery traditionally associated with the lead Dalek, generally referred to in classic-era stories as the Dalek Supreme – but the added feature of a set of four clunky gold-coloured attachments positioned around the central section of the casing is decidedly ugly. So prominent are these attachments that one keeps expecting them to serve some specific plot purpose, but they never do, and this has to be adjudged a completely unwarranted elaboration. Over the years, there have been a number of other attempts to introduce modifications to Raymond P Cusick's original Dalek design – one of the most notable of these being the addition of power-collection discs to their backs in 'The Dalek Invasion of Earth' (1964) – but these have invariably proved unsuccessful, which perhaps just goes to demonstrate that it is impossible to improve on perfection.[88]

'The Dalek Invasion of Earth' is actually alluded to in 'The Stolen Earth', when the Doctor recalls that someone – i.e. the Daleks – tried to move the Earth once before.[89] This thus becomes, astoundingly, the third story of Series Four to make explicit reference to one transmitted over 40 years earlier.[90] Even some of the dialogue of 'The Dalek Invasion of Earth' is quoted here, with the Daleks rejoicing in becoming 'the masters of Earth' and calling on 'the males, the females, the descendants' to emerge from their homes to be taken prisoner. More generally, the Second World War-inspired invasion imagery of that earlier classic is evoked in shots of Daleks patrolling the ravaged streets of Britain and of their saucer-shaped spacecraft flying overhead and firing down rays of destruction – although naturally the visual effects work is far more impressive this time around, thanks to some further excellent CGI contributions by The Mill and yet more pyrotechnic barrages fired off by Danny Hargreaves and his Any Effects colleagues. The Mill have also made a fine job of representing the assemblage of 'lost' planets brought by the Daleks to the Medusa Cascade, as the viewer finally gets to discover the significance of these oft-mentioned phenomena – not to mention that of the disappearing bees, which turn out to be alien creatures that have fled the Earth in anticipation of impending disaster, in what must surely be a homage by Davies to Douglas Adams' idea of the dolphins leaving Earth prior to its demolition in *The Hitchhiker's Guide to the Galaxy* (BBC Radio 4, 1978).

Last but by no means least amongst the episode's many noteworthy points is its jaw-dropping ending. No aspect of *Doctor Who* seems to have preoccupied the British media and general viewing public more in recent years than the question of how long David Tennant will remain in the role of the Doctor, and who will step in to succeed him when he finally moves on. It was therefore a particularly astute move on Davies's part to build the mid-story cliffhanger of this series finale around a shock regeneration, kept tightly under wraps by removing the scene in question from all preview copies of 'The Stolen Earth' provided to the press. In an episode largely devoted to setting things up in readiness for the closing instalment, this is undoubtedly the most tantalising teaser of all. Ultimately, however, its effectiveness, like that of the episode as a whole, can be judged only in the light of how well, or otherwise, it is all resolved in 'Journey's End' ...

---

[88] Apparently Cusick himself at one point toyed with the idea of introducing a Dalek Supreme with a differently-shaped dome section in 'The Daleks' Master Plan' (1965/66), but that idea was ultimately abandoned.

[89] The Time Lords actually succeeded in moving the Earth through space at one point, renaming it Ravolox in the process, as recounted in 'The Trial of a Time Lord' (1986), but it is clear from the context that that is not what the Doctor is referring to here.

[90] 'The Fires of Pompeii' makes mention of the events of 'The Romans' (1965), while 'Planet of the Ood' refers to those of 'The Sensorites' (1964).

4.13 – JOURNEY'S END

Writer: Russell T Davies
Director: Graeme Harper

DEBUT TRANSMISSION DETAILS

BBC One
Date: 5 July 2008. Scheduled time: 6.40 pm. Actual time: 6.40 pm.

BBC Three
Date: 6 July 2008. Scheduled time: 7.30 pm. Actual time: 7.31 pm.

Duration: 63' 03"

ADDITIONAL CREDITED CAST

Noel Clarke (Mickey Smith), Camille Coduri (Jackie Tyler), Gareth David-Lloyd (Ianto Jones), Eve Myles (Gwen Cooper), Thomas Knight (Luke Smith), Adjoa Andoh (Francine Jones), Julian Bleach (Davros), Valda Aviks[91] (German Woman), Shobu Kapoor[92] (Scared Woman), Elizabeth Tan[93] (Chinese Woman[94]), Michael Price[95] (Liberian Man), Nicholas Briggs (Dalek Voice), Barney Edwards[96] (Dalek Operator), Nick Pegg[97] (Dalek Operator), David Hankinson[98] (Dalek Operator), Anthony Spargo[99] (Dalek Operator), John Leeson[100] (Voice of K-9), Alexander Armstrong (Voice of Mr Smith)

Daleks created by Terry Nation
K-9 created by Bob Baker and Dave Martin

PLOT

The Doctor channels excess regeneration energy into the jar containing his spare hand, so that he is healed but does not have to change his appearance. Jackie Tyler

[91] Not credited in *Radio Times*.
[92] Not credited in *Radio Times*.
[93] Not credited in *Radio Times*.
[94] Name given in dialogue as 'Anna Zhou'.
[95] Not credited in *Radio Times*.
[96] Not credited in *Radio Times*.
[97] Not credited in *Radio Times*.
[98] Not credited in *Radio Times*.
[99] Not credited in *Radio Times*.
[100] Not credited in *Radio Times*.

and Mickey Smith meanwhile arrive from their parallel universe in time to save Sarah Jane from the Dalek patrol she encountered, and Gwen and Ianto find that they are protected in the Hub by an impenetrable time lock program developed by their late colleague Toshiko Sato. The Daleks transfer the TARDIS to the Crucible, where the Doctor, Rose and Jack emerge to face them. Donna is trapped inside, though, when the door closes apparently of its own accord. Davros consigns the TARDIS to be destroyed in the core of the Crucible, but when Donna touches the jar containing the Doctor's hand, it triggers a biological metacrisis: the jar shatters and the hand grows into a complete duplicate Doctor. The duplicate Doctor then moves the TARDIS away from the Crucible and constructs a device with which to disable the Daleks' reality bomb - a weapon they intend to use to annihilate the whole of creation but for their own race. Martha threatens to destroy the Earth using the Osterhagen Key - a device that will trigger 25 strategically-placed nuclear warheads beneath the planet's crust - while Sarah Jane and Jack threaten to blow up the Crucible with a warp star pendant. Davros easily neutralises these threats, however, imprisoning the Doctor, his duplicate and his companions in the vault of the Crucible and blasting Donna with a bolt of energy fired from his fingertips. This bolt of energy has the unforeseen effect of completing the two-way metacrisis, changing Donna into the DoctorDonna - an amalgam of the Doctor's mind within Donna's body. By operating a control console in the vault, the DoctorDonna is able to deactivate the reality bomb and render the Daleks powerless. The Doctor, his duplicate and the DoctorDonna then work together to send all the stolen planets back to their proper points in space and time, but the Supreme Dalek blasts the equipment when there is still one planet left to be returned: Earth. Jack blows up the Supreme Dalek, and while the Doctor is in the TARDIS, the duplicate Doctor triggers a reaction that will destroy all the other Daleks as well - thus fulfilling a prophecy of the deranged Dalek Caan, who has been secretly manipulating the timelines to this end as he wishes to put a stop to the evil of the Daleks. As the Crucible blows up, the Doctor, the duplicate Doctor, the DoctorDonna and all their friends escape in the TARDIS. They use the ship to tow the Earth back to its rightful coordinates, aided by Gwen and Ianto in the Hub and Luke, K-9 and Mr Smith in Sarah Jane's attic. Sarah Jane, Martha, Jack and Mickey all bid farewell to the Doctor, who then takes his duplicate, Rose and Jackie back to Bad Wolf Bay in the parallel universe. The duplicate being half-human, he has only one heart and lacks the ability to regenerate, so he and Rose can now live out the remainder of their lives together. The Doctor and the DoctorDonna depart, but the DoctorDonna's human brain proves unable to cope with all the Time Lord thoughts within it, and the Doctor is forced to wipe her mind of them, and also of all her memories of him and the TARDIS. He returns Donna home to Wilf and Sylvia, then leaves in the TARDIS, alone once again.

<u>QUOTE, UNQUOTE</u>

- **DoctorDonna:** 'Part human, part Time Lord. And I got the best bit of the Doctor. I got his mind.'
  Sarah Jane: 'So there's three of you?'
  Rose: 'Three Doctors.'
  Jack: 'I can't tell you what I'm thinking right now.'

Doctor: 'You're so unique, the timelines were converging on you: human being with a Time Lord brain.'

- **Doctor:** 'Davros, come with me! I promise I can save you.'
  Davros: 'Never forget, Doctor, you did this! I name you forever: you are the destroyer of worlds!'
- **Sarah Jane:** 'You know, you act like such a lonely man, but look at you, you've got the biggest family on Earth.'
- **Duplicate Doctor:** 'I look like him, I think like him. Same memories, same thoughts, same everything. Except I've only got one heart.'
  Rose: 'Which means?'
  Duplicate Doctor: 'I'm part human. Specifically the ageing part. I'll grow old and never regenerate. I've only got one life, Rose Tyler. I could spend it with you, if you want.'
  Rose: 'You'll grow old at the same time as me.'
  Duplicate Doctor: 'Together.'
- **Doctor:** 'I had to wipe her mind completely: every trace of me or the TARDIS, anything we did together, anywhere we went, had to go.'
  Wilf: 'All those wonderful things she did.'
  Doctor: 'I know. But that version of Donna is dead, because if she remembers, just for a second, she'll burn up. You can never tell her. You can't mention me or any of it, for the rest of her life.'
  Sylvia: 'But the whole world's talking about it. We travelled across space.'
  Doctor: 'It'll just be a story. One of those Donna Noble stories, where she missed it all again.'
  Wilf: 'But she was better with you.'
  Sylvia: 'Don't say that!'
  Wilf: 'No, she was!'
  Doctor: 'I just want you to know that there are worlds out there, safe in the sky because of her. That there are people living in the light and singing songs of Donna Noble, a thousand million light years away. They will never forget her, while she can never remember. And for one moment, one shining moment, she was the most important woman in the whole wide universe.'
- **Wilf:** 'Oh, but Doctor, what about you now? Who have you got? I mean, all those friends of yours ...'
  Doctor: 'They've all got someone else. Still, that's fine. I'm fine.'
  Wilf: 'I'll watch out for you, sir.'
  Doctor: 'You can't ever tell her.'
  Wilf: 'No, no, no. But every night, Doctor, when it gets dark, and the stars come out, I'll look up, on her behalf. I'll look up at the sky, and think of you.'
  Doctor: 'Thank you.'

CONTINUITY POINTS

- The Doctor says of his stalled regeneration: 'Used the regeneration energy to heal myself, but as soon as that was done, I didn't need to change ... So, to stop the energy going all the way, I siphoned off the rest into a handy bio-matching receptacle; namely my hand, my hand there, my handy spare hand.' This spare hand was cut off by the Sycorax leader in a swordfight in 'The

Christmas Invasion', obtained by Torchwood and kept in a jar in the Hub in Cardiff until the *Torchwood* Series One finale 'End of Days', and then taken on board the TARDIS by Captain Jack in 'Utopia'. It was briefly stolen by the Master at the end of the latter episode, but subsequently retrieved by the Doctor.

- Ianto discovers from consulting Torchwood's computer system that the Hub is protected by a 'time lock ... the ultimate defence program'. He recalls that Tosh was working on it – prior to her death in the *Torchwood* Series Two finale 'Exit Wounds' – but that he was unaware she had finished it. The effect of this system is to seal the Hub in a 'time bubble' in the event of an attack, so that nothing can get in or out.
- The Daleks trap the TARDIS in a 'temporal prison', which the Doctor describes as 'some sort of chronon loop', and then transport it to the Crucible. The Doctor tells Rose: 'Last time we fought the Daleks they were scavengers, and hybrids, and mad. But this is a fully-fledged Dalek empire, at the height of its power. Experts at fighting TARDISes; they can do anything. Right now, that wooden door is just wood.'
- The circular, yellow-fronted dimension jump devices used by Mickey and Jackie are modified versions of the type first seen in 'Doomsday'. These were invented by the parallel universe Torchwood to enable travel between one universe and another before they became sealed. Mickey says that they '[rip] a hole in the fabric of space' and that they need half an hour to recharge between jumps.
- Rose explains that the parallel universe Torchwood have been developing a device called the 'dimension cannon' to enable her to cross to the Doctor's universe and find him. This retrospectively accounts for her appearances in 'Turn Left' and 'The Stolen Earth'. She adds: 'Suddenly it started to work, and the dimensions started to collapse, not just in our world, not just in yours, but the whole of reality; even the void was dead. Something is destroying everything'. The void was established in 'Army of Ghosts'/'Doomsday' to be a dimension outside all the universes. When Donna asks Rose to clarify what the device revealed about her, Rose says: 'The dimension cannon can measure timelines, and it's weird, Donna, but they all seem to converge on you.'
- The Daleks in this story use their established unit of time, the rel.
- The Doctor taunts Davros by suggesting that he is the Daleks' 'pet' and that he is essentially a prisoner in the vault of the Crucible. Davros counters this by saying that he and the Supreme Dalek have an 'arrangement'. This reflects the uneasy relationship between Davros and the Daleks seen in classic-era *Doctor Who.*
- The Supreme Dalek says that the Crucible has 'a heart of z-neutrino energy'.
- When Donna touches the jar containing the Doctor's hand imbued with the siphoned-off regeneration energy, it creates a duplicate Doctor via a process that he describes to her as 'instantaneous biological metacrisis', adding, 'I grew out of you'. He realises that he has only one heart and that his body is 'part Time Lord, part human'. The Doctor himself is genetically half-human on his mother's side, as established in the 1996 TV movie, but has a predominantly Time Lord body with two hearts – although his eyes are human. This was presumably the result of normal sexual reproduction and clearly differs from

the type of hybridisation seen here, as the duplicate Doctor says that he is 'unique'.[101] It must also differ from the process seen in 'Evolution of the Daleks', where the Doctor added Time Lord DNA to the Daleks' human army to create a new human-Time Lord species; in that case, the bodies of the people concerned were still primarily human. Equally, it must differ from the process that resulted in the birth of Jenny in 'The Doctor's Daughter'; in that instance, Jenny had a physical form akin to that of a Time Lord, including two hearts, but the Doctor implied that she did not have a Time Lord mind or the ability to regenerate.

- It is uncertain whether or not the Doctor's part-completed regeneration seen here counts as one of the maximum 12 allowed to a Time Lord, as established in 'The Deadly Assassin' (1976).
- The Doctor deduces that the reality bomb uses the 27 stolen planets in alignment to flatten z-neutrino energy from the Crucible into a single stream and transmit it out into the universe. Davros explains: 'Every atom in existence is bound by an electrical field. The reality bomb cancels it out. Structure falls apart ... Full transmission will dissolve every form of matter ... across the entire universe, never stopping, never faltering never fading. People, planets and stars will become dust, and the dust will become atoms, and the atoms will become nothing; and the wavelength will continue, breaking through the rift at the heart of the Medusa Cascade into every dimension, every parallel, every single corner of creation. This is my ultimate victory, Doctor: the destruction of reality itself!' This implies that it is only in the Doctor's universe that the Daleks have developed the reality bomb, but that its effects threaten to spread out and destroy all the parallel universes as well. This process started to occur ahead of time in Rose's universe, which runs slightly in advance of the Doctor's, causing the onset of 'the darkness'. This recalls the way the effects of the 'Pyrovillian alternative' rippled back through time from an ultimately negated timeline in 'The Fires of Pompeii'. Toward the end of the story, the DoctorDonna says: 'The walls of the world are closing again, now that the reality bomb never happened. It's dimensional retroclosure. See, I really get that stuff now.'
- Mistakenly believing that Captain Jack is dead, the Daleks send his body for incineration. It is unclear whether he is actually consigned to the incinerator or manages to scramble clear of it after the door closes behind him; the latter seems more likely, as his clothes are still intact when he subsequently escapes (although there have been some indications in *Torchwood* that, for reasons unknown, his clothes are exceptionally resistant to damage).
- Sarah Jane has brought with her from her home to the Dalek Crucible a warp star contained within a pendant given to her by a 'Verron Soothsayer ... for the End of Days'. This may well have been the same (unseen) Verron Soothsayer

[101] In Marc Platt's *New Adventures* novel *Lungbarrow* (Virgin Publishing, 1997), it is indicated that the Time Lords are normally born from genetic looms but that the Doctor is different from the others, as signified by the fact that unlike them he has a navel. It is implied that he was once a mysterious figure known as the Other, who effectively committed suicide by throwing himself into the looms and was then reborn as the Doctor. It may be that it was the Other who had a human mother.

who gave her the puzzle-box featured in the 'Whatever Happened to Sarah Jane?' story of *The Sarah Jane Adventures*. Captain Jack tells Mickey that a warp star is a 'warpfold conjugation trapped in a carbonised shell ... an explosion waiting to happen'.

- The duplicate Doctor constructs a 'z-neutrino biological inversion catalyser' and explains: 'Davros said that he built those Daleks out of himself. His genetic code runs through the entire race. If I can use this to lock the Crucible's transmission onto Davros himself ... Biggest backfire in history!'
- It requires at least three UNIT operators at different stations to activate the Osterhagen system. Martha explains the Osterhagen Key: 'There's a chain of 25 nuclear warheads placed in strategic points beneath the Earth's crust. If I use the key, they detonate and the Earth gets ripped apart ... The Osterhagen Key is to be used if the suffering of the human race is so great, so without hope, that this becomes the final option.' The relatively small number of 25 nuclear warheads would not normally be sufficient to destroy the Earth, or even to do much damage to it in geological terms, so either the 'strategic points' mentioned by Martha must have some significance unknown to scientists in our universe (perhaps exploiting special flaws in the planet's structure?) or else the military forces of the *Doctor Who* universe must have a far more powerful kind of nuclear weapon available to them.
- The timeline of Earth history seen in the Series One episode 'Dalek' must by this point have been completely overwritten. Set in Utah in 2012, that had wealthy alien artefact collector Henry Van Statten trying to find out what a Dalek was, whereas following 'The Stolen Earth'/'Journey's End' (if not 'Army of Ghosts'/'Doomsday') that must be fairly common public knowledge – despite the implication in 'Journey's End' that some sceptics will continue to try to deny the existence of alien life even in the face of the seemingly incontrovertible evidence now presented to them. Presumably if the Doctor were to revisit Utah in 2012, things would be very different.
- The DoctorDonna explains that the human biological metacrisis was a two way process: she is now part Time Lord, part human: 'But, it just stayed dormant in my head till the synapses got that little extra spark, kicking them into life.' That spark was provided by Davros blasting Donna with a bolt of energy. However, while she has the Doctor's mind, her body is still human, and it eventually becomes clear that her brain is unable to cope with all the Time Lord thoughts within it. The Doctor says, 'There's never been a human-Time Lord metacrisis before now, and you know why', and the DoctorDonna replies, 'Because there can't be'.
- The device used to send the stolen planets (bar Earth) back to their proper points in space and time (and presumably to collect them in the first place) is identified by the DoctorDonna as a 'magnetron'. The Daleks were first seen to use a 'time vortex magnetron' in 'Day of the Daleks' (1972). The Time Lords also once used a magnetron to move Earth to a different point in space and time, as recounted in 'The Trial of a Time Lord' (1986).
- On seeing Gwen on the TARDIS monitor screen, the Doctor asks: 'Tell me, Gwen Cooper, are you from an old Cardiff family?' She replies: 'Yes, all the way back to the 1800s.' Exchanging a grin with Rose, the Doctor says: 'Ah, thought so: spacial genetic multiplicity. It's a funny old world.' This is a

reference to the fact that Gwen looks very similar to Gwyneth from 'The Unquiet Dead' (owing to both characters having been played by the same actress, Eve Myles). Although taken by some fans to mean that there is a blood relationship between Gwen and Gwyneth, this was not Russell T Davies's intention when writing the line. Quoted on the official *Doctor Who* website, he explains: 'It's not familial as we understand it. There's no blood tie. Spatial genetic multiplicity means an echo and repetition of physical traits across a time rift.'

- There now seems to be a distinct coolness between Rose and Mickey. They do not speak to each other at any point during the episode, and when Mickey decides to stay in the Doctor's universe, rather than return to the parallel world, where his gran has now passed away, he says: 'There's nothing there for me now; certainly not Rose.'
- In the time since she last saw the Doctor, Jackie has had a baby boy, named Tony. Her husband Pete has been looking after him while she has been away.
- The DoctorDonna mentions the planet Felspoon and says that it has 'mountains that sway in the breeze'.

PRODUCTION NOTES

- Made with 'The Stolen Earth' as part of Block 9 of production.
- Aside from specials, this is the longest *Doctor Who* episode ever.
- Credited over the opening titles are David Tennant, Catherine Tate, Freema Agyeman, John Barrowman, Elisabeth Sladen and Billie Piper. Then, as on 'The Stolen Earth', a number of additional actor credits are superimposed after the opening titles: these are for Noel Clarke, Camille Coduri, Adjoa Andoh, Eve Myles and Gareth David-Lloyd.
- The scenes of the Doctor taking Donna back to the Nobles' home and later leaving in the rain were shot at the usual Nant-Fawr Road location on 27 and 28 February 2008, along with material for 'The Stolen Earth'. Southerndown Beach, Ogmore Bay, Bridgend once again became Bad Wolf Bay for Rose's farewell scene, recorded on 5 March. The shot of Wilf and Sylvia outside their house, looking up into the sky as the Dalek ships depart, was taped outside 18 Hawthorn Road, Pontypridd on 12 March, again along with material for 'The Stolen Earth'. The scene of the TARDIS being transported to the Crucible was part of the material recorded on 13 March on the High Street, Penarth. Castell Coch in Tongwynlais, Cardiff was the location used for the Osterhagen base in Germany. Recording took place there on 14 and 18 March. As scripted, these scenes were originally to have featured a quaint, Hansel and Gretel-style cottage, but Castell Coch was used instead as no suitable cottage could be found within a reasonable travelling distance of the show's production base. The Alpha Steel plant on Corporation Road, Newport was the venue for taping of some of the Crucible interiors, which was done on 17 March. Morgan Jones Park in Caerphilly was the place where the Doctor dropped off Sarah Jane, Captain Jack, Martha and Mickey after the defeat of the Daleks. It is unclear whether this was intended to represent an area close to Sarah Jane's address in Ealing or one close to the Torchwood Hub in Cardiff, or indeed elsewhere; at any rate, it seems that some of the Doctor's friends will still have quite a bit of

travelling to do before they finally get home! Martha's farewell to Francine was part of the material shot on 25 and 26 March at a house in Cwrt-y-Vil Road, Penarth. The scene of Sarah Jane, Jackie and Mickey giving themselves up to a Dalek patrol was shot on Robinswood Crescent, Penarth on 25 March, along with that of Sarah Jane's initial encounter with the patrol in 'The Stolen Earth'.

- The studio recording for this story was carried out at Upper Boat on 18 to 22, 25, 28 and 29 February, 3, 4, 6, 7, 10, 11, 20, 21, 24 and 27 to 29 March and 1 May 2008.
- *Blue Peter* presenter Gethin Jones stood in as a Dalek Operator in one scene in the Crucible, as part of a preview feature for the long-running children's magazine show.
- Musician Collum Sanson-Regan doubled for David Tennant in the scenes where the Doctor and his duplicate were both required to be in shot at the same time.
- When Davros asks the Doctor to reflect on how many people have died in his name, flashback clips are shown of Jabe from 'The End of the World', the Controller from 'The Parting of the Ways', Lynda from 'The Parting of the Ways', Sir Robert MacLeish from 'Tooth and Claw', Mrs Moore from 'The Age of Steel', Mr Skinner, Ursula Blake and Bridget from 'Love & Monsters', the Face of Boe from 'Gridlock', Chantho from 'Utopia', Astrid from 'Voyage of the Damned', Luke Rattigan from 'The Poison Sky', Jenny from 'The Doctor's Daughter', 'River Song' from 'Forest of the Dead' and the Hostess from 'Midnight'.
- When the Doctor removes all the Time Lord thoughts from Donna's brain, flashback clips are shown of Donna from most of her previous episodes back to 'The Runaway Bride'.
- The last official working day on *Doctor Who* for both producer Phil Collinson and star Catherine Tate was 21 March 2008, although Collinson continued to be involved in post-production matters right up to the time of this episode's transmission.
- Early drafts of the script for this episode contained a flashback sequence revealing how Davros sustained his disfiguring injuries on the Daleks' home planet Skaro.
- Russell T Davies originally intended that in the Bad Wolf Bay scene the Doctor would leave his duplicate and Rose with a small piece of the TARDIS, so that they could use it to grow their own ship. This idea was dropped in the course of editing. Another change made at a late stage was the removal of a shot where, having been returned to her home with her memories of the Doctor wiped, Donna hears the TARDIS dematerialising; director Graeme Harper and producer Phil Collinson were keen to retain this, but were overruled by Davies and his fellow executive producer Julie Gardner. The episode was originally supposed to close on a cliffhanger, with two Cybermen appearing behind the Doctor inside the TARDIS. Although recorded, this was ultimately dropped by Davies at the urging of regular *Doctor Who Magazine* contributor Benjamin Cook, with whom he was collaborating on the book *The Writer's Tale* (BBC Books, 2008).

- The episode ends with the captions 'Coming Christmas 2008', 'The Return' and 'Of the Cybermen', interspersed with a selection of preview clips from the forthcoming Christmas special, 'The Next Doctor', unnamed at the time.

OOPS!

- Much is made of the question of who caused the TARDIS doors to close, trapping Donna inside, after the ship's arrival in the vault of the Crucible. The Doctor accuses the Daleks of being responsible, while they in turn suspect him of trying to trick them. In the end, though, it is never explained who did it …
- The Doctor says that the Ood predicted the creation of the DoctorDonna. However, it was he who first started using the phrase 'Doctor Donna' in 'Planet of the Ood', and the Ood simply copied him, apparently mistaking this for a 'joint' name.
- Although Wilf and Sylvia can both be relied upon not to remind Donna of her time with the Doctor after she is returned to them at the end of the story, there are many other people who might inadvertently do so, including all the guests who were at her cancelled wedding to Lance Bennett and (assuming that the Doctor has not, unseen on screen, cautioned them against contacting her) Sarah Jane, Martha, Mickey and Captain Jack. (Perhaps, though, the block the Doctor has put on those memories is stronger than he initially suggests; otherwise, her seeing him at her home, albeit that he introduces himself as 'John Smith' rather than as 'the Doctor', would surely be enough to trigger them in itself.)

PRESS REACTION

- 'DoctorDonna is the ingenious feat of plot-twistery that we've been waiting for, but the technobabble she spews … is like someone laughing hysterically at you: "None of this matters! Whee!" And sometimes you can't help thinking, would this be more interesting if it were actually watertight, or at least made gestures in that direction? As it is, there is no predicting what's going to happen, no device that can't be whipped out of someone's pocket to block a hole or destroy the universe or erase the past. Marshalled against the forces of darkness, the Doctor's private army, almost squad-sized, make the odds seem strangely in their favour. Wielding supercomputers, necklace-bombs, nuclear weapons and even K-9, our ex-companions do what humans do, which is what the Doctor refused to do at the end of "The Parting of the Ways", and seems to have emerged as the climactic theme of the series. Sometimes, the Doctor needs people to stop him, but those same people, thanks to his influence, will then be prepared to do the dirty jobs he can't face. Like war, for example. All the self-congratulation ("Don't Torchwood look great?" "You're all brilliant!"), while occasionally cloying, has a point to it. Even if the Doctor isn't aware of it, he's grooming killers, as you might if you found yourself facing down the hordes of death on a daily basis.' Thom Hutchinson, *DeathRay* Issue 15, September 2008.
- 'Oh dear. If "The Stolen Earth" pumped us up with excitement, then "Journey's End" eventually, after some promise, took a pin and slowly

deflated us. Because as the episode wound itself into its back third, once all the scores seemed to have been settled, it was clear that this wasn't going to be the classic series finale we'd been teased with. And while it was better than last year's "Last Of The Time Lords" (even if it didn't necessarily feel like it immediately after the end credits), this was still a major missed opportunity, and a real disappointment.' Simon Brew, Den of Geek website, 5 July 2008.

- 'As usual, *Doctor Who* served up a lot more than mere excitement. There was also plenty of heartbreak and heroism – clearly discernible emotions, even to the inhabitants of Planet Adolescence and its near-neighbour, Planet Post-Adolescence (where this particular critic happens to reside). And herein lies one of the secrets of *Doctor Who*'s success: amid the special effects and gloopy grotesques, lie richly defined characters behaving in readily identifiable ways. It had been widely flagged beforehand that someone was going to take a final bow last night. Most of the thinking money was on David Tennant but in the end it was Catherine Tate's excellent Donna who copped it – or rather had her memory wiped. Tennant meanwhile sails on for another series. Few will mourn his non-passing. He has proved to be an excellent Doctor, bug-eyed with intensity when circumstances demanded it, yet also full of zip and sparkle.' John Preston, Telegraph.co.uk website, 7 July 2008.
- 'Donna's apotheosis, quoting formulae as if to the manner born, and using her temp typing skills to dispatch the Daleks, gave Catherine Tate her finest hour. The warmth and humour she has brought to the series will be missed, though I won't mourn the absence of dialogue insisting on how special she is. For it was Donna not the Doctor who left the show, abandoned back on earth with her mind wiped of memories. This was one of the bows Davies left neatly tied. He also sealed Rose (Billie Piper, a less vibrant presence than in her heyday) into her parallel universe with the human Doctor, where they can snog to the end of their days. Sarah Jane Smith, Martha and Captain Jack were all gently propelled into their own spin-off series, where they will no doubt continue to thrive. Which left Russell T Davies exactly where he most likes being: with his Doctor. His conception of Doctor Who is of a complex being who is always ultimately alone as he wrestles with the business of salvation. "How many have died in your name?" asks Julian Bleach's eerie Davros. But that obsessive nagging away at the morality of being a Time Lord can seem repetitive and limiting. The Russell T Davies *Doctor Who* has been a glory, but when the fifth series returns (in 2010, after a number of specials next year) he will be a different man – whether or not the charismatic David Tennant continues to play him. "Journey's End" was a delirious conclusion to Davies's reign, a rollercoaster through his favourite themes. I wouldn't have missed it for the world, but I await the reinvention.' Sarah Crompton, Telegraph.co.uk website, 7 July 2008.
- 'Well, I think we can safely say there was something for everyone in that, can't we? Hands up who wanted two pints of Tennant in the finale of *Doctor Who*? You got it! Hands up those who thought Donna would help fufil the three-fold man prophecy? Done and done! And anyone who wanted *Matrix* bullets, exploding Daleks, Davros screaming in elation and despair, Gita from *EastEnders* vaporised by a reality bomb, a two-way biological metacrisis, John Barrowman, warp stars, Osterhagen Keys, Catherine Tate doing impressions

of David Tennant and vice versa, planets popping like balloons and more *dei ex machini* than you could shake a sonic screwdriver at, found them all spread lavishly on the Whovian buffet table by Russell T Davies, like a host who has thrown dietary and budgetary constraints to the wind for one final, farewell blowout. There was even a cameo appearance by K-9, looking even better for his age than Sarah Jane. I can't, to be brutally honest with you, work out exactly what happened. The jargon-heavy mid-section rather did for my chances of keeping a grip on the minutiae, but that's nothing that three days on the internet forums won't sort out.' Lucy Mangan, guardian.co.uk website, 7 July 2008.

- 'The last three episodes of this series of *Doctor Who* have been outstanding. It was great to see all the cast get back together. I love it when a show can do that. Also, as always with *Who*, there were lots of clever clues and tie-ins all the way through. I have to admit, I wasn't a fan of Catherine Tate from the start, and I'm still not too keen on her by the end, but she served her purpose so I'll give her that. Not to be too smug, but I actually guessed the Doctor wasn't going to regenerate and Donna was going to be the one who goes. It's not that hard, basically take anything show creator Russell T Davies says in an interview and take the opposite view, so when he starts going on about David Tennant leaving you know he isn't yet.' Karen Dunn, *Now* magazine website, 5 July 2008.

ANALYSIS

With the *Doctor Who* production team having made it their firm policy to keep advance plot information close to their chests, there is invariably much speculation within the show's online fandom about any forthcoming story - and never more so than when it is a series finale. Usually this speculation is so wild, and ultimately proves to be so far wide of the mark, that it is not worth taking seriously. However, in May 2008, around the time that 'The Unicorn and the Wasp' was transmitted, a rumour started to spread about the overarching plot of the last few episodes of Series Four that seemed a lot more credible than usual. The gist of this was as follows:

> Harriet Jones, still angry at being deposed by the Doctor, steals the Master's ring from his funeral pyre, starts hearing the sound of drums and senses that this emanates from an army of Daleks, led by Davros, who were trapped beneath the Medusa Cascade during the Time War and are now on the point of breaking free. Meanwhile, in the Library, Donna reads in River Song's discarded diary that she should have been killed by the Racnoss Empress when she first met the Doctor. She determines to ask the Doctor about this, but he suddenly vanishes. Rose communicates with Donna via the TARDIS monitor screen, explaining that the walls between parallel universes are breaking down. Guided by Rose, Donna operates the TARDIS controls, and after a number of failed attempts, in which they both see alternative timelines showing what their lives would

> have been like had they never met the Doctor, the Time Lord is restored to the ship. He had been drawn beneath the Medusa Cascade by Davros and his new ally, Harriet Jones, who has been part-converted into a red Supreme Dalek. It is the Daleks' efforts to escape from the Medusa Cascade that are causing all the parallel universes to become intertwined. A number of previously-defeated enemies of the Doctor start to reappear from alternative timelines in which they were victorious, while some of his past companions, including Martha, Jack and Sarah Jane, join forces to try to stop the chaos, along with Rose, Jackie and Mickey, who can now cross between the universes. One of the enemies that reappears is the Racnoss Empress who, having also allied herself with Davros, activates a hitherto-dormant Metebelis spider that has been sitting invisibly on Donna's back ever since their first encounter. Donna starts to act as a traitor within the Doctor's group, but he realises this and manages to injure the spider, while stopping short of killing it, as that would also kill Donna. The Doctor decides that in order to put things to rights, he and his friends need to travel to the Medusa Cascade and seal it once again. On arriving, though, he hesitantly concludes that the only way to do this is to give it a human life. This is how it was sealed during the Time War: he and his companion Grace Holloway both jumped into it, but it kept only Grace and spat him out again, causing him to regenerate from his eighth incarnation to his ninth, as seen in a flashback. The Doctor's friends all selflessly offer to be the one to enter the Medusa Cascade, but Donna's arguments prove persuasive: she has less to live for than the others, as she is only a temp, Wilf and Sylvia have both been killed during the course of the action and she does not want to have to spend the rest of her life with an injured spider on her back! She kisses the Doctor goodbye, falls into the Medusa Cascade and seals it with her death. All the universes are restored to the point when Donna should have been killed by the Racnoss Empress in 'The Runaway Bride'. However, wracked by guilt, the Doctor breaks a fundamental law of time. He goes back to 24 hours before her death, plucks her from her timeline, destroys the Racnoss Empress and gets Jack to drug Donna with retcon so that she will remember none of this. He then leaves her at her home with Wilf, who is laid up with the flu while the rest of her family are waiting at the church for her wedding that will never happen.

In the end, of course, this all turned out to be a hoax. But whoever came up with that fake storyline certainly deserves some credit. Not only does it encompass all the characters and elements that, at the time, were known or rumoured to be featured in the concluding episodes of the series, and all the scenes witnessed being recorded by those who had been present on location, but it also addresses a number of big fan preoccupations, such as the identity of the woman who took the Master's ring from his funeral pyre at the end of 'Last of the Time Lords' and the possibility of the eighth and ninth Doctors returning in cameo appearances. Furthermore, it reads very much like a Russell T Davies plot, with just the right sort of dramatic and emotional beats one would expect. In fact, so taken in by it were many of those who heard about it that they became convinced that it was true, and moreover really *hoped* that it was true, as it seemed to hold out great promise for a really thrilling and poignant climax to the series. However, perhaps the most remarkable thing about it, and the main reason why it is worth mentioning here, is that it demonstrates how the series could have been wrapped up using all the same characters and elements but, arguably, in a far more coherent and satisfying way than was actually achieved in the transmitted episodes.

The problems with 'Journey's End' start right at the beginning. It would not be overstating things to say that the regeneration cliffhanger to 'The Stolen Earth' had got the whole nation buzzing with excitement and anticipation - recalling celebrated precedents such as the 'Who shot JR?' mystery in *Dallas* back in the 1980s - and this is borne out by the huge audience of 10.57 million who tuned in to 'Journey's End' to see its resolution, making *Doctor Who* the number one rated programme of the week for the first time in its entire history. But one can only suppose that the words 'cop out' must have rung around many living rooms up and down the country as, within the first couple of minutes, it became clear that David Tennant was not really leaving the show after all, and that the whole thing had been just one big tease. It seems that even many fans, let alone members of the general viewing public, had been taken in by this - perhaps surprisingly so, as it was quite common knowledge on the online forums that Tennant would be appearing in 'Journey's End', and indeed that he had already been spotted recording scenes on location for the 2008 Christmas special; not to mention the fact that it seriously strains credibility to suppose that the BBC might actually have cast a new Doctor without any hint of this having leaked out into the press. As delighted as the great majority were to learn that they had not in fact seen the last of Tennant's brilliant portrayal of the Doctor, it was hard to shake the feeling that this had all been a huge anticlimax.

Thankfully, the 'fake' regeneration, with the Doctor simply draining the excess energy off into his spare hand, does at least prove to be not entirely superfluous to the plot, as it subsequently leads on to the creation of the duplicate Doctor, and then of the DoctorDonna - the ultimate expression of the running Series Four theme of alien forms of reproduction. However, these developments bring problems of their own. For one thing, to turn this into a multi-Doctor story, almost like a new-era take on 'The Three Doctors' (1972/73), when there are already so many other players jostling for space in the narrative - further added to in this episode by the arrival of Jackie Tyler and Mickey Smith from the parallel universe - makes the whole thing seem even more overblown than it did before. More than that, though, the respective roles that the duplicate Doctor and the DoctorDonna play in the proceedings are deeply unsatisfactory.

The idea that the duplicate Doctor has a darker state of mind akin to that of the ninth Doctor when Rose first met him, so that he is prepared to wipe out the Daleks without giving a second thought to the fact that he is actually committing genocide, is fair enough in itself - although the implied description of the ninth Doctor as being 'full of blood and anger and revenge' seems exaggerated to say the least. The snag is that it completely undermines the claim that the duplicate has the 'same memories, same thoughts, same everything' as the original, bar the lack of a Time Lord's second heart and extended lifespan. In fact, the duplicate and the original do not even act as if they consider themselves to be equals; the duplicate meekly defers to the original, who in turn treats him like a recalcitrant younger sibling. What's more, the duplicate has clearly absorbed a degree of Donna's personality, as established in the scene where he starts to talk in the same manner as her. None of this would really matter, but for the crucial fact that it makes the original's idea to pair the duplicate off with Rose and abandon them both in the parallel universe, and Rose's apparent acceptance of this imperfect compromise, decidedly creepy. Recalling her own reaction in the accompanying *Doctor Who Confidential* programme, Billie Piper comments, 'I always felt like she shouldn't be kissing that number two, and also, he's not the same, it's all a bit weird' – which, quite apart from being the closest that *Doctor Who Confidential* has ever come to including a negative comment about *Doctor Who*, is absolutely spot on.

The duplicate Doctor may be the only one that Rose can ever have, but he's not the one she really wants, and she is basically manipulated into accepting him – for the time being, at least – by being taken back to Bad Wolf Bay, scene of her enforced separation from the Doctor at the end of 'Doomsday', and given no real choice in the matter. This is far from being the 'happy ending' for Rose that some commentators have sought to suggest, and certainly not for the Doctor. The situation isn't even improved by the supposed redeeming factor for Rose that the duplicate, unlike the original, is able to say that he loves her, the obvious flaw in this argument being that he doesn't actually say it at all; the best he can manage is to whisper it in her ear, as if embarrassed to speak the words out loud, leaving the viewer simply to infer what has been said. In short, Davies completely blows this incredibly important scene. It is as if someone had made a new version of the classic movie *Casablanca* (1943) and reworked the ending to have Ingrid Bergman's Ilsa packed off with the previously-unseen twin brother of Humphrey Bogart's Rick. Not only does it fall far short of the incomparable, heart-rending original, but sadly it rather cheapens the memory of it.

Donna becoming the DoctorDonna does at least give one aspect of the Doctor a chance to experience being ginger – an ambition he admitted to in 'The Christmas Invasion', in reference to his recent regeneration – and also arguably fulfils that much-discussed possibility of the show having its first 'female Doctor'. However, there are a number of unfortunate aspects to the way this unique character is handled. The idea that the personalities of the Doctor and Donna become intermixed is used by Davies to give David Tennant an opportunity to mimic Catherine Tate's performance and vice versa, but sadly this pushes them into rather too broad an area of comedy, verging on spoof. Throughout Series Four, Tate has ironically always been at her weakest when given humorous material to perform, tending to overplay it somewhat, and that is again the case here. The blame lies squarely with Davies's script, though, for the appalling scene in which the DoctorDonna, spouting reams of technobabble, wrecks Davros's entire scheme by tapping gleefully on some oversized buttons on a master keyboard laughably positioned in the Crucible's vault, then reduces the Daleks to figures of fun by causing them to spin about uncontrollably – an incident that must surely have displeased the estate of their creator Terry Nation, which has always been, quite rightly, very keen to preserve their menace by vetoing their depiction in a humorous light. Not only does this essentially repeat the uninspiring resolution of both 'Partners in Crime' and 'The Fires of Pompeii', in which the Doctor likewise defeats the aliens by pushing a few buttons on a control console, but far more damagingly it belittles the threat of the Daleks and undermines the idea of the Doctor having had to make huge and traumatic sacrifices in order to destroy them in the past. In effect, it raises the question, if the DoctorDonna can merrily neutralise a huge Dalek army here and thwart its apocalyptic intentions without even breaking a sweat, why couldn't the Doctor have found some way to end the Time War that did not involve his entire race being wiped out, and why did it take the terrible cost of Rose becoming the Bad Wolf and him then having to give up his ninth life to overcome the Daleks in 'The Parting of the Ways'? A kind of answer to this is provided when the DoctorDonna notes that the Doctor is 'lacking that little bit of human, that gut instinct that goes hand-in-hand with planet Earth' and claims that she can think of ideas that he and his duplicate 'couldn't dream of in a million years'; but, all the same, the undoing of the Daleks' grand plan seems altogether far too easy here, notwithstanding the hope-sapping sequence where Davros disarms and imprisons each of the Doctor's companions in turn and even the surprise reinforcement of his duplicate. The fact that this episode subverts such iconic aspects of new-era *Doctor Who* as the Doctor's relationship with Rose and the horrific legacy of the Time War – a mistake that even that fan hoax storyline managed to avoid – shows just how badly misjudged it really is.

Having said this, the creation of the DoctorDonna is not without its own high cost, as becomes apparent in the distressing scene in the TARDIS where she starts to get overwhelmed by all the Time Lord thoughts teeming within her physically human brain – an idea rather cleverly foreshadowed in 'Forest of the Dead' when the Doctor explains the inability of CAL to reverse the failure of the Library's computer by saying, 'She's got over 4,000 living minds chatting away inside her head; it must be like being ... well, me.' (River Song's voiceover comment in that earlier episode that 'the skies of all the worlds might just turn dark' if the Doctor ever accepted the inevitability of death also starts to look prescient in view of what happens in 'The Stolen Earth'/'Journey's End', but perhaps that is a coincidence.) The Doctor's solution to this problem, to block all those thoughts from Donna's mind but also, for fear of them being reawakened, to deprive her of all her memories of her life with him, leaving her as she was prior to 'The Runaway Bride', affords a logically coherent and deeply moving ending to Donna's story – and, notably, one that is very similar to that described in the hoax storyline, making one wonder if that was actually compiled with the benefit of some inside knowledge. And yet it still strikes a rather discordant note – just as it did when essentially the same thing was done with the second Doctor's companions Jamie and Zoe at the end of 'The War Games' (1969) – as to rob Donna of all the wonderful experiences she has had on her journeys through time and space, and even more so of all the positive growth she has undergone as a person, seems decidedly cruel; and one thing *Doctor Who* should *never* be is cruel to its regular characters. It also completely glosses over the tricky question of how Donna will be able to rationalise such things as the fact that her family are now living in a different house from the one they occupied at the time of 'The Runaway Bride', that her father has died in the interim and that all her suitcases and clothes have mysteriously vanished; one can only assume that the Doctor has edited out all the memories involving himself and the TARDIS but left in place the other, unrelated ones, somehow making it possible for Donna's mind to stitch all the fragments back together into a new pattern.

The revelation that the Daleks are planning to use a 'super-weapon' in the form of the reality bomb recalls to some extent their intention to deploy the time destructor in 'The Daleks' Master Plan' (1965/66). Again, though, Davies pushes this rather too far. The idea that the device would destroy the whole of reality except for the Daleks themselves goes beyond even the hypothetical notion posited by the Doctor in 'Genesis of the Daleks' (1975) of a virus that would wipe out all other forms of life, and inevitably leads one to wonder what they would do with themselves if they actually succeeded. With no more planets left to conquer and no more inferior races left to enslave, it seems their only option would be to develop a sudden interest in art or take up a hobby in order to pass the time …

One of the most interesting parts of the episode comes when Davros accuses the Doctor of hypocritically preaching peace while at the same time using his human companions to fight his battles for him: 'The man who abhors violence, never carrying a gun. But this is the truth, Doctor: you take ordinary people and you fashion *them* into weapons. Behold your children of time, transformed into murderers. I made the Daleks, Doctor. You made this.' It seems that the other running Series Four theme of the Doctor's ambivalent attitude toward weapons, raised with increasing emphasis in earlier episodes including in particular 'The Fires of Pompeii', 'The Sontaran Stratagem'/'The Poison Sky' and 'The Doctor's Daughter', is to have a dramatic pay-off here. Once more, though, Davies drops the ball just when he is about to cross the line. Davros having launched such a scathing attack on the way the Doctor goes about his perennial fight against the evils of the universe, the viewer expects the Time Lord to respond with an equally robust justification of his methods, perhaps pointing out that he always acts for the greater good, that he encourages his companions to view violence as something to be used only in self-defence or as a last resort, and that he cannot dictate their actions as – unlike the Daleks – they have minds of their own and can choose what to do for themselves. As it is, though, the only thing he can offer in defence of himself and his companions is the decidedly lame, 'They're trying to help'. In the accompanying *Doctor Who Confidential* documentary, Davies comments that he felt there was actually no good answer to Davros's accusations, because they were essentially true. It could even be said that, in the end, the Doctor uses his own duplicate as a weapon to wipe out the entire Dalek race, notwithstanding the fairly muted anger he expresses when he learns what has happened. It is, after all, difficult to see how else the threat still posed by Davros and the Dalek army could have been effectively defused. This, though, represents a very jaundiced view of the Doctor's *modus operandi*; another fundamental aspect of *Doctor Who* that this episode arguably sells rather short.

Even with all these problems and shortcomings, 'Journey's End' packs so much into its extra-long running-time that it still offers quite a lot to admire and enjoy. As in 'The Stolen Earth', Julian Bleach delivers an absolutely phenomenal performance as Davros, and thankfully he is given rather more to do in this second instalment. It is great, too, to see Davros shooting bolts of energy from his fingertips at one point, as he did previously in 'Revelation of the Daleks' (1985); a nice piece of continuity and an exciting moment in its own right. The unfortunate thing about Davros in classic-era *Doctor Who* was that the character became overused; after his introduction, the Daleks never got to have another story without him. However, although he seems to be killed in the closing stages of 'Journey's End', it would be a great pity if this were to be his only new-era appearance, as Bleach's interpretation is a positive triumph, and cries out for a rematch.

Also wonderful to see are the scenes of the Doctor and Rose properly reunited at last and sharing another adventure together, albeit more briefly than one would like. Billie Piper really shines here, and the episode boasts further terrific performances from Elisabeth Sladen, Freema Agyeman and John Barrowman too. A particular highlight is the sequence where Sarah Jane and Davros refer back to their previous encounter in 'Genesis of the Daleks' (1975). Another is the one where Martha arrives at the Osterhagan station in Germany. To have a patrol of Daleks flying through a forest outside Nuremberg ranting in German was an absolutely inspired idea on Davies's part, effectively paying homage to Terry Nation's original conception of the creatures as a metaphor for Nazism while gifting the viewer a highly memorable image. Equally outstanding is the part where Captain Jack deliberately gets himself exterminated in order to escape from the vault of the Crucible, realising that the Daleks will be unaware that he cannot die – although this is at the cost of upsetting Rose, who is likewise ignorant of the fact. It is an enormous pleasure, too, to see the return of Camille Coduri as Jackie and Noel Clarke as Mickey, these brilliant characters having been almost as badly missed as Rose herself since their last appearance in 'Doomsday'. Again, it is just a pity that with so many different elements jostling for space in the script, they aren't afforded all that many scenes – although happily when they do appear, they get to deliver some excellent and often very amusing dialogue perfectly in keeping with their established personalities. The fact that both Mickey and Martha leave with Captain Jack at the end of the story seems to set up some intriguing possibilities for future series of *Torchwood*, although whether or not these will be followed up on remains to be seen ... Bernard Cribbins and Jacqueline King are once more superb as Wilf and Sylvia, particularly in the poignant closing scenes where Donna is returned home with her memories of the Doctor wiped. Last but by no means least, it is always pleasing to see the ever-chipper K-9 pop up for another appearance in the show – and although again this is no more than a cameo, it seems that in his case, rights complications would have ruled out anything more extensive, even if the jam-packed nature of the script had not effectively precluded it.

But while the episode has many memorable moments, fine performances, great exchanges of dialogue and spectacular set-pieces, the fact remains that the script signally fails to pull these together into a coherent and satisfying plot. A scene that perfectly illustrates this disjunction is the one where the Doctor, his duplicate, the DoctorDonna and all the 'children of time' – Sarah Jane, Rose, Captain Jack, Martha, Jackie and Mickey – are piloting the TARDIS in concert, towing the Earth back to its proper point in space and time, with the aid of Gwen, Ianto and the rift manipulator in the Torchwood Hub and Luke, K-9 and Mr Smith in Sarah Jane's attic. To witness the full complement of the tenth Doctor's companions and friends – his surrogate 'family' – gathered together and working in perfect harmony like this (although Jackie is only allowed to watch!), all to the accompaniment of a stirring piece of incidental music by Murray Gold, is an incredibly moving experience, and will have brought a tear to the eye of many a viewer. The explanation that the TARDIS is able to function to its full capacity here because it is designed to have a separate pilot stationed at each of its six control panels simultaneously is also a very clever notion (and one previously hinted at in some of the tie-in novels).[102] It is pleasing, too, that Davies does not simply press a 'reset button' and have the events of the story erased from history, as he did in 'Last of the Time Lords' (except for those people who were on board the *Valiant*). When one really thinks about what is being depicted in plot terms, though, it all starts to seem far less satisfactory. For one thing, the fact that the Earth is the only one of the 27 stolen planets that the Doctor is unable to return to its rightful coordinates using the Daleks' own equipment is deeply contrived. Worse still, though, the idea of the TARDIS towing the Earth through space at faster-than-light speed, while keeping its atmosphere intact and without anything more than minor tremors being felt by those on the ground, and then instantly restoring the gravitational balance of the solar system and returning the Moon to its proper orbit, presumably along with dozens of artificial satellites as well, goes way beyond the bounds of scientific plausibility. Of course, one can always invoke the oft-quoted third law of prediction formulated by science fiction author Arthur C Clarke, that any sufficiently advanced technology is indistinguishable from magic - and there can surely be few races with technology more advanced than that of the Time Lords. There is also the possibility that the Earth is not actually towed through space at all but through the TARDIS's more usual element of the time vortex - although unprotected exposure to that has always been indicated to be lethal in the past. But there nevertheless comes a point, even in a show like *Doctor Who*, where what is being presented on screen is so wildly far-fetched and over-the-top that the suspension of disbelief becomes simply impossible; and that is the problem with 'Journey's End' in a nutshell.

Davies throws in everything bar the proverbial kitchen sink in this episode (although he was at least persuaded to remove the planned cliffhanger ending featuring the Cybermen), and in the final analysis, it is a bit of a mess; a glorious mess at times, but a mess nonetheless.

---

[102] This does however go against the intentions of the original TARDIS set designer Peter Brachacki, who decided to place all the controls on a central console, rather than on a number of separate panels spread about the room, precisely because he envisaged that the ship was intended to be piloted by one person, who could easily move around the compact console operating switches, checking guages etc as required.

BBC PROMS SPECIAL 2008 MUSIC OF THE SPHERES

Writer: Russell T Davies
Director: Euros Lyn

DEBUT TRANSMISSION DETAILS

BBC Radio Three and BBC iPlayer.
Date: 27 July 2008. Scheduled time: 11.40 am. Actual time: 11.41 am.

Duration: 7′ 10″

ADDITIONAL CREDITED CAST

Jimmy Vee (The Graske), Philip Hurd-Wood (Voice of the Graske).

PLOT

The Doctor is in the TARDIS composing a piece of music when a Graske gets into the ship by teleport. The Graske demands to know the source of the beautiful sound it can hear, and the Doctor explains that it is the Music of the Spheres: the gravity patterns produced by the motion of celestial bodies, fed through the TARDIS's harmonic filter. The Graske claims to have come here to warn the Doctor about a dangerous space portal opening up within the TARDIS. The Doctor sees that the portal links to the Royal Albert Hall in London, where a Proms concert is in progress. He converses with the audience via the portal and throws through the pages of music he has been composing. These are picked up by the members of the orchestra, who play the Doctor's composition, 'Ode to the Universe', while the Doctor conducts, using his sonic screwdriver as a baton. The Doctor then notices that, while he has been distracted, the Graske has slipped through the portal to the Royal Albert Hall. The Graske begins making mischief on the stage with a water pistol stolen from the Doctor's pocket. The Doctor reverses the polarity of the neutron flow and pulls the Graske back into the TARDIS, then reverses the creature's teleport signal and sends him all the way to the other side of the galaxy. He finally closes the space portal, telling the Royal Albert Hall audience to remember that the Music of the Spheres is all around them.

QUOTE, UNQUOTE

- **Doctor:** 'I said to Beethoven, I said, "I can rattle off a tune".' He said, "Pardon?"'
- **Doctor:** 'Oi! Graske! Stop it! Behave! Oh, he wasn't trying to warn me, he was

trying to find a shortcut to Earth. If he escapes, he'll go round the whole planet, causing trouble, stealing sweets, making smells ...'

- **Doctor:** 'Music isn't just orchestras and pop stars and special people with albums and downloads and concerts. It's you. 'Cause the Music of the Spheres is all around you. When you're on your own, just close your eyes, and you'll hear it. Music, inside your head. 'Cause everyone's a musician. Everyone's got a song inside them. Every single one of you. Bye!'

CONTINUITY POINTS

- This is the third appearance of a Graske in the *Doctor Who* universe: the first was in the interactive adventure 'Attack of the Graske' and the second in the 'Whatever Happened to Sarah Jane?' story of *The Sarah Jane Adventures*, both written by Gareth Roberts.
- The Doctor says that he was present at the very first Proms in 1895 and played the tuba: 'I was brilliant!'
- The Doctor uses the phrase 'reverse the polarity of the neutron flow', which is more commonly associated with his third incarnation (although in fact it was used only twice by that incarnation on screen, in 'The Sea Devils' (1972) and 'The Five Doctors' (1983)).

PRODUCTION NOTES

- This special was made specifically to be shown on a large screen above the stage at a *Doctor Who*-themed concert at the Royal Albert Hall on 27 July 2008, as part of the annual BBC Proms series. It was designed to be interactive, with live-action effects on stage tying in with the action on screen, such as pages of music manuscript being blown down onto the orchestra at the point when the Doctor throws them through the space portal. Jimmy Vee appeared as the Graske on stage, running around with a yellow water pistol supposedly stolen from the Doctor's pocket. This was identical to the one featured in the TV episode 'The Fires of Pompeii'.
- The official *Doctor Who* website made the special available to view online to coincide with it being played at the Royal Albert Hall, but removed it immediately afterwards. The sound from the Royal Albert Hall (including audience reaction) was also included in BBC Radio Three's live broadcast of the entire concert, a recording of which could then be accessed for up to seven days afterwards via the 'listen again' feature on the station's own website. The concert is due to get a TV broadcast at Christmas 2008.
- The scene was recorded on a single day on the TARDIS set, the only actors involved being David Tennant as the Doctor and Jimmy Vee as the Graske. Philip Hurd-Wood provided the voice of the Graske in post-production, having previously done so for 'Whatever Happened to Sarah Jane?'. A small amount of CGI work was done by The Mill for the teleport and space portal effects, but otherwise the production was a minimal one.
- To mark the fiftieth anniversary of the inauguration of the BBC Radiophonic Workshop, Delia Derbyshire's original arrangement of the *Doctor Who* theme music was used over the closing credits of the special – the only time so far

that an arrangement other than one of Murray Gold's has been used on a new-era *Doctor Who* episode. (Russell T Davies had originally intended to use a remix of Derbyshire's arrangement as the standard theme music for the new-era show back in 2005, but changed his mind after hearing an alternative offered by Gold, who had already been engaged as the regular incidental music composer.)

PRESS REACTION

- 'Despite the Ood, TARDIS, Daleks and Davros, the most affecting moment [of the Prom] comes in a five-minute [sic] *Doctor Who* ... special, called "Music of the Spheres". Here, David Tennant delivered, to a rapt audience, one of Russell T Davies's trademark homilies to self-expression and joy ... And what could have been a wonderful, yet surreal and overwhelming, introduction to orchestral music – with its standing ovations, intervals and architecture – was brought back down to a rather lovely question. Did you like this orchestra, kids? What would you do with one?' Caitlin Moran, *The Times*, 28 July 2008.

ANALYSIS

Following on from the tenth Doctor's introductory *Children in Need* scene in 2005, the interactive Christmas adventure 'Attack of the Graske' at the end of the same year and the second *Children in Need* special 'Time Crash' in 2007, 'Music of the Spheres' is the latest in what might now be considered an irregular series of *Doctor Who* mini-episodes produced by Russell T Davies and his team for specific one-off purposes (and where 'Attack of the Graske' and 'Music of the Spheres' itself are concerned, not subsequently made available on DVD for the benefit of those who missed out on them at the time[103]). Far more so than in the other cases, one really needed to be present on the occasion in question, in the audience at the Royal Albert Hall concert, in order to appreciate fully the impact of 'Music of the Spheres', complete with the live-action elements and the delighted responses of the assembled throng. Even viewed 'cold', however, it is great fun, with a cracking script by Davies, which goes just about as far as it is possible to go in terms of audience interaction without actually breaking the 'fourth wall', and a truly exuberant performance by David Tennant, which belies the fact that this was recorded right at the end of the gruelling Series Four production schedule, after the 2008 Christmas special 'The Next Doctor'. The musical subject of the piece is perfectly in tune with the principal purpose of the concert itself – to appeal particularly to children who might be unfamiliar with classical music – and the whole thing is beautifully pitched. It is wonderful, too, to hear Delia Derbyshire's original arrangement of the show's theme music used over the closing credits; it remains the best version there has ever been, and should never have been replaced. In short, after the excesses of 'Journey's End', transmitted only three weeks earlier, 'Music of the Spheres' comes as a welcome breath of fresh air.

---

[103] The 'Tardisode' teasers produced for the Series Two episodes have also yet to be made available on DVD at the time of writing.

SERIES OVERVIEW

One of the main things for which Series Four will be remembered is Catherine Tate's portrayal of Donna Noble. To say that Tate's engagement for a regular role in the show was contentious, particularly after the mixed reaction to her one-off appearance in 'The Runaway Bride', would probably be an understatement. In my book *Third Dimension: The Unofficial and Unauthorised Guide to Doctor Who 2007* (Telos Publishing, 2007), I commented on this as follows:

> We now know that ... the Doctor's main companion [for Series Four] will be Catherine Tate's Donna Noble. This is not a prospect that fills me with joy. I well remember the terrible sinking feeling I got, back in 1986, on being told by someone over the phone that Bonnie Langford would be joining *Doctor Who* to partner Colin Baker's Doctor. These days we tend to learn of breaking news not over the phone but over the internet, but the feeling I got was exactly the same when, on 4 July 2007, I switched on my computer and read of Tate's imminent return to the series. Like Langford, Tate is best known for something other than her dramatic acting ability - in this case, for her work as a comedienne - and, again like Langford, she is the sort of performer who seems to have the unfortunate knack of causing extreme irritation to a sizeable minority of the general viewing public. I would consequently have had serious misgivings about her becoming a regular in *Doctor Who* even if I personally had greatly enjoyed her performance in 'The Runaway Bride' and felt that she worked well alongside David Tennant - which ... I most certainly did not. It is notable that, of all the Series Three episodes, 'The Runaway Bride' received the joint lowest Appreciation Index figure amongst general viewers and was also the lowest-ranked amongst fans in the Outpost Gallifrey forum polls. If this was due to some extent to the 'Tate factor', then it does not bode at all well for Series Four.
>
> It seems highly likely ... that Davies's decision to offer Tate a regular role in the series was motivated far more by her star-name status than by a desire to see Donna back *per se*; and if, as he and other production team members have suggested in interviews, the intention is that she and the Doctor should continue the Katharine-Hepburn-and-Spencer-Tracy-style 'screwball comedy' sparring that was attempted, and fell so flat, in 'The Runaway Bride', it raises the dreadful prospect of a return to the frequent 'bickering in the TARDIS' scenes that marred many of the Doctor-and-companion relationships of the 1980s. I very much hope that, in a year's time, I will be eating

> my words on this; but, as things stand, this looks to me to be the first really major, potentially ruinous, mistake that Davies has made since taking over the series.

So, am I eating my words? Well, to some extent. Due in part to Russell T Davies having effectively re-imagined her as a far more likeable person, and in part to Tate having adopted a far less strident tone of performance, Donna in Series Four was by no means the disaster I had feared. However, Tate still had a tendency to deliver her more overtly humorous lines in an over-the-top, comedy character style, particularly in the earlier-recorded episodes when she was still to some extent finding her feet, and there never seemed to be a great deal of on-screen chemistry between her and David Tennant. Moreover, even when she was at her very best, Tate never quite *became* Donna in the way that Billie Piper became Rose or Freema Agyeman became Martha. Regardless of the quality of her performance in any given scene - and it was undeniably superb at times, although it never quite warranted the lavish praise that Davies and his colleagues heaped on it at seemingly every opportunity - one was always conscious that it *was* a performance; that this was an actress playing a part, rather than a fully convincing character. Tate is a woman with a huge personality, as comes across very clearly in interviews and in her sketch show work, and ultimately that could not be fully subsumed within the role of Donna. In addition, while it would obviously have been a mistake to bring in a new companion who was effectively a clone of either Rose or Martha, those character types having been done more or less to perfection already, the idea of having a more mature woman travelling with the Doctor, who was less overawed by him, had no romantic interest in him and was more ready to challenge him over his actions, didn't work quite as well as it might have seemed it would on paper. The Doctor-companion dynamic was thrown slightly off balance, and it was never entirely clear *why* Donna was so desperately keen to keep travelling in the TARDIS; if her main motivation was simply to escape from her mundane life as an office temp in Chiswick, surely she could have found some other way to do it that did not involve her being exposed to such a succession of dangerous and traumatic situations. All in all, then, I still feel it was a misjudged decision to bring Donna back as a regular companion, and that there were other options open to the production team that would have reaped greater rewards, albeit that it worked out a lot better than I had anticipated.

The other key consideration regarding Series Four is that it is Russell T Davies's last full series as showrunner, Julie Gardner's last as his fellow executive producer and Phil Collinson's last as producer. When *Doctor Who* returns in 2010, after a transitional run of specials, it will have a completely new team of people in charge, who are bound to bring a somewhat different sensibility to it. This is therefore very much the end of an era.

It is impossible to overstate the magnitude of the mark that Davies has made on *Doctor Who* history. In the space of just a few short years, he has taken a show that had been out of regular TV production since the end of the 1980s, persuaded the BBC to revive it, reinvented it to appeal to a 21st Century mass audience, managed at the same time to retain its essential ethos and delight the vast majority of its established fans, and elevated it to a previously undreamt-of level of public adulation and critical acclaim. In fact, *Doctor Who* has now gone beyond being just a successful TV show. More so than at any other time in its long history – even the Dalekmania days of the mid-1960s – it is now a *bona fide* cultural phenomenon. It is almost impossible to walk down a busy British high street today without seeing children wearing *Doctor Who* T-shirts, carrying Dalek backpacks or swapping *Battles in Time* trading cards, or their parents scanning the shelves of W H Smith's for the latest issue of *Doctor Who Magazine* or one of the many tie-in books or games inspired by the show. In short, *Doctor Who* has become a part of the fabric of British family life; and this is a legacy that will endure for many years, if not decades, to come. This has also been an era in which *Doctor Who* has achieved unparalleled popularity overseas, gaining greater exposure than ever before in established territories such as the USA and Australia and finding a market in many countries where it was previously unknown. It is now well on the way to becoming a truly global phenomenon.

It seems astonishing to think that a mere five years ago, no-one had ever heard of such now-iconic, household-name characters as Rose Tyler and Captain Jack Harkness, such memorable new monster races as the Slitheen and the Ood and such resonant concepts as the last great Time War and the Bad Wolf – all devised by Davies. [104] While it would obviously be wrong to underestimate the contributions of Gardner, Collinson and the many others who have been involved in the making of the show, both behind and in front of the cameras, there is no doubt that much of the credit for the incredible success it has enjoyed is owed to Davies himself. It is he who has set the artistic vision, overseen every aspect of the production, written the majority of the episodes and rewritten (to a greater or lesser extent) almost all of the others. It is his unique creative voice that has infused every facet of new-era *Doctor Who* and won the hearts of TV audiences the world over.

By the end of Series Four, though, it is definitely starting to seem that Davies's approach to the show has been taken just about as far as it can possibly go, and that maybe it is indeed time for a change. Commendably, Davies and his team have endeavoured to make each of their four series the best that it could be, striving each year to outdo what they achieved the year before; but while in many respects this has yielded amazing results, it has at the same time led to the stories becoming increasingly complex in construction, dark in tone and wrapped up in the show's own mythology, perhaps inevitably culminating in the overblown self-indulgence seen in 'The Stolen Earth'/'Journey's End' – astutely characterised by incoming showrunner Steven Moffat as Davies seeing what would happen if he 'pressed all the buttons at once'. During the course of writing this book, I happened to re-watch the relatively unassuming Series One episode 'The Long Game', and was surprised to find that I had enjoyed it more than even the best of the Series Four episodes.

---

[104] The premise of a Time War that culminated in the Doctor destroying the Time Lords' home planet Gallifrey was actually first featured in BBC Books' Eighth Doctor Adventures tie-in range. The Daleks were not identified as participants in that conflict, however, and Davies has stated that he considers it to be distinct from the last great Time War referred to in the TV show – analogous to the way the First and Second World Wars were fought in quick succession on Earth. That said, it is possible to reconcile the two without too much difficulty, and some fans choose to regard them as the one and the same.

Admittedly I have never subscribed to the majority fan view that holds 'The Long Game' to be one of the weakest ninth Doctor's outings – it has always been something of a favourite of mine – but it seemed to me, on seeing it again, that it had a pleasing accessibility, lightness of touch and directness of storytelling that the show has really lost as time as gone by.

This is not to deny that Series Four is in many respects a showcase of brilliant, imaginative scripting and admirable thematic richness – as seen particularly in the series-spanning focus on the Doctor's attitude toward weapons and the persistent contrasting of the pitfalls of unnatural forms of alien procreation with the strength of human family bonds – not to mention a triumph of fine performances and outstanding production values. Nevertheless, while Series Three probably ranks as the best of new-era *Doctor Who* to date, Series Four is on balance probably the weakest – notwithstanding its huge ratings success – mainly because it tries just a bit to hard and thus tends to go a bit overboard.

But, of course, this is not quite the end of Davies's era as *Doctor Who*'s showrunner. There are still the five specials to go before he bows out and leaves the way clear for Moffat to bring his own vision to the production. It will be interesting to see how Davies approaches these specials. Most likely, he will treat them as self-contained stories that essentially mark time as far as the development of the show's ongoing mythology is concerned. 'Journey's End' having done what its title implies and brought closure to the storylines of all the regular characters introduced by Davies over the course of his four series in charge, wiping the slate clean for Moffat to introduce whatever new ones he chooses in Series Five, the chances are that the specials will feature a succession of 'one off' companions akin to Astrid in 'Voyage of the Damned' – starting with Rosita, played by Velile Tshabalala, in the 2008 Christmas special 'The Next Doctor' – leaving Moffat to present his own new ongoing companion(s) in the 2010 episodes. Similarly, it seems unlikely that the specials will introduce any new story arcs or running threads designed to carry forward into Series Five.

That said, Series Four has itself introduced some new characters that seem to cry out for return appearances. The closing scene of 'The Doctor's Daughter' clearly sets up the possibility of further adventures involving Jenny, and there have already been press rumours that she is to feature in at least one of the specials. Given that the original plan to kill her off was changed specifically at Moffat's suggestion, it also seems quite possible that he will be want to bring her back again during his time as showrunner. Then there is River Song, a character created by Moffat himself, who is already known to have a long future association with the Doctor that has yet to be seen on screen. Depending on the availability of actress Alex Kingston, it seems more than likely that she too will be putting in some further appearances.

Probably the most crucial question, though, is who will play the Doctor in Moffat's episodes. It has already been announced by the BBC that Tennant will appear in all five of Davies's specials, and as this book was being finalised for printing, the announcement came from Tennant himself that he would not be continuing with the role into 2010.Whoever is chosen to succeed him will certainly have a tough task on his (or her?) hands; Tennant's brilliant performances throughout Series Four have confirmed him to be arguably the best Doctor the show has ever had, and he will be an incredibly hard act to follow.

There will doubtless be no shortage of people eager to offer Moffat advice on all aspects of his stewardship of the show – for my own part, I would love to see him bring back Paul McGann as the Doctor, have the TARDIS interior set redesigned to resemble more closely the iconic classic-era original and reinstate Delia Derbyshire's incomparable first arrangement of the theme music, to mention just three of many things – but his wisest course of action would probably be to ignore all this and do just what Davies has done: trust his own creative instincts and surprise everyone with a wealth of wonderful new characters and stories reflecting his own unique take on *Doctor Who*. Given the superlative quality of all his contributions to the show to date, it seems safe to predict that the viewing public has a real treat in store, and many more exciting adventures in space and time to look forward to.

PART FIVE
APPENDICES

APPENDIX A
DOCTOR WHO CONFIDENTIAL

As in the previous three years, each episode of this latest series of *Doctor Who* was accompanied by its own dedicated documentary. *Doctor Who Confidential* remained in the vanguard of this type of programming, each standard instalment having a generous running time of around 43 minutes, and the Christmas special on 'Voyage of the Damned' lasting almost a full hour - so, for the most part, the documentaries were about the same length as the episodes they were covering! Although there were no format-stretching experiments for Series Four, as there had been for Series Three with the outstanding, David Tennant-directed 'Do You Remember the First Time?', the show continued to present an informative and entertaining account of various aspects of the making of *Doctor Who*, illustrated by plentiful behind-the-scenes and programme clips and supported by numerous cast and production team interviews. For the second year running, the *Confidential* team even got to capture some overseas recording, although in this instance they travelled on the coat-tails of the *Doctor Who* crew, whereas the previous year, for 'Daleks in Manhattan'/'Evolution of the Daleks', it had been the other way around.

The full-length versions of these programmes were shown only once; as in previous years, condensed versions, each roughly ten minutes long, were prepared for repeat slots, under the informal title *Confidential Cutdown*. Because these shorter edits omitted the contemporary music tracks featured in the full-length ones, it would again be these versions that would be lined up for inclusion in the *Complete Series* DVD box set due to be released in the autumn, in order to avoid potential music clearance problems and associated fees. This time, though, anyone who missed the full-length versions on their debut screening could at least catch up on them, during the week that followed, via the BBC's new iPlayer service or the on-demand packages offered by digital TV providers such as Virgin Media.

SERIES CREDITS

Narrated by: Anthony Head

PRODUCTION TEAM[105]

Camera: James Daniels (all except 4.03, 4.04), Nick Jardine (4.00, 4.01, 4.03, 4.04, 4.05, 4.07, 4.10, 4.11), Andy Smith (4.00, 4.02, 4.06, 4.12, 4.13), Eric Huyton (4.01, 4.04, 4.05, 4.06, 4.07, 4.08, 4.09, 4.10, 4.11, 4.12, 4.13), Andy Clifford (4.02, 4.11, 4.12,

[105] Where an episode number (or more than one) appears in brackets after a person's name in the listing, this means that they were credited only on the episode (or episodes) indicated. Otherwise, the person concerned was credited on all 14 episodes.

4.13), John Podpadec (4.02), Dewi Davies (4.06, 4.08, 4.09, 4.12, 4.13), Jaimie Gramiston (4.06), Aled Jenkins (4.06, 4.08, 4.09, 4.11, 4.12, 4.13), Mark Chandler (4.10), Huw Walters (4.10)
Sound: Kevin Meredith (all except 4.02), Sean Millar (4.00), Steve Hoy (4.00, 4.02, 4.06, 4.12, 4.13), Jon Thomas (all except 4.00), Rob Craig (4.02, 4.06, 4.11, 4.12, 4.13), Deian Humphreys (4.08), Brian Murrell (4.08, 4.10, 4.12, 4.13), Dafydd Parry (4.09), Roger van Koningsveld (4.12), Will Planitzer (4.12)
Runner: Scott Handcock, Stuart Laws (all except 4.00), Robert Wootton[106] (4.01, 4.10, 4.11, 4.12, 4.13), Poppy Chandler (4.10, 4.11, 4.12, 4.13)
Edit Assistant: Sam Jones
Researcher: Ian Hay, Nathan Landeg, Robin Owen Ellis (4.01, 4.02, 4.03, 4.04, 4.05, 4.07, 4.10), Jamie Lynch (4.10)
Assistant Producer: Paul Giddings (all except 4.00, 4.05), Hannah Williams (all except 4.07), Paul Symonds (4.01, 4.02, 4.04, 4.05, 4.06, 4.07, 4.09, 4.10, 4.12)
Production Team Assistant: Amanda Buckley, Rachel Evans (4.11, 4.12, 4.13)
Production Accountant: Elaine Stephenson
Production Co-ordinator: Tors Grantham, Amanda Buckley (4.07)
Production Manager: Kirsty Reid
Production Executive: Paul Williams
Editor: Rob Franz (4.00, 4.09, 4.11), Lizzie Minnion (4.01), James Brailsford (4.02, 4.05), Rahim Mastafa (4.03, 4.08), John Parker (4.04, 4.07, 4.12), William Ward-Lewis (4.06), Mike Crawford (4.10), Gary Skipton (4.13)
Additional Editing: James Brailsford (4.00), Lizzie Minnion (4.00)
Colourist: Simon Meek (4.00), Jon Everett (all except 4.00, 4.13), Richard Doel (4.13)
Dubbing Mixer: Mark Ferda

Edit Producer: Ailsa Jenkins (4.00, 4.10), Paul Symonds (4.03, 4.08, 4.11, 4.13), Nathan Landeg (4.06), Jamie Lynch (4.06), Cat Chappell (4.09), Donovan Keogh (4.12)
Executive Producer: Mark Cossey
Executive Producer for *Dr Who*: Russell T Davies, Julie Gardner

Produced and Directed by: Mark Procter (4.02), Ailsa Jenkins (4.04), Paul Giddings (4.05), Hannah Williams (4.07)
Producer: Zoë Rushton
Series Producer: Gillane Seaborne

BBC Wales

[106] Credited on 4.01 as 'Rob Wootton'.

EPISODE GUIDE

The episode durations quoted below are for the full versions as originally transmitted (not the shorter, *Confidential Cutdown* versions used for most subsequent repeat screenings and for DVD releases). They may be a couple of seconds different from the timings of the complete programmes on the BBC's master tapes, as each episode tended to be cut into very slightly by the preceding and/or following continuity caption and announcement.

4.00 - [UNTITLED]

DEBUT TRANSMISSION DETAILS

BBC Three
Date: 25 December 2007. Scheduled time: 8.30 pm. Actual time: n/k
Duration: 56' 42"

NOTE

- Featured the additional credit: 'With Thanks To IPC Media'.

4.01 - A NOBLE RETURN

DEBUT TRANSMISSION DETAILS

BBC Three
Date: 5 April 2008. Scheduled time: 7.10 pm. Actual time: 7.11 pm.
Duration: 43' 55"

PUBLICITY BLURB

In the first of a new series, *Confidential* features the welcome return of Catherine Tate as the unstoppable Donna Noble and gets up close and personal with the Doctor's latest companion – from her first days on set through to her battle against an army of sinister Adipose.

4.02 - THE ITALIAN JOB

DEBUT TRANSMISSION DETAILS

BBC Three
Date: 12 April 2008. Scheduled time: 7.35 pm. Actual time: 7.36 pm.
Duration: 43' 19"

PUBLICITY BLURB

Doctor Who Confidential travels the long road to Rome to witness the making of the Doctor's latest volcanic voyage. Filming at the famous Cinecittà Studios, the production team face an Italian job of colossal proportions, and *Confidential* is on set to feel the heat. Plus David Tennant heads up Pompeii and climbs Mount Vesuvius in this latest *Doctor Who Confidential* exclusive.

4.03 – OODS AND ENDS

DEBUT TRANSMISSION DETAILS

BBC Three
Date: 19 April 2008. Scheduled time: 7.05 pm. Actual time: 7.07 pm.
Duration: 42′ 33″

PUBLICITY BLURB

The *Confidential* crew travel to the Ood-Sphere to examine the return of the mysterious Ood to *Doctor Who*. They discover how a quarry in South West Wales in the middle of summer gets turned into a winter wonderland, and how David Tennant gets turned into an all action hero.

4.04 – SEND IN THE CLONES

DEBUT TRANSMISSION DETAILS

BBC Three
Date: 26 April 2008. Scheduled time: 7.05 pm. Actual time: 7.06 pm.
Duration: 43′ 04″

PUBLICITY BLURB

Join *Confidential*, as we take you exclusively behind the scenes as Martha greets the Doctor again and meets his latest companion, Donna Noble. As confusion abounds, the Time Lord, Donna and Martha join forces in a battle to save the human race.

4.05 – SONTAR-HA!

DEBUT TRANSMISSION DETAILS

BBC Three
Date: 3 May 2008. Scheduled time: 7.05 pm. Actual time: 7.06 pm.
Duration: 42′ 57″

PUBLICITY BLURB

For the first time in over 20 years, the Sontarans are back as *Confidential* explores the return of the ultimate warrior race. We speak to David Tennant and Colin Baker and go behind the scenes to look at the explosive Sontaran invasion against UNIT forces.

4.06 - SINS OF THE FATHERS

DEBUT TRANSMISSION DETAILS

BBC Three
Date: 10 May 2008. Scheduled time: 7.30 pm. Actual time: 7.30 pm.
Duration: 42′ 50″

PUBLICITY BLURB

Confidential are present at the birth of a new chapter in history as we see the Doctor's daughter Jenny bound onto our screens. We speak to David Tennant and Georgia Moffett to see how this new relationship develops.

4.07 - NEMESIS

DEBUT TRANSMISSION DETAILS

BBC Three
Date: 17 May 2008. Scheduled time: 7.45 pm. Actual time: 7.45 pm.
Duration: 42′ 55″

PUBLICITY BLURB

Join *Confidential*, become an armchair detective and find out exactly what goes into creating a classic murder mystery. Find out what it's like behind the scenes with such a big ensemble cast and discover the mysterious events surrounding the real Agatha Christie.

4.08 - SHADOW PLAY

DEBUT TRANSMISSION DETAILS

BBC Three
Date: 31 May 2008. Scheduled time: 7.45 pm. Actual time: 7.47 pm.
Duration: 42′ 54″

PUBLICITY BLURB

The *Confidential* team materialise with the Doctor and Donna on the set of the eerie Library planet to confront the monsters of the dark, the vicious Vashta Nerada. We examine where the library was located, how the shadows were created and the contribution of writer Steven Moffat to the series.

4.09 - RIVER RUNS DEEP

DEBUT TRANSMISSION DETAILS

BBC Three
Date: 7 June 2008. Scheduled time: 7.45 pm. Actual time: 7.46 pm.
Duration: 43′ 04″

PUBLICITY BLURB

Fresh from Stateside success and back in the UK to film her part in *Doctor Who*, we talk to Alex Kingston and discover more about her time travelling archaeologist River Song.

4.10 - LOOK WHO'S TALKING

DEBUT TRANSMISSION DETAILS

BBC Three
Date: 14 June 2008. Scheduled time: 7.55 pm. Actual time: 7.54 pm.
Duration: 42′ 59″

PUBLICITY BLURB

Join *Doctor Who Confidential* as we take you behind the scenes of one of the creepiest episodes yet! As well as exclusive backstage footage, the show also reveals how the sound team put together the complicated soundscape of the hit show.

4.11 - HERE COME THE GIRLS!

DEBUT TRANSMISSION DETAILS

BBC Three
Date: 21 June 2008. Scheduled time: 7.30 pm. Actual time: 7.31 pm.
Duration: 42′ 35″

PUBLICITY BLURB

Join *Doctor Who Confidential* as it witnesses Earth slowly unravelling through the eyes of a Doctor-less Donna. This week, the show travels backstage with the TARDIS and takes a stroll down the exotic Shan Shen Alley. It also welcomes back an old friend to the show with the return of Rose Tyler.

4.12 - FRIENDS AND FOE

DEBUT TRANSMISSION DETAILS

BBC Three
Date: 28 June 2008. Scheduled time: 8.00 pm. Actual time: 7.59 pm.
Duration: 42′ 54″

PUBLICITY BLURB

As the Doctor faces up to his greatest ever challenge, and companions from past and present join forces to defend the Earth, the *Confidential* crew lift the lid on the deadly Daleks, and gets the inside story on the galaxy's greatest menace.

4.13 - END OF AN ERA

DEBUT TRANSMISSION DETAILS

BBC Three
Date: 5 July 2008. Scheduled time: 7.45 pm. Actual time: 7.45 pm.
Duration: 43′ 14″

PUBLICITY BLURB

Confidential goes behind the scenes of the nail biting finale to Series Four as we see the Doctor's arch-enemy bring the universe to the brink of extinction. Featuring interviews with David Tennant, Russell T Davies and Phil Collinson.

APPENDIX B
RATINGS AND RANKING

In each of its first three series following its triumphant return in 2005, *Doctor Who*'s ratings and Appreciation Index (AI) figures had exceeded all expectations, confirming that it had been not only a critical success and a winner with the fans but also, and no doubt most importantly from the BBC's perspective, a huge hit with the general viewing public in the UK. It had proved to be a rare example of a show capable of achieving the highly-prized 'double whammy' of attracting a very big audience and keeping it highly entertained. Not only that, but its figures had seen a steady year-on-year improvement overall, until by the end of Series Three, it seemed that they must surely have attained a level that could not be bettered. Astonishingly, however, Series Four saw them climb still further, taking the show to a peak of popularity arguably higher than it had ever reached before in its entire 45-year history.

The table below records what happened. It lists, for the BBC One and BBC Three debut transmissions of each of the 14 episodes (including the Christmas special): the estimated total number of viewers aged four and over (corrected and adjusted to include those who recorded the episode to watch within the week following transmission) in millions (RATING); percentage share of the total TV audience at the time of transmission (S); chart position amongst all programmes transmitted the same day on the same channel (D); overall chart position amongst all programmes transmitted the same day on all terrestrial channels (for the BBC One transmissions) or all digital channels (for the BBC Three transmissions) (D/O); chart position amongst all programmes transmitted the same week (Monday to Sunday inclusive) on the same channel (W); overall chart position amongst all programmes transmitted the same week (Monday to Sunday) on all terrestrial channels (for the BBC One transmissions) or all digital channels (for the BBC Three transmissions) (W/O); and the audience appreciation index as a percentage (AI). The entries marked n/k are not known, as the relevant data are unavailable.

EPISODE	CHANNEL BBC-	RATING	S	D	D/O	W	W/O	AI
'Voyage of the Damned'	One	13.31 m	52%	2nd	2nd	2nd	2nd	85
	Three	n/k	n/k	n/k	n/k	n/k	n/k	n/k
'Partners in Crime'	One	9.14 m	41%	1st	1st	5th	10th	88
	Three	1.40 m	6%	2nd	4th	2nd	5th	88
'The Fires of Pompeii'	One	9.04 m	39%	1st	2nd	4th	10th	87
	Three	1.03 m	5%	3rd	6th	4th	8th	89
'Planet of the Ood'	One	7.50 m	35%	1st	2nd	4th	12th	87
	Three	1.30 m	6%	2nd	2nd	3rd	3rd	89
'The Sontaran Stratagem'	One	7.06 m	37%	1st	2nd	6th	17th	87
	Three	1.04 m	5%	1st	2nd	3rd	6th	n/k
'The Poison Sky'	One	6.53m	34%	1st	2nd	7th	18th	88
	Three	1.09 m	5%	1st	1st	2nd	4th	n/k
'The Doctor's Daughter'	One	7.33 m	40%	1st	2nd	4th	10th	88
	Three	0.95 m	5%	1st	6th	4th	10th	n/k
'The Unicorn and the Wasp'	One	8.41 m	38%	1st	2nd	2nd	7th	86
	Three	0.82 m	4%	3rd	6th	6th	10th	n/k
'Silence in the Library'	One	6.27 m	28%	2nd	5th	9th	27th	89
	Three	1.35 m	6%	1st	1st	1st	2nd	n/k
'Forest of the Dead'	One	7.84 m	42%	1st	1st	5th	10th	89
	Three	0.82 m	4%	1st	1st	4th	7th	n/k
'Midnight'	One	8.05 m	40%	1st	1st	3rd	5th	86
	Three	1.07 m	5%	1st	1st	2nd	2nd	n/k
'Turn Left'	One	8.09 m	38%	1st	1st	3rd	4th	88
	Three	0.92 m	4%	1st	1st	4th	4th	88
'The Stolen Earth'	One	8.78 m	42%	1st	1st	2nd	2nd	91
	Three	1.01 m	4%	1st	1st	3rd	3rd	93
'Journey's End'	One	10.57 m	49%	1st	1st	1st	1st	91
	Three	1.21 m	5%	1st	1st	2nd	2nd	92

Source for viewing figures: Broadcasters' Audience Research Board (BARB)
Source for AI figures: BBC

The following table indicates how many viewers each episode attracted not only on its BBC One and BBC Three debut transmissions but also on its first BBC Three repeat – which (with the exception of 'Voyage of the Damned') was on the following Friday evening – and via the BBC's interactive iPlayer service. This gives an overall total viewing figure - otherwise known as audience reach - for the whole period.[107] The figures for 'Voyage of the Damned' are not strictly comparable to those for the other 13 episodes as, being a Christmas special, it naturally had different transmission slots, and also an extra repeat on BBC One. The relevant figures are nevertheless included here for the sake of completeness. 'The Stolen Earth' and 'Journey's End' were also given an extra BBC One repeat, together, on Sunday 13 July 2008. All figures in the table are in millions.

EPISODE	BBC ONE DEBUT	BBC THREE DEBUT	BBC THREE REPEAT	BBC ONE REPEAT	BBC iPLAYER	ALL
'Voyage of the Damned'	13.31	n/k	n/a	2.41	n/k	>15.72
'Partners in Crime'	9.14	1.40	0.74	n/a	0.50	11.78
'The Fires of Pompeii'	9.04	1.03	0.54	n/a	0.41	11.02
'Planet of the Ood'	7.50	1.30	0.64	n/a	0.39	9.83
'The Sontaran Stratagem'	7.06	1.04	0.53	n/a	0.48	9.11
'The Poison Sky'	6.53	1.09	0.51	n/a	0.45	8.58
'The Doctor's Daughter'	7.33	0.95	0.53	n/a	0.53	9.34
'The Unicorn and the Wasp'	8.41	0.82	0.64	n/a	0.42	10.29
'Silence in the Library'	6.27	1.35	0.59	n/a	0.55	8.76
'Forest of the Dead'	7.84	0.82	0.50	n/a	0.41	9.57
'Midnight'	8.05	1.07	0.38	n/a	0.42	10.02
'Turn Left'	8.09	0.92	0.38	n/a	0.52	9.91

[107] General research into viewing figures has shown that the great majority of viewers who tune in for repeats are additional, i.e. that they have not already seen the programme on one or more of its earlier transmissions. Some sources suggest that the figure is at least 90 percent.

'The Stolen Earth'	8.78	1.01	0.74	1.62	0.71	12.86
'Journey's End'	10.57	1.21	0.62	2.66	0.84	15.90
Average over 13 episodes*	**8.05**	**1.08**	**0.56**	**0.33**	**0.51**	**10.54**

* Not including 'Voyage of the Damned'
Source: Broadcasters' Audience Research Board (BARB)

Instantly apparent from these tables is that the Christmas special, 'Voyage of the Damned', performed exceptionally well - no doubt due in part to the inclusion of pop icon Kylie Minogue in its cast list, as well as to its status as part of a special schedule of festive programming. In fact, it achieved *Doctor Who*'s highest ever chart position to that point, the previous best having been the fifth place gained by Part Two of 'The Ark in Space' (1975).[108] More impressive still, not only was it the second-highest-rated programme of the week - being bested only by the one that immediately followed it, the Christmas Day edition of *EastEnders*, which won 14.38 million viewers - it was the second-highest-rated of the whole *year*, and the fourteenth-highest-rated of the decade; an incredible achievement for a *Doctor Who* episode. In addition, although the figures for the BBC Three repeat and iPlayer viewings are unavailable, these will probably have added at least another million to the total, giving 'Voyage of the Damned' a phenomenal audience reach of around 17 million. This makes it arguably the most watched episode in the entire history of *Doctor Who*, the previous highest-rated episode, Part Four of 'City of Death' (1979), having had 16.10 million viewers, albeit for a single transmission. Even if only its BBC One debut transmission figure of 13.31 million is counted, 'Voyage of the Damned' still stands as the eighth-highest-rated *Doctor Who* episode ever, when TV audiences in general have declined considerably from their levels in earlier decades. Its breathtaking audience share of 52% is also the highest ever won by the show in the multi-channel era.

Just as outstanding, if not more so, are the figures gained by the series finale, 'Journey's End', which went one better than 'Voyage of the Damned' by actually topping the ratings chart for the week of its transmission - an amazing feat that until recently would have been beyond the wildest dreams of any *Doctor Who* fan or, no doubt, any production team member. Although its audience share, debut transmission rating and audience reach figures are all slightly below those for 'Voyage of the Damned', they are still highly impressive; and, what's more, they were achieved without the benefit of the latter's prestigious Christmas Night slot, having been gained instead in the mid-June summer holiday season when TV audiences in general are usually much lower.

---

[108] With an audience of 11 million, the 'Time Crash' mini-episode actually comprised the most watched few minutes of TV during its transmission week. For official ratings purposes, however, it was counted not as a separate programme in its own right but as part of the *Children in Need* telethon, which had a lower figure overall.

Leaving aside 'Voyage of the Damned', the average debut transmission rating for Series Four proper was 8.05 million on BBC One – which compares with 7.95 million for Series One, 7.71 million for Series Two and 7.55 million for Series Three – and 1.08 million on BBC Three – which compares with 0.58 million for Series One[109], 0.63 million for Series Two and 0.92 million for Series Three. The combined total was thus well over half a million higher than for each of the previous three series. This rises to almost two million if one takes into account also the Friday evening BBC Three repeats, the additional BBC One repeats of the last two episodes and the BBC iPlayer viewings, making Series Four unquestionably the most successful to date. *Doctor Who* has thus once again maintained and reinforced its position as a big-hitter in the ratings war, and one of the BBC's flagship drama productions, rivalling *EastEnders* for pre-eminence.

On BBC One, the highest rating for an individual Series Four episode (excluding 'Voyage of the Damned') was, as previously mentioned, 13.31 million for 'Journey's End', while the lowest was 6.27 million for 'Silence in the Library', giving a spread of 7.04 million. This compares with a high of 10.81 million, a low of 6.81 million and a spread of 4.00 million for Series One; a high of 9.24 million, a low of 6.08 million and a spread of 3.16 million for Series Two (excluding 'The Christmas Invasion'); and a high of 8.71 million, a low of 6.62 million and a spread of 2.09 million for Series Three (excluding 'The Runaway Bride'). Taking into account all the viewings that each Series Four episode had within its debut week[110] (again excluding 'Voyage of the Damned'), the overall audience reach peaked at 15.90 million for 'Journey's End' and bottomed out at 8.58 million for 'The Poison Sky', giving a spread of 7.32 million. The Series Four spread is thus by far the widest to date, although this is accounted for mainly by the exceptionally high ratings gained by 'Journey's End' which, incredibly, was seen by almost twice as many people as 'The Poison Sky'. There is little variation between the figures achieved by the lowest-rated episodes in each of the four series, these all falling around the 6.5 million mark.

The average audience share on BBC One was 39%, with a high of 49% for 'Journey's End' and a low of 28% for 'Silence in the Library'. This compares with an average of 40%, a high of 45% and a low of 36% for Series One; an average of 41%, a high of 45% and a low of 33% for Series Two; and an average of 39%, a high of 41% and a low of 35% for Series Three. Series Four thus maintained the show's strong performance in this regard, without however improving on the Series Three average. Once more, 'Journey's End' had an exceptionally good figure. The 28% share for 'Silence in the Library', on the other hand, was exceptionally low; a dip accounted for by the fact that it was transmitted opposite the final of ITV1's hugely popular *Britain's Got Talent* show, which proved to be the first effective competition the commercial channel had managed to mount against *Doctor Who* since its return in 2005. The average share on BBC Three was 5%, varying from a low of 4% to a high of 6%. This

---

[109] This figure, although it likewise relates to the regular Sunday evening repeat, is not strictly comparable, because the Series One episodes from 'World War Three' onwards actually had their debut BBC Three transmission in a late night Saturday slot. This attracted only 0.2 million viewers on average, but it is possible that it may have slightly reduced the audience for the Sunday evening screening.

[110] Strictly, eight days in the case of the additional BBC One repeats of the last two episodes.

is identical to the performance of Series Three on the digital channel and compares with an average of 4%, a low of 3% and a high of 5% for Series Two; equivalent figures are not available for Series One. (All these figures exclude the Christmas specials.)

With the sole exception of 'Silence in the Library', *Doctor Who* was always BBC One's top-rated programme on Saturday, and usually amongst its top five for the week. Again leaving aside 'Silence in the Library', it was always in the top 20 programmes across all channels for the week, with as many as nine out of the 13 episodes (or ten out of the 14 if one includes 'Voyage of the Damned') achieving a coveted top ten place - far more than in any previous series. The frequent changes in the show's BBC One time slot this year, which saw some episodes being scheduled to start at 6.20 pm - the earliest slot yet accorded *Doctor Who* since its return in 2005, as Russell T Davies publicly bemoaned - seem to have had less impact than feared on the viewing figures. 'Partners in Crime', one of the episodes transmitted in the 6.20 pm slot, won a higher rating than either of the previous two series-openers, 'New Earth' and 'Smith and Jones'. 'Planet of the Ood', 'The Sontaran Stratagem' and 'The Poison Sky' may, however, have suffered somewhat from the earlier start time. As previously mentioned, ITV's very successful *Britain's Got Talent* continued to rival *Doctor Who* for dominance of the Saturday evening ratings, generally knocking it down to second place even though, apart from in its final week, it was not scheduled in direct competition.

Similarly, *Doctor Who* was almost always the top-rated Sunday programme on BBC Three, and amongst the top five for the week (on a couple of occasions being knocked down a place by *Doctor Who Confidential*, which tended to have quite similar figures - see below), and invariably in the top ten across all digital channels for the week. This was essentially in line with the pattern established in the first three series.

The average AI figure on BBC One was 88 (compared with 82 for Series One, 84 for Series Two and 86 for Series Three) and on BBC Three, for the six episodes for which figures are known, 90 (compared with 86 for Series Two and 87 for Series Three; no equivalent figure is available for Series One). Given that the average AI figure for all drama programmes broadcast by BBC One and ITV1 is 77, these are exceptionally good results; and they also continue to show a steady year-on-year improvement, indicating that the viewing public's enjoyment of *Doctor Who* has been growing with each successive run, from an already high base. Although comprehensive comparative data are not available, Series Four's figures may very well be the best ever achieved by such a highly-rated drama series. The slightly higher figure for BBC Three is not unexpected: programmes with smaller ratings tend to get higher AI figures, all other things being equal, as their audiences generally have a higher proportion of viewers who are predisposed to like them (as opposed to casual viewers who have tuned in more on a whim).

On BBC One, the highest AI figure was 91 for 'The Stolen Earth' and 'Journey's End' and the lowest was 85 for 'Voyage of the Damned'. This compares with a high of 89 and a low of 76 for both Series One and Series Two and a high of 88 and a low of 84 for Series Three. On BBC Three, the highest was an amazing 93 for 'The Stolen Earth' and the lowest was 88 for 'Partners in Crime' and 'Turn Left' - although figures for most episodes are unknown. This compares with a high of 91 and a low of 79 for Series Two and a high of 90 and a low of 84 for Series Three; equivalent figures for Series One are not available. 91 is the highest AI figure that *Doctor Who* has ever gained on BBC One.

Based on the BBC One debut transmission figures, the general viewing public's order of preference for the episodes, working downwards from favourite to least favourite, was:

1. = 'The Stolen Earth'
1. = 'Journey's End'
3. = 'Silence in the Library'
3. = 'Forest of the Dead'
5. = 'Partners in Crime'
5. = 'The Poison Sky'
5. = 'The Doctor's Daughter'
5. = 'Turn Left'
9. = 'The Fires of Pompeii'
9. = 'Planet of the Ood'
9. = 'The Sontaran Stratagem'
12. = 'The Unicorn and the Wasp'
12. = 'Midnight'
14. 'Voyage of the Damned'

An indication of the relative merits of the episodes from the point of view of fans can be gleaned from the online episode polls conducted on the Outpost Gallifrey-associated Doctor Who Forum – the most popular *Doctor Who* fan forum on the internet – at www.doctorwhoforum.com. An average of 4167 voters participated in these polls, ranging from a low of 3477 for 'The Poison Sky' to a high of 5508 for 'Journey's End'. Each episode was given a mark of between one and five by each voter, with five being the highest. The percentages in the table below have been calculated by adding together the total number of marks received by each episode (as of 4 September 2009) and dividing by the maximum that could have been achieved if everyone who voted had given the episode a five.

EPISODE	FAN RATING
'Voyage of the Damned'	72.32 %
'Partners in Crime'	71.94 %
'The Fires of Pompeii'	84.64 %
'Planet of the Ood'	78.68 %
'The Sontaran Stratagem'	79.08 %
'The Poison Sky'	80.12 %
'The Doctor's Daughter'	72.42 %
'The Unicorn and the Wasp'	75.55 %
'Silence in the Library'	91.38 %
'Forest of the Dead'	91.04 %
'Midnight'	82.44 %
'Turn Left'	88.09 %
'The Stolen Earth'	92.40 %
'Journey's End'	80.67 %

Based on these figures, the fans' order of preference for the episodes was:

1. 'The Stolen Earth'
2. 'Silence in the Library'
3. 'Forest of the Dead'
4. 'Turn Left'
5. 'The Fires of Pompeii'
6. 'Midnight'
7. 'Journey's End'
8. 'The Poison Sky'
9. 'The Sontaran Stratagem'
10. 'Planet of the Ood'
11. 'The Unicorn and the Wasp'
12. 'The Doctor's Daughter'
13. 'Voyage of the Damned'
14. 'Partners in Crime'

As for Series Three, and unlike for Series One and Series Two, this ranking does not correspond particularly closely to the one for the general viewing public (see above), although certain episodes - 'The Stolen Earth', 'Silence in the Library' and 'Forest of the Dead' - come at or near the top in both, and certain others - 'Voyage of the Damned' and 'The Unicorn and the Wasp' - come at or near the bottom in both. Perhaps the most significant point to note here is that the fans clearly thought that the overall standard of Series Four was on a par with that of Series Three and that there was a greater consistency of quality than ever before: the spread of the figures in the fan ranking - from a still-very-respectable low of 72 percent ('Voyage of the Damned') to a fantastic high of 92 percent ('The Stolen Earth') - is four points less than for Series Three - which went from a low of 71 percent ('The Runaway Bride' and 'Evolution of the Daleks') to a high of 95 percent ('The Family of Blood') - eight points less than for Series Two - which went from a low of 65 percent ('Fear Her') to a high of 93 percent ('Doomsday') - and five points less than for Series One - which went from a low of 68 percent ('Boom Town') to a high of 93 percent ('Dalek'). However, it would seem that, by a narrow margin, Paul Cornell's remarkable Series Three contributions 'Human Nature' and 'The Family of Blood' remain the most popular episodes to date amongst dedicated fans.

The full ratings statistics produced by BARB for the main BBC One transmissions (which go into too fine a level of detail to be reproduced in their entirety here) reveal three other points of particular note, each of which is fully consistent with the equivalent findings for Series Three.

First, *Doctor Who* consistently scored well above the average for drama programmes under a range of viewer response headings, including 'Made a special effort to watch', 'High quality programme', 'Feels original and different', 'Would like to discuss', 'Liked the storyline', 'Liked the characters' and 'Would recommend'. The two main exceptions were 'Learned something new' and 'Programme was thought-provoking', under which headings the episodes tended to score around or just below the average for drama - although, bucking this trend, 'Turn Left', 'The Stolen Earth' and 'Journey's End' all scored exceptionally well under 'Programme was thought-provoking'.

Secondly, the average number of children aged four to 15 amongst viewers for these BBC One transmissions (excluding 'Voyage of the Damned') was 1.58 million, and the average share of the total children's audience an astonishingly high 58 percent, making *Doctor Who* by far the most popular TV programme amongst children each week. Boys outnumbered girls by an average of seven percentage points amongst viewers in this age range. In one case – 'The Doctor's Daughter' – this disparity between the sexes was as high as 18 percentage points, although in one other case – 'Silence in the Library' – girls actually outnumbered boys, by four percentage points, indicative of the fact that there was quite a wide spread in these figures.

Thirdly, where adult viewers were concerned, the position was reversed: excluding 'Voyage of the Damned', the average proportion of the total BBC One viewing audience (all ages) who were men was 49 percent and the average proportion who were women was 51 percent. For the BBC Three screenings, however, the split was 52 percent to 48 percent in men's favour, whereas for Series Three it had been very close to even. Children aside, the series was most popular amongst those in the 35 to 44 age range – some of whom will, of course, have been parents watching with children as a family – but had a good spread of viewers across all other age ranges as well. This belies the once-stereotypical image of the typical *Doctor Who* viewer as being an adolescent male science fiction fan.

To conclude this section, set out below, for what it's worth, is this author's own ranking of the episodes, again working downwards from favourite to least favourite – although I should perhaps add that my views on this tend to change from time to time!

1. 'Forest of the Dead'
2. 'Planet of the Ood'
3. 'The Fires of Pompeii'
4. 'Silence in the Library'
5. 'Turn Left'
6. 'Midnight'
7. 'The Doctor's Daughter'
8. 'The Poison Sky'
9. 'The Sontaran Stratagem'
10. 'The Stolen Earth'
11. 'Partners in Crime'
12. 'Voyage of the Damned'
13. 'Journey's End'
14. 'The Unicorn and the Wasp'

DOCTOR WHO CONFIDENTIAL

The main ratings data for the debut transmissions of the fourth series of *Doctor Who Confidential* were as follows. (The terms in the heading have the same meanings as in the equivalent table above for *Doctor Who* itself.)

EPISODE	RATING	SHARE	AI
[Untitled]	0.35 m	2 %	83

A Noble Return	0.96 m	5 %	84
The Italian Job	0.63 m	3 %	n/k
Oods and Ends	0.71 m	4 %	84
Send in the Clones	0.59 m	3 %	81
Sontar-Ha!	0.61 m	4 %	n/k
Sins of the Father	0.64 m	4 %	n/k
Nemesis	0.69 m	3 %	n/k
Shadow Play	0.57 m	3 %	n/k
River Runs Deep	0.87 m	5 %	n/k
Look Who's Talking	0.59 m	3 %	n/k
Here Come the Girls	0.85 m	5 %	87
Friends and Foe	1.27 m	7 %	90
End of an Era	1.46 m	8 %	88
Average*	**0.80 m**	**4%**	**86**

* Not including the Christmas special, which was transmitted on Christmas Day 2007.
Source for viewing figures: Broadcasters' Audience Research Board (BARB)
Source for AI figures: BBC

Children aged four to 15 inclusive made up 24 percent of the audience, slightly lower than for the third series. The split between male and female viewers (all ages) was 54 percent to 46 percent, very close to the third series' split of 53 percent to 47 percent.

These excellent figures – higher in some cases than for the BBC Three transmissions of *Doctor Who* itself – maintained *Doctor Who Confidential*'s record of success, the average viewing figure of 0.80 million for the debut transmissions representing a steady improvement on the third series' 0.70 million, the second series' 0.63 million and the first series' 0.54 million. As in previous years, repeat screenings – in edited, *Confidential Cutdown* format – also drew significant numbers of additional viewers.

APPENDIX C
ORIGINAL NOVELS

During the period of the build up to and transmission of Series Four, BBC Books published a further nine titles in their ongoing range of tenth Doctor hardback novels, plus another of the paperback 'Quick Reads' books. Summary details are as follows.

16: FOREVER AUTUMN

Writer: Mark Morris
Publication date: 6 September 2007
Series Consultant: Justin Richards; Project Editor: Steve Tribe; Cover Design: Lee Binding

PUBLICITY BLURB

It is almost Halloween in the sleepy New England town of Blackwood Falls. Leaves litter lawns and sidewalks, paper skeletons hang in windows, and carved pumpkins leer from front porches. The Doctor and Martha soon discover that something long-dormant has awoken, and this will be no ordinary Halloween. What is the secret of the ancient tree and the book discovered tangled in its roots? What rises from the churchyard at night, sealing the lips of the only witness? Why are the harmless trappings of Halloween suddenly taking on a creepy new life of their own? As nightmarish creatures prowl the streets, the Doctor and Martha must battle to prevent both the townspeople and themselves from suffering a grisly fate ... Featuring the Doctor and Martha as played by David Tennant and Freema Agyeman in the hit series from BBC Television.

NOTES

- Also released by BBC Audio on 3 March 2008 as an abridged audiobook CD set read by Will Thorp.
- Also issued in a paperback edition by the Book Club in June 2008 as part of a box set of ten *Doctor Who* novels.

17: SICK BUILDING

Writer: Paul Magrs
Publication date: 6 September 2007
Series Consultant: Justin Richards; Project Editor: Steve Tribe; Cover Design: Lee Binding

PUBLICITY BLURB

Tiermann's World: a planet covered in wintry woods and roamed by sabre-toothed tigers and other savage beasts. The Doctor is here to warn Professor Tiermann, his wife and their son that a terrible danger is on its way. The Tiermanns live in luxury, in a fantastic, futuristic, fully-automated Dreamhome, under an impenetrable force shield. But that won't protect them from the Voracious Craw. A huge and hungry alien creature is heading remorselessly towards their home. When it arrives, everything will be devoured. Can they get away in time? With the force shield cracking up, and the Dreamhome itself deciding who should or should not leave, things are looking desperate ... Featuring the Doctor and Martha as played by David Tennant and Freema Agyeman in the hit series from BBC Television.

NOTES

- Also released by BBC Audio on 3 March 2008 as an abridged audiobook CD set read by Will Thorp.
- Also issued in a paperback edition by the Book Club in June 2008 as part of a box set of ten *Doctor Who* novels.
- The working title of this book was *The Wicked Bungalow*, which was vetoed by Russell T Davies.

18: WETWORLD

Writer: Mark Michalowski
Publication date: 6 September 2007
Series Consultant: Justin Richards; Project Editor: Steve Tribe; Cover Design: Lee Binding

PUBLICITY BLURB

When the TARDIS makes a disastrous landing in the swamps of the planet Sunday, the Doctor has no choice but to abandon Martha and try to find help. But the tranquillity of Sunday's swamps is deceptive, and even the TARDIS can't protect Martha forever. The human pioneers of Sunday have their own dangers to face: homeless and alone, they're starting to see that Sunday's wildlife isn't as harmless as it appears. Why are the others behaving so strangely, and what is the creature in the swamps that is so interested in the humans, and the new arrivals? The Doctor and Martha must fight to ensure that human intelligence doesn't become the greatest danger of all. Featuring the Doctor and Martha as played by David Tennant and Freema Agyeman in the hit series from BBC Television.

NOTES

- Also released by BBC Audio on 3 March 2008 as an abridged audiobook CD set read by Freema Agyeman.
- Also issued in a paperback edition by the Book Club in June 2008 as part of a box set of ten *Doctor Who* novels.

19: WISHING WELL

Writer: Trevor Baxendale
Publication date: 26 December 2007
Series Consultant: Justin Richards; Project Editor: Steve Tribe; Cover Design: Lee Binding

PUBLICITY BLURB

The old village well is just a curiosity – something to attract tourists intrigued by stories of lost treasure, or visitors just making a wish. Unless something alien and terrifying could be lurking inside the well. Something utterly monstrous that causes nothing but death and destruction. But who knows the real truth about the well? Who wishes to unleash the hideous forces it contains? What terrible consequences will follow the search for a legendary treasure hidden at the bottom? No-one wants to believe the Doctor's warnings about the deadly horror lying in wait – but soon they'll wish they had ... Featuring the Doctor and Martha as played by David Tennant and Freema Agyeman in the hit series from BBC Television.

NOTES

- Also released by BBC Audio on 10 July 2008 as an abridged audiobook CD set read by Debbie Chazen.
- Also issued in a paperback edition by the Book Club in June 2008 as part of a box set of ten *Doctor Who* novels.

20: THE PIRATE LOOP

Writer: Simon Guerrier
Publication date: 26 December 2007
Series Consultant: Justin Richards; Project Editor: Steve Tribe; Cover Design: Lee Binding

PUBLICITY BLURB

The Doctor's been everywhere and everywhen in the whole of the universe and seems to know all the answers. But ask him what happened to the Starship *Brilliant* and he hasn't the first idea. Did it fall into a sun or black hole? Was it shot down in the first moments of the galactic war? And what's this about a secret experimental drive? The Doctor is skittish, but if Martha is so keen to find out, he'll land the TARDIS on the *Brilliant*, a few days before it vanishes. Then they can see for themselves ... Soon the Doctor learns the awful truth. And Martha learns that you need to be careful what you wish for. She certainly wasn't hoping for mayhem, death, and badger-faced space pirates. Featuring the Doctor and Martha as played by David Tennant and Freema Agyeman in the hit series from BBC Television.

NOTES

- Also released by BBC Audio on 10 July 2008 as an abridged audiobook CD set read by Freema Agyeman.
- Also issued in a paperback edition by the Book Club in June 2008 as part of a box set of ten *Doctor Who* novels.

21: PEACEMAKER

Writer: James Swallow
Publication date: 26 December 2007
Series Consultant: Justin Richards; Project Editor: Steve Tribe; Cover Design: Lee Binding

PUBLICITY BLURB

The peace and quiet of a remote homestead in the 1880s American West is shattered by the arrival of two shadowy outriders searching for 'the healer'. When the farmer refuses to help them, they raze the house to the ground using guns that shoot bolts of energy instead of bullets ... In the town of Redwater, the Doctor and Martha learn of a snake-oil salesman whose patent medicines actually cure his patients. But when the Doctor and Martha investigate, they discover the truth is stranger, and far more dangerous. Caught between the law of the gun and the deadly plans of intergalactic mercenaries, the Doctor and Martha are about to discover just how wild the West can become ... Featuring the Doctor and Martha as played by David Tennant and Freema Agyeman in the hit series from BBC Television.

NOTES

- Also released by BBC Audio on 10 July 2008 as an abridged audiobook CD set read by Will Thorp.

REVENGE OF THE JUDOON

Writer: Terrance Dicks
Publication date: 28 February 2008
Series Consultant: Justin Richards; Project Editor: Steve Tribe; Cover Design: Lee Binding

PUBLICITY BLURB

The TARDIS brings the Doctor and Martha to Balmoral in 1902. Here they meet Captain Harry Carruthers - friend of the new king, Edward VII. Together they head for the castle to see the king - only to find that Balmoral Castle is gone, leaving just a hole in the ground. The Doctor realises it is the work of the Judoon - a race of ruthless space police. While Martha and Carruthers seek answers in London, the Doctor finds himself in what should be the most deserted place on

Earth - and he is not alone. With help from Arthur Conan Doyle, the Doctor and his friends discover a plot to take over the world. With time running out, who will fall victim to the revenge of the Judoon? Featuring the Doctor and Martha as played by David Tennant and Freema Agyeman in the acclaimed hit series from BBC Television.

NOTES

- A paperback in the 'Quick Reads' range launched by the National Literacy Trust charity on World Book Day 2006 with the stated aim to 'provide fast-paced, bite-sized books by bestselling writers for emergent readers, anyone who had lost the reading habit or simply wanted a short, fast read'.

22: MARTHA IN THE MIRROR

Writer: Justin Richards
Publication date: 10 April 2008
Series Consultant: Justin Richards; Editor: Stephen Cole; Project Editor: Steve Tribe
Cover Design: Lee Binding

PUBLICITY BLURB

Castle Extremis - whoever holds it can control the provinces on either side that have been at war for centuries. Now the castle is about to play host to the signing of a peace treaty. But as the Doctor and Martha find out, not everyone wants the war to end. Who is the strange little girl who haunts the castle? What is the secret of the book the Doctor finds, its pages made from thin, brittle glass? Who is the hooded figure that watches from the shadows? And what is the secret of the legendary Mortal Mirror? The Doctor and Martha don't have long to find the answers - an army is on the march, and the castle will soon be under siege once more ... Featuring the Doctor and Martha as played by David Tennant and Freema Agyeman in the hit series from BBC Television.

23: SNOWGLOBE 7

Writer: Mike Tucker
Publication date: 10 April 2007
Series Consultant: Justin Richards; Project Editor: Steve Tribe; Cover Design: Lee Binding

PUBLICITY BLURB

Earth, 2009. Global warming is devastating the climate. The polar ice caps are melting. In a desperate attempt at preservation, the governments of the world have removed vast sections of the Arctic and Antarctic and set them inside huge domes across the world. The Doctor and Martha arrive in Snowglobe 7 in the Middle East, hoping for peace and relaxation. But they soon discover that it's not only ice and snow that have been preserved beneath the Dome. While Martha struggles to help with an infection sweeping through the Dome, the Doctor discovers an alien threat that has lain hidden since the last ice age. A threat that is starting to thaw. Featuring the Doctor and Martha as played by David Tennant and Freema Agyeman in the hit series from BBC Television.

24: THE MANY HANDS

Writer: Dale Smith
Publication date: 10 April 2008
Series Consultant: Justin Richards; Project Editor: Steve Tribe; Cover Design: Lee Binding

PUBLICITY BLURB

Edinburgh, 1759. The Nor' Loch is being filled in. If you ask the soldiers there, they'll tell you it's a stinking cesspool that the city can do without. But that doesn't explain why the workers won't go near the place without an armed guard. That doesn't explain why they whisper stories about the loch giving up its dead, about the minister who walked into his church 12 years after he died ... It doesn't explain why, as they work, they whisper about a man called the Doctor. And about the many hands of Alexander Monro. Featuring the Doctor and Martha as played by David Tennant and Freema Agyeman in the hit series from BBC Television.

25: THE GHOSTS OF INDIA

Writer: Mark Morris
Publication date: 4 September 2008
Series Consultant: Justin Richards; Project Editor: Steve Tribe; Cover Design: Lee Binding

PUBLICITY BLURB

India in 1947 is a country in the grip of chaos - a country torn apart by internal strife. When the Doctor and Donna arrive in Calcutta, they are instantly swept up in violent events. Barely escaping with their lives, they discover that the city is rife with tales of 'half-made men', who roam the streets at night and steal people away. These creatures, it is said, are as white as salt and have only shadows where their eyes should be. With help from India's great spiritual leader, Mohandas 'Mahatma' Gandhi, the Doctor and Donna set out to investigate these rumours. What is the real truth behind the 'half-made men'? Why is Gandhi's role in history under threat? And has an ancient, all-powerful god of destruction *really* come back to wreak his vengeance upon the Earth? Featuring the Doctor and Donna as played by David Tennant and Catherine Tate in the hit series from BBC Television.

26: SHINING DARKNESS

Writer: Mark Michalowski
Publication date: 4 September 2008
Series Consultant: Justin Richards; Project Editor: Steve Tribe; Cover Design: Lee Binding

PUBLICITY BLURB

For Donna Noble, the Andromeda galaxy is a long, long way from home. But even two and a half million light years from Earth, danger lurks around every corner ... A visit to an art gallery turns into a race across space to uncover the secret behind a shadowy organisation. From the desert world of Karris to the interplanetary scrapyard of Junk, the Doctor and Donna discover that appearances can be deceptive, that enemies are lurking around every corner – and that the centuries-long peace between humans and machines may be about to come to an end. Because waiting in the wings to bring chaos to the galaxy is The Cult of Shining Darkness. Featuring the Doctor and Donna as played by David Tennant and Catherine Tate in the hit series from BBC Television.

27: THE DOCTOR TRAP

Writer: Simon Messingham
Publication date: 4 September 2008
Series Consultant: Justin Richards; Project Editor: Steve Tribe; Cover Design: Lee Binding

PUBLICITY BLURB

Sebastiene was perhaps once human. He might look like a 19th Century nobleman, but in truth he is a ruthless hunter. He likes nothing more than luring difficult opposition to a planet, then hunting them down for sport. And now he's caught them all – from Zargregs to Moogs, and even the odd Eternal ... In fact, Sebastiene is after only one more prize. For this trophy, he knows he is going to need help. He's brought together the finest hunters in the universe to play the most dangerous game for the deadliest quarry of them all. They are hunting for the last of the Time Lords – the Doctor. Featuring the Doctor and Donna as played by David Tennant and Catherine Tate in the hit series from BBC Television.

APPENDIX D
ORIGINAL COMIC STRIPS

During the 12 month period covered by this book, *Doctor Who* fans could enjoy no fewer than four different comic strip series presenting new adventures for the tenth Doctor and his companions. These appeared in: Panini's *Doctor Who Magazine*, which (under various different titles) had been home to a *Doctor Who* comic strip since 1979; *Doctor Who Adventures*, a fortnightly comic aimed at a pre-teen audience, published by BBC Magazines; *Battles in Time*, a fortnightly trading-card magazine pitched toward slightly older children, published by G E Fabbri; and *Doctor Who*, a US-only comic book series, published by IDW (who also brought out a series of classic *Doctor Who* comic books featuring the fourth Doctor in stories reprinted, with newly-added colour, from earlier incarnations of *Doctor Who Magazine*). Listed below are details of the stories from each of these four titles in turn.

DOCTOR WHO MAGAZINE

BUS STOP!

Story: Rob Davis
Art: John Ross; Colours: James Offredi; Lettering: Roger Langridge; Editors: Clayton Hickman and Scott Gray
Publication[111]: Issue 385; 22 August 2007

PLOT

Alien mutants from the 27th Century attempt to destroy President Lithops on Mars by travelling back in time to 21st Century London and assassinating his ancestor, the Mayor, and thereby wiping out his entire lineage. The Doctor creates a decoy by making a 'soup' out of the Mayor's DNA and taking it on a bus, but finds himself pursued by two of the assassins. Martha, left on Mars with the President and a policeman named DI Moloch, is able to gain access to the time machine that the aliens have been using. She rescues the Doctor by bringing him back to the 27th Century. The Doctor then destroys the time machine, causing the assassins left in the 21st Century to vanish.

[111] The publication dates given here for *Doctor Who Magazine* are those printed on the covers of the issues in question. The issues generally went on sale about a month earlier than the cover dates.

THE FIRST

Story: Daniel McDaid
Pencils: Martin Geraghty; Inks: David A Roach; Colours: James Offredi; Letters: Roger Langridge; Editors: Clayton Hickman and Scott Gray
Publication: Issues 386-389; 19 September 2007, 17 October 2007, 14 November 2007, 12 December 2007.

PLOT

The TARDIS brings the Doctor and Martha to the Antarctic in September 1915. There they meet the famous explorer Ernest Shackleton and the crew of his ship *Endurance*, who have been attacked by a huge, many-tentacled creature on the ice. The expedition ventures out after the creature – a mutated whale, as the Doctor later deduces – but it is destroyed by its alien controllers, the Skith. The Skith capture the human party and take them below the ice to their spaceship, at the heart of which is the Mindcore, the repository of all Skith knowledge. The Skith are galactic explorers rather than conquerors, but they aim to be the first to reach any given planet; on learning that the Doctor is also an alien, and has been on Earth before them, the Skith leader declares his expedition a failure. The Skith destroy all the planets they explore, turning them into frozen husks, in order to prevent other races from acquiring the same knowledge as them, and this is what they now intend to do to Earth. The Doctor communes with the Mindcore and attempts to overcome it, but to no avail – until Shackleton comes to his aid. Then he is able to send the Skith ship, the *Oppressor One*, through a space rift, heading into the Sun. The Mindcore retreats to the Skith ownworld, leaving the Doctor and Shackleton alone on the disintegrating ship. Martha, however, is able to direct the TARDIS to the ship and effect a rescue.

DEATH TO THE DOCTOR!

Story: Jonathan Morris
Art: Roger Langridge; Colours: James Offredi; Editors: Tom Spilsbury and Scott Gray
Publication: Issue 390; 9 January 2008.

PLOT

A group of aliens, all of whom have suffered defeats at the hands of the Doctor, gather for a secret meeting at a quarantined research base called Truro on a remote planet. They resolve to join forces and defeat their mutual adversary, chanting 'Death to the Doctor'. One of their number is then killed in an accident, however, and the others assume that the Doctor is responsible and is hiding amongst them. Gripped by paranoia, the creatures end up killing each other. The TARDIS arrives, and the Doctor and Martha find a base full of dead aliens. The Doctor sadly reflects that if only he had got there sooner, he might have been able to save them …

UNIVERSAL MONSTERS

Story: Ian Edginton
Artwork: Adrian Salmon; Lettering: Roger Langridge; Editors: Tom Spilsbury and Scott Gray
Publication: Issues 391-393; 6 February 2008, 5 March 2008, 2 April 2008.

PLOT

The Doctor and Martha arrive on a wooded planet where the inhabitants of the solitary village are being terrorised by a mysterious beast known as the Hound of Thane - the Thane being a nobleman who used to watch over them but now lives in seclusion in a great Keep nearby. The Hound - in truth a cyborg called Viktor - makes a raid on the village and captures Martha, taking her back to the Keep, where she meets the Thane. The Doctor goes to the Keep to rescue his companion and discovers that the villagers are being kept pacified by a neuropathic generator. Disregarding Martha's attempts to warn him against this, he destroys the device - and the villagers all transform into vicious monsters. The Thane explains that he is a Thane-class replicant, a product of Cyrene genetic technology, and Viktor is a Xhosa bio-mechanical construct. The Cyrene and Xhosa were at war for centuries before reaching a pact, and this left them with a terrible legacy: the Cyrene Khamirae, savage, gene-spliced shape-changers made for war. As it was deemed immoral to kill the creatures, they were placed on this planet to live out their lives, in the mistaken belief that they were sterile. The Thane has now been watching over them for 50 generations, periodically cloning himself each time he grows old and needs to be replaced. The Doctor repairs the neuropathic generator, using energy from the planet's red moons to jump-start it, although Viktor is destroyed in the process. The villagers, restored to their humanoid forms, refuse the Doctor's offer to summon a rescue ship, as this planet is now their home. Viktor pledges to look after them for the rest of his natural life, having decided not to clone himself again.

HOTEL HISTORIA

Story and art: Dan McDaid
Lettering: Roger Langridge; Editors: Tom Spilsbury and Scott Gray
Publication: Issue 394; 30 April 2008.

PLOT

Hotel Historia offers rich clients from 2008 a chance to visit different periods of Earth history. The operation is run by an alien calling herself Majenta Pryce, using a Chronexus 3000 time travel device - which the Doctor quickly realises is malfunctioning, allowing the clients and those they encounter on their visits to interact, which should not be possible. A group of Graxnix conquerors from the 41st Century invade the Hotel, delighted to have a chance to destroy London all over again. The Graxnix were minor players in the Time War, held back by their primitive time travel technology. They now want to take the Chronexus, but the

Doctor repairs and reprograms it so that it traps the Graxnix outside time, rendering them invisible and intangible, and then shuts down permanently. Majenta is arrested by cosmic bailiffs.

THE WIDOW'S CURSE

Story: Rob Davis
Pencil Art: Martin Geraghty; Inks: David A Roach; Colours: James Offredi; Lettering: Roger Langridge; Editors: Tom Spilsbury and Scott Gray
Sycorax created by Russell T Davies
Publication: Issues 395-398; 28 May 2008, 25 June 2008, 23 July 2008, 20 August 2008.

PLOT

The Doctor and Donna are amongst a group of tourists on a ferry trip to the Caribbean island of Shadow Cay - which the Doctor knows should not exist. A group of zombies meanwhile retrieve an alien object discovered on the nearby Granma Island. Arriving on Shadow Cay, the Doctor is astonished to discover a perfect replica of Westminster Abbey. Donna and the other tourists are locked inside the building, where they are confronted by a group of female Sycorax. The Doctor meanwhile realises that everything on the island is a façade created by the Sycorax using magma-sculpting software. This is actually one of their rock spaceships, and the zombies are corpses psychically controlled by the Sycorax. Donna and the tourists are brought before the Haxan Craw, witch queen of the Sycorax. The device found on Granma Island, the Foraxi Yox, is a kind of black box recorder for the ship that previously visited the Earth carrying all the Sycorax males of this clan. On playing back images from the device, the Haxan Craw learns that the humans destroyed that ship in an act of betrayal, after the Doctor killed her husband, the Sycorax leader - to whom Shadow Cay is a shrine, Westminster Abbey having been where he fell to his death. The Haxan Craw intends to send a plane full of zombies to London, carrying a virus that removes the immune system but prevents death, condemning the human race to live in agony for hundreds of years. The plane takes off, but with Donna and one of the tourists, Norah, as stowaways. The Doctor gains access to the spaceship's systems and directs the zombies to restrain the Sycorax. Donna and Norah meanwhile get control of the plane and turn it back to the island. The Doctor uses the magma-sculpting software to create a huge pair of hands and catch the plane mid-flight, bringing it safely back to the ground. Another of the tourists, Jean, whose husband has been killed by the Sycorax, causes the Haxan Craw to plunge to her death as the spaceship takes off. The Doctor, Donna and the surviving tourists swim back to the ferry as the spaceship explodes, the Doctor having given the magma-sculpting software the impossible task of copying everything on Earth.

NOTE

- This is a sequel to the TV story 'The Christmas Invasion'.

THE TIME OF MY LIFE

Story: Jonathan Morris
Art: Rob David; Colours: Geraint Ford; Lettering: Roger Langridge; Editors: Tom Spilsbury and Scott Gray
Publication: Issue 399; 17 September 2008.

PLOT

The Doctor, left alone in the TARDIS with only his memories of his amazing adventures with Donna, is surprised to receive a hologram farewell message from her, recorded in case she did not get a chance to say a proper goodbye.

DOCTOR WHO ADVENTURES

THE LAST SOLDIER

Script: Martin Day
Art: John Ross; Colours: Alan Craddock; Lettering: Paul Vyse
Publication: Issues 34-35; 19 July 2007, 2 August 2007

PLOT

The Doctor and Martha arrive on a far off planet where two groups of creatures - one of beautiful, humanoid appearance made of living metal, and the other of huge, monstrous appearance made largely of bone - are fighting a war with curious rules: their weapons do not kill, only stun, placing their targets in a kind of suspended animation. Eventually there is only one creature left on each side. The Doctor persuades them to make peace and shake hands. When they do so, they are transformed, combining into a single creature containing elements of both. The Doctor explains that the war was really a battle of the sexes: on this planet, only the last male and the last female to come through the conflict are able to pass on their genetic material. The other creatures all revive from suspended animation and await the birth of a new generation.

SIGNS OF LIFE

Script: Trevor Baxendale
Art: John Ross; Colours: Alan Craddock; Letters: Paul Vyse (Part One), Ben Ireland (Part Two)
Publication: Issues 36-37; 16 August 2007, 30 August 2007

PLOT

The Doctor and Martha are visiting Liverpool in the 1960s to see the Beatles playing in the Cavern. Martha is trapped in a long-range teleport beam and disappears, but the Doctor follows the signal in the TARDIS and manages to intercept it and rescue her. He learns from the TARDIS's instruments that the beam originated on the planet Gelezen, which is surrounded by an impenetrable time field. The Gelezen are a clone race who reputedly used human DNA as a template for their entire species. In short, they are DNA vampires. Martha is again seized by the teleport beam, from inside the TARDIS itself. She finds herself on Gelezen, where the clone surgeons tell her that their race is dying. They want to forcibly extract her DNA - as she has travelled in time, this will enable them to live forever - but she fights them off and destroys the time field generator, allowing the Doctor to materialise in the TARDIS. The Doctor uses a sample of his own DNA to replicate the human gene matrix as self-regenerating DNA in the surgeons' cloning machine, saving their race from extinction.

SHIPWRECK!

Script: Trevor Baxendale
Art: John Ross; Colours: Alan Craddock; Letters: Paul Vyse
Publication: Issues 38-39; 13 September 2007, 27 September 2007.

PLOT

The TARDIS materialises aboard the *Seamancer*, a fishing trawler out of Portsmouth, in the grip of the worst storm the Atlantic Ocean has seen for 30 years. The TARDIS needs some repairs, but the Doctor's work is interrupted as the trawler hits a rock and sinks, stranding all the occupants on an island. The Doctor quickly realises that they are actually on an alien planet. In the midst of the storm, the malfunctioning TARDIS has transported the *Seamancer* 420,000 light years across the galaxy. Suddenly a group of octopus-like creatures appear, declaring this to be oceanworld of Surobos and condemning the alien intruders to death. When the Doctor and the others explain that they have come here by accident, a stay of execution is granted: they have until moonfall to leave the planet. One of the Suboran creatures, Jalkis, defies its leader by helping the Doctor to swim down to the wreck of the *Seamancer*, distracting the vicious Skilus creatures that live in the water. The Doctor retrieves the TARDIS and uses it to bring the injured Jalkis back to the shore. Martha stitches the heroic Jalkis's wounds. The Doctor then uses a gravity beam projected from the TARDIS to retrieve the *Seamancer*, reverses the materialisation field to take it back to Earth and applies a localised time reversal to repair the hull.

COLD WAR

Script: Mark Michalowski
Art: John Ross; Colours: Alan Craddock; Letters: Paul Vyse
Publication: Issues 40-41; 11 October 2007, 25 October 2007.

PLOT

The TARDIS materialises on an icy landscape on an alien planet. The ice is melting and Martha slips and falls from a cliff. She is saved by a purple-skinned, green-haired creature call Paltoq riding on the back of a pterodactyl-like creature. Paltoq explains that he comes from the nearby citadel of Isqaron and that the ice is melting because the Sky God Asharoth has decreed that his race are sinners and should fall beneath the waves. The Mouth of Asharoth appears as a great orange glow in the sky. The Doctor persuades Paltoq to take them to the Isqaron Empress, Thamli. Thamli, however, concludes that the Doctor and Martha are escaped slaves of Asharoth and decrees that they must be taken back to their master, along with Paltoq as a sacrifice. Martha and Paltoq manage to escape, but the Doctor is thrown into the Mouth of Asharoth, which he realises is actually a dimensional gateway. He finds himself in a laboratory on Earth and discovers that the scientists are using the whole of Isqar as a giant air-conditioner for the Earth - pumping heat through the gateway as a solution for global warming. He is helped by one of the scientists, Professor Kate Curran, who realises that what they are doing is wrong, and manages to close the gateway for good, leaving just enough time for him to return through it to Isqaron to be reunited with Martha and Paltoq.

WASTE NOT

Script: Trevor Baxendale
Art: John Ross; Colours: Alan Craddock; Letters: Paul Vyse
Publication: Issues 42-43; 8 November 2007, 22 November 2007.

PLOT

The Doctor and Martha arrive in the far-distant future on the planet Zetheda, which has been used as a giant landfill site for the rubbish of nearby worlds. There they meet the rodent-like Ratlings, who idolise a large, glowing object as the Great Orb of Refuse. The Doctor realises that this is an old interstellar distress beacon from an Earth spaceship that crashed on the planet almost ten thousand years ago. The Ratlings are evolved descendants of the human crew. A spaceship arrives in response to the beacon. Its occupants, the Optimi, want to colonise the planet, and are horrified to find that it is a rubbish dump. They determine to clear it and destroy the Ratlings. The Doctor realises that the Optimi are also evolved descendents of the human race - or part of it, at least. The spaceship that crashed here was one of theirs. It incorporated a terraforming device, and this has continued working, changing the inside of the planet into a paradise. This presents the perfect solution: the Optimi can live in the paradise below ground, while the Ratlings continue to occupy the rubbish planet on the surface.

A KLYTODE CHRISTMAS

Script: Trevor Baxendale
Art: John Ross; Colours: Alan Craddock; Letters: Paul Vyse
Publication: Issues 44-45; 6 December 2007, 13 December 2007.

PLOT

The Doctor is doing some Christmas shopping with Martha in Oxford Street in the year 3781 when he bumps into two old friends, Jimmy and his robot mate Bert X-5, who now have their own business installing sanitary systems in government facilities. Bert is worried that Jimmy has been acting strangely since they started a job in the new Ecopower Station franchise, wandering off and getting lost in restricted reactor areas. The Doctor deduces that Jimmy is under some form of telekinetic mind control. He, Martha and Bert follow Jimmy the next day and see him entering the bio-reactor room, where they are horrified to discover the Klytode - a gestalt being that wants to turn Earth into a toxic wasteland. The vengeful creature has used its telekinetic powers to control Jimmy and conceal itself here. It brings the Prime Klytode - the gestalt brain that controls its kind - through from hyperspace to begin spewing toxic gas over the planet. The Doctor uses the bio-reactor's power core, linked to the computer brain of one of the Kyltode's robot servants destroyed by Martha and the now-recovered Jimmy, to reverse the hyperspatial link and send the Prime Klytode back where it came from. The Klytode performs an emergency teleport and escapes. The Doctor and Martha stay to celebrate Christmas with Bert and Jimmy.

NOTE

- The previous story featuring Bert, Jimmy and the Klytode was entitled 'Snag Finders' and appeared in Issues 26 and 27 of *Doctor Who Adventures.*

THE MONSTER UPSTAIRS

Script: Trevor Baxendale
Art: John Ross; Colours: Alan Craddock; Letters: Paul Vyse
Publication: Issues 46-47; 3 January 2008, 17 January 2008.

PLOT

Nine-year-old Violet Hopley believes there is a monster lurking upstairs at her family home. Her father answers a knock at the door and the Doctor bursts in and runs upstairs, saying that he is tracking the energy signature of a rogue Extron parasite. The creature is there, with the terrified Violet before it, trying to achieve 'full gene transmutation'. The Doctor explains that it transmutes in order to survive, combining with an intelligent, living mammal, usually an infant. This particular Extron is on the run from the galactic penal institute of Inkarsera. The Doctor is powerless to intervene as the Extron teleports away from the house, taking Violet with it to the distant planet Onla-toch, which it previously devastated - something it regards as its greatest achievement, but also its downfall, as it was arrested by the Judoon and sentenced to eternal imprisonment. The Doctor takes the TARDIS to Inkarsera and, having learnt from its records of the scene of the Extron's crime, is then able to follow it to Onla-toch and save Violet. Violet helps by fitting the creature with a pair of biometric manacles, obtained by the Doctor from Inkarsera, which automatically teleport it back to the prison. The Doctor returns Violet to her grateful parents.

HOT METAL

Script: Christopher Cooper
Art: John Ross; Colours: Alan Craddock; Letters: Paul Vyse
Publication: Issues 48-49; 24 January 2008, 31 January 2008.

PLOT

The TARDIS collides with a planet made of papier-mâché in the middle of a major galactic bypass. In amongst the rubbish the Doctor finds a discarded copy of the *Daily Eon* free newspaper, the sports pages of which bear a photograph of a green, rabbit-like creature who is actually able to communicate through the image. The creature introduces himself as Ray Royce, head sports writer, and explains that he and hundreds of other journalists are trapped at the News Factory, where the *Eon* is printed. The Doctor journeys to the Factory in the TARDIS and finds a vast Crystalline Memory device in which the neural matrices of all the journalists are stored. His presence is detected by RoboCopiers, who digitise him, adding him to the memory as a new journalist with 900 years' worth of stories to tell. The Doctor uses his sonic screwdriver to take him to the sports page to meet up with Ray. SubEd entities arrive to try to delete this 'erroneous copy', but the Doctor and Ray eventually make their way to the Editorial to meet the Proprietor. The Doctor's intervention has caused the *Eon*'s systems to shut down, and he suggests that the Proprietor launches a recycling business instead.

THE HALLS OF SACRIFICE

Script: Martin Day
Art: John Ross; Colours: Alan Craddock; Letters: Paul Vyse
Publication: Issues 50-51; 7 February 2008, 14 February 2008.

PLOT

The TARDIS brings the Doctor to a planet where the sonic screwdriver earns him unwanted attention from some vicious bat-like creatures called Shrikes. He meets a young humanoid called Kaze who takes him to a nearby village. The villagers' leader, Genji, dwells in a building called the Halls of Sacrifice, where each year the fittest of their number are chosen to undergo training in order to defend them against the Shrikes. Kaze is disappointed not to be amongst the chosen ones at the latest ceremony, but as he and the other rejected candidates are led away, the Doctor becomes suspicious and tries to intervene. He and Kaze are then thrown into a sort of anti-gravity chute that takes them to the true heart of this society – a Worldbuilder-class starship. Genji explains that the population came to this planet decades ago but found only the Shrikes, which damaged the ship. They have been trying to repair it ever since. Those young people rejected as warriors become scientists and thinkers instead. The subterfuge is to fool the Shrikes, who are more intelligent than they seem. With the aid of the TARDIS, the Doctor repairs the starship and gets it away from the planet. He also ejects a couple of roomfuls of junk from the TARDIS, providing energy for the Shrikes to feed on.

THE OLD KINGS OF SKARAB

Script: Martin Day
Art: John Ross; Colours: Alan Craddock; Letters: Paul Vyse
Publication: Issues 52-53; 21 February 2008, 28 February 2008.

PLOT

The Doctor arrives on a planet where he is attacked by an gorilla-like beast and rescued by an explorer called Mason Burns who is searching for the final resting place of the Old Kings of Skarab, a terrifying power who once ruled the entire planet but whose civilisation has been lost. Mason and the Doctor find the Kings' tomb, where they narrowly avoid falling foul of a number of traps and other security measures. As Burns inadvertently presses a release switch, the Doctor realises that this is not a tomb but a prison - and they have just freed one of the inmates. The Kings were dictators who were overthrown by their subjects and now want to reassert their authority. Their once-humanoid subjects have now evolved into the gorilla-like creatures, however, and this time they overpower and kill the Kings.

REIGN OF THE STONE MONKEY

Script: Christopher Cooper
Art: John Ross; Colours: Alan Craddock; Letters: Paul Vyse
Publication: Issues 54-55; 6 March 2008, 13 March 2008.

PLOT

In ancient China, an old man named Chan Li tells his grandchildren a story of when, as a boy, he met the Doctor, who was an old friend of his uncle's. Their area, Gansu province, was beset by demons, who had taken control of the population, raised taxes and stolen crops. Li told the Doctor that the demons were at the Temple in Qingyang and offered to take him there. The Doctor accepted. Together they gained access to the Temple, the Doctor having realised that the soldiers' thoughts were being controlled by the so-called demons - who turned out to be three alien creatures, led by one calling himself the Monkey King. The Doctor undertook to compete with the aliens in a series of challenges on the basis that, if he won, they would leave peacefully. One of these challenges involved taming a man-eating dragon in a cave. When an explosion erupted from the cave, everyone assumed the Doctor had been killed. In fact, however, the 'dragon' was the aliens' spaceship and the explosion was caused by its defence system, which the Doctor managed to disable. The Doctor trapped the aliens in their ship and sent them into space on autopilot, telling them that the authorities would be there to arrest them when they got home. As the grandchildren fall asleep, the Doctor arrives to visit his old friend Chan Li, who is now Governor of the province.

EVERY DOG HAS ITS DAY

Script: Trevor Baxendale
Art: John Ross; Colours: Alan Craddock; Letters: Paul Vyse
Publication: Issues 56-57; 20 March 2008, 27 March 2008.

PLOT

While they are out walking, young Tom Blakeney's dog Sammy finds what appears to be a strange stone, but the Doctor arrives and identifies it as a silicoid space-folder from the planet Omikros - one half of a key that can fold space like paper and create a bridge. Sammy then finds the other half of the key and succumbs to physical possession by a creature called Ramadra from the Omikron Invasion Force. Ramadra brings both halves for the key together, hoping to enable the rest of the Force to join him, but the Doctor manages to close the bridge using his sonic screwdriver after only a few of the creatures have come through. By appealing to what remains of Sammy within Ramadra, Tom manages to buy the Doctor enough time to separate the two halves of the key again and destroy the circuitry. The Omnikron are pulled back to their own planet, 150 million light years away, and Sammy is restored to his true form.

THE POISON PLANET

Script: Trevor Baxendale
Art: John Ross; Colours: Alan Craddock; Letters: Paul Vyse
Publication: Issues 58-60; 3 April 2008, 10 April 2008, 17 April 2008.

PLOT

Answering a distress signal, the Doctor arrives on the treacherous planetoid Death's Door and discovers the corpse of a scientist called Dr Kaleb Loss and his sample canister. He takes them both back to the scientist's research base, InFECT, on the planet Mustron V. He finds the base apparently deserted, but suddenly comes face to face with a fearsome creature. Having escaped this, he meets one of the base's scientists, Rachel 'Red' Barlow, who has been in hiding - not from the creature, which is a Vox that acts as a guard dog, but from a faceless spacesuited figure who has been terrorising her and her colleagues. She explains that they have been working on finding a cure for a space plague that is spreading through the Outer Worlds. The Doctor finds the other three scientists, who have also been in hiding, and tells them of the death of Kaleb. When he goes to show them the body, however, it has disappeared. Could this be the work of the faceless spaceman? The Doctor and Red retrieve Kaleb's sample canister, which contains samples of the mineral strynthium that will enable the scientists to complete their work, but get ejected from an airlock by the faceless spaceman. The Doctor uses his sonic screwdriver to get them back inside, where the spaceman is unmasked as Jennifer Arden, one of the scientists, who had fitted her space helmet with a refraction visor. She thought that it was taking too long to develop the cure for the space plague, which had already claimed her brother as one of its victims, and wanted to speed up the work. As she puts the finishing touches to the cure, she accidentally releases a sample of the plague and becomes infected. However, the Doctor uses the cure on her, and she recovers. The scientists then prepare to transmit details of the cure around the galaxy.

SEA-RAH

Script: Trevor Baxendale
Art: John Ross; Colours: Alan Craddock; Letters: Paul Vyse
Sea-Rah created by Lewis Grainger
Publication: Issue 61; 24 April 2008.

PLOT

A young boy named Lewis is beachcombing when a huge, mace-wielding monster emerges from the sea. The Doctor arrives and rescues the boy, explaining that the monster is the Sea-Rah, a genetically engineered guardian from the Treasure Vaults of Rhosis. Its mace should contain the Time Stone of Isop, but it is missing; it fell through a hole in time and ended up here. The Sea-Rah is now searching for it, and will follow it anywhere in time and space. Lewis tells the Doctor that he found the Stone on the beach. The Doctor takes him on board the TARDIS and they journey to the deserted planet Kerun Za where, with the Stone returned to its mace, the Sea-Rah can live in peace and harmony.

NOTE

- The Sea-Rah was thought up by young Lewis Grainger as the winning entry in a competition run by *Doctor Who Adventures* to create a new monster for the comic strip.

THE GREAT MORDILLO

Script: Trevor Baxendale
Art: John Ross; Colours: Alan Craddock; Letters: Paul Vyse
Publication: Issue 62; 1 May 2008.

PLOT

Opera singer Anton Mordillo aspires to be one of the world's greatest tenors. The Doctor attends one of his performances at the Vienna State Opera, which is enthusiastically received by the audience. Afterwards, backstage in Mordillo's dressing-room, he uses his sonic screwdriver to reveal the singer's true form: a large, purple-skinned alien. The Doctor knows that Mordillo is a deserter from the Penal Mines of Dredge, who was being punished for his crimes as a member of the Thieves Guild of Kardol and a con-artist in seven different star systems. The creature explains that he had been sold into a life of criminal slavery. He escaped from the Mines only because he had been framed for a crime that he *didn't* commit. He fled to Earth, where over the past five years he has managed to make an honest career out of the happy accident that he could sing. The Doctor decides against alerting the Judoon to Mordillo's presence here, allowing him to reassume his human disguise and continue entertaining audiences with his rare talent.

NIGHTMARE ON THE BOULEVARD

Script: Brendan Sheppard
Art: John Ross; Colours: Alan Craddock; Letters: Paul Vyse
Publication: Issues 63-64; 8 May 2008, 15 May 2008.

PLOT

Donna asks the Doctor to take her to Hollywood. They arrive in the year 2012 but find the place virtually deserted. A waiter in a coffee shop tells them that this is due to the influence of a woman named Amelia Hubble, who arrived three years earlier. They visit Amelia at her home, and the Doctor realises that she is actually a Cion – a creature that sucks all thoughts and ideas out of her victims' brains, leaving them mindless. The Cion attacks the Doctor, but Donna intervenes and saves him. The Cion then vanishes. By searching her computer, the Doctor discovers that the she was planning a to steal the mind of famous director Alan Crawford. He confronts her at Crawford's home, and on learning that she is the last of her kind, persuades her to restore the minds of all those she has attacked, in return for which he promises to link her up to the internet, giving her all the creative energy she needs. A year later, the Doctor offers to take Donna to see the movie *Space Bugs*, directed by Alan Crawford and written by his new wife Amelia Crawford-Hubble. She declines, saying that she hates sci-fi.

WINDSWEPT

Script: Christopher Cooper
Art: John Ross; Colours: Alan Craddock; Letters: Paul Vyse
Publication: Issues 65; 22 May 2008.

PLOT

The TARDIS brings the Doctor and Donna to a strangely deserted dairy farm near a wind farm. They meet a terrified worker who tells them that the farm was attacked by creatures who sucked the electricity out of all the appliances. He describes the creatures as tall and metallic, with spinning blades at the top, and the Doctor realises that the 'wind farm' he saw earlier was actually nothing of the sort. As Donna discovers from a newspaper that they are in 1970, the farm again comes under attack from the creatures. The Doctor repels them using the sonic screwdriver. He realises that they are super-evolved weeds, and that their blades are petals. Their seed pods ride the cosmic winds, and now they threaten to overrun the Earth. The Doctor sprays them with milt from a full tanker, killing them.

THE CONTINUITY CAP

Script: Christopher Cooper
Art: John Ross; Colours: Alan Craddock; Letters: Paul Vyse
Publication: Issues 66-67; 29 May 2008, 5 June 2008.

PLOT

The TARDIS, in the form of a red phone box, deposits the Doctor on 21st Century Earth with his companion, an eight-foot-tall armoured lobster called Falanx. The Doctor realises that something has gone very wrong with local space/time. This realisation causes Falanx to transform into Donna - although she retains the creature's claws instead of her hands. She spots a poster advertising a business called ReThinx, offering people a chance to undo decisions they wish they'd never made. Investigating, the travellers meet Kevin, a member of the Friends of Authoritative Decisions (FAD), who are holding a demonstration against ReThinx. Kevin explains that the company has a device that allows people to alter their own past decisions, changing their entire lives, hence why Earth's history is now such a mess. The Doctor and Donna gain access to the ReThinx building, where they meet the founder and proprietor, Sir Stephen Cropper. Sir Stephen admits that the secret of his business is a small cap that he found in a bed and breakfast in Cardiff. The Doctor identifies this as the Continuity Cap, created by a race called the Hyffons in the Dark Times to undo a catastrophic war; it fell into the wrong hands, and their race vanished in a puff or its own continuity. The Doctor persuades Sir Stephen to put things to rights by revisiting his original discovery of the cap and undoing his decision to put it on. History is thus restored to its proper course.

WORMHOLE

Script: Trevor Baxendale
Art: John Ross; Colours: Alan Craddock; Letters: Paul Vyse
Publication: Issues 68-69; 12 June 2008, 19 June 2008.

PLOT

The Doctor and Donna are in the 99th Century visiting the Stellion Gate, the entrance to a naturally occurring space-time wormhole that connects one end of the galaxy to the other and is used as a short cut by spacecraft. They meet an Angrodox Ambassador named Volfus who explains that he is here to gain an assurance from the Gate's owners, the Fatkat Corporation, that they will not try to lay claim to the Angrodox territory through which the wormhole passes. Suddenly an emergency is declared - the Gate has malfunctioned and spaceships have gone missing. Volfux and the Fatkat representatives accuse each other of trickery, but the Doctor discovers that there is a massive spatial flux within the wormhole itself. The Doctor, Donna and Volfus go through the Gate in Volfus's ship. Inside the wormhole they find the trapped spaceships, which have been attacked by the Nematode Horde, quantum nematodes otherwise known as the Star Worms. These are the larval stage of an ancient race of energy beings that exist beyond space, and the wormhole is a kind of incubator for them. The Doctor persuades the Star Worms to use their own energy to send the trapped spaceships back through the Gate. The wormhole will now be useless as a hyperspace flyover, but the Angrodox and the Fatkats decide to work together to set up light-speed stations across Angrodox space.

NOTE

- The Fatkat Corporation previously featured in the story *Minus Seven Wonders* in Issues 32 and 33 of *Doctor Who Adventures*.

THE BLACK HOLE GANG

Script: Christopher Cooper
Art: John Ross; Colours: Alan Craddock; Letters: Paul Vyse
Publication: Issues 70-71; 26 June 2008, 3 July 2008.

PLOT

The Doctor and Donna are taking a steam train journey across the Wild West when the train is boarded by a pair of robotic treasure hunters, Butch and Sundance, seeking the Febree Orb, one of the most incredible energy cells ever invented. The Doctor finds the Orb concealed aboard the train, and also happens to have another of them, this one broken, in his pocket. A spaceship flies overhead, and Butch tells the Doctor that it belongs to the Black Hole Gang. The Gang seize the train using a teleport vortex and manage to get hold of the working Orb. They want to use it as the power source for an mining machine, The Rig, which will enable them to harvest the molten core of any planet, starting with Earth. The Doctor begs them not to use the Orb, but they disregard him. When they insert the Orb into The Rig, however, it immediately goes flat, then starts to recharge itself from the Gang's nuclear reactor, causing it to become unstable and run wild. The Gang make for their escape pods, while the Doctor, Donna, Butch and Sundance get away on the train.

CITIZEN'S ARREST

Script: Christopher Cooper
Art: John Ross; Colours: Alan Craddock; Letters: Paul Vyse
Publication: Issues 72-73; 10 July 2008, 17 July 2008.

PLOT

The TARDIS brings the Doctor and Donna to the planet Theta Magnon 7 in the year 3269 where, having mistaken the Doctor for a fleeing felon named Obadiah Jones, the police try to arrest them. They are rescued by a mysterious figure in a dark hat and trenchcoat who also believes the Doctor to be Obidiah and tells them he is making a 'CitiZen's arrest'. When his flying car lands again, they are surrounded by figures wearing superhero-style costumes. These are the Thargs, who have modelled themselves on comic book characters because comic books – and all other sorts of literature beginning with the letter 'C' – have been outlawed for centuries here, ever since the CitiZen supercomputer came on-line. The computer was built to uphold the letter of the law, but there was a programming error in the Literature Law section, and 'C' was left out. As this included computer manuals, no-one was able to fix it. But now Obidiah has found a copy of the missing appendix, and hopes to use this to win a legal case to have 'C' reinstated. The Doctor, Donna and the Thargs make their way through the sewers to CitiZen Headquarters. They meet up with Obidiah, and the Doctor and Donna take him before the CitiZen user interface. The Doctor causes the computer to shut down by pointing out that logically there must be a gap in the system between 'B' and 'D'. He is then able to sort out the problem.

THE LAVENDER HILL BLOB

Script: Christopher Cooper
Art: John Ross; Colours: Alan Craddock; Letters: Paul Vyse
Publication: Issues 74-76; 24 July 2008, 31 July 2008, 7 August 2008.

PLOT

The Doctor and Donna arrive in 1951 in the London area of Battersea, which is being terrorised by a mysterious creature dubbed the 'Lavender Hill Blob' by the locals. They meet a policeman, but he vanishes after the Blob suddenly appears. The Doctor and Donna follow the Blob, which the Doctor believes must be an alien shape-shifter, and meet a woman named Edna Wilberforce, who has apparently been struck down by the creature. Leaving Donna with the recovering Edna, the Doctor searches for the missing policeman. He quickly realises that the policeman actually transformed into the Blob, which is indeed a shape-shifter and has now taken on the form of Edna. The Doctor returns just in time to protect Donna, threatening to destroy the Blob by throwing a bucket of soapy water over it. The Blob explains that it was simply trying to escape. It has rebelled against the others of its kind as it can no longer support their practice of colonising a succession of planets and absorbing all their water. It takes the Doctor and Donna to the secret base of the invasion force, but finds it deserted. The invaders have assumed human form and are now advancing on Parliament, intending to replace all the country's leaders. Aided by the residual energy of her dead partner Amuul, the Blob now known as Edna attacks the Nucleus of her race, who has taken on the form of Prime Minister Clement Atlee. The Nucleus resists, bringing together all the others of its kind into a single Collective, and the Doctor destroys this with a bottle of detergent. He manages to save Edna and Amuul in a mug and takes them to another world, many light years away, to start a new life.

SHARK BAIT

Script: Christopher Cooper
Art: John Ross; Colours: Alan Craddock; Letters: Paul Vyse
Publication: Issues 77; 14 August 2008.

PLOT

Having arrived on a pirate ship, *The Intrepid Fox*, the Doctor and Donna are suspected of being responsible for the unexplained disappearances of some of the crew. They are forced to walk the plank, but have a narrow escape when leaping shark-cum-squid monsters - the true culprits - emerge from the sea and carry off the ship's captain and some of the others. The Doctor goes below the surface in a diving suit to investigate, and discovers a malfunctioning Jaeklo teleport unit, dumped by a passing spaceship. This is leaking a tachyon teleport field and causing any creature that comes within its radius to mutate - hence the monsters. Despite being affected by the teleport field himself and almost being turned into coral, the Doctor manages to fix the unit. All the mutations are then reversed, and the Doctor determines to take the unit away in the TARDIS and dispose of it more responsibly. Donna meanwhile has been helping the surviving pirates to fend off attacks from the monsters, and they offer her a job as their new captain. She turns it down, saying that she is first mate on the perfect ship already.

ATTACK OF THE MANGE MITES!

Script: Martin Day
Art: John Ross; Colours: Alan Craddock; Letters: Paul Vyse
Publication: Issues 78-79; 21 August 2008, 28 August 2008.

PLOT

The Doctor and Donna arrive on the International Space Station, 50 years in the future, where they are greeted by Truman Truss, the American head of the base. The hull is breached by a swarm of alien insects, like huge mange mites, and the Doctor is sucked out into space. Truss takes a rocket out and rescues him before he is killed by the vacuum. Back on board the Space Station, they see that the insects have sealed the hole they made in the hull and are now heading for the kitchens. There, they bypass the food and start to gorge on the contents of the waste bins. Truss is initially in favour of eradicating the creatures with insecticide, but is dissuaded from doing so when the Doctor points out that they could be useful in helping the human race to explore further into space: they can survive in the vacuum, mend holes in metal, consume rubbish ... and they even breathe out oxygen. The Doctor is even tempted to keep one himself as a pet, but Donna objects.

BY ORDER OF THE BONEMENDERS

Script: Martin Day
Art: John Ross; Colours: Alan Craddock; Letters: Paul Vyse
Publication: Issues 80-82; 4 September 2008, 11 September 2008, 18 September 2008.

PLOT

The Doctor takes Donna to the Feu, supposedly one of the most peaceful and relaxing planets in the cosmos. There they are granted an audience with Cosmae, leader of the Ancient Order of Bonemenders, a group dedicated to psychic healing. The Doctor is feeling unwell - he starts to forget words and can sense something strange inside his mind - and while he is resting, Donna goes for a walk, only to encounter a hideous floating head, which quickly flies away. It later seems that the monster may have been an illusion, as no-one else can see it. The Doctor is speaking increasingly erratically, as is Cosmae, whose brain appears to have been tampered with. Suddenly Donna sees that the Doctor now has coloured rings around one of his eyes and his mouth, similar to markings on the Bonemenders' faces. Donna takes the Doctor back to the TARDIS, where he is protected from most forms of mind control, and he recovers. He explains that the floating head is a parasite called a Kra Durr, or Brain Worm. It must have been brought to Feu years ago by a patient, and has been feeding on the Bonemenders' minds ever since. By using the TARDIS's circuits to link his mind to those of the Bonemenders, the Doctor is able to repel the Brain Worm. The Bonemenders are returned to normality, and the Doctor and Donna depart.

THE ALICE IN WONDERLAND CIRCUIT

Script: Martin Day
Art: John Ross; Colours: Alan Craddock; Letters: Paul Vyse
Publication: Issue 83; 25 September 2008.

PLOT

A power spike affects the TARDIS's controls and causes it to make an emergency landing. It also breaks the Dimensional Interface Override - otherwise known as the Alice in Wonderland Circuit - which helps to regulate the interplay between the real world and the dimension within the TARDIS; as a result, the Doctor and Donna both grow to giant size. Venturing outside while she is still able to squeeze through the door, Donna encounters a man whom the Doctor immediately identifies as Minos, the universe's only dealer in spare parts for time machines - which is why the TARDIS has brought them here. Although initially annoyed that the surprise of the Doctor's arrival has caused him to break a vow of silence he has kept for the last seven years, Minos agrees to supply a new Alice in Wonderland Circuit for the TARDIS, returning the time travellers to their proper size.

WASHED AWAY!

Script: Michael Stevens
Art: John Ross; Colours: Alan Craddock; Letters: Paul Vyse
Publication: Issues 84-85; 2 October 2008, 9 October 2008

PLOT

The TARDIS arrives beside a mountain river on a planet somewhere in the Myolthen System. Donna gets knocked into the water by a freak wave, but the Doctor jumps in and rescues her. The TARDIS has been swept away by the wave, and the two time travellers set off down the mountain, hoping to find it at the bottom. While a mysterious stranger looks on from a distance, they encounter a group of fierce-looking sheep-like creatures, but manage to scare them away. As night falls, they lose their way, and fall over the edge of a cliff above the raging river. They manage to hold on, and are hauled to safety on a rope thrown to them by the stranger. The stranger introduces himself as a fisherman named Jeb, a native of the planet Zentos 3, whose space pod has also been swept away by a freak wave. The Doctor deduces that the waves must be caused by a balancing pool on a pivot somewhere in the natural rock formation. He is worried that, with rain now falling, there may be more to come. In the morning, the Doctor, Donna and Jeb make their way down to the river via a treacherous set of steps carved into the cliff face. At the bottom, they all get caught by another of the waves, but are rescued from the river by a huge bear-like creature - one of this planet's indigenous inhabitants. The creature points them to a pool where both the TARDIS and Jeb's space pod have washed up, and they bid their farewells.

TITANOLEUM TOURISTS

Script: Michael Stevens
Art: John Ross; Colours: Alan Craddock; Letters: Paul Vyse
Publication: Issues 86-87; 16 October 2008, 23 October 2008

PLOT

The Doctor has taken Donna to the opening of a new tourist attraction: the Acropolis of Xentha, one of the ancient wonders of Galaxy 12, where the statue-like forms of 200 warriors cast in pure Titanoleum were recently unearthed after being buried for 5,000 years. While the Doctor meets a child called Jeri, who parents are missing, Donna is hypnotised by a sinister figure and led away. Jeri shows the Doctor a door leading into a locked private area. Having opened it with his sonic screwdriver and ventured inside, he is shocked to see a line of hypnotised visitors, including Jeri's parents, filing into a machine where they are being transformed into new Titanoleum warriors! The culprits are a group of Teglatrons who have set this up as a pilot scheme to create exhibits for their clients' museums. Donna, having been rescued by the Doctor, creates a diversion while he sabotages the Teglatrons' machine and releases the tourists from their hypnotic thrall. The Teglatrons are then rounded up and put permanently out of business, while Jeri's family are reunited.

BATTLES IN TIME

HEAD START / JEWEL OF THE VILE / LOCK, STOCKS AND BARREL / END GAME

Written by: Mike Tucker
Inks: Lee Sullivan; Colours: Alan Craddock
Publication: Issues 22-25; 4 July 2007, 18 July 2007, 1 August 2007, 15 August 2007.

PLOT

The Doctor and Martha are lured to the planet Brendock Seven by a distress call from an archaeologist, Professor Dinsdale. The Doctor helps Dinsdale to gain access to a sealed chamber below some giant stone heads. Inside they find the Vortex Cannon – a legendary weapon that could destroy the universe – although thankfully the Treed Crystals that power it have decayed. Dinsdale transforms into a monstrous Zaan warrior and seizes the weapon, gloating that his race are close to obtaining a new supply of the Crystals. He takes off in a nearby Zaan spaceship and, despite the stone heads – in reality a defence mechanism – coming alive and trying to stop it, manages to get away in an escape pod. The Doctor and Martha follow in the TARDIS to the planet Garvrath – the only place where Treed Crystals can be found. They attend a movie premiere where the star, Miss Honey Vox, is wearing a huge Treed Crystal as a pendant. Later, on her yacht, they warn her that someone might try to steal the Crystal. Even as they speak, a small turquoise creature called Jebelex the Pulthasian cuts through the hull of the vessel with a matter transmuter and takes the Crystal from Honey's safe. Martha tries to retrieve it, but Jebelex manages to get away by giving her the matter transmuter instead. Evading two pursuing Zaan, Jebelex blasts off in a spaceship. The Doctor determines to follow by tracking his DNA. This brings them to the planet Karaten, where the Doctor is taken prisoner by the native inhabitants and offered as a sacrifice to a creature composed of blue liquid that has already devoured Jebelex and the crystal. Martha uses the matter transmuter to solidify the creature, rescuing the Doctor and enabling him to retrieve the Crystal. The Zaan arrive and take Martha away with them as a hostage, telling the Doctor to bring the Crystal to their home world or face the consequences. He materialises the TARDIS in a huge arena where Martha is being held prisoner. He gives the Crystal to the Zaan and releases his companion. Ignoring the Doctor's warnings, the Zaan activate the Vortex Cannon – but the weapon proves to be a trap and seals their planet in a time loop forever. The Doctor and Martha escape in the TARDIS.

THE MILLENNIUM BLAG / SECOND WAVE / OPERATION LOCK-UP / CRIME AFTER CRIME

Written by: Steve Cole
Inks: Lee Sullivan; Colours: Alan Craddock
Publication: Issues 26-29; 29 August 2007, 12 September 2007, 26 September 2007, 10 October 2007.

PLOT

On Earth in the year 2000, the Doctor and Martha are witness to two robberies carried out by different groups of aliens. They trick the rival groups into crashing their getaway vans into each other. Deciding that the 'contest' cannot continue, the aliens activate a Trilexic teleport beam and disappear. The Doctor resolves to follow them. The TARDIS arrives on a schooner in the Caribbean Sea in July 1800. The Doctor and Martha are taken prisoner by the crew, but the vessel then comes under attack from two others, of anachronistic design, each piloted by one of the competing groups of aliens, firing proton cannons. The Doctor propels a mixture of food from the schooner's gun and clogs the intake valve of the cannon on one of the attacking ships, causing it to explode. He then puts the schooner on collision course with the other ship and uses the sonic screwdriver to cause that one to blow up too. The aliens again teleport away, and the Doctor and Martha give chase in the TARDIS. Their next destination is Japan in the year 3000, where the two groups of aliens attack a bank, one using a remote-controlled robot and the other a mind-controlled zombie. However, it is the Doctor and Martha themselves who are the aliens' target, not the bank. They take refuge in the vault. The aliens try to gas them, but the Doctor uses a beam from his sonic screwdriver, focused and magnified by the gems in the vault, to cut through the floor, enabling them to escape. The aliens once more teleport away, but this time the Doctor and Martha travel with them in their teleport field. They find themselves on a neutral-space capsule bridging three different types of alien warship. Big Yedari, one of the most wanted crime lords in future history, is on board. He has organised the contest between the two races of aliens, the Verx and the Alsh, to help him decide which of them he should employ to rob the Earth in all its eras. The Doctor claims that the Alsh leader tried to cheat by hiring him and Martha to sabotage the contest. This causes the Verx and the Alsh to come to blows, and the Doctor and Martha use this distraction to get away, taking a teleporter from one of the creatures in the process. The Doctor cuts loose the creatures' three warships, seals off the capsule and uses the stolen teleport to take him and Martha to the Yedari ship. He then renders the other teleports useless, trapping the aliens on the capsule, and signals their location to the nearest space cops. He and Martha then prepare to teleport to Earth to collect the TARDIS.

HOUSE PESTS

Written by: Jason Loborik
Inks: Lee Sullivan; Colours: Alan Craddock
Publication: Issue 30; 24 October 2007.

PLOT

The Doctor and Martha arrive on the planet Lumana where the cute and friendly Luma and his fellow natives, the Loomish, help them by scaring away some vicious bat-like creatures with a blast on a horn. Luma asks that in return they get rid of a monster called the Slaken that lives in a cave and preys on his people. The Doctor and Martha agree, somewhat reluctantly, and visit the Slaken in its cave. The

Slaken tells them that they have been tricked and asserts that the bat-like creatures are the Loomish's friends. Returning to the TARDIS, the two travellers find it overrun by the Loomish, who have wrapped it in garlands of flowers. The Doctor takes the Loomish's horn outside, and when Martha blows on it, Luma and his friends come running. The Slaken, who actually looks after the Loomish, gives them all pots of food as the Doctor and Martha take their leave.

MINOR TROUBLE / INHUMAN SACRIFICE / CRIMES AND PUNISHMENT

Written by: Claire Lister
Inks: Lee Sullivan; Colours: Alan Craddock
Publication: Issues 31-33; 7 November 2007, 21 November 2007, 5 December 2007.

PLOT

The Doctor and Martha visit the Ancient Worlds theme park on the planet Dewy, where everyone is obsessed with Earth history. The Doctor has heard rumours of things going wrong here, and these are borne out as they are attacked by a group of aliens masquerading as mythical creatures such as the Cyclops. They escape into a replica of the Labyrinth of Minos, meeting some tourists who have been hiding there since the theme park guards became aggressive. They are attacked by a Minotaur-like creature identified by the Doctor as a Tauride – normally a peaceful species. There is a dart embedded in the creature's hide, and the Doctor realises that it must contain a stimulant. He removes it, and the Tauride is rendered passive. The creature helps them to escape from the Labyrinth, but on entering the Aztec zone they are denounced as criminals by the green-skinned, eye-patched Chiffala mercenary in charge of the park. They disguise themselves in costumes bought from a gift shop, the Doctor as an Aztec priest and Martha in a leopard-skin outfit. The Doctor confronts the Chiffala so that Martha can free a party of schoolchildren who have been imprisoned in a cage, then they flee to the Ancient Egypt zone, where tourists are being attacked by robots in the form of mummies and Egyptian gods. The Chiffala thrive on conflict, and this one decided to make his own when he crash-landed here, transforming the once-peaceful planet into a place where all the most horrific parts of Earth history are re-enacted. Having disguised themselves again, this time as robot mummies, the Doctor and Martha are able to overpower the Chiffala, whose race are surprisingly vulnerable to concussion. They take him in the TARDIS to a real-life historical torture chamber, promising to return for him ... in three to six months' time.

THE DIAMONDS OF SARTOR/QUARSIAN MISSION/ANDROID OF DEATH

Written by: Jason Loborik
Inks: Lee Sullivan; Colours: Alan Craddock
Publication: Issues 34-36; 19 December 2007, 9 January 2008, 23 January 2008.

PLOT

The Doctor, travelling alone, arrives on the planet Sartor, where he finds human colonists being attacked by androids controlled by Quarsian pirates from their spaceship. The pirates are intent on stealing the planet's diamonds. The Doctor works with a human scientist named Nadia to try to repair their force-field. The androids eventually manage to break through and gain access to the humans' control centre, but the Doctor uses his sonic screwdriver and Nadia her sonic disruptor to blow them apart. The Doctor borrows the sonic disruptor and one of the diamonds and takes Nadia to the Quarsian spaceship in the TARDIS. The diamond responds to a concentration of Zortron energy from the ship's engine rooms, and the Doctor and Nadia make their way there, dodging the slow-moving Quarsians. The Doctor explains that Zortron energy is perfect for powering massive cargo ships at light speed but requires thousands of heavy storage vessels to contain it. By contrast, just a small number of the Sartor diamonds could harness enough energy for an entire fleet. The Doctor ascends the side of one of the storage vessels and plugs the diamond into its energy inlet to form a dam. The engines will blow at any moment, but the Doctor and Nadia are prevented from escaping when the Quarsians' captain arrives and takes them prisoner. Worse still, the Quarsians have made an android double of the Doctor with which to infiltrate the humans' base. The Doctor overpowers the android, and he and Nadia escape back to the planet in the TARDIS as the spaceship's engines explode. The android Doctor has teleported ahead of them and tries to convince the humans that he is the genuine article. The truth is established, however, when the Doctor reveals that, unlike him, the android has nothing in its pockets bar the sonic disruptor that it took when they struggled earlier. He goads the android into blasting one of the diamonds, which then explodes, destroying the android in the process. The Doctor bids farewell to Nadia and leaves in the TARDIS.

BLOOMS OF DOOM!

Written by: Keiran Grant
Inks: Lee Sullivan; Colours: Alan Craddock
Publication: Issues 37; 6 February 2008.

PLOT

The TARDIS alerts the Doctor to massive distortion in the time fields but brings him to the seemingly innocuous venue of a garden centre in Croydon. He and the shop assistant, Horace, are attacked by a giant plant in humanoid form but destroy it with a blast of weed killer. The Doctor identifies it as a super-evolved tulip. More of the plants rise up, and the Doctor explains that someone has been interfering with time, evolving them millions of years in a few seconds. The plants vanish as more time spillage causes them to evolve another billion years into air particles. Elsewhere in the garden centre the Doctor discovers a crashed Fraxis Pod – an unreliable type of time machine from the 51st Century that was ultimately banned. Inside it he finds its dead pilot. The pod is the source of the problem, but the Doctor loops the energy back into its Zygma-drive and causes it to age into dust. This 'mop up' has also reversed the time spillage, restoring the garden centre to normality.

NOTES

The references to the unreliable time machine originating in the 51st Century and having a Zygma-drive tie in to the TV story 'The Talons of Weng-Chiang' (1977).

DUSTY DEATH / COLD ASSASSIN / DESIGNS OF THE DUST / A SUITABLE SHOWDOWN

Written by: Steve Cole
Inks: Lee Sullivan; Colours: Alan Craddock
Publication: Issues 38-41; 20 February 2008, 5 March 2008, 19 March 2008, 2 April 2008.

PLOT

The TARDIS brings the Doctor to an empty, and very dusty, building on a barren alien world, where he is assailed by automated defence systems. He deduces that this is a computer-controlled prison. He manages to shut down the defence systems and then leaves in the TARDIS, not realising that the prison's computer is registering an escape … A crystalline-bodied frog-like creature named Koto the Bounty Hunter appears inside the TARDIS and accuses the Doctor of freeing a war criminal. Ignoring the Doctor's protestation that the prison was empty, Koto starts to absorb all light, heat and air from inside the TARDIS. The Doctor dons a spacesuit and, by blasting Koto with a fire extinguisher and bombarding it with ice and snow, sends it back to wherever it came from. He next arrives at the Asteroid Bazaar, where his suit, still covered with dust from the prison, seems to take on a life of its own. The dust is actually the disassembled form of Skalesh, dictator of Delossa, who was deposed and imprisoned by his own people. Each movement the Doctor makes in his suit feeds Skalesh with kinetic energy and makes him grow stronger. The animated suit takes the Doctor into a notorious den of arms dealers where Skalesh demands the deadliest weapons. The Doctor however contrives to have a fire truck spray him with water, temporarily disabling Skalesh and allowing him to remove the suit. The animated suit then takes off on its own, Skalesh vowing revenge on the people of Delossa. He steals a warship, complete with a force of robo-assassins, but the Doctor follows in the TARDIS. On arriving on Delossa, Skalesh finds that it has been taken over by the Madrojar - his own people left 400 years ago, having accelerated their evolution and become gas-creatures. The Madrojar sentence Skalesh to eternal imprisonment, and the Doctor is able to retrieve his suit.

THE CREATIVE SPARK

Written by: Simon Furman
Inks: Lee Sullivan; Colours: Alan Craddock
Publication: Issue 42; 16 April 2008.

PLOT

The TARDIS brings the Doctor to the edge of Lake Geneva in Switzerland in 1816.

He finds an alien machine generating an artificial storm, and beside it a large, humanoid alien who is obviously in great pain. A woman from a nearby house is drawn by the commotion and faints at the sight of the 'monster'. The Doctor adjusts the machine, ending both the storm and the alien's pain. The alien introduces himself as ZZazik and explains that in his haste to feed after completing a cross-dimensional journey he put his elemental intensifier on too high a setting and overdosed. The Doctor assures him that no harm has been done. Later, the woman, Mary Wollstonecraft Shelley, is back in her house and begins writing a new story inspired by what she has seen, *Frankenstein, or The Modern Prometheus*.

ANY OLD IRON / MERCHANT OF MENACE

Written by: Keiran Grant
Inks: Lee Sullivan; Colours: Alan Craddock
Publication: Issues 43-44; 30 April 2008, 14 May 2008.

PLOT

The TARDIS's auto-repair circuits cause it to materialise on a barren planet where a replacement can be found for its malfunctioning chrono-loop spectrometer. The Doctor and Donna are teleported aboard a huge robot-like vessel where the owner introduces himself as Silas Wrench, collector of rare metal marvels. When Donna suggests that he is a just a junk dealer, Wrench tries to blast her and the Doctor with a gun. They flee into another part of the vessel, where the Doctor finds a horobot - a type of robotic time traveller - that begs him to save it from Wrench. Wrench catches up with them, however, and worse still, he has captured the TARDIS. The Doctor gives Wrench a TARDIS key, but when he tries to insert it in the lock, the meson recognition defence system renders him unconscious. On recovering, Wrench determines to sell his captives to the Slave Masters of Zooveron. The vessel takes off, but the horobot grapples with Wrench and causes it to crash. The Doctor and Donna just manage to escape in the TARDIS. The horobot is destroyed, but the Doctor finds within it the chrono-loop spectrometer he needs. Wrench also escapes from the wreck to fight another day.

THE BLACK SEA / STING OF THE SERPENT / ATTACK OF THE RATS / THE ZANTRAAN INVASION

Written by: Jason Loborik
Inks: Lee Sullivan; Colours: Alan Craddock
Publication: Issues 45-48; 28 May 2008, 11 June 2008, 25 June 2008, 9 July 2008.

PLOT

The Doctor and Donna track an alien space pod to a North Sea oil rig, where it has crash-landed and ruptured one of the crude oil tanks beneath the surface. A giant oily creature rears up from the water, seizing some of the rig workers. Analysing a sample with the sonic screwdriver, the Doctor finds that alien molecules are fusing with the crude oil from the ruptured tank and mutating: the pod's pilot is seeking a new host body. The Doctor and Donna hose the oil with a detergent mixture, causing it to disperse and thus releasing the rig workers. Suddenly news arrives that another alien pod has crash-landed, in Arizona. The Doctor and Donna hurry to the scene in the TARDIS to find themselves menaced by a gigantic rattlesnake, the host for another of the alien creatures, whose original form lies dead inside the pod. The Doctor sets the pod to auto destruct, then he and Donna run to a safe distance as it explodes and destroys the snake. Back in the TARDIS, the Doctor detects and alien mothership about to enter Earth's atmosphere. However, another of the alien pods has crash-landed, this time in Paris, and he materialises the TARDIS there in time to see two giant rats emerge from the ground. Aided by UNIT troops, the Doctor and Donna gain access to the pod. The Doctor contacts the mothership and speaks with the Queen of the Zantraani, telling her that all her scout ships crashed; the scouts tried to find new forms to inhabit, but became terrible mutations. The pod is drawn up to the mothership by a tractor beam. On learning that Earth is not the pure world she thought it was, the Queen determines to cleanse it with her ship's weapons, making it suitable as a new home for her race. The Doctor realises that the creatures are not only wary of germs, they also have a hyper-sensitive sense of smell. He gains control of their ship and lands it in a farmyard, allowing pigs and chickens to come on board. Repulsed by the small, the aliens make a hasty exit, returning to their home planet Zantrah.

PAWNS OF THE ZENITH / SWARM OF THE ZENITH / PREY OF THE ZENITH / LAIR OF THE ZENITH

Written by: Neil Corry
Inks: Lee Sullivan; Colours: Alan Craddock
Publication: Issues 49-52; 23 July 2008, 6 August 2008, 20 August 2008, 3 September 2008.

PLOT

Outside New New Scotland Yard in 22nd Century London, a shoot-out is in progress between the police and four fugitives. One of the fugitives, shouting that the human race should 'prepare for the Zenith', is knocked unconscious when she bumps into the TARDIS as it materialises. The other three lift off in an air-car, but suddenly it explodes. Passing themselves off as police officers, the Doctor and Donna see the surviving fugitive being interrogated inside the station. She identifies herself as a member of the personnel staff there, and claims to have no memory of what happened before. Suddenly she and two policemen become possessed by the Zenith and threaten the Doctor and Donna with guns. The Doctor fends them off with the sonic screwdriver, but out in the street, a crowd of Zenith-possessed people block the way to the TARDIS. The Doctor 'borrows' an air-car. Once he and Donna are in flight, however, the Zenith take over the car's systems and cut its power, causing it to plummet toward the ground. Donna manages to activate the emergency override, and the car lands safely. The Doctor has deduced that the Zenith are using the Earth's network of communications satellites to control people via phone patches affixed to their hands. Things go from bad to worse as the Zenith signal starts to rewrite the controlled subjects' DNA, turning them into monstrous Zenith themselves. Donna and the Doctor are caught, given phone patches and transformed into Zenith, but the Doctor's mind is strong enough to reverse the process. He takes Donna in an air-car to the Telecom Tower, where he sets up a computer firewall that stops the Zenith's signal from getting through, thwarting their scheme to take over the Earth and become lords of time.

DOCTOR WHO

ISSUE 1

Written by: Gary Russell
Art by: Nick Roche; Art assist by: Joe Phillips; Inking assist by: German Torres; Colours: Charlie Kirchoff; Letters: Chris Mowry; Editor: Chris Ryall
Publication: February 2008.

PLOT

The Doctor takes Martha to a space station diner in search of the best chocolate milkshake she has ever tasted, but his suspicions are aroused when he sees a Gizou shape-changer poorly disguised as a reptile. They follow the creature, only to find that it has been reduced to a pile of dust. A Sycorax appears and takes them both prisoner. It has been collecting the last known survivors of various species, holding them in stasis on its asteroid ship and then using Gizou to imitate them, in order to con numerous collectors into buying what they believe are the last examples of otherwise extinct life-forms. The Gizou have a habit of escaping, though, and must then be dealt with. The Doctor outwits the Sycorax, plugging his sonic screwdriver into the asteroid ship's controls and entering a pre-set course for a research planet where the captive aliens will be helped to readjust. The Sycorax leaps back on board the ship just before it departs, hoping to use the Time Lord technology of the sonic screwdriver to its own advantage, but the device self destructs. The Sycorax is left to the mercy of its alien captives as their stasis tubes open and they are freed ...

NOTE

The Sycorax were first seen in the TV story 'The Christmas Invasion'.

ISSUE 2[112]

Written by: Gary Russell
Art by: Jose Maria Beroy; Art assist by: Joe Phillips; Inking assist by: German Torres; Colours: Charlie Kirchoff; Letters: Neil Uyetake; Cover: Nick Roche; Editor: Chris Ryall

---

[112] The strips from Issues 2 to 6 inclusive of the IDW comic book series form a single story. When they were later compiled into a graphic novel, along with those from Issue 1, this was given the overall title *Agent Provocateur*; however, this title was not used on the individual issues.

Publication: March 2008

PLOT

The populations of a number of planets around the universe are suddenly disappearing, leaving just one individual behind in each case. The Doctor and Martha, meanwhile, are in London in 1974. The city comes under attack from a giant cat apparently made of sand, which suddenly disappears. The Doctor and Martha then visit an exhibition of lifelike statues, also made of sand. They are watched by a black cat and meet a strange man and woman who transform Martha into one of the statues. The man explains that nearly 4000 years earlier in Ancient Egypt, the Princess Hentopet was angered by her father and, through a subterfuge involving the cat-god Bast, killed him. Bast was actually Bubastion of the Pantheon, a creature dispatched by the Shadow Proclamation to oversee Earth's forward development, and he, Hentopet and her slave Sheeq were cursed to be linked forever. Hence their presence here in 1974. Suddenly Hentopet and Sheeq are also transformed into statues. The Doctor talks to the cat, Bubastion, and promises to take him home if he will restore all the people he has trapped as statues. He agrees, but while the others are indeed restored, the two Ancient Egyptians are not, and Bubaston disappears. Sheeq is able to give the Doctor a final warning to trust no-one, then he and Hentopet crumble to dust. Busbastion watches as the TARDIS dematerialises, taking the Doctor and Martha to the point of origin of the force-field that held the statues together. Meanwhile, the Pantheon gather, Bubastion having reported that he has found the agent they need ...

ISSUE 3

Written by: Gary Russell
Art by: Stefano Martino; Colours: Charlie Kirchoff; Letters: Chris Mowry; Cover: Nick Roche; Editor: Chris Ryall
Publication: April 2008

PLOT

On New Savannah, there are just a few hours to go until the start of the year five billion, when the planet will be ceded to the Earth Empire. While the Doctor goes to investigate the scene of a bomb blast, Martha is arrested by Catkind police, ostensibly for her own safety. At the police station, she learns that those Catkind who opposed the hand-over to Earth returned to the planet's savannah, contained behind a force-field, where it is believed they died within a few months. The Doctor manages to track Martha down. He has discovered that the bomb blast was designed to allow a group of conspirators to obtain the mechanism to lower the force-field. As midnight arrives, the force-field comes down and giant armoured cats attack the city from the savannah. This wasn't what the conspirators planned. The Doctor and Martha go to confront their leader, a Cat-Nun, but she is killed and they then find themselves in a limbo presided over by Bubastion. The Pantheon want to take over the business world of this planet and remove the population, believing that this will enable them to control the galaxy. Busbastian will not reveal why, but says that they have been testing the Doctor, and that so far he has passed with flying colours. The Doctor and Martha escape back to the planet as the limbo closes off. The giant cats - not the spirits of the dead returned, but holographically-disguised hydraulic weapons controlled by Bubastian - have been destroyed, but the place is devastated.

NOTE

- This issue features the Catkind, as seen in the TV stories 'The End of the World', 'New Earth' and 'Gridlock'.

ISSUE 4

Written by: Gary Russell
Art by: Mirco Pierfederici; Colours by: Tom Smith; Letters by: Neil Uyetake; Cover: Nick Roche; Editors: Chris Ryall and Denton J Tipton
Publication: May 2008

PLOT

The TARDIS brings the Doctor and Martha to the planet Omphalos, seemingly populated entirely by hostile robots. They eventually meet a green-skinned humanoid, Professor Tharlot, who asks if they too are survivors of the galactic holocaust that has seen worlds ravaged, populations decimated and energy lost. They admit that they are ignorant of this. Tharlot introduces the sole survivors of ten other worlds, with whom he is in contact via a video screen. The Doctor, however, realises that Tharlot is not as trustworthy as he seems and has been spying on him and Martha on their recent journeys. As Tharlot makes a swift exit, Martha reveals to the Doctor that the robots are not hostile after all but simply need someone to direct them. The robots also confirm that Tharlot is not a professor but a criminal who was imprisoned until the rest of the planet's population disappeared. Tharlot manages to destroy the robots. He confronts the Doctor and Martha, throwing them an electronic device that he says they will need to lead them to 'the leash'. If they fail to find this, they will never see the TARDIS again. Suddenly the floor opens up beneath them and the Doctor and Martha fall into a spatial vortex. Tharlot falsely reports to a mysterious Mr Wain that he has the Doctor and the TARDIS secure on Omphalos. Mr Wain in turn reports this to the Pantheon. Meanwhile, the ten devastated planets are positioned in a straight line, and their combined gravitational pull affects the fabric of space, allowing something to start to break through from outside the universe ...

ISSUE 5

Written by: Gary Russell
Art by: Mirco Pierfederici; Colours by: Tom Smith; Letters by: Amauri Osorio; Cover: Nick Roche; Editors: Chris Ryall and Scott Dunbier
Publication: July 2008

PLOT

The Doctor and Martha find themselves on the Cumbrian coast of England in 1957. When Martha receives a glancing gunshot wound to the forehead, the Doctor takes her for treatment to a building nearby, which appears to be a Ministry of Defence base. This is in fact a front for the Pantheon, who finally tell the Doctor and Martha what is going on. Aware that an evil primeval being is breaking through from outside the universe, they hired Mr Wain to find someone with exceptional abilities to combat this. He selected the Doctor and Martha, and proceeded to put them through a series of tests. In addition, Mr Wain secured the help of the scientist Tharlot from Omphalos to design a huge sonic cannon to be used in the fight, and this weapon has been constructed here at the base in 1957. Tharlot, however, has double-crossed the Pantheon, and has his own uses for the weapon, which he now threatens to turn on either the Doctor or Martha.

ISSUE 6

Written by: Gary Russell
Art by: Stefano Martino; Colours by: Tom Smith; Letters by: Neil Uyetake; Cover: Nick Roche; Edits: Scott Dunbier
Publication: August 2008

PLOT

The Doctor deflects the beam from the sonic cannon using his sonic screwdriver. Tharlot teleports away, taking the weapon with him. The Doctor gets the Pantheon to return him and Martha to Omphalos to retrieve the TARDIS. The abducted populations of the ten planets then join them in a huge battle against Tharlot and his robot army. Tharlot is killing indiscriminately with the sonic cannon, but the weapon is turned against him by the Doctor using the sonic screwdriver, and he is destroyed. The Doctor then uses the two sonic devices together to repel the creature from outside the universe and seal the tear in space and time. The abducted populations, whose collective psychic trauma has been providing the power for the sonic cannon, are then returned to their respective home worlds, and the Doctor tells the Pantheon that he hopes never to see or hear of them again. Mr Wain has meanwhile returned to his home, although it seems that he still has plans for the Doctor and Martha ...

APPENDIX E
OTHER ORIGINAL FICTION

In addition to the novels and comic strip stories covered in the preceding Appendices, there were a number of other places where original, officially-sanctioned new series *Doctor Who* fiction could be found during the period covered by this book.[113] Details are given below.

DOCTOR WHO AUDIOBOOKS

Having previously brought out audiobook versions of titles from BBC Books' *Doctor Who* range, BBC Audio went one better on 8 May 2008 with the release of a double-CD set presenting a story exclusive to the audio medium. This having proved successful, a follow-up was issued on 9 October 2008.

PEST CONTROL

Written by: Peter Anghelides
Read by: David Tennant
Produced by: Kate Thomas; Project editor: Gary Russell; Executive producer: Michael Stevens; Music and sound effects composed and performed by Simon Hunt; Doctor Who theme music by Murray Gold

PUBLICITY BLURB

The TARDIS is lost in battle on a distant planet. When the Doctor sets off in pursuit, Donna is left behind, and finds herself accepting a commission in the Pioneer Corps. Something is transforming soldiers into monstrous beetles, and she could be the next victim. Meanwhile, the Doctor steals a motorbike and stages a jailbreak. Well, how hard can it be to find the TARDIS, rescue Donna, and negotiate a peace? But that's before the arrival of a brutal and remorseless mechanical exterminator, bent on wiping out the insects. It may be that nothing can stop it, because this robot's solution for the infestation is very simple: kill everything. Featuring the Doctor and Donna, as played by David Tennant and Catherine Tate in the hit series from BBC Television, this story has been written specially for audio, and is read by David Tennant.

---

[113] There was also one unlicensed fiction-orientated publication that received widespread distribution in the UK and contained some new series-related material. This was *I am the Doctor: The Unauthorised Diaries of a Time Lord*, published by Zone Publishing, written by John Peel and illustrated by Pete Wallbank, which purported to present diary entries written by each of the ten TV Doctors plus the Peter Cushing-played movie incarnation.

THE FOREVER TRAP

Written by: Dan Abnett
Read by: Catherine Tate
Produced by: Kate Thomas; Project editor: Steve Tribe; Executive producer: Michael Stevens; Music and sound effects composed and performed by Simon Hunt; Doctor Who theme music by Murray Gold

PUBLICITY BLURB

When the TARDIS is invaded by a holographic marketing scam, the Doctor and Donna find themselves trapped on the Edifice, a purpose-built complex of luxury apartments in space. Their new environs leave much to be desired: millions of beings from across the universe have been gathered to live side by side in similar apartments. Instead of creating neighbourly affection, it's led to terrible battles being waged in the corridors and on the stairwells. The Doctor and Donna must cross the paths of deadly alien mobs as they search for the Edifice's ultimate authority. Who - or what - lies at the heart of the incredible complex? What destructive scourge is eating away at the Edifice itself? And are the Doctor and Donna trapped forever in this living hell? *The Forever Trap* features the Doctor and Donna, as played by David Tennant and Catherine Tate in the hit BBC television series *Doctor Who*. Written specially for audio by Dan Abnett, it is read by Catherine Tate.

DOCTOR WHO FILES BOOKS

The *Doctor Who Files* are a range of children's books, each of which covers one character or other aspect of *Doctor Who*, presenting various factual items, 'Test Your Knowledge' quizzes and the like, and also one short piece of original fiction.

NEEDLE POINT

Written by: Justin Richards
Publication: *Doctor Who Files: Martha*; BBC Children's Books; 30 August 2007.

PLOT

A group of aliens resembling giant grasshoppers arrive on Earth and disguise themselves by changing their appearance into that of a little old lady - the same little old lady in each case. They then set about gathering enough etheric energy to report back to their fleet commander in space, using sets of knitting-needle-like etheric antennae. The Doctor and Martha arrive and, while the Doctor tries to detect the source of the etheric energy, Martha waits at a café. Her suspicions aroused by all the identical little old ladies she sees passing by, Martha follows one of them and finds the group of aliens in a room at the back of an antiques shop. She seizes a gun from one of them as it prepares to fire on her. In the ensuing struggle, one of the aliens drops its etheric antennae, which then come into contact with each other, causing the energy to dissipate and the aliens themselves to disappear.

BEST FRIENDS

Written by: Justin Richards
Publication: *Doctor Who Files: Captain Jack*; BBC Children's Books; 30 August 2007.

PLOT

In 1895, the mind of a young boy named Anthony Bradshaw is infiltrated by an alien energy creature called a Lawphoram, which starts to feed on his thoughts, progressively weakening him. An unscrupulous man named Edward Hardiman uses Anthony as the centrepiece of a music hall act, offering a prize of a hundred guineas to anyone who succeeds in asking the boy a question he cannot answer - a challenge no-one meets, as the Lawphoram can read the audience members' minds, and also knows of future events, and so is able to tell Anthony what to say. Jack attends a performance and wins the prize by asking when he will die - a question with no answer. Hardiman attempts to smuggle Anthony away, as he does not really have a hundred guineas, but Jack catches him and frees the boy. He then uses his vortex manipulator to extract the Lawphoram from Anthony's mind.

BIRTH OF A LEGEND

Written by: Justin Richards
Publication: *Doctor Who Files: The Cult of Skaro*; BBC Children's Books; 30 August 2007.

PLOT

A Dalek Commander succeeds in destroying a group of Mechonoids on the planet Magella and is then summoned to Skaro by the Emperor where it and three other Daleks, similarly noted for their exceptional battle skills, are told that they are to become the Cult of Skaro - the ultimate Dalek weapon in a forthcoming war. The Dalek Commander is to be given the name Sec, while the others are to be known as Jast, Thay and Caan. Dalek Sec is given a new casing made of black Metalert - superior to the usual Dalekanium because it is infused with flidor gold and sap from the extinct Arkellis flower.

NOTES

- The Mechonoids first appeared in the TV story 'The Chase' in 1965.
- Metalert and its infusion with flidor gold and sap from the Arkellis flower were first mentioned in the comic strip saga 'The Daleks' in *TV Century 21* in 1965.

THE SECRET OF THE STONES

Written by: Justin Richards
Publication: *Doctor Who Files: The TARDIS*; BBC Children's Books; 30 August 2007.

PLOT

Martha suggests using the TARDIS to solve a historical mystery, and the Doctor agrees. They eventually settle on the mystery of why Stonehenge was erected. To avoid the possibility of interfering with events, the Doctor decides that they should simply observe from inside the TARDIS, briefly materialising at the site on the same day each year during the era of the stone circle's construction and using the scanner to take a 'snapshot' of the work in progress. This they do, but fail to realise that someone has spotted the TARDIS on one of its first visits and that it is the annual appearances of the ship itself that have inspired the creation of the monument.

NOTES

- This story contains brief references to a number of earlier trips the Doctor has made into Earth's history, including an incident on board the *Mary Celeste* as seen in 'The Chase' (1965). It also alludes obliquely to the Monk - another Time Lord - having aided in the construction of Stonehenge with an anti-gravity lift, as described in 'The Time Meddler' (1965).

BLIND TERROR

Written by: Justin Richards
Publication: *Doctor Who Files: The Sontarans*; BBC Children's Books; 3 July 2008.

PLOT

Sontarans Commander Churl and Lieutenant Stavv follow a battle-damaged Rutan ship down to its crash-landing site at a farm on Earth. One of the Rutans is still alive, and Churl hunts for it while Stavv is tasked with copying coded information from its ship's computers. Churl encounters a young blind girl, whose mother died when the ship crashed and whose father was killed by the Rutan survivor. Stavv appears with a wounded leg, having apparently been attacked by the Rutan. Churl, however, realises that this is actually the Rutan in disguise - the Rutans have been developing a shape-shifting capability but have yet to perfect it, hence the flaw in the leg. Churl restores the young girl's sight, and she kills the disguised Rutan with a shotgun, avenging her parents' deaths. Churl leaves, asking the girl to ensure that Stavv gets an honourable burial if his body is found.

DISAPPEARING ACT

Written by: Justin Richards
Publication: *Doctor Who Files: The Ood*; BBC Children's Books; 3 July 2008.

PLOT

Fergus Antelect is a magician who performs his act at posh hotels, assisted by his servant Ood Delta. His 'tricks' are all achieved by getting Ood Delta to convince the audience via telepathic projection that they are seeing something other than what is actually happening on stage. Antelect is also using his act as a cover to steal items of jewellery from rich audience members, who are convinced by Ood Delta that they have actually left the items back in their rooms. The Doctor and Donna attend one of the performances and, by usurping Antelect's telepathic control over Ood Delta, the Doctor is able to uncover his villainy. The magician is arrested by Special Agent Ratner of the Galactic Enforcement Agency.

DOCTOR WHO - DECIDE YOUR DESTINY BOOKS

In 2007, BBC Children's Books began publishing a new range of *Doctor Who* fiction aimed at younger readers than the BBC Books novels series. The *Decide Your Destiny* tagline reflected the fact that these followed the 'find your fate' principle whereby the reader was given a series of options in the text that allowed them to decide which of a number of different plotlines they followed. This was explained on the back of each book as follows: 'Join the Doctor and Martha on their travels through time and space and influence the story with your decisions. Choose a direction and let the adventures begin ...' The words 'and Martha' were dropped, and 'their' changed to 'his', on books 9 to 11, reflecting the fact that Martha does not feature in these three stories.

1: THE SPACESHIP GRAVEYARD

Writer: Colin Brake
Publication date: 5 July 2007

PUBLICITY BLURB

When the TARDIS engines fail, you find yourselves on a planet littered with abandoned spaceships. But where are the crews? And why has the TARDIS crashed there, too? Explore the spaceship graveyard to find out ...

NOTE

- This was a replacement for a book entitled 'Frozen Earth' by Kay Woodward, which was cancelled.

2: ALIEN ARENA

Writer: Richard Dungworth
Publication date: 5 July 2007

PUBLICITY BLURB

You're on an alien prison ship in the midst of a mutiny! The ringleader, Mr Big, has created an arena, where aliens from all over the universe are fighting each other. Only your quick wits, and a little help from the Doctor and Martha, can help you escape the arena!

3: THE TIME CROCODILE

Writer: Colin Brake
Publication date: 5 July 2007

PUBLICITY BLURB

The space zoo isn't like any zoo you've ever visited on Earth. For a start, some of the animals can talk! Explore the zoo and work out who can be trusted and who has a hidden agenda ...

4: THE CORINTHIAN PROJECT

Writer: Davey Moore
Publication date: 5 July 2007

PUBLICITY BLURB

When the TARDIS lands in an undersea community known as the Corinthian Project, it doesn't take you long to realise there are some very strange things going on. Explore the Project and see if you can uncover the truth.

5: THE CRYSTAL SNARE

Writer: Richard Dungworth
Publication date: 4 October 2007

PUBLICITY BLURB

People all over the world were amazed at the exhibits on display at the Great Exhibition – and they didn't even see the alien visitors! Help the Doctor and Martha put a stop to the aliens' plans, before they wreak havoc on humankind ...

6: WAR OF THE ROBOTS

Writer: Trevor Baxendale
Publication date: 4 October 2007

PUBLICITY BLURB

On a distant world populated by robots, war has been raging for many years. Can you, the Doctor and Martha discover why the robots are fighting and end the war once and for all?

7: DARK PLANET

Writer: Davey Moore
Publication date: 4 October 2007

PUBLICITY BLURB

Earth is divided. The Upsiders live in luxury while the Downsiders scavenge in the dark world below. Can you help the Doctor and Martha bring the two conflicting sides back together?

8: THE HAUNTED WAGON TRAIN

Writer: Colin Brake
Publication date: 4 October 2007

PUBLICITY BLURB

Pioneers travelling across the American mid-West report ghost sightings, but you, the Doctor and Martha believe it's extra-terrestrial activity. Can you track down the aliens before it's too late?

9: LOST LUGGAGE

Writer: Colin Brake
Publication date: 6 March 2008

PUBLICITY BLURB

When the TARDIS goes missing in a busy spaceport, the Doctor and you must race against time and across space to find it, before the Doctor's incredible spaceship is lost forever ...

10: SECOND SKIN

Writer: Richard Dungworth
Publication date: 6 March 2008

PUBLICITY BLURB

When you find yourself on a 23rd Century space station, you soon realise a dangerous alien parasite has taken over most of the people on board. Can you and the Doctor destroy it before it reaches Earth?

11: THE DRAGON KING

Writer: Trevor Baxendale
Publication date: 6 March 2008

PUBLICITY BLURB

Your journey takes you to the planet Elanden, where people live side by side with dragons. But hunters from a neighbouring planet are attacking … Can you restore peace to these two clashing worlds?

12: THE HORROR OF HOWLING HILL

Writer: Jonathan Green
Publication date: 6 March 2008

PUBLICITY BLURB

Help the Doctor and Martha discover the truth behind the legend of Howling Hill, before the horror that stalks the night catches up with you …

NOTE

- This was a replacement for a book entitled 'Racing Moon' by Davey Moore, which was cancelled.

THE DOCTOR WHO STORYBOOK 2008

This book, published by Panini, followed the same format as the previous year's equivalent title, presenting seven short pieces of text fiction with illustrations, plus a comic strip story entitled *Sunscreen*, featuring the tenth Doctor and Martha. The introduction, *A Letter from the Doctor*, was provided by Russell T Davies. Story credits were as follows.

CATS AND DOGS
Written by Tom McRae. Illustrations by Andy Walker.

THE BODY BANK
Written by Gareth Roberts. Illustrations by Dan McDaid.

THE BOX UNDER THE TREE
Written by Robert Shearman. Illustrations by Martin Geraghty.

ZOMBIE MOTEL
Written by Paul Magrs. Illustrations by Ben Wilsher.

SUNSCREEN
Written by Jonathan Morris. Pencil art by Martin Geraghty.

THE IRON CIRCLE
Written by Nicholas Briggs. Illustrations by Adrian Salmon.

KISS OF LIFE
Written by Justin Richards. Illustrations by Andy Walker.

DEEP WATER
Written by Nicholas Pegg. Illustrations by Brian Williamson.

THE DOCTOR WHO STORYBOOK 2009

This third entry in the *Storybook* series followed the now-familiar format of the previous two, with seven illustrated pieces of prose fiction and one comic strip story, *The Immortal Emperor*. These all starred the Doctor and Donna apart from the last, *The Puplet*, which was a solo outing for the Doctor. *Cold* was notable for being the first piece of officially-sanctioned new-era *Doctor Who* fiction to feature an Ice Warrior, one of the most popular classic-era monsters. This year's *A Letter from the Doctor* introduction was supplied by Steven Moffat. Story credits were as follows:

HELLO CHILDREN, EVERYWHERE
Written by Paul Magrs. Illustrations by Brian Williamson.

GRAND THEFT PLANET!
Written by James Moran. Illustrations by Daryl Joyce.

COLD
Written by Mark Gatiss. Illustrations by Ben Wilsher.

THE IMMORTAL EMPEROR
Written by Jonathan Morris. Artwork by Rob Davis.

BING BONG
Written by Gareth Roberts and Clayton Hickman. Illustrations by Daniel McDaid.

ISLAND OF THE SIRENS
Written by Keith Temple. Illustrations by Adrian Salmon.

HOLD YOUR HORSES
Written by Nicholas Pegg. Illustrations by Jon Haward.

THE PUPLET
Written by Gary Russell. Illustrations by Andy Walker.

DOCTOR WHO - THE OFFICIAL ANNUAL 2008

Whereas the only fiction included in the previous year's equivalent title from BBC Children's Books had been some reprint comic strip stories from *Doctor Who Adventures*, this time there were two original comic strip stories, *Myth Maker* and *Swarm Enemies*, plus one original text story, *The Planet that Wept*. Details were as follows:

MYTH MAKER
Written by Davey Moore. Illustrations by John Ross. Colours by James Offredi.

THE PLANET THAT WEPT
Written by Justin Richards.

SWARM ENEMIES
Written by Davey Moore. Illustrations by John Ross. Colours by James Offredi

DOCTOR WHO - THE OFFICIAL ANNUAL 2009

Maintaining a year-on-year improvement in quality, the latest *Official Annual* offered the most substantial content yet, including three original comic strip stories, *The Greatest Mall in the Universe, The Time Sickness* and *Death Disco,* and two pieces of original prose fiction, *One Upon a Time ...* and *Most Beautiful Music*. Credits were as follows:

THE GREATEST MALL IN THE UNIVERSE
Written by Colin Brake. Illustrations by John Ross. Colours by James Offredi.

ONCE UPON A TIME ...
Written by Justin Richards.

THE TIME SICKNESS
Written by Trevor Baxendale. Illustrations by John Ross. Colours by James Offredi.

MOST BEAUTIFUL MUSIC
Written by Justin Richards.

DEATH DISCO
Written by Alan Barnes. Illustrations by John Ross. Colours by James Offredi.

THE *DAILY TELEGRAPH* CHRISTMAS STORY 2007

Following on from his 2006 *Doctor Who* Christmas story in *The Sunday Times*, Paul Cornell this time contributed a piece to the *Daily Telegraph*, where it was published on 22 December 2007, accompanied by an illustration pencilled by Mike Collins and inked by David A Roach.

THE HOPES AND FEARS OF ALL THE YEARS

PLOT

The Doctor arrives at the home of a young boy called Tom Wake on Christmas Eve 1920 and finds his sonic screwdriver hanging from the Christmas tree with a gift tag attached, the note suggesting that he will save Tom and his family from danger many times at Christmas over the next 90 years. This causes him to visit Tom at Christmas on an annual basis thereafter, but on only one occasion does he encounter any danger, saving his life in Burma during the Second World War. In 2007, he takes Tom, now a very old man, back to his home in 1920 to try to solve the mystery of how this all came about. Tom then makes a copy of the original gift tag, attaches it to the sonic screwdriver and hangs it from the tree - this is how it got there in the first place. Tom has tricked the Doctor into visiting him each year throughout his life; but this has been a true Christmas present for the Doctor, as it has enabled him to witness and play a small part in the kind of normal family life that he could never have himself.

ABOUT THE AUTHOR

Stephen James Walker became hooked on *Doctor Who* as a young boy, right from its debut season in 1963/64, and has been a fan ever since. He first got involved in the series' fandom in the early 1970s, when he became a member of the original Doctor Who Fan Club (DWFC). He joined the Doctor Who Appreciation Society (DWAS) immediately on its formation in May 1976, and was an attendee and steward at the first ever *Doctor Who* convention in August 1977. He soon began to contribute articles to fanzines, and in the 1980s was editor of the seminal reference work *Doctor Who – An Adventure in Space and Time* and its sister publication *The Data-File Project*. He also became a frequent writer for the official *Doctor Who Magazine*. Between 1987 and 1993 he was co-editor and publisher, with David J Howe and Mark Stammers, of the leading *Doctor Who* fanzine *The Frame*. Since that time, he has gone on to write and co-write numerous *Doctor Who* books and articles, and is now widely acknowledged as one of the foremost chroniclers of the series' history. He was the initiator and, for the first two volumes, co-editor of Virgin Publishing's *Decalog* books – the first ever *Doctor Who* short story anthology range. More recently, he has written *Inside the Hub*, the definitive factual guide book on the *Doctor Who* spin-off *Torchwood*. He has a degree in Applied Physics from University College London, and his many other interests include cult TV, film noir, vintage crime fiction, Laurel and Hardy and an eclectic mix of soul, jazz, R&B and other popular music. Between July 1983 and March 2005 he acted as an adviser to successive Governments, latterly at senior assistant director level, responsible for policy on a range of issues relating mainly to individual employment rights. Most of his working time is now taken up with his role as co-owner and director of Telos Publishing Ltd. He lives in Kent with his wife and family.

Other Cult TV Titles From Telos Publishing

Back to the Vortex: *Doctor Who* 2005
Second Flight: *Doctor Who* 2006
J Shaun Lyon

Third Dimension: *Doctor Who* 2007
Monsters Within: *Doctor Who* 2008
End of Ten: *Doctor Who* 2009
Cracks in Time: *Doctor Who* 2010
River's Run: *Doctor Who* 2011
Time of the Doctor: *Doctor Who* 2012 and 2013
Stephen James Walker

The Television Companion (*Doctor Who*) Vols 1 and 2
David J Howe, Stephen James Walker

The Handbook (*Doctor Who*) Vols 1 and 2
David J Howe, Stephen James Walker, Mark Stammers

Talkback (*Doctor Who* Interview Books) Vols 1, 2 and 3
Ed. Stephen James Walker

The Target Book (*Doctor Who* Novelisations)
David J Howe

Doctor Who Exhibitions
Bedwyr Gullidge

Inside the Hub (Guide to *Torchwood* Season 1)
Something in the Darkness (Guide to *Torchwood* Season 2)
Stephen James Walker

A Day in the Life (Guide to Season 1 of 24)
Triquetra (Guide to *Charmed*)
A Vault of Horror (Guide to 80 Great British Horror Films)
The Complete Slayer (Guide to *Buffy the Vampire Slayer*)
Keith Topping

Liberation (Guide to *Blake's 7*)
Fall Out (Guide to *The Prisoner*)
By Your Command (Guide to *Battlestar Galactica*, 2 Vols)
Alan Stevens and Fiona Moore

A Family at War (Guide to *Till Death Us Do Part*)
Mark Ward

Destination Moonbase Alpha (Guide to *Space 1999*)
Robert E Wood

Assigned (Guide to *Sapphire and Steel*)
Richard Callaghan

Hear the Roar (Guide to *Thundercats*)
David Crichton

Hunted (Guide to *Supernatural* Seasons 1-3)
Sam Ford and Antony Fogg

Bowler Hats and Kinky Boots (Guide to *The Avengers*)
Michael Richardson

Transform and Roll Out (Guide to The Transformers Franchise)
Ryan Frost

Songs for Europe (Guide to the UK in the Eurovision Song Contest: 4 Volumes)
Gordon Roxburgh

Prophets of Doom (Guide to *Doomwatch*)
Michael Seely and Phil Ware

All available online from www.telos.co.uk